BEST-KEPT SECRET

BEST-KEPT SECRET

CANADIAN SECRET INTELLIGENCE

IN THE SECOND WORLD WAR

John Bryden

LESTER

PUBLISHING

Canadian Cataloguing in Publication Data

Bryden, John, 1943–
Best-kept secret : Canadian secret intelligence
in the second world war

1st Canadian ed.
Includes index.
ISBN 1-895555-29-9

1. World War, 1939–1945 – Secret Service – Canada.
2. Espionage, Soviet – Canada   3. Intelligence service – Canada.
I. Title.

D810.S7B79 1993   327.12'0971   C93-093119-X

Lester Publishing Limited
56 The Esplanade
Toronto, Ontario M5E 1A7

Printed and bound in Canada
93 94 95 96 5 4 3 2 1

To H. S. Armstrong

*A friend, gentleman, and scholar
of the old school*

CONTENTS

ACKNOWLEDGEMENTS

I BEGAN THIS PROJECT in late 1989 by telephoning the records branch of the Communications Security Establishment and asking to see all of its wartime files connected with code- and cipher-breaking. There was a long pause after I finished speaking, then the person on the other end of the line simply said, "Holy Cow." Subsequently, the CSE released to me photocopies of several thousand documents which it was in the process of declassifying, on the understanding that they would be deposited in a public archive when I was done with them. Otherwise, no deals were struck. I made it clear from the outset that any still-secret information I discovered in any way, from any source, I would feel free to use. The CSE edited hard and I dug hard. I would like especially to thank Ronald Browne, then in charge of CSE's records management. He was tough, but always fair, in applying the rules of secrecy defined by the Access to Information Act.

The Access to Information personnel at the National Archives also gave crucial help by releasing seemingly unimportant files that turned out to be invaluable. They also applied the Access to Information rules strictly, and exercised their independence and judgment in ways that ultimately worked to my great advantage.

I am particularly indebted to Major Catherine Allan, formerly with the Directorate of History, Department of National Defence, for an early lead that I was able to mine to great depth. Nancy Hill, Gilbert Robinson's daughter, gave vital assistance by searching her father's papers and coming up with several items of great importance. Natalie de Marbois was similarly generous in allowing me access to her father's diaries and photo albums.

The financial support given this project by the Canada Council was essential. I could not otherwise have afforded the trips to London and Paris that were so necessary if I was to understand how completely the Canadians had penetrated the diplomatic ciphers of Charles de Gaulle.

I would also like to congratulate the Hamilton Public Library for its excellent collection of books on the Second World War. Librarians must wonder sometimes whether their acquisition strategies are appreciated. I was saved an immense amount of time and travel by having so many wartime secondary sources so near at hand. Barbara Hehner's eagle eye on the manuscript was also much appreciated.

Finally, I would like to thank the Canadian Security Intelligence Service for the way in which I was covertly checked out. It was done with great finesse; had I not been expecting it, I never would have suspected. Once it was established that I was simply an ordinary citizen going about his legitimate business, the coverage was dropped. I thereby lost a most interesting new acquaintance.

INTRODUCTION

T HIS IS A BOOK of many secrets, disclosed here for the first time. It is based almost entirely on original documents. What's reported here is fact, not hearsay.

Most books on Allied secret intelligence during the Second World War deal with American and British activities, not Canadian. Some of these, to be sure, cite documents copiously, but the best of them give only an illusion of completeness. The release of intelligence documents to archives in the United States and Britain has been carefully controlled so that the stories written from them tell only what the security authorities in those two countries want the public to know. Much has been concealed.

In the last two decades, for instance, there have been excellent accounts of how the Americans and British broke the codes and ciphers of the Germans and Japanese during the Second World War. But these books have dealt mainly with breaking *enemy military* messages; scant mention has been made of the parallel and equally vital endeavours to obtain intelligence by intercepting letters and telegrams, and by breaking the diplomatic ciphers of neutral and friendly nations. The documents that tell the non-military side of the wartime secret intelligence story are still generally withheld in the United States and Britain.

There has also been much misinformation. British books on secret intelligence tend to be especially misleading: they have often been written by former intelligence officers schooled in what to avoid, and

I

sometimes by writers who have been deliberately fed selected material by the British security authorities. The United States is somewhat more open, but the whole picture in both countries is incomplete.

That leads to Canada. For over forty-five years after the Second World War, Canadians believed that Canada had no secret agency actively engaged in gathering foreign intelligence. Only the RCMP's security service—later the Canadian Security Intelligence Service—was known to be involved in secret work, chiefly to do with domestic security and counter-espionage. CSIS is still regarded as Canada's only secret service agency by much of the public.

About six years ago, a few newspapers made mention of another secret agency—the Communications Security Establishment. The headquarters of the CSE is a complex of buildings surrounded by a high fence on Heron Road in Ottawa. Government authorities deflected inquiries about what was done there, causing much speculation in the press. Meanwhile, several Canadian historians reported encountering wartime documents indicating the existence during the Second World War of a small code- and cipher-breaking facility called the Examination Unit. It was initially dismissed as being inconsequential. The Examination Unit, it turns out, was the CSE's predecessor.

My original intention for this book was to make the connection between the code- and cipher-breaking of the Examination Unit of fifty years ago and the activities of today's Communications Security Establishment. It quickly became more than that. My research disclosed that Canada had been an intimate partner of Britain and the United States in almost all areas of secret intelligence during the Second World War, and that this partnership persisted through the Cold War. Canada had, and likely still has, one of the most sophisticated intelligence-gathering organizations of the Western democracies.

The key to telling this broader story is the fact that the available documents in Canada on secret intelligence are fewer, but far wider ranging, than those which have been released in the United States and Britain. And because the wartime intelligence services of the three countries cooperated closely, the Canadian documents provide a much fuller picture of what was happening in the United States and Britain than has so far been revealed in those two countries. Thus a

Canadian story became an American and British one as well.

The Canadian security authorities have been just as tight-fisted about the release of information as their U.S. and British colleagues. Documents released by the CSE under Canada's Access to Information Act were rigorously vetted, and contain thousands of deletions by word, paragraph, and page. However, obscure files discovered in the National Archives which had been declassified long ago allowed me to fill in many of the blanks in the CSE documents. Similarly, files in archives in the United States, Britain, and France helped unlock some of the information still withheld in Canada. Ironically, the process of comparing many incomplete documents in order to determine the content of all of them is precisely the technique used by codebreakers. It was a three-year task.

The following is a typical example of my research procedure. The CSE released an October 12, 1944 letter to Lester Pearson from Norman Robertson which, paraphrased, went something like this:

> [*Blank*] in Ottawa this week warned that the Examination Unit could expect no further cooperation with [*blank*] unless it broke off its liaison with [*blank*] because [*blank*] is bitterly opposed to sharing traffic with [*blank*].

A completely unrelated document of early October 1944 in the National Archives mentioned that the British DMI (Director of Military Intelligence) was to visit Robertson on his way back to Britain from Washington. Other documents in other files revealed that the Canadians were unofficially liaising with the Office of Strategic Services, the wartime American spy agency. Still other documents revealed that U.S. Military Intelligence was then adamantly opposed to sharing any intercepted radio traffic with the OSS. This information, put together and matched by letter-count to the blanks in the CSE document, enabled me to read the letter to Pearson in full. The paraphrase above would now look like this:

> [*John Sinclair*] in Ottawa this week warned that the Examination Unit could expect no further cooperation with [*the SSA*] unless it

broke off its liaison with [*the OSS*] because [*G-2*] is bitterly opposed to sharing traffic with [*the OSS*].

In this document, SSA stands for the U.S. Signal Security Agency and G-2 for U.S. Military Intelligence.

Hundreds of partially declassified documents—British and American as well as Canadian—could be filled out in this way. The endnotes which accompany the text describe the most notable examples.

Because the Examination Unit specialized in deciphering enemy secret service and diplomatic messages rather than military ones, I found it necessary to describe wartime censorship—the interception and reading of both letters and telegrams—in detail. Censorship was a complementary operation essential to the successful interpretation of both military and non-military intelligence obtained by other means. Allied documents on censorship are still secret in Britain; they are not in Canada. Censorship, indeed, begins the story about Canada's involvement in secret intelligence. Inevitably, information about American and British censorship activities came to light and is described here as well.

Much of what is told in the following pages about British wartime intelligence activities will be new to historians. Not only have the British authorities severely restricted the release of relevant documents, but they have also systematically withheld the names of the people who were involved in secret intelligence. This has made it almost impossible for British historians to reconstruct an adequate sequence of events from what is available. Consequently, I have always used the names of individuals in this book, in the hope that this may help it serve as a kind of *Michelin Guide* for American and British writers dealing with incomplete secret-intelligence documents in their own countries.

I have another reason for wanting to include the names of individuals. Espionage, and counter-espionage, are as old as recorded history. The stories in this book are, above all, about people.

CHAPTER ONE

JUST LISTENING

SEPTEMBER 1939 — DECEMBER 1940

No one seriously considered that Canada would play a role in secret intelligence when war against Germany was declared on September 10, 1939.

Spies, counter-espionage, code- and cipher-breaking—this was the stuff of European nations and novels. It was not the concern of a vast, sparsely populated land surrounded on three sides by oceans and sharing a single border with the like-minded and friendly United States. The Royal Canadian Mounted Police, it is true, had kept tabs on Communist trouble-makers during the 1930s, but that was about the limit of Canada's commitment to national security. There was nothing secret about it.

In Britain, France, Germany, and the United States, there was at least a long tradition of intelligence-gathering through their embassies and consuls abroad. Canada did not have embassies. Having only recently become a Dominion—with true self-government rather than colonial status—Canada was new to being in charge of its own foreign affairs. The Department of External Affairs was as fresh-faced as a schoolboy. Its missions abroad were still styled "legations"—the diplomatic equivalent of a country's admission that it is still a teenager.

On the eve of war in 1939, the Canadian government had no formal mechanism for foreign intelligence-gathering. Canada still viewed the rest of the world through the eyes of Britain, mainly from Foreign Office summaries and from the Secretary of State for Dominion Affairs. For foreign military matters, Canada relied on reports from the War Office and the Admiralty, plus copies of the discussions of Britain's Committee for Imperial Defence. It gathered nothing on its own.[1]

Actual espionage—and its cousin, counter-espionage—was unthinkable. There was no equivalent in Canada (or in the United States, for that matter) to the British secret services: MI6, the Secret Intelligence Service, responsible for running agents and outright spying, and MI5, the Security Service, with its elaborate collection of dossiers on suspected subversives in Britain and the Commonwealth. Both had been in existence for two decades, and sprang from traditions of secrecy that spanned centuries.[2]

Secret intelligence in Britain was light-years ahead of Canada in yet another way. When Prime Minister Neville Chamberlain came home from Munich in 1938, waving a scrap of paper and declaring "Peace in our time," the Royal Navy was listening intently to the encoded radio signals of the German Navy. Chamberlain had deliberately toadied up to Nazi dictator Adolf Hitler to buy time for rearmament. The Navy's job was to obtain confirmation that war had been averted. The ultra-modern pocket battleship *Deutschland* was then in Spain on a goodwill cruise. A recall to Germany to pick up its regular crew would surely mean that Hitler intended to break his word. There was no increase in messages from Germany and the *Deutschland* continued to communicate normally with its planned ports of call. The British concluded that Hitler had been put off for now.[3]

Britain had dozed for the previous twenty years, neglecting new weapon development, but the country had not been in a deep slumber. The Royal Navy (the "Admiralty"), in particular, never lost sight of the need to study the radio traffic of its potential enemies. Ships at sea could communicate with land in no other way. Moreover, fleet units needed to remain in touch with each other, as well as with home base. The result was a continuous stream of encoded messages that could be analysed for hints of an enemy's intentions.

Intelligence obtained from radio interception in those days had an unusual label. It was called "Y intelligence." The term arose during the

First World War, when it was discovered that a radio transmitter could be pinpointed by aiming the antennae of two widely spaced receivers toward the incoming signal. Plotted on a map, the bearing and cross-bearing thus obtained intersected on the source of the transmission and formed a "y."

By the beginning of the Second World War, however, obtaining cross-bearings on radio transmissions had reached such a degree of sophistication that the practice acquired its own name—"direction finding." Y intelligence then came to mean the interception and inter-pretation of all forms of radio messages *exclusive* of direction finding. The British used the term "wireless" for radio which, to save confusion, the Canadian authorities also adopted. Thus Y intelligence, radio intelligence, and wireless intelligence were synonymous.

The primary form of wireless intelligence was traffic analysis. This involved the study of the characteristics of intercepted transmissions rather than reading their actual content. The stations sending and receiving, the broadcast frequencies, call signs, types of ciphers, and so forth often indicated what was going on, even though the messages themselves remained unintelligible. Traffic analysis had disclosed the *Deutschland*'s movements. Nevertheless, it was preferable by far to be able to decipher an opponent's messages. This came to be called "spe-cial intelligence"—cryptanalysis.[4]

During the First World War the Admiralty had set up the first modern code- and cipher-breaking unit—innocuously named Room 40. A *code*, it should be explained, is a system of writing in which nor-mal words or letters are replaced by arbitrarily chosen symbols. A *cipher* involves scrambling or replacing letters or numbers according to fixed rules. The two terms have often been used interchangeably, as have *code-breaking* and *cryptanalysis*.

From 1915 onward, Room 40 had regularly read the wireless traffic of the German Navy. Unfortunately, the confused decisions of big-gun admirals repeatedly deprived the British of their advantage. At the Bat-tle of Jutland, the German High Seas Fleet had escaped destruction, even though Room 40 had provided prompt warning of the fleet's intentions. Even worse, the Germans had inflicted more damage than they had received. It was a bitter lesson.

In the interwar years, the Admiralty built direction-finding stations in Britain and Bermuda. Theoretically, at least, it had the Atlantic covered. The Pacific was another matter. In 1925 the Admiralty asked Canada to build a wireless and direction-finding station at Esquimalt, the Canadian naval base on Vancouver Island, to work with a similar station at Singapore that was code-named STONECUTTERS. Cross-bearings could then be obtained on wireless transmissions in the Pacific and off the west coast of South America. The staff at Esquimalt was trained by the Royal Navy and the raw wireless intercepts and direction-finding data were sent directly to the Admiralty for processing.[5]

After the First World War, the Admiralty continued to do its own traffic analysis, but it was no longer responsible for cryptanalysis. Room 40 had been dismantled in 1918, only to reappear immediately with some of the same staff under a new name, the Government Code and Cipher School. The job of this new organization was to keep alive the expertise already developed and to keep track of any new advances in cryptography. Its staff was small, about thirty people, and it was the responsibility of the British Foreign Office. Although it worked on some military traffic, most of its effort was directed at breaking diplomatic messages.

Successive British governments had prepared for war in other ways. Even before the First World War, they had encouraged British telegraph companies to lay undersea cables by providing subsidies and loan guarantees. As a result, on the eve of war in 1939, most of the world's transoceanic telegraph cables touched either Britain itself or Commonwealth territory. The United States, for instance, was linked to the Far East and Europe mainly by the undersea cables that left from Vancouver or Nova Scotia, with the exception of two single cables: one to France via the tiny French islands of St. Pierre and Miquelon in the Gulf of St. Lawrence, and another from New York to Italy via the Azores and the Strait of Gibraltar. Since South America was only linked to the United States, most telegrams leaving the Western Hemisphere passed through Canada.[6]

It was the same with the mails. Letters from North America to Europe normally went through Great Britain or Bermuda. Gibraltar was the funnel through which the letters of Mediterranean countries passed. Trinidad gathered mail from South America. Vancouver forwarded much of the mail from the United States and Mexico bound for the Far East. Hong Kong and Singapore were also major centres for international mail.[7]

All this gave Britain potential access to much of the world's international communications. In time of war, Britain would be in a position to intercept and examine the mail and telegrams of enemies and friends alike.

Cooperation with Canada was essential. Vancouver, with its mail and telegraph channels to the Far East, was a vital centre in what was termed the "Empire Censorship Scheme." Even before Hitler's rise to power, the authorities in Britain had proposed to Canada that the two countries cooperate on postal and telegraph censorship in the event of an international emergency. But it was only after Hitler's sabre-rattling during the Munich Crisis that censorship rules, modelled on similar ones in Britain, were drawn up and incorporated in the Defence of Canada Regulations. They would be immediately activated by passage of the War Measures Act.[8]

Censorship, as the British then used the term, meant preventing the release of information through private communications that could be useful to the enemy. Thus both Canadian and British regulations required all messages going out of the country to be in plain language so that their contents could be read by the censors. If they contained sensitive economic or military information, the censors were to cut out the offending passages or stop the messages. Only diplomats were allowed the use of codes or ciphers. The rules in Canada did not apply to traffic on the so-called transit lines—Italian and British cables that began in the United States and only incidentally left the continent via Nova Scotia.

Shortly before the war, the British expanded the concept of censorship. The Munich Crisis prompted the reorganization of British Imperial Censorship under the War Office and a reassessment of its function. In March 1939 the Censorship authorities ruled that private mail and cable communications were to be intercepted and read, primarily to gather information that would be useful to British government ministries and to the armed forces. Preventing useful information getting out of the country would only be of secondary importance.[9]

The British regulations had an important appendix: copies of all intercepted messages deemed "prejudicial to public safety or the operations of His Majesty's Forces" were to be passed to MI5, the Security Service. This "public safety" provision meant that Britain intended to use intercepted communications to keep track of subversive elements on the home front. These could range from spies to people engaged in legitimate political dissent.[10]

The Canadian authorities considered censorship to be mainly a preventive measure. Although the Canadian regulations provided for reading intercepted messages for "contents of value ... to the prosecution of the war," it would be three years before an organization was set up that could coordinate and distribute censorship intelligence for the use of Canadian Government agencies. For a long time, the British authorities would remain the primary clients.[11]

The Munich Crisis prompted Canada's Department of National Defence to take a surprising step beyond what the British had requested. The department decided secretly to hire and train former telegraph operators to act as telegraph censors. The moment war was declared, these people were to be installed in the offices of the major telegraph companies and vet all messages leaving Canada. Lieutenant Colonel W. W. Murray, a veteran of the First World War and then a Parliamentary reporter with the Canadian Press news agency, was recruited to head this shadow organization.[12]

The British authorities, however, never considered that Canada might use any of the intelligence it gathered. The person, for example, that the Admiralty provided in 1939 to serve as Canada's director of Naval Intelligence was a Royal Navy specialist in merchant shipping. In the event of war, Commander E. S. (Eric) Brand was to look after the Canadian end of convoy assembly and protection. He had no previous experience nor instructions pertaining to intelligence-gathering. Before he left for Canada, however, the Admiralty asked him to persuade the Canadians to set up an additional wireless-receiving and direction-finding station on the East Coast, possibly at Halifax.[13] Nevertheless, the Admiralty expected that the raw data so obtained would be sent to Britain for analysis.

In 1939 the Canadian Navy was ludicrously small. Naval Service Headquarters was a large room above a row of shops in downtown Ottawa, filled with the desks of clerks and naval ratings. Rear Admiral Percy Nelles, the naval Chief of Staff, had a small office in one corner. The Canadian fleet comprised six destroyers and a handful of minesweepers. The total paper strength of the Navy consisted of 366 officers and 3,477 men, including reservists.

Commander Brand arrived in Ottawa in July 1939. Less than two months later, Canada was at war. The call-up of reservists immediately provided him with an assistant, Lieutenant Commander John (Jock) Barbe-Pougnet de Marbois of the Royal Navy Reserve. De Marbois was fifty-one years old and had most recently been a language teacher at Upper Canada College, a private boys' school in Toronto.

Jock de Marbois was unusual. Born on an island near Mauritius in the Indian Ocean, he had run away to sea at age twelve. By the time he was seventeen, he had been around the world twice in sailing vessels and had survived two shipwrecks and a bloody mutiny in which the captain and all the ship's officers died. During the First World War, he had served as a British liaison officer aboard a Russian cruiser and had fled the Bolshevik revolution with his fiancée, a Russian countess. After the war he settled for a time in Nigeria before finally coming to Canada. He spoke French, Spanish, German, and Russian fluently, and had a smattering of Arabic, Turkish, and about a dozen Far Eastern languages.[14]

De Marbois was one of those people who loved to tell about his past but had the misfortune rarely to be believed. He enthralled the boys of Upper Canada College with tales of typhoons at sea, rescue by cannibals, and escapes from Argentinian desperadoes. His colleagues at Naval Headquarters were sceptical. Yet the stories were true and de Marbois could tell them vividly. Even how he got his nickname was the stuff of a good yarn in his unpublished autobiography:

> Mr. McGraw became my guardian angel. He hailed from Scotland and during all these years of sailing in the southern seas, coming in contact with all kinds of languages, he had not in the least modified his strong Scottish accent. On my arrival on board, I was introduced to him as a new boy wishing to be a sailor.

He grunted and said to me, "What's yerr name?"

I meekly answered, "John."

"John!" exclaimed he. "John! Ye'll no' be John here'r'r on this packet, laddie, ye'll be Jock and that's aw!"[15]

Brand put de Marbois in charge of wireless interception. The choice could not have been better. De Marbois was the kind of person who gripped an idea absolutely and ran with it, no matter what the opposition. Things began to happen quickly.

Within days of his arrival in Ottawa, de Marbois was negotiating with the Department of Transport for the use of its East Coast stations for naval direction finding. Responsible in peacetime for Canada's national and international radio communications systems, the Department of Transport had a number of stations fitted with direction-finding equipment scattered across the country. The department readily yielded to de Marbois's request, also agreeing to build a new station specifically for the Navy at Hartlen Point near Halifax. In the meantime, de Marbois toured the existing Department of Transport stations to explain to the civilian operators their new duties. Within two weeks, bearings on suspicious wireless transmissions from the Atlantic were being sent to the Admiralty. They were also received at Naval Headquarters in Ottawa.[16]

The Admiralty sought only three things from the fledgling Canadian Navy wireless intelligence organization: the bearings, the call signs, and the broadcast frequencies of enemy transmissions. It did not ask for copies of the actual traffic because the ciphers of the German Navy had not yet been broken. For the next year-and-a-half, the wireless war in the Atlantic would mainly be fought by direction finding and traffic analysis.

De Marbois wanted to do more that just pass raw data on to the Admiralty. With Commander Brand's approval, he styled his tiny operation the Foreign Intelligence Service. De Marbois did his own traffic analysis and plotted the movement of enemy shipping, creating, in effect, a prototype naval operational intelligence centre. He also received foreign language newspapers (German, Russian, Japanese) from the United States so that he could read them for shipping intelligence. Lieutenant C. H. (Herbie) Little, a thirty-two-year-old Canadian Navy reservist and de Marbois's former German-language student at Upper Canada College, was soon posted to Naval Headquarters to help him. As Little later recalled, the room he and de Marbois shared was "just wide enough to accommodate two desks, a hat rack and a phonograph."

It all seemed small and amateurish. Little's main job was to read the newspapers and transcribe German-language broadcasts picked up and recorded by the Department of Transport listening stations. However, he soon chalked up an important intelligence score of his own. At the outbreak of war, the authorities at Newfoundland had seized a small German freighter, the *Christoff von Doornum*. Its confidential papers had been collected and sent to Ottawa. Little's first task at Naval Headquarters was to examine them for anything of value.

> ... bit by bit, [I] assembled a revealing picture of the enemy's secret plans and procedures for merchant ships in wartime. These included some instructions about mines that no one at NSHQ could help me with. I extracted that particular section and included it verbatim with my summary which was forwarded to the Admiralty.... It was no wonder we had been baffled by the mines: the passage to which I invited attention referred to Germany's new invention, the magnetic mine, and was very helpful in drawing up countermeasures.[17]

By mid-November, de Marbois could sit at his desk in their tiny room and persuade himself that a map on the wall opposite showed the tracks of German submarines moving out of the Bay of Biscay to the South Atlantic and the coast of Africa. It was wishful thinking. Although the Admiralty was providing the call signs and wireless procedures of German U-boats—necessary for effective direction finding—it was not sending him the bearings taken in Britain. Canadian bearings for the North Atlantic were not enough by themselves. There was brief but keen excitement at Naval Headquarters, however, when the Department of Transport direction-finding stations played a key role in tracking the pocket battleship *Graf Spee* across the South Atlantic, pursued by a covey of British cruisers. They were elated when the doomed battleship was cornered and scuttled.

De Marbois's insistence on doing his own traffic analysis paid one important dividend. In the welter of enciphered messages that crossed his desk, de Marbois noticed some that were in quite different ciphers and obviously had nothing to do with the German Navy. Direction finding indicated that some appeared to be coming from Mexico. It was soon obvious that, along with everything else, the Department of Transport receiving stations were picking up messages from the secret transmitters of enemy spies or sympathizers.

By this time the Navy was not the only Canadian service interested in enciphered messages. During the Munich Crisis, the Canadian Army, which was about the same size as the Canadian Navy, had proposed setting up its own wireless intelligence organization. The idea languished after the naval Chief of Staff insisted that direction finding was more important. At the outbreak of war, however, the Army's Director of Signals revived the plan, and a small wireless monitoring team was installed in the basement of the Signal Corps radio station at Rockcliffe Airport, Ottawa. Staffed by only sixteen operators, it was strictly experimental, but the little unit soon discovered that the airwaves were charged with the jumbled letters of enciphered messages. Since none of these could be identified, or even separated, an officer was dispatched to Britain to find out how to handle them.[18]

Meanwhile, Colonel Murray's censors were in place and doing their jobs at the major telegraph centres in Toronto, Montreal, and Vancouver. Messages of interest were copied and sent to the newly formed Information Section of Military Intelligence, which was then to pass them along to Britain and to whatever Canadian government department or agency might have use for them. Then the Canadian Army authorities took a further step, one that the British had not proposed and, indeed, may never even have considered.

Two transit lines passed through Nova Scotia: a British cable from North Sydney and an Italian-owned cable called Horta 2, which went from Canso to the Azores (Horta) and thence to Italy via the Strait of Gibraltar. They were called transit lines because their telegraph offices were actually in the United States; there was no message handling in Canada. Traffic between the United States and Italy went via Canso, while traffic to and from Spain went via North Sydney and Britain. In defiance of international convention, the Canadian censors, in "utmost secrecy," tapped both lines.

This move originated with Colonel Maurice Pope, then secretary to the Canadian Chiefs of Staff Committee and acting as the Army's Director of Military Operations and Intelligence. Before the war Pope had drawn up Canada's censorship regulations with their provision exempting transit lines. However, because Spain and Italy were Fascist states sympathetic to Hitler, Pope was tempted to defy the rule. As early as November 1939, he described the intelligence obtained from the transit lines as being of "inestimable value."[19]

Pope next turned his attention to the activities of the experimental wireless station at Rockcliffe. At his prompting, the Signal Corps officer who had been sent to Britain to learn about British wireless interception procedures received a startling telegram in early December. It came from Canada's Chief of the General Staff and read, in part:

> ... desire you secure all possible information regarding cypher and code systems used by other nations, particularly Germany, together with data which may assist in breaking down these systems. Consult Brigadier Crerar, CanMilitary, to whom letters on subject in the mail. Above duties should not be permitted to delay return to Canada more than a few days.

Brigadier H. D. G. Crerar, head of Canadian Military Headquarters in London, promptly wired back:

> War Office says useless to expect him to obtain any useful knowledge methods solving cyphers in a few days.

Citing the heavy volume of enciphered traffic being heard at Rockcliffe and by the Navy's Department of Transport stations—some of which was missing "the British Isles entirely"—Colonel Pope had proposed to the Chiefs of Staff that Canada solicit British help to set up its own cryptanalysis unit, specifically to attack German, Italian, and Spanish traffic.[20]

While it was a little silly to expect one man to absorb twenty-five years' worth of cryptanalysis experience from the Government Code and Cipher School in "a few days," Pope's suggestion was received seriously by the British. It was true that Canada was hearing traffic which could not be picked up in Britain. Short-wave wireless transmissions tended to bounce back and forth between the ionosphere and the earth; this was known as the "radio skip" phenomenon. Depending on a signal's broadcast frequency, some locations were deaf to it while others further away could hear it clearly.

The British appreciated the offer of help. The operational head of the Government Code and Cipher School at this time was Commander Alastair Denniston, a veteran of Room 40. Denniston had been frantically recruiting more staff for the Government Code and Cipher School to handle the huge increase in enciphered traffic brought on by the war. Most of it was still unreadable, whether from Germany or her potential allies. However, Denniston stated that if the Canadians wanted to get into the cipher-breaking game, they must first have a "high-grade cryptographer of long experience" who would then require at least three months of instruction in Britain.[21] There was no such person in Canada.

The Canadians were daunted when they realized the magnitude of the task. They were also impressed by arguments that deciphered messages could be acted upon only by the British authorities. Pope's idea was dropped.

The Canadian Army chose instead the more manageable alternative of working with the British on wireless interception. Responsibility for the Rockcliffe station was transferred from the Signal Corps (which continued to supply the personnel) to Military Intelligence. Arrangements were made for the station to coordinate its coverage of suspicious transmissions with that of Britain's Radio Security Service (RSS), then under the operational intelligence department of the War Office (MI8, code-named TROOPERS). The RSS comprised a handful of army personnel in charge of the listening stations of Britain's General Post Office and about one thousand civilian volunteers with their own short-wave receivers. It was specifically responsible for intercepting and collating the messages of Germany's spies—the so-called "illicit" or "clandestine" traffic—and that became the main preoccupation at Rockcliffe.[22]

Because the Canadian Army had no direction-finding stations of its own, Commander de Marbois was approached to supply bearings as required from the listening stations under his control. He also turned over any obviously clandestine messages he received, duplicating them to the RCMP. All of this data was to go via the Army to the Radio Security Service in Britain for evaluation and processing.[23]

As for Canadian Postal Censorship, for the first few months of the war it confined itself to a haphazard examination of mail going to Germany and the neutral countries in Europe and Asia for breaches of security. It came under the Post Office and such leadership as it had came from a Censorship committee, consisting of the Postmaster and representatives from the Departments of Transport and External Affairs, plus one person from the Department of National Defence. This committee met rarely and gave little guidance.[24]

The turning point came in early February 1940, with a visit to Britain by Canada's Chief Postal Censor, F. E. Jolliffe. He toured the entire British Censorship operation. It was an eye-opener. He found British Postal and Telegraph Censorship organized under the War Office and concentrated at two centres. The first, Postal Censorship or MC5 (for Military Censorship 5), in a large building in Edge Lane, Liverpool, examined all mail to and from censorable countries—basically every country bordering Germany, as well as those in sympathy with her. It also examined prisoner-of-war correspondence and mail taken off neutral ships. MC5 employed 2,109 workers and in the first three months of the war had examined four million pieces of mail.

Jolliffe also visited an intriguing sub-department at Liverpool University called the Testing and Code Facility. This was a laboratory that detected secret inks by chemical treatment or by passing suspect letters under an ultraviolet lamp. It also examined mail for secret codes, known from the First World War to be sometimes concealed in apparently inconsequential text or even in the pencil strokes of a drawing. "It is the boast of this section that they have never failed to break a code," Jolliffe reported.

However, the real nerve-centre of British Censorship was elsewhere.

At the beginning of the war, the famous and forbidding London prison Wormwood Scrubs was emptied of inmates. Walls between the cells were knocked down and made into offices. Here Jolliffe found the headquarters of Telegraph Censorship (MC4), the Information and Records Branch (MC3), and Censorship headquarters itself (MC1).

The Information and Records Branch most impressed Jolliffe. Here postal and telegraph intercepts from all over the world were collected, filed, and collated; then they were sent to the using agencies, accompanied by remarks from the files. It was far more sophisticated than anything being done in Canada. Jolliffe probably felt a little gratified when he was asked if he could arrange for the Information and Records Branch to receive copies of the traffic intercepted by the Canadians from the Italian cable out of Canso.[25]

There was one thing that Jolliffe did not see. Wormwood Scrubs was also the wartime home of MI5, the Security Service. It had moved in at the beginning of the war, along with its copious registry of suspect persons assembled over two decades. What an opportunity it had now. The Information and Records Branch was collecting private data from all over the world, and not just on German sympathizers. As Jolliffe was soon to learn, it was gathering information on every manner of radical group or individual, British or foreign, right, left, or centre. Wormwood Scrubs had become the Security Service's memory centre.[26]

Locating the key departments of British Postal and Telegraph Censorship so close to MI5 had its disadvantages, however. After the first four months of war, an internal War Office investigation found that British Censorship was spending too much time examining private letters for security reasons rather than for gathering intelligence. The Censorship authorities were given a stiff reminder that "security concerns are not paramount." Instead, they were to focus on the interception of communications from neutral countries, including mail and telegrams simply passing through Britain, in order "to track neutral countries acting on behalf of the enemy."[27] The idea was to gather information that could be useful for restricting the flow to Germany of scarce commodities and raw materials.

Jolliffe arrived for his tour two months after this rebuke and, on returning to Canada, reported that the British Censorship authorities were "keenly interested" in the activities of Canadian Censorship and were most "anxious" (repeated three times) to receive the Italian traffic the Canadians were intercepting on the Canso cable.

Canadian Postal Censorship suddenly expanded. It no longer confined itself to outgoing mail and, by the end of June 1940, was reading letters *from* Denmark, Holland, Belgium, Italy, Spain, Switzerland, Sweden, Yugoslavia, Hungary, Romania, and Russia. Transit mail between the Orient and Latin America via Vancouver was also to be examined.[28] All content of interest was copied and sent to British Censorship Headquarters (code-named BLANKETING) at Wormwood Scrubs.

To ensure that the Canadians knew what was worthwhile, a British liaison officer was posted to Canada to advise on both postal and telegraph censorship.[29] The Canadians were also supplied with a set of "Ministerial Requirements": lists of subjects that using agencies in Britain wanted British Censorship to search for in letters and telegrams. The following is only a sample:

General

Report shortage of railway facilities and road improvements in
    Spain, Portugal, North Africa, and Russia;

Movements of German troops in Finland;

Shortage of Swedish shipping in the Baltic;

German movements through Italy;

Italian efforts to reinforce Sicily;

Cancellation of Japanese sailings;

Purchase by Japanese of maps of British or Dutch possessions.

MI5 (Security Service)

Effect of war in occupied countries;

Military disposition and troop strengths in Eire, plus attitude of
    civilian population to German and British defeats and victories;

Anything that pertains to treason, mutinous incitement, sabotage,
    hostile propaganda, dangerous people in British service, unlawful use of codes, ciphers, radios, pigeons, and lights;

Activities of Communist, Pacifist, Celtic Nationalist, and extreme
   right-wing organizations throughout world;
Foreign political organizations in the British Empire;
Letters from Spain or Portugal, especially if of an inconsequential
   nature....

Admiralty
Anything to do with the war at sea.

Dominions Office
Effect of enemy propaganda in Europe;
General correspondence from Eire except for "mere vituperation
   from illiterate Irishmen with an anti-British bias."

The British authorities were interested in more than information
related to the war. They used the opportunity of legalized mail and
telegraph interception to check the temperature of the Empire:

Union of South Africa Office
Private correspondence dealing with Communist activities involving
   the native races;
References to the South African Defence Forces and their bases;
Private correspondence dealing with political and economic condi-
   tions in the Belgian Congo, Madagasgar, etc., as well as trade
   reports to and from Africa;
Diamonds.

India Office
Any political information involving the Indian National Congress,
   the Muslim League, the Pan Islamic Movement;
Anything suspicious re Afghanistan;
Movements and activities in any part of the world by people who
   have influence in India.

And so the requirements go on, for nearly every major department
of the British government. These lists were continuously updated

throughout the war. They provide a unique insight into the preoccupations of Britain's senior politicians and civil servants, many of them still highly secret. Even fifty years later, in 1991, these "Ministerial Requirements" had not yet been released in Britain.[30]

Canada's early interest in any of this intelligence was marginal. External Affairs was the main recipient, and this department made its interests known through its representatives on the Censorship committee. These were very modest up to May 1940, during the period known as the Phoney War.[31] Germany had successfully invaded Denmark and Norway, but otherwise its armies had remained quiet on the frontier with France. The British and French armies were watching and waiting, reluctant to make the first move. Except for the mounting struggle in the Atlantic against German submarines and surface raiders, and the fact that Canada had sent troops to Britain, the war seemed remote.

Blitzkrieg began. Lightning war. On May 13, 1940, German tanks burst across the French border at the heel of Belgium and were soon speeding eastward to the coast. The French Army reeled. The British Expeditionary Force in Belgium suddenly found the enemy behind it. Italy declared war and attacked France in the south. The British forces retreated to Dunkirk, then fled across the English Channel. By the middle of June, it was all over.

Canadian Telegraph Censorship made a stunning contribution in these fearful days. On May 18 Italian dictator Benito Mussolini warned Britain that he intended to attack France. This meant war with Italy. When this news reached Canada, Colonel Murray promptly produced the entire Italian order-of-battle. He was able to name and locate every division and sub-unit in the Italian armed forces, both at home and abroad. When Italy formally declared war on June 10, Britain knew exactly what new forces she faced and where they were placed.[32]

William Waldie Murray was a remarkable man. Aged forty-nine, square-faced and stocky, he had emigrated to Canada in 1913 from Scotland, joining the 97th Algonquin Rifles shortly after the outbreak of the First World War. He was in the thick of the action in many of the worst killing fields: the Somme, Vimy Ridge, Passchendaele, Hill 70, Amiens, and others. The odds were that he should have been killed in any one of these battles. Yet he did more than simply survive. He was commissioned in the field, repeatedly cited for bravery under fire, and received the Military Cross and Bar.[33]

Obtaining an enemy's order-of-battle is one of the primary aims of military intelligence and was a remarkable coup for Colonel Murray. The secret of his success was that, before hostilities began, Mussolini had been anxious to obtain American dollars to finance military production. He concocted a scheme whereby Italians in the United States were asked to deposit U.S. dollars to the Italian government's account and name a beneficiary in Italy who would receive the same value in lire plus a forty per cent bonus. The idea had tremendous appeal to Italian-Americans wanting to send money to poorer relatives in Italy. However, American banks insisted on full names and addresses on the remittances and, since many of the named beneficiaries were military personnel serving with their units, Colonel Murray was able to copy this information off the New York–Canso–Italy cable and use it to plot the locations—and even movements—of Italian military formations.

> Soon particulars of the Italian army were being card-indexed and colored pins began to go up on maps. The pins were thickest on the French frontier; and there were concentrations of troops in the Piedmont, in the vicinity of Aosta, Novara and Turin and on the Mediterranean Coast. Similarly, the invasion routes to Yugoslavia were becoming crowded. There was heavy mobilization around Glorizia, Udine and Belluno. We were able to plot Mussolini's dispositions in the Libyan desert and Ethiopia.[34]

It was a superb piece of intelligence, as fine as anything produced during the war short of intelligence obtained by cryptanalysis. It did not save France, but it certainly alerted Britain to the challenge it was soon to face in the Middle East and even anticipated the Italian invasion of Yugoslavia. The information shaped the outcome of the war, for it enabled General Percival Wavell to know exactly what Italian army and air force formations he faced during the successful battles he waged to oust the Italians from Egypt and Ethiopia in 1940–41.[35]

Wavell was a brilliant general, now recognized as one of Britain's best. With only a handful of British and Australian divisions, he destroyed ten Italian divisions and captured nearly 315,000 prisoners, always because he attacked first where the Italians were most vulnerable. It is now known that comprehensive intelligence about Italian dispositions was the key to his successes. While some of this was provided by decrypts of Italian military communications, the information obtained from Censorship was highly regarded by the Middle East operational commanders, being specifically mentioned in the official history, *British Intelligence in the Second World War* (1979). Indeed, in a lecture to the Imperial Defence College after the war, the Chief British Censor, Sir Edwin Herbert, cited the use of telegraph intercepts to determine the Italian order-of-battle as one of Censorship's most outstanding wartime accomplishments. He neglected to mention, however, that it was an achievement of Canadian Censorship, not British.[36]

The collapse of France brought the war home to Canadians. Britain was alone in Europe and facing defeat. Canada was now its largest ally. The Canadian First Division in England was one of the few organized fighting forces left on the island. If Hitler launched an immediate leap across the Channel, it would be mostly Canadians fighting on the beaches at Dover.

Canadian politicians suddenly came face to face with the decisions of war. On June 18 the French cruiser *Emile Bertin* docked at Halifax. On board were approximately 240 tons of gold bullion—part of the French gold reserves worth $305 million (U.S.). The captain of the ship had orders to deliver his cargo to Canada for safekeeping, but before unloading could begin, he received another message directing him to sail for Martinique in the West Indies.

What was left of the French government was then fleeing to Bordeaux. It was not known whether the still untouched and powerful French Fleet would join Britain or submit to the inevitable surrender of France. Perhaps the new orders to the captain had been faked by the Germans. The Canadian authorities pleaded with him to stay in harbour while they tried to get his new orders countermanded. Meanwhile, the shore guns were manned.

Prime Minister Mackenzie King and his cabinet swayed this way and that over the next few days. Should the *Emile Bertin* be sunk if it attempted to sail? The naval authorities at Halifax were told to be ready to take "any necessary action, however strong" to prevent its departure. When a Canadian naval officer boarded the ship with this warning, the French captain received it sombrely, drawing himself up and declaring that he did not intend to be "branded a traitor":

> ... he told (Captain) Read that he had no alternative but to force his way out if necessary. He did not intend to leave for a short time but would tell Read before he did. Read asked him to wait until he had sent a report of the discussions to Ottawa, and said it would be silly to have a rumpus before the question was fully examined.

Before such noble resolve, the Canadian politicians wilted. Mackenzie King hurriedly insisted that he never meant for "actual force" to be used. The Canadians sought the advice of the British. It was up to Canada, the Admiralty said, but the cruiser *Devonshire* was close by if they needed its services. Mackenzie King was appalled. Shoot at an ally? What would the Americans think? The *Emile Bertin* was allowed to sail. A suspicious *Devonshire* shadowed it all the way to Martinique.[37] And there the gold remained for the rest of the war.

Mackenzie King and his war cabinet had encountered firsthand one of the agonizing consequences of France's defeat. Would French soldiers and sailors, still out of reach of the Germans, join Britain and her allies, or would they obey the commands of a government suing for peace? It was a question of conscience for the French that was to bedevil Allied plans and policies for the next three years. The incident also tested—and found wanting—the ability of Canada's war cabinet to act independently. In the years that followed, Mackenzie King and his ministers met regularly for earnest discussion, but the real decisions of war were henceforth made in London or Washington.

Germany and Italy were now masters of Europe, and Britain was alone except for her Commonwealth allies. The fighting shifted to the North

Atlantic as U-boats increased in number and skill. Merchant ships gathered in Halifax like frightened sheep, eyeing with dread the dark waves to the east. Almost all Department of Transport wireless stations were put on naval listening assignments. If the waiting submarines could be located, the convoys could be routed to avoid them. The demand for direction-finding bearings from Canadian stations became acute. Bermuda served as the control station and plotted the fixes received from Admiralty DF stations in Jamaica and British Guiana as well as those from Canada. Then de Marbois asked that Bermuda start sending him the bearings it was taking.

De Marbois had become ambitious. He complained openly to the Admiralty about the direction-finding work being done by Bermuda and questioned whether it should remain the controlling station. It was connected to Halifax by an undersea telegraph cable, and getting a fix on a submarine transmitting in the Atlantic required quick reflexes. The moment an operator in Halifax heard a suspicious signal, its frequency was sent to Bermuda even as the Halifax station turned its antenna toward the source. The message came out on a teletype machine beside the British operator in Bermuda, who immediately tuned to the same frequency and searched with his aerial. If both were fast enough, cross-bearings that pinpointed the source would be the result.[38]

Everything depended on the quality of equipment, the personnel, and speed. U-boat messages were notoriously brief—as little as twenty-two seconds. An operator might spend hours hunched over his radio set, his head clamped in padded earphones, ears numbed by an incessant hiss. Then suddenly the static would leap to life in a staccato of Morse code. The man's hand would slam onto a buzzer and an assistant would jump to the teletype machine, banging the frequency numbers out on the keys. Within a couple of seconds the person in Bermuda would begin his search.

De Marbois usually had at least two other Department of Transport direction-finding stations linked to Halifax by teletype circuit and noticed, so he said, that their cross-bearings often did not match those from Bermuda. An interminable exchange of memos followed, most of them written by de Marbois and edged with sarcasm about the alleged incompetence of the personnel in Bermuda. After six months he won his point, and the Canadian direction-finding stations were given the right to operate independently. De Marbois's tactics, however, had made his colleagues at Naval Headquarters uncomfortable. Here was no team player. De Marbois was a terrier who ragged his opponents to death.

It was a peculiar victory. Both de Marbois and Brand were Royal Navy types and here they were arguing for Canadian independence *from* the Royal Navy. The Admiralty's head of wireless intelligence, Captain Humphrey Sandwith, was puzzled by the continual wrangling between Naval Headquarters in Ottawa and Bermuda, especially since a Canadian had deliberately been selected to head the Bermuda operation. Besides, even though de Marbois had a map on the wall of his little office and was doing his own position-plotting of enemy units, the Admiralty was in charge of the war at sea. Only the plotting boards and U-boat tracking room in London actually mattered.[39]

Cooperation between the Army's Rockcliffe wireless station and the Radio Security Service in Britain was much better. Throughout the fall of 1940, there was a free exchange of data on suspicious transmissions. Some of these were from Mexico and South America, but the Canadians identified one as coming from Long Island, New York. The British reported this to the U.S. Federal Bureau of Investigation which replied that it knew the "exact location" of the transmitter. The FBI agreed with British suggestions, however, that nothing should be done to interfere with the clandestine station until the situation had been fully investigated and the extent of the organization behind it ascertained.[40]

The Ottawa area was an excellent listening location, with both the Rockcliffe station and the larger Department of Transport station hearing far more traffic than they could handle. The Rockcliffe group added several more receivers and about a dozen new operators. It also came under the command of Lieutenant E. N.(Ed) Drake, a serious young man with a flair for getting the most out of subordinates. In the fall of 1940, Colonel Murray was transferred out of Telegraph Censorship and put in charge of the Army's wireless intelligence program.

It was probably at Murray's urging that Drake's Rockcliffe team now began to listen to Spanish wireless stations. With Italy's entry into the war, the British had cut the Italian cable out of Canso near Gibraltar. This put pressure on the Spanish in North America to send their plain-language commercial messages by wireless. On their own initiative, Murray and Drake collected this traffic to see if they could compile Spain's order-of-battle in the same way as had been done with Italy's. They were 100 per cent successful.

It was a spectacular achievement. After four months' work, Murray sent the War Office (MI8) page after page listing the entire Spanish Army by regiment, corps, and division, plus where they were posted in Spain and Morocco. He did the same for the Spanish Air Force and Navy, and also identified the head of Spain's much-feared security service (Count Mayalde). He even named and located the officer in the Spanish Army responsible for overseeing executions—a vivid reminder that Spain had recently emerged from one of the bloodiest civil wars of the century.

The War Office acknowledged that the information was "very interesting" and "valuable." Indeed it was. Spain had been actively negotiating with Hitler. If it had decided to enter the war on Germany's side, this would certainly have closed the western end of the Mediterranean to the British, forcing them to rely on the long trip around Africa to supply their troops then fighting the Italians in Libya. Gibraltar was also likely to be directly attacked. If Spain had declared war—as then appeared likely—Colonel Murray's intelligence would have been invaluable.[41]

If the Rockcliffe station could extract such excellent results from plain-language commercial messages, how much greater the prospects if the Army had experts who could read the plethora of enciphered traffic being received at Rockcliffe. On this matter Drake and Murray were on the same wavelength. In early November 1940, Drake, now a captain, made a quick visit to the still-neutral United States. In Washington he met General Joseph Mauborgne, the Chief Signals Officer and the man in charge of the U.S. Army's cryptanalysis unit, the Signal Intelligence Service. Yes, the general assured him, Canada would undoubtedly benefit by having its own cipher-breaking bureau. He offered to supply Drake with secret pamphlets that described some of the latest techniques.

Drake wrote a glowing report. His proposal for a tri-service cryptographic bureau went up to the Chiefs of Staff. It was strongly backed by the Army's Director of Military Operations and Intelligence, with the suggestion that appropriate people could be recruited from the Dominion Bureau of Statistics. The RCMP might also want to get involved. The Navy, however, sat on the idea with a thud. The Navy's Director of Plans wrote:

> ... the matter was dropped [earlier] for three reasons. One was the size of the organisation that would be required; another the necessity of employing personnel with a very specialised knowledge; and the main reason was that the existence of a complete set-up for this work in the United Kingdom would mean that we should only be duplicating a large part of their work.

Captain Brand, speaking for Naval Intelligence, scribbled the following on the margin of that memo:

> Concur with DPD—I doubt whether there is much to be got out of it this war. Everybody has paid too much attention to rendering their cyphers unbreakable.

On November 29, 1940, the Chiefs of Staff killed the idea. "We should continue to use United Kingdom facilities for this work," they ruled, adding that "the cost of such an organization in Canada could not be justified at this time."[42]

The problem was the Navy brass did not know what they were talking about when it came to cryptanalysis. The Government Code and Cipher School in Britain was not nearly large enough to work on all the German and Italian codes and ciphers of potential value, much less those of Axis-leaning neutral countries like Spain, Portugal, Japan, the Soviet Union, and defeated France. Its total personnel at this time was about eighty, more than half of them untrained amateurs recently recruited from the universities. The Government Code and Cipher School was still a teaspoon operation.

Unfortunately, there was no one in Canada with the right kind of experience to realize all this.

CHAPTER TWO

CODEBREAKER
FOR HIRE

JANUARY — JUNE 1941

I T WAS VALENTINE'S DAY, 1941, but there was no love in the letter that arrived by special messenger on the desk of Brigadier General Sherman Miles in the Army Building, Washington. It was from FBI director J. Edgar Hoover and warned that Herbert Yardley was back in town.

A confidential informant "associated with the newspaper profession" had told Hoover that the press had heard Yardley had been hired by the War Department. The newsmen were prepared to pounce. Hoover's letter continued:

> No one among the reporters can understand why the War Department or any other government agency would hire Yardley for any confidential work after the disgraceful manner in which he sold out the Federal Government after his employment in a confidential capacity during the last war. When this story breaks, it will probably be in such a vein that it will ridicule those people who are responsible for Yardley's present employment.

"I thought you should have the benefit of this information," Hoover piously offered.[1]

The report was both vicious and spurious. The FBI had known for more than two months that America's most notorious cryptographer had returned from China and had moved into the Washington apartment of an old girlfriend. Moreover, just two weeks earlier, the FBI had learned from a senior officer in the Signal Corps that Yardley had been given a secret contract to do a special job for the War Department. But it was a contract only, the officer had stressed; Yardley had not been hired and was in no sense an "employee."

As for Hoover's description of journalists seething with righteous indignation over the War Department's hiring practices, the picture does not ring true. What with America's precarious neutrality and half the world at war, the news story surely would have been about *why* someone with Yardley's particular talent had been hired, rather than *whether* he should have been.[2]

Hoover's note appears to have been calculated to elicit a negative response. If so, it passed beneath eyes that were especially receptive. As Assistant Chief of Staff (G-2)—the head of U.S. Military Intelligence—General Miles had been spying on Yardley long before the FBI. His filing cabinet already contained at least two reports marked "Secret" from the military attachés in Chungking, laced with comments like "subject has a decided weakness for women," "drank heavily" and "do not trust him." Hoover did not have to worry about Miles giving Yardley a job.

What had a balding, greying, fifty-two-year-old man done to merit such covert hostility? In intelligence circles, the worst of all possible crimes. Yardley had snitched. He had written a book which told all.

The American Black Chamber (1931) is a classic in the annals of secret intelligence. It is mostly the story of Yardley's First World War experiences as the head of the War Department's cryptanalysis bureau. Written in a crisp, anecdotal style, it is a very readable narrative of early code- and cipher-breaking, wireless and cable interception, secret inks, and spy-catching. These revelations were enough to make it an instant best seller but, unfortunately for him, Yardley went too far.

Yardley had a natural gift as a cryptographer; a "cipher brain," as he used to call it. As a lowly telegraph clerk in the State Department in 1916, he drew attention to himself by showing that he could break all the U.S. diplomatic codes. The feat so impressed his superiors that when the United States joined the war against Germany in 1917, he was placed in charge of the War Department's code and cipher bureau. He was then only twenty-eight, and soon was leading highly successful attacks against German diplomatic and espionage codes, and against the techniques of secret writing.

He was so successful, indeed, that his unit was retained by the Army after the war, camouflaged as a civilian agency based in New York that specialized in compiling commercial codes. Partly financed by the State Department, its real job was to break the code and cipher messages of the diplomatic community in Washington. This function was an echo of the so-called *chambres noires* or "black chambers" that various European governments had operated during the eighteenth century. These would secretly intercept and copy the letters of diplomats, and attempt to break the rather rudimentary codes and ciphers then in use. Yardley was assigned precisely the same task, except that the messages he received were copies of diplomatic cables illegally supplied by the telegraph companies through the connivance of the State Department.

Intercepting other people's mail in peacetime was fair game to monarchs, but the emerging nation-states of the late nineteenth century saw themselves as conducting international affairs on a higher, more gentlemanly plane. Both Britain and France, for example, closed their black chambers in 1844, as did most other countries at about the same time. The privacy of correspondence was deemed sacrosanct, an ethical idea that persists to this day. Thus it was forbidden fruit that U.S. government officials knowingly nibbled as they read the decodes that came from Yardley's little group. From 1917 to 1929, his American black chamber broke the codes and ciphers of Argentina, Brazil, Britain, Chile, Cuba, Costa Rica, France, Germany, Japan, Liberia, Mexico, Nicaragua, Panama, Russia, San Salvador, Santo Domingo, and Spain. Yardley received a second Distinguished Service Medal for his efforts.

Yardley's greatest triumph was cracking Japan's diplomatic code. For Westerners, Japanese is a difficult language. In its written phonetic form, called *kana*, it is represented by about seventy-three letters or pairs of letters standing for specific sounds and syllables. Even though he spoke no Japanese, the ambitious and relentless Yardley had bet his job that he would break the code within a year. He was successful, narrowly, and the dividends were immediate and profound.

In the years immediately following the First World War, Japan was a perplexing and unknown power. A mere seventy years earlier, it had been an isolated island, its people still in the middle ages with bows and arrows, swords, chivalry, and feudalism. Fifty years later, in 1905, Japan manned a fleet of British-built battleships that annihilated a Russian fleet. It also landed an army near Vladivostok and, in a bloody harbinger of the Western Front a decade later, used machine guns and artillery to destroy a Russian army.

Japan joined the Allies in the First World War and continued to manage modern weapons with ease. This was disconcerting to the Western nations. Here was a new world power completely outside European political and military traditions. No one quite knew what to do about Japan when, in 1921, it was suddenly necessary to treat her as a high-ranking nation in the postwar armament discussions. Britain's answer was to deal with her secretly, against the interests of the United States.

Yardley, having cracked the Japanese code, reported everything. Over their morning coffees, State Department officials could read Japanese reports of discussions with the British, and marvel at the audacity of the Foreign Office as it ridiculed American proposals, or smile with condescension at Japanese naivete in seeking to achieve "perfect harmony" among the three powers. When the Japanese delegation to the Washington Arms Conference stonily insisted on a 10–7 capital ship ratio with the United States, Yardley's decodes told of uncertainty, indecision, and then panic behind the scenes. The Americans, forewarned, insisted on a 10–6 ratio. The Japanese caved in.[3]

All this, including reproducing the text of the intercepted telegrams, was reported in *The American Black Chamber*. When the book came out, there was hell to pay.

It is interesting to speculate on whether Yardley's indiscretions materially contributed to the war that eventually engulfed the United States and Japan. His description of the 1921 arms negotiations reveals that Japan was bargaining in good faith, whereas Britain and the United States were not. *The American Black Chamber* was an immediate best seller in Japan and there was a brief flare of official outrage. Then a decade of silence. The Japanese had put on the mask, already worn so skillfuly by the two great English-speaking powers.

For the time being, however, the U.S. authorities could only rage helplessly at Yardley's book. It was terribly damaging to their foreign relations, and not just with Japan. To illustrate how codes were broken, Yardley had selected a page from a reconstructed Foreign Office code book, thereby demonstrating that U.S. officials had been reading Britain's diplomatic correspondence as well. Equally reprehensible, the book was arrogant and sneering in its portrayals of the men who pulled the strings of U.S. government. It depicted them as oafs who little appreciated the value of the intelligence that his cryptographic skills provided, mental midgets beside his shining intellect. The book, in fact, was an act of revenge.

Yardley had been fired. Despite his brilliant behind-the-scenes contribution to the war effort and the immense edge his decrypts had given U.S. foreign policy, a change in the White House had abruptly cut support for his little black chamber. The new Secretary of State under Herbert Hoover, Henry Stimson, was surprised and shocked to learn that his department was spying on foreign diplomats in Washington. He felt this was morally improper and ordered State Department funding to be halted forthwith. "Gentlemen do not read each other's mail," Stimson is reported to have said.

The line is famous, but there is no proof Stimson actually said it. It may have been coined by Yardley himself because it certainly captures the kind of pompous attitude he believed was behind the shutting down of his operation. Being an egotist, he naturally assumed that all his troubles came from on high. In that, however, he was quite wrong.

The man ultimately responsible for Yardley's misfortunes was his new boss, Lieutenant Colonel O. S. Albright, who took over the communications section of the Military Intelligence Division in the summer of 1928. He immediately decided that cryptanalysis in peacetime should be confined to training, and that it should be done without obtaining the current cable messages of foreign governments, which "technically violated the law." This, of course, meant that Yardley's group would no longer have "live" material to work on and could no longer produce intelligence. Albright recommended that the group be detached from Military Intelligence and placed under the Signal Corps.

The recommendation to truncate Yardley's cryptanalysis unit was approved on April 5, 1929, more than a month before Stimson's decision to withdraw State Department funding. On May 10, Army regulations were formally changed to put all code and cipher work under the chief signal officer, including the small code- and cipher-compiling section already in the Signal Corps. Albright then threw Yardley the crumb of less than half his former salary if he cared to stay on as an instructor. Yardley reacted by writing *The American Black Chamber* and it was Albright, plus Colonel A. T. Smith, then chief of Military Intelligence (G-2), who set the Army nipping at his heels.[4]

Students of craven behaviour will find the actions of Albright and Smith fascinating. Apparently in response to prepublication publicity, four days before excerpts of Yardley's book were to appear in *The Saturday Evening Post*, Albright wrote a for-the-file memo to Smith, in which he recounted his reasons for wanting to stop Yardley's work on current codes and ciphers. He justified himself by citing Stimson's *subsequent* judgment that such operations were "unethical." Then he told of Yardley's unhappy reaction and his attempt to dissuade Yardley from writing about the black chamber, concluding: "Mr. Yardley, as yet, has committed no overt act which is reprehensible, and in fact may never do so. But there is a chance he may do so." Albright was covering himself.

When *The American Black Chamber* did appear, the furore was probably more than either Albright or Smith had expected. On August 28, 1931, obviously in response to a peremptory request, Smith sent a memo to the Chief of Staff that failed to mention the Army's decision on reorganization and stated only that Yardley's black chamber had been closed at the instigation of the Secretary of State when the funds it supplied were withdrawn. He backed this up with an analysis that showed that the State Department had contributed two-thirds of the operating costs.

Three days later, presumably after having received this rather incomplete information, the acting Secretary of War, F. H. Payne, took the scenario one step further when he wrote to Stimson: "On Oct. 31, 1929, the Department of State terminated its further participation in the matter, thereby necessitating the closing of the New York office and the discharge of all the civilian personnel, including Yardley." In fact, the Army had closed Yardley's office in June, giving the staff three months' severance pay. Thus did a series of half-truths become a lie, and the State Department unknowingly took full responsibility for the questionable and inept decisions of the War Department.

The ugliest aspect of this story is that Albright and Smith then tried to crucify Yardley. Three years later, when the cryptographer tried to follow up with another book, entitled *Imperial Japanese Secrets*, Colonel Smith got wind of it. He secretly wrote the publisher, Bobbs-Merrill, and warned that Yardley was believed to be in possession of official government documents and therefore in contravention of the Espionage Act. The implied threat was unmistakable. Bobbs-Merrill replied that it had already rejected the manuscript.

Yardley's manuscript was now in the hands of another publisher, the Macmillan Company, and here similar tactics were employed. This time the Attorney-General was also involved. Macmillan ultimately agreed to turn the manuscript over to the United States Attorney for New York and both publisher and author were summoned before a grand jury. The manuscript itself was sent on to the War Department. It was never returned, even though the grand jury found no grounds for charges.

Yardley never fought the seizure very vigorously. He may have been afraid to do so. He had just received a visit from two army officers who had demanded he give back the government documents he had used in writing *The American Black Chamber*. Yardley, sensing a trap, insisted he had no such documents.

And it had been a trap, set by Albright and Smith. In response to a query from them, the Army's Judge Advocate-General had advised that Yardley could be liable to twenty years in jail for *The American Black Chamber*, if it could be proved that he had absconded with the "originals" of government documents. Otherwise, Smith and Albright had been told, his position was little different from that of any employee who had been privy to his company's secrets and then let go. Yardley was probably entitled to say what he pleased.

Later, the judge advocate helpfully added that if Yardley could be persuaded to admit to having such documents in front of suitable witnesses, he could be arrested and convicted. The entrapment arrangements, however, ought only to be made "verbally."[5]

So it was that two army officers, trailed by two civilian witnesses, arrived at Yardley's apartment. He invited them in and, when all were settled, they told him they had come to collect the government documents he had. They must have looked a little too anxious. They also stressed that they wanted the *original* documents. Yardley refused to take the bait. Not me, he said. When he closed the door on the disappointed soldiers, Yardley must have realized he was in deep, deep trouble.

By now, some of the most powerful men in government were out for his blood, and they weren't too scrupulous about how they were going to get it. In the same week the entrapment attempt occurred, the new Chief of the General Staff, General George C. Marshall, suggested to the assistant secretary of state that they confer with the Justice Department for "joint action" against Yardley.[6] In the end, they were only able to arrange to have a bill rapidly pushed though Congress which made it a crime for a government employee to disclose confidential information pertaining to codes and ciphers, on pain of a $10,000 fine or ten years in prison.[7]

Yardley, like a wise rabbit, went to ground. Army intelligence officers were told to be on the lookout for any other books he might try to publish. In the years that immediately followed, there were two harmless spy novels, *The Red Sun of Nippon* and *The Blonde Countess.* The latter was even made into a Hollywood movie, *Rendezvous*, starring William Powell and Rosalind Russell. Then nothing. Yardley spent the next few years as a real estate broker living quietly in New York.

Natural-born cryptographers, however, are a little like professional assassins. They are drawn to political instability and the threat of war. Only under such circumstances are their unique talents suitably appreciated and paid for. As the 1930s crumbled toward conflict in Europe, Yardley found new employment on the other side of the world. Japan had invaded China. Once again Yardley found himself at work on

Japanese codes and ciphers. Once again U.S. Military Intelligence (G-2) opened its file on him.

Assuming the cover-name Herbert Osborn and pretending to be a dealer in hides, Yardley arrived in Chungking in 1938. He was soon leading a successful attack on Japanese military codes for the nationalist Chinese under the leadership of Chiang Kai-shek. His direct boss was General Tai Li, head of the Generalissimo's secret service and probably the most feared man in all China. Tai Li had a gift for making opponents of the regime disappear. He was popularly known as "The Killer" or "Number One Hatchet Man" in a country where beheading was still a common form of execution. Yardley and Tai Li got along extremely well.

The Hatchet Man smiled faintly and I grinned back.

"Tell the general I think Wang Ching-wei should be killed before he does China too much harm."

"The general says (the interpreter explained) you are the first foreigner he has met who believes that personal enemies of his country should be liquidated."

"Why not?" I returned. "In war an assassin's bullet is no more than a soldier's, to my way of thinking, and quite as patriotic. Western tradition says differently. There is an unwritten law that the leaders should go unharmed while the pawns slit each other's throats. Napoleon bled Europe for years without suffering a scratch. One assassin's bullet would have saved countless lives and untold suffering. In the American Civil War the Confederate general Robert E. Lee, by his military genius, dragged out the war for four long years. Assassination is not pleasant, but neither is war."

This called for another *kam-pei*. Ling had quit long ago; the general blinked and gulped his brandy, and I must have been far gone myself. I heard myself say, as from a distance, "Ask the general if his men use silencers."

"Silencers? What is that?" Ling asked.

"Well, it's like this," I began gropingly. "I come from a family of poachers in southern Indiana. We know how to make a contraption..."[8]

The foregoing, from his autobiography, is classic Yardley. Even today his thinking would be considered unconventional, if not outrageous. Then in his early fifties, he enjoyed poker, sex, hard liquor, life in general, and intellectual challenges. One suspects that people with more pedestrian minds instantly disliked him.

Nevertheless, it was his chumminess with Tai Li that would have especially concerned the chief of Military Intelligence (G-2) in Washington. Today's ally may be tomorrow's enemy and, while how to make a silencer was not especially secret, Yardley was loose of tongue on more delicate matters. "Some time ago," he wrote General Tai, "I was asked if the contents of letters could be read without opening the envelope. I beg to report that this can be done by 'infra Red' photography. If you are interested in full information, Miss Edna in Washington will gladly introduce Major Shaio to the right people." Since this particular use of infrared photography was still not generally known, one can imagine what went through General Sherman Miles's mind when a copy of Yardley's letter to General Tai arrived on his desk.[9]

The military attachés at the American embassy in Chungking had the job of spying on Yardley. They did not confine themselves to describing his work for the Chinese: "He is very restless, drinks a great deal, interposed with short periods of total abstinence. Sex is a major obsession with him and his conversation is filled with vulgar and bawdy references to women." And later, in another report: "… many Chinese women visit his apartment, but as far as is known, no foreign women."[10]

All this covert attention, however, sprang from something more than lingering anger over Yardley's disclosures in *The American Black Chamber*. Both the U.S. Navy and the Army had long been preparing for the war that was sure to come. Each operated a wireless interception network and each had cryptanalysis bureaus studying the codes and ciphers of America's most likely enemies.

The Army group, still under the Signal Corps, was called the Signal Intelligence Service, and in 1940 it consisted of slightly more than 300 people, half to monitor the airwaves and half to work on the codes and ciphers so obtained. The chief cryptographer was William Friedman, during the interwar years the only man who matched and then exceeded Yardley in ability. They had known each other for years and after the First World War Yardley had tried unsuccessfully to recruit both Friedman and his wife Elizabeth for his black chamber. Friedman instead joined the Signal Corps as a compiler of codes and ciphers rather than a breaker of them.

Yardley believed that part of his misfortune came about because Friedman had "undermined" him. There is some evidence that this is true. On the other hand, had Yardley accepted the offer of half-salary and gone along with the transfer from Military Intelligence to the Signal Corps, he undoubtedly would have benefited when General Joseph O. Mauborgne took over as Chief Signal Officer. Mauborgne had been a brilliant cryptanalyst in his own right during the First World War and had no myopia about the need for code- and cipher-breaking. In 1937 he vastly expanded the program and, had Yardley been available, Mauborgne likely would have put him in charge. Instead, Friedman was given the task and it was Friedman, not Yardley, who in due time earned honours, distinction, and the thanks of his country.

The U.S. Navy's wireless intercept and code-breaking section was twice as big again as the Army's, and for good reason. Throughout the 1930s, as the world rearmed and Germany became increasingly aggressive, any armchair strategist could see that the United States was certain to be drawn into a new world war, especially if it included Russia and Japan as adversaries. Any war in the Pacific would have to be fought almost entirely by the Navy. The admirals were therefore alive to the need for wireless intelligence-gathering facilities. The Navy had been eavesdropping on Japanese fleet movements since 1927 and, while no documents have yet been released in the United States that specifically mention it, documents in Canadian archives show that by 1940 the U.S. Navy was listening in on the Russians as well.[II]

The organization responsible for this activity was OpNav-20-G, a deliberately confusing mouthful, usually shortened to Op-20-G. In 1940 this label stood for the headquarters of a wireless intercept network that covered some of the Atlantic but even more of the Pacific, with code-breaking units in Hawaii, the Philippines, and Washington.

All along, while Yardley railed publicly and privately against the failure of U.S. authorities to appreciate the need for code- and cipher-breaking, there had been steady and substantial development in the field. The closing of Yardley's black chamber was but a single blink in what otherwise was a clear vision of military necessity. On the eve of war, the United States was again reading Japan's most secret code and cipher messages.

Yardley, however, was on the outside and a potential embarrassment. At any moment, he was liable to draw unwelcome attention to the subject of cryptography. Should the Japanese react by suddenly changing all their codes, the work of years could perish.

In 1940 Yardley appears to have arrived back in the United States believing that he could again be of service to his country. His "true love," Edna Ramsaier, worked in the cryptographic section of the Signal Corps, and it was probably through her that he contacted General Mauborgne. The latter gave him a six-month contract to prepare a report on how to break the Japanese military codes he had encountered in China. Yardley hoped the assignment would lead to a permanent job, but that could never be.[12]

Yet Yardley's career was far from over. This middle-aged outcast, this pariah in his own land, was to be the founder of a wireless intercept and code- and cipher-breaking organization which, after the Second World War, would become the third most sophisticated in the non-Communist world. It survives to this day, but not in the United States or Britain. In Canada.

———————

Norman Robertson, Canada's acting undersecretary of state for External Affairs, fingered the letter from London. Spread out below it on his desk were a dozen War Office flimsies bearing the text of telegrams sent to Vichy by René Ristelhueber, the representative in Ottawa of the new government in conquered France. The letter was dated February 1, 1941. The messages were all more than a month old.

"It looks as if the War Office are showing some reluctance to continue to decode these telegrams," the writer of the letter, Lester Pearson, complained. "In a number of cases blank spaces are left which, I think, could have been supplied from the context, especially as the same person, no doubt, has been doing the deciphering from the beginning."

Pearson was then first secretary to Vincent Massey, Canada's High Commissioner in London. One of his jobs was to make sure that Canada's needs were looked after in its dealings with the various bureaucracies of the Imperial government. In this case, the bureaucracy was the Government Code and Cipher School, and Canada's needs were definitely not being met.

"It is unfortunate in this connection that the more interesting telegrams in the present batch should be the ones with the most blanks," Pearson went on. Then he quoted a War Office official: "'We are wondering whether your people in Ottawa have any idea of setting up a cryptographic bureau of your own; if so, we think we could be of considerable help to you.'"[13]

Do it yourself, in other words. The British cryptographers at GC&CS, submerged as they were in a deluge of intercepts from German-occupied Europe, had better things to do than worry about the activities of a French diplomat in far-off Canada. The new German-dominated government of France had moved its administrative headquarters from Paris to the resort town of Vichy, and its messages to French colonies in the Middle East, West Africa, North Africa, and the West Indies were a thousand times more important to the war. There were also the naval codes of the still-intact French Fleet to be broken and read. There just wasn't the staff—perhaps twenty to thirty actual cryptanalysts—to handle everything. Ottawa–Vichy traffic must have been pretty close to the bottom of the heap.[14]

To Robertson, however, it was important. The soft-spoken thirty-six-year-old had been catapulted into the undersecretary's post by the fatal heart attack of his boss, O. D. Skelton, a few days earlier. It was a job for which he had few apparent qualifications: he was prematurely bald, deaf in one ear, and had a soft, babyish face that invited bullying rather than confidence. He was, however, a graduate of Oxford and had spent time with the Brookings Institution before joining External Affairs in 1929. Now, mainly because he happened to be in the right place at the right time, he was directly answerable to Canada's Prime Minister. Mackenzie King also held the portfolio of Secretary of State for External Affairs and he had an obsession with Vichy.

Five months earlier, after the fall of France, a British and Free French force had attempted to land at Dakar, the great French naval base on the west coast of Africa. The leader in exile of the Free French, General Charles de Gaulle, had convinced Winston Churchill that the garrison would certainly choose liberty over loyalty to the Nazi-backed Vichy government in France. He was wrong. The garrison put up a stubborn fight, gave more than it got, and forced the British fleet to withdraw with two destroyers and a battleship seriously damaged.

Dakar was a fiasco. In his diary Mackenzie King congratulated himself for having gone "on record in advance" as being opposed to the scheme. What it confirmed to the Canadian Prime Minister, as it did to Churchill, was that Frenchmen world-wide had lost their *élan*, their spirit. The capture of Paris by the Germans in June 1940 had cut the very heart out of French resistance and loyalty to the Allied cause. Dakar showed that the soldiers who yesterday were faithful comrades-in-arms might tomorrow be adversaries.

Almost fifty years after the war, it seems all but forgotten that defeated France was once a serious potential enemy. Germany had overrun continental France but the French colonies, with their considerable military and economic resources, were out of reach. Britain had hoped they would join the Allied cause, but instead most opted for obedience to Vichy. The British then chose to believe that the majority of Frenchmen would want to carry on the fight, or at least stay out of it. This was illusion. Not only was there resistance at Dakar, but in retaliation 100 French bombers from North Africa raided Gibraltar. Churchill concluded that the attack on Dakar should not be resumed. Open war with Vichy in 1940 would have made Britain's hold on the Mediterranean impossible. Churchill had no choice but to back off.[15]

In fairness to the French people, Hitler had been lucky in more than blitzkrieg in the conquest of France. The leader who stepped forward to come to terms with the victorious Germans was Marshal Henri Pétain, hero of the First World War. In 1917 he had single-handedly saved the French armies from mutiny and collapse, and was subsequently seen by the French as one of the architects of Allied victory in 1918. Now he sought to save France again, this time by preaching collaboration rather than resistance. As leader of the new Vichy government, Pétain had the credentials to appeal to the patriotism of Frenchmen, to ask them to be loyal to country above all else, to urge them not to join the Allied cause. He was highly successful, persuading the majority that a German victory over Britain and its allies was inevitable. As the Canadian Chiefs of Staff observed sententiously, the result was that the French were "more and more tending to make a friend of the Mammon of Unrighteousness in the hope thereby of improving their position."[16] In the course of the war the Allies had to use armed force to regain every major French colony.

Mackenzie King worried incessantly that Vichy France might go beyond neutrality and actually come into the war on Germany's side. Britain had broken off diplomatic relations, but Churchill had encouraged the Canadian Prime Minister to recognize the Vichy regime so that there would be a Vichy official in Ottawa who would serve as a "window" on what was happening across the Channel. Mackenzie King accepted the assignment, even though there was a possibility that the Vichy government might try to influence attitudes in French-speaking Quebec.[17] This danger gave him an excellent reason for wanting to be able to read the enciphered messages the Vichy representative sent back to France.

Robertson did not act immediately on the letter from Pearson. He had many other new responsibilities, so it was more than a month before he found time to pass along Pearson's letter to the Army's Director of Military Intelligence. He was unaware that the idea of a code and cipher bureau had twice been rejected. Yet the concept was very much alive.

The third attempt to give Canada a code and cipher bureau was coming from an unexpected quarter. The Chiefs of Staff had turned down the idea the previous November, but even as they did so it was being debated separately at the National Research Council. The unravelling of ciphers, after all, is a scientific endeavour and Canada's government-run research centre in Ottawa had suddenly found itself with more than enough money to spend on off-the-wall projects.

The British army that straggled across the Channel from Dunkirk in 1940 was a defeated army. The First Canadian Division under General Andrew McNaughton suddenly became half the total forces in

Britain capable of resisting German invasion.[18] Canadians saw their tiny contingent of troops in the same glow as the heroes of Thermopylae. This brought forward an unusual outburst of patriotism.

At the suggestion of a friend in government, John David Eaton, head of the privately owned T. Eaton Co. department store chain, and Sir Edward Beatty, president of the Canadian Pacific Railway, each agreed to put up $250,000 from their private fortunes to finance military research. Samuel Bronfman, head of Seagrams, the Canadian distillery giant, promptly matched their gifts, and soon other corporate donations had swelled the fund to over $1 million.[19]

The money came with no strings attached and was a godsend to the National Research Council. The NRC had been set up in 1916 to promote scientific research in Canada, and in 1932 had opened laboratories of its own in a new building on Ottawa's Sussex Drive. Initially, its work was primitive and of little value, but from 1935 on, under its new head, General McNaughton, the NRC had begun to acquire a leadership role in Canadian scientific research.

The NRC worked by means of associate committees. These bodies coordinated research in the NRC labs with similar research in industry and the universities. There were associate committees on aviation medicine, applied mathematics, chemistry, physics, and so on, with the members being drawn from scientists at the NRC and from private institutions. When war broke out in 1939, this system proved ideal for mobilizing Canada's meagre scientific resources for military purposes. But there was little money. Even after the defeat of France, the Mackenzie King government remained parsimonious about funding research. The money from Eaton, Beatty, and Bronfman suddenly made all the difference.

In 1940 $1 million was a very large sum. The new acting president of the NRC, C. J. Mackenzie, immediately used it to launch an ambitious program of research into poison gas, bacterial warfare, radar, ballistics, optics, new explosives, and a host of other projects. The money was administered and new programs approved by the War Technical and Scientific Development Committee, consisting of the major donors—Eaton, Bronfman, and Beatty; an officer from each of the three services; a person from External Affairs; and three senior scientists—Mackenzie, chemist Otto Maass, and the discoverer of insulin, Sir Frederick Banting.

It was the External Affairs member of the committee, Hugh Keenleyside, who first suggested cryptography as a scientific project worthy of the committee's sponsorship. In mid-January 1941, Keenleyside reminded the committee that some months earlier he had proposed a search in Canada for people knowledgeable about codes and ciphers. Had anything been done about it, he wondered? Mackenzie promised to find out and report back at the next meeting.

Meanwhile, Keenleyside approached the Navy with the idea. His inquiry was passed along to Captain Brand of Naval Intelligence, who told him of the November 1940 Chiefs of Staff decision. Brand said that the matter had been "deferred" indefinitely.[20]

The impression of inertia that Brand gave Keenleyside was deceptive. On the very day that he was handling Keenleyside's query, Brand asked the Department of Transport to persuade the Federal Communications Commission in the still-neutral United States to help out on the coverage of illicit wireless messages from spies in Mexico and South America. He also proposed providing similar listening assignments as they cropped up "if your friends care to assist us further."[21]

Brand's interest in what was essentially non-naval wireless material stemmed from a split in his own intelligence staff. During the preceding year, the Canadian Navy's wireless listening and direction-finding capability had expanded dramatically. The new Navy-staffed station at Hartlen Point in Halifax had become operational, while existing Department of Transport stations had received better equipment and more staff. Moreover, because the Government Code and Cipher School in Britain was now making headway against various naval codes and ciphers, the Admiralty was demanding the raw traffic from German, Japanese, French, and American sources as well as bearings.[22] This meant that Brand's deputy, Commander de Marbois, had little time for anything other than wireless intelligence. All the peripheral activities of his Foreign Intelligence Service were taken over by Lieutenant Herbie Little, including liaison with the Army's wireless intelligence unit at Rockcliffe. Little did not mind. He and the man in charge over at Rockcliffe, Captain Ed Drake, were about the same age and shared the same curiosity about the enciphered traffic from German spies still being intercepted and sent to the Radio Security Service in Britain.

One clandestine transmitter was especially interesting. Naval direction finding had located it on the East Coast of the United States, somewhere near New York. Having a German spy that close was exciting, and both Little and Drake pined for the chance to read what he was sending. Then, through the RCMP, Little learned that the spy was actually under the control of the Americans. His transmitter had been set up to relay messages to Germany from other spies in the United States and Mexico. It was hoped that some of these transmissions could be cracked and the FBI asked the RCMP to help. Constable Robert McLaren was assigned to the task and de Marbois arranged for Little to assist McLaren as German translator.[23]

Little was thrilled by the opportunity, although it is doubtful that either man accomplished much, for neither knew anything about cryptanalysis. Nevertheless, to encourage his subordinate, de Marbois proposed to Brand that Little head a separate "general intelligence section" to tackle non-naval intercepts. De Marbois could then focus exclusively on naval direction finding and traffic analysis. This was done.[24]

Mackenzie of the National Research Council, meanwhile, had written to all the universities in Canada, asking if they had anyone on their staffs knowledgeable about cryptography. He did not have much luck. The head of the mathematics department at the University of Toronto suggested two young professors, but otherwise drew a blank. Then Little called Mackenzie to ask if the NRC had any mathematicians who could help him decipher some intercepted messages.

Little's request was the first Mackenzie had heard of the Navy's interest in cryptanalysis, and he reacted decisively. At the next meeting of the War Technical and Scientific Development Committee, on March 27, 1941, he recommended that $10,000 be set aside for Project G-1003, the establishment of a cryptographic bureau. The others at the meeting nodded their agreement. Canada's own special intelligence service was born.[25]

No one knew how to proceed. Mackenzie, as requested, matched

Constable McLaren and Lieutenant Little with Dr. Richard Rudey, one of the NRC's mathematicians, and together they chipped away at some of the enemy intercepts. The middle-aged Rudey was well-respected at the NRC but when it came to cryptanalysis, he had neither knack nor knowledge. The trio made little progress.

Keenleyside called a meeting in late April of the "inter-departmental committee on cryptography," to which he invited Brigadier Maurice Pope, now attached to the Army's General Staff. Pope, obviously remembering the advice he had received from the British a year earlier, suggested that they confine their efforts to "comparatively simple activities" such as trying to break the clandestine messages from Latin America and the United States. Yet this had already proved beyond the capabilities of Little's team of amateurs.[26]

The two young professors recommended to Mackenzie by the University of Toronto broke the impasse. They were both keen to help when they learned that the NRC had been looking for cryptographers. H. S. M. Coxeter and Gilbert de B. Robinson hardly knew anything about codes and ciphers, but they knew Abraham Sinkov, a mathematician under William Friedman with the U.S. Army's Signal Intelligence Service. On their own initiative they wrote him, and Sinkov replied that he believed training pamphlets on cryptanalysis were already being gathered for the Canadian government and that they should inquire into the matter.[27]

This was news to Mackenzie. As soon as he heard of it, he alerted Little and then arranged to get letters of accreditation for Coxeter and Robinson from External Affairs and the Canadian legation in Washington. Go down and talk to Sinkov, he told them. Within two weeks, on May 1, 1941, the academics were on their way.

By this time, there was a much more sophisticated awareness in Canada of the intelligence potential of wireless interception. The year had begun with indifference and doubt at the highest level; four months later even the deputy minister of defence (Army) was warning all government departments that they must use high-grade ciphers when sending messages by radio. "There is grave possibility that every message transmitted is available to … enemy sympathizers. It is safe to assume that the signals emanating from Ottawa, Winnipeg, Halifax, etc. are just as strong in enemy countries as they are in Canada."[28]

The reason for the sudden concern is clear. Enemy countries could hear radio signals from Canada just as easily as Canadians could hear theirs. And the receivers manned by army, navy, and Department of Transport personnel crackled with a constant stream of messages, day and night, on all practical bands. Dot-dot, dash-dot—almost all were in Morse code and the listeners knew that they came from U-boats announcing sinkings, enemy raiders, spies calling home, diplomats reporting negotiations, or German air and army units organizing attacks. Some of the messages were from enemies—Germany and Italy—and some from potential enemies—Japan and Russia.[29]

"You literally could reach up and pluck messages from the air," Little was to recall many years later. Yet the Canadians could not read them.

Thus it was that two young university professors found themselves in the office of the Chief Signal Officer, U.S. Army, Washington, D.C., on a fine sunny day in May. The meeting did not go well. General Mauborgne was grey, gruff, and professional. His first question was whether they were following up the contact he'd had six months earlier with Captain Drake. Who? Captain E. N. Drake, General Mauborgne said. Canadian Army. Signal Corps. Drake had requested an outline for the organization of a cryptographic unit and it had been prepared long ago. Yet there had been no formal request through channels.

Robinson and Coxeter were embarrassed. What was the general talking about? The two young professors awkwardly improvised an explanation: the National Research Council was trying to obtain information on its own account to help the government formulate policy. It probably did not fool Mauborgne, but at least it got the meeting over that bumpy bit of ground.

Mauborgne refused to give the Canadians any details about the cryptographic service under his command. The conversation remained on general lines and was not encouraging. He told them they would need a skilled instructor and at least fifty people. It would probably take a year to train them, although if really pushed it might be managed in four to five months. And, no, he had no one he could spare to send to Canada; nor would he allow a Canadian to come to study their techniques. He could supply training manuals, make some suggestions regarding organization, and that was that.

Coxeter and Robinson must have shown their disappointment. Mauborgne softened. He had been in the military side of codes and ciphers for the last twenty-five years and was not about to discourage enterprise. He had also heard from someone recently who might perfectly fit the bill for the Canadians, someone who had made a misstep in the past for which, in Mauborgne's opinion, he had "perhaps suffered unduly."[30]

The man he had in mind, Mauborgne told the Canadians, was an expert cryptographer and a fine organizer. He was right here in Washington. The general even had his address. His name?

Herbert O. Yardley.

CHAPTER THREE

SPIES IN ABUNDANCE

JUNE – OCTOBER 1941

FRIEDRICH KEMPTER was a spy. Code-named King, or KOE-NIG, the thirty-seven-year-old German had been working in Brazil for the German espionage agency, the Abwehr, for more than a year. He was good at his job.

Kempter's primary task was to report on the cargos, departure times, and destinations of merchant ships that called at Brazilian ports. He had built up an efficient network of sub-agents to serve as his eyes and ears. The information they obtained was sent to Germany to be relayed to the U-boats lying in wait in the mid-Atlantic. Kempter's organization was so comprehensive that his Abwehr controllers in Hamburg labelled him "Message Centre Brazil."

On June 22, 1941 he was sitting before his transmitter, the apparatus neatly nestled in a small black suitcase. His finger rested lightly on the sending key. It was 7.45 p.m. and he was about to send a message. Beside him, on a piece of paper, was the enciphered text, a meaningless jumble of letters in groups of five. But it was not shipping information this time. Hamburg had asked him to do a discreet investigation of some of his colleagues operating in Brazil.

Kempter now began to work the key. Tap-tap, tap-tap. Rapidly.

After about a minute he stopped. Long messages increase the chance of enemy interception. He waited, then started again. Tap-tap, tap-tap. Then he was done.

Six thousand miles north of Kempter, a soldier in the Royal Canadian Corps of Signals stopped writing. He listened intently, pencil poised. There was only static in his earphones now.

The following day a yellow message form bearing the jumbled letters left the Army's experimental Special Wireless Station at Rockcliffe airport, Ottawa, and was delivered to a sparsely furnished room in the new National Research Council buildings on Montreal Road. There it came under the eye of a slightly built man in his early fifties: Herbert Yardley. He probably smiled when he saw it. The cipher type was familiar to him. A few days of pencil work, and the plaintext lay before him. It read:

> The gentlemen from Siemens are Hans Muth and Benno Sobisch who give us valuable assistance and must not be deterred from collaboration. From these men we learned details on colleagues [break in transmission here] … in fatherland work with stations. Engels establishes liaison with the Embassy. Then there is Karl Muegge under the direction of a gentleman from whose name is unknown. To this group belongs Schwab of the firm Munlos.

While the text of the message was still incomplete, and the translation awkward, Yardley was reading the real names of five of the German agents working for the three major spy rings then in Brazil. Three of them—Muth, Sobisch, and Schwab—could easily be located because the message connected them to the companies they worked for. These three could easily lead to the other two. And the man named Engels (code-named ALFREDO) was the leader of a spy ring even more important than Kempter's.[1]

Yardley knew the value of what he was reading. Unlike most of the decrypts from this period to be found in Canadian archives, this one is marked "Secret" and appears to have been kept separate from the main files. Yardley, moreover, had deciphered Hamburg's request for the information the day before, so he could not possibly have missed the significance of Kempter's answer.

The Canadian legation in Washington had already been alerted to expect "some very interesting decyphers" as soon as a way was found to convey them to the appropriate U.S. authorities.[2] Within two weeks of starting up under Yardley, Canada's new cryptanalysis bureau had produced significant results. What remained to be seen was whether—and how—the Allies profited from them.

Yardley owed his presence in Canada to General Mauborgne's recommendation two months earlier. After leaving the Washington office of the head of the U.S. Signal Intelligence Service, Professors Robinson and Coxeter immediately phoned Yardley, who agreed to meet them at the Canadian legation that afternoon. He impressed them. In their report the next day to the National Research Council, the two academics strongly urged that Yardley be invited to Ottawa for further talks. They also stressed that they had learned it was "almost useless" to attempt a cryptographic project without the proper expertise which Yardley, they said, possessed "in the highest degree."

Hume Wrong, the legation's first secretary, sounded a warning, however. In a separate message to External Affairs—which ultimately was seen by both Norman Robertson and the Prime Minister—Wrong noted that Yardley was "in disfavour" in certain circles of the U.S. government because of the disclosures in *The American Black Chamber*. "Should the question arise of Major Yardley's appointment on a regular basis," he wrote, "I believe that it would be desirable to consider carefully whether we should consult the State Department before making any definite offer." For the time being, however, External Affairs ruled that no mention of the matter would be made to the American authorities.[3]

"Even between friendly governments, there's very little cooperation in such things," Yardley told his listeners in Ottawa a week later. "One government would be so afraid of its sources of information, it would hesitate to let another government know it was breaking down certain codes and ciphers." His comment was made during debate on whether the United States was already intercepting and deciphering Japanese diplomatic traffic. In the months and years ahead, the Canadians were to discover much truth in Yardley's words.

Canada's fledgling cryptographic committee had gathered in Room

123 of Parliament Hill's gothic and gloomy East Block, the Canadians to size up Yardley, the American to sell his hosts on an idea they only dimly understood. Hugh Keenleyside of External Affairs chaired the meeting. Also present were T. A. Stone, the External Affairs representative on the Censorship committee, Colonel Murray of Military Intelligence, Captain Brand of Naval Intelligence, and Lieutenant Little.

Yardley listened sympathetically as Little told how he, Drake, and McLaren had been struggling with enciphered messages from enemy agents in Latin America. It was a good place to start, the American agreed, but suggested that they should also consider working on Japanese messages. It was a field in which he'd had some experience and the Japanese had a legation in Ottawa. Its encoded messages to Tokyo were already being copied by Telegraph Censorship, so there would be plenty of raw material.

Canada, of course, was not yet at war with Japan. That was nearly seven months in the future, but they all knew that ambitious Japan, with a navy that rivalled that of Germany, was a growing menace in the Pacific. Keenleyside asked Yardley what was the minimum number of people he needed to run cryptographic attacks on both German clandestine transmissions and the Japanese diplomatic messages. Yardley said six, including himself.

Yardley then slyly took the opportunity to suggest that the Canadians try to hire Miss Edna Ramsaier from the U.S. Signal Intelligence Service as his assistant. She had worked with him in the 1920s, he explained, and was an expert on Japanese ciphers. General Mauborgne would be loath to release her, he said, but it was worth a try.[4]

In fact, Mauborgne probably would have been delighted to release her. When Yardley had returned from China and moved in with his former girlfriend, the FBI had checked her out and discovered she was a cryptanalyst with the War Department. This had been reported to U.S. Military Intelligence (G-2) which undoubtedly fingered her as a security risk because of her relationship with Yardley.[5] And there was reason to worry. Mauborgne's cryptanalysts under William Friedman were enjoying better success with Japanese traffic than Yardley and the Canadians ever dreamed possible. They had broken Japan's highest grade machine cipher (code-named PURPLE) and were regularly reading the messages between Tokyo and the Japanese embassy in Washington.

Yardley impressed his listeners. The next day the same group met again, with the addition this time of two people of sufficient authority to give the go-ahead: Maurice Pope of the Army's General Staff, newly promoted to brigadier, and Norman Robertson, the acting undersecretary of state for External Affairs. They agreed that Yardley should be hired and a small staff assigned to him. These would include the two University of Toronto mathematicians, Miss Ramsaier if she were available, a translator from the RCMP, and three clerk/typists.

They also decided that the unit should come under the administrative control of the National Research Council while reporting to External Affairs. Robertson stressed the need for absolute secrecy while Keenleyside proposed that the unit's existence be kept from the Chiefs of Staff. Brigadier Pope protested that he would at least have to mention it to the Army chief. Robertson yielded on that point, but then agreed that Yardley take an assumed name. Here, perhaps, it was not just the Germans he was concerned about. The acting undersecretary of state for External Affairs had decided to hire Yardley without officially informing the U.S. State Department.[6]

Yardley began work on June 11, 1941. He and Edna Ramsaier, Gilbert Robinson, Constable McLaren of the RCMP, plus a few others were set up in a room in the annex of the new National Research Council building on Montreal Road in Ottawa. A supervisory committee was organized to include representatives from Censorship and the RCMP, plus Colonel Murray from Military Intelligence and Lieutenant Little from Naval Intelligence. T. A. Stone—always referred to as "Tommy" Stone—was the nominee from External Affairs and was to serve as chairman.

For a cover name, Yardley's team was called the "Examination Unit." It was to receive copies of all code and cipher messages intercepted by Censorship or by the wireless listening stations. Yardley adopted his old alias, Herbert Osborn, and on June 16 received his first samples of Kempter's enciphered messages. Eleven days later he had broken them.[7]

By remarkable coincidence, the FBI had received its first decrypts of South American spy messages just two weeks earlier. These had come by way of the small cryptographic unit of the Coast Guard which was then directed by William Friedman's wife, Elizabeth, also an accomplished and gifted cryptanalyst. The intercepts themselves had been supplied by the Radio Intelligence Division of the Federal Communications Commission (FCC), the civilian agency in the United States which in peacetime had the same responsibility for licensing and overseeing domestic radio communications as Canada's Department of Transport and Britain's General Post Office.

Soon after Germany overran France in June 1940, President Roosevelt had approved a $1.6 million expansion of the FCC's intercept facilities. The following October, the FBI received a trickle of messages from German agents in Mexico via the FCC and the Coast Guard. Then, in January 1941, the program was formalized by the creation of the Defense Communications Board, which was to oversee the monitoring and decrypting of wireless traffic from secret agents throughout the Western Hemisphere. The FCC made the intercepts, the Coast Guard deciphered them, and the FBI did the subsequent investigations on behalf of the State Department. Thus a third wireless intelligence service was created in the United States, which existed independent of the Navy's Op-20-G and the Army's Signal Intelligence Service.[8]

The Coast Guard's code- and cipher-breaking unit was set up by the Treasury Department during the Prohibition years, when rum-runners dodged Coast Guard vessels to unload their cargos of illegal liquor on the then-dry shores of the United States. This was a lucrative criminal activity during the late 1920s and early 1930s, and its sophisticated business techniques included radio communication in code between the rum-running vessels offshore and their customers on land. In 1927 the Prohibition authorities hired Elizabeth Friedman to try to break some of these codes, and she was so successful—leading to the arrest of a number of vessels—that the Treasury Department set up a permanent cryptanalysis unit, under her direction, to work with the Coast Guard. This was still operating in 1941.[9]

They must have had unusual conversations over supper, Mr. and Mrs. Friedman. In 1941 she was in charge of cipher-breaking attacks on German espionage traffic and he on Japanese diplomatic messages, plus whatever else the U.S. Army sent his way. Both their offices were in Washington. Herbert Yardley and Edna Ramsaier were likewise a man and woman united by cryptography. She had joined his black chamber in 1919, then an exceptionally pretty woman of nineteen, and had helped with the Japanese codes. Yardley was already married then, and Edna also later married someone else, but the attraction was mutual and eventually they drifted together after their marriages fell apart. One can say of both couples—how can one resist it?—that it was love at first cipher.

Roosevelt made two other major decisions on intelligence matters as a result of Germany's 1940 successes in Europe. He expanded the FBI's mandate to include counter-espionage work outside U.S. territory—specifically Latin America—and agreed to allow the British to set up their own secret service agency in the United States. The director of this new agency, which came to be called British Security Coordination (BSC), was the wealthy Canadian businessman, William Stephenson. He and a small team moved into offices in the Rockefeller Center in New York. Their primary assignment, in cooperation with the FBI, was to counter Axis subversion and the dockside sabotage of ships loading for Britain in U.S. ports.

Unlike most European powers, the United States did not then have a secret service. Foreign intelligence-gathering was the responsibility of individual government departments—the State Department for political information, the Army and Navy for military matters. There was little provision for espionage and none for counter-espionage outside the U.S. The FBI had some of the dossier-collecting functions of MI5, Britain's Security Service, but the Bureau was more a national police force than a national security agency.

Stephenson and his men, by contrast, were appointees of MI6, Britain's Secret Intelligence Service. While their mandate was cooperation with the FBI on security and counter-espionage matters, it extended also to intelligence-gathering. The United States was still neutral and the Axis countries had embassies in Washington. There were Axis sympathizers among the general public, in Congress, and in government. By the end of 1940, British Security Coordination had expanded sufficiently to be organized into three divisions: security, special operations, and secret intelligence.

Whether Hoover was aware of the full scope of BSC activities is unknown, but Stephenson brought one thing to the table that the FBI director could not resist. In the United States it was illegal to interfere with private communications, including the mails; there was no general censorship organization equivalent to British Imperial Censorship. In exchange for the Americans' arranging to have all of their trans-Atlantic mail pass through Bermuda and Trinidad, the British established major censorship centres at these two places. They fed the copied contents of suspicious letters to the FBI, which led to the arrests of several German secret agents operating in the United States.[10] From mid-1940 to early 1941, however, neither British nor American counter-espionage was effective in Latin America. The FBI gave a number of its agents crash courses in Spanish and Portuguese and dispatched them to the various Latin American countries under false identities, but they probably stood out like sore thumbs. There is no evidence in the available records that they accomplished anything.

The British did no better. Stephenson's intelligence territory was mainly the United States, with limited extension to Central America and to British colonies in the West Indies. As for South America, the entire continent was covered by one London-controlled MI6 agent pretending to be a passport control officer at the British embassy in Montevideo. Moreover, mail could avoid British Censorship by going directly from Brazil to Europe via LATI, the Italian-owned air service, or via Condor, the German-owned one. Axis espionage activities in South America were virtually a closed book.[11]

The FBI, for all its inexperience, scored one very important counter-espionage coup at this time. In mid-1940 the German spy, William Sebold, surrendered to the American authorities and agreed to work as a double agent. Sebold's job had been to provide a wireless relay link between spies in North America and their controllers in Germany. This was the "Long Island" traffic being picked up in Canada by Drake and worked on by Little and McLaren. The FBI had Sebold's code-book but it did not have the cipher keys to the messages he was relaying.[12] The Canadian attempt to help was both welcome and appreciated.

It was Elizabeth Friedman of the Coast Guard, however, who actually broke the traffic. The decrypts she produced in the spring of 1941 disclosed an elaborate spy ring with links across the United States and in Mexico and Central America. In a few months enough messages had been decrypted for the FBI to pounce. The spies in the United States were rounded up in June. This success, plus the favourable report of two FBI agents who visited Britain's Government Code and Cipher School in February,[13] undoubtedly convinced the Bureau that, when it came to spy-chasing, cryptanalysis was the best way to go.

Meanwhile, the Abwehr was turning increasing attention to South America. Its espionage effort there had so far been half-hearted. Intelligence from Europe and the Middle East had been far more important during the first two years of war. Now the fighting had shifted from land to sea as the British fought to maintain their supply lines across the Atlantic. Germany's U-boat building program had found its stride, and more and more British merchant vessels, engulfed in flame and smoke, were sliding under the Atlantic's dark waves.

Shipping intelligence was suddenly at a premium. One of the world's greatest trade routes followed the eastern coast of South America. The Abwehr now made a concentrated effort to expand its spy networks on the southern continent, especially in Brazil. In the interests of speed, they were also supplied with wireless transmitters.

Germany's secret agents in South America were just getting used to the new method of contacting home when the Examination Unit started up. Almost immediately their messages came under attack by Yardley and the Coast Guard cryptanalysts under Elizabeth Friedman. The Canadian group, indeed, was initially more successful in obtaining raw intercepts, possibly because Captain Drake's wireless intercept station at Rockcliffe was on a wartime footing, whereas the stations of the Federal Communications Commission were not. In a few months this would change.[14]

In the weeks that followed breaking Kempter's cipher, Yardley dazzled his new employers. Everyone was taken by surprise at the wealth of intelligence he extracted from the meaningless jumbles of letters and numbers that crossed his desk.

Most striking was an enormous flow of sailing reports from Kempter: the *City of Paris* to Capetown, the *Palma* to England, the *T. J. Williams* to Port of Spain, the *City of Toronto* to Buenos Aires, and so on. Other spies in other Brazilian ports joined in. The reports rapidly grew from the tens to the dozens to the hundreds, and all in Ottawa who received the decrypts knew that they were touched with death, that those in Germany who controlled the U-boat wolf packs in the Atlantic were also reading them, and deploying their forces accordingly.

Some of the reports from Kempter and other agents graphically evoked the Atlantic war:

Message No. 153 Date 4–7 Time 21.30

> This morning the auxiliary cruiser *Carnarvon Castle* arrived from the high seas. The visible main armaments are eight 15 centimetre guns, four in the bow and four astern.

It did not take much imagination to visualize a submarine commander greedily digesting that bit of information as his vessel punched its way through the Atlantic's great waves. If it was the *Carnarvon Castle* that next loomed over the horizon, he would know to use a torpedo and submerged attack, rather than his gun. It would be safety first, sinkings second, for the prudent submariner.

Kempter also reported the results of the Atlantic battle:

Message No. 159 Date 8–7 Time 23.00

> *Scottish Star* docked in Brazil. Visible on starboard were machine gun hits.

Again it took little imagination to see an intelligence officer in the German Navy matching this message against a U-boat commander's description of a midnight attack, and its picture of staccato flashes of gunfire against a vague shape hulking in the dark.

It was difficult for the members of the Examination Unit committee to decide who should get the intercepts. At first they thought that all should go to External Affairs for distribution. Then they decided to give one copy each to Military and Naval Intelligence, which would then forward them to the appropriate intelligence officers attached to the British Joint Staff Mission in Washington. The majority of the decrypts dealt with reports on shipping, but when the committee realized that some also gave clues to the identities of the spies and their methods, these messages were given to the RCMP to pass on to the FBI.[15]

Suspicious letters intercepted by Postal Censorship also came to Yardley's little group to be examined for hidden meanings and codes. The entire collection of enciphered Japanese diplomatic messages intercepted since 1939 by Telegraph Censorship was sent over. Samples of all unreadable wireless transmissions, heard on whatever frequency by the Army's Rockcliffe receiving station, were also submitted so that Yardley could rule on whether the messages were military or diplomatic, in code or cipher, resolvable or not.

In June, just as Yardley was starting up, Hitler launched his surprise attack against Russia and that summer there was a surge of Abwehr intercepts from the other side of the world. When deciphered, these turned out to be from secret agents behind Russian lines, alerting the advancing German armies to the locations and defenses of airports and other strategic centres. Because Russia had so recently been a potential enemy, and because the Germans were moving faster than the information could be put to use, the Canadians were hard-pressed to know what to do with the messages. Before long, they dropped the coverage. Yardley's prowess in breaking ciphers had outrun his new employers' ability to put them to use.[16]

When Yardley asked whether he could get some American cigarettes duty-free, Norman Robertson himself took the time to put the request to the assistant commissioner of customs. After noting that American "Herbert Osborn" was engaged on "some highly secret intelligence work," Robertson wrote:

> I should add that in making this request, Mr. Osborn made it quite
> clear to me that he did not want to press the point or make a nui-

sance of himself. He was hopeful that after a certain length of time he might be able to smoke Canadian cigarettes with some pleasure but up until now he said that the education of his taste had been a very slow process.

The reply, when it eventually came back, was a polite but firm refusal. Regulations were regulations, even for an undersecretary of state.[17]

Robertson had every reason to bestow small favours on Yardley. As the senior officer in External Affairs, he could not have failed to appreciate that the American was supplying him with the greatest of all diplomatic treasures: secret intelligence that one country can offer another for, as they say in sports, "future considerations." Even as he made the request for Yardley's cigarettes, Robertson was sending his third batch of decrypts to the Canadian legation in Washington.

"Channels of reference of these messages are gradually being worked out," Robertson wrote Hume Wrong in Washington on July 24, 1941, "but it will take some time before we can be sure they are reaching the proper people." To this end, Robertson authorized an "off the record" approach to British Security Coordination for its advice.[18] As later events were to prove, this was the first that BSC learned of the substantial and dangerous espionage activity in South America. It was undoubtedly news as well to the Admiralty's intelligence liaison officer in Washington, Captain E. G. Hastings.[19]

The content of the decrypts was impressive. By mid-summer Yardley was supplying lengthy lists of merchant shipping departures from South American ports, particularly from Brazil. He also provided glimpses of the Abwehr controllers in Germany, directing their growing spy networks:

Pernambuco to Hamburg
Message No. 126 Date 21–6 Time 24.00

State whether VESTA can be given details of our work. A report on U.S.A. bases in Brazil will be sent by mail.

(Sent to Postal Censorship to be relayed to British Censorship in

Bermuda and to the Canadian legation in Washington to be passed on to U.S. "authorities.")

Hamburg to Brazil
Message No. 122 Date 14–7 Time 16.10

Concerning Message No. 157. Bombsight. First, according to which principle is it built? Second, [continued] is it a modification of an instrument invented in the U.S.A.? Third, are other official services interested?

Caution. The offer may have been made to nail down OTIS as German Agent. Caution.

(Sent to military attaché of the Canadian legation to be given to U.S. Military Intelligence.)

Hamburg to Brazil
Message No. 125 Date 15–7 Time 16.22

There exists in the Port of Rio an English Spy Service under Captain PENY (or PINY) who is with the Embassy....

(Sent to the Canadian legation in Washington to be forwarded to British embassy in Rio.)

In another letter to Washington, Robertson again assured Wrong that "all messages which contain any mention of individuals, Fifth Column or Intelligence activities are referred to the Royal Canadian Mounted Police, and the information contained in them is forwarded to the F.B.I."[20] There were now plenty of these. The German agents had such confidence in the security of their ciphers that they were incredibly indiscreet:

Hamburg to Brazil
Message No. 93(?) Date 20–6 Time ?

OTIS has received recognition for sending concealed and disguised reports.

The false names HAERING and KEMPTER stand for TIMKEN and KOENIG.

How long has KOENIG lived in South America?

Rio de Janeiro to Hamburg
Message No. 187 Date 24–7 Time 21.30

Your message No. 134. Full name Charles Herring. Name is transcription. P.O. Box belongs to Timken.

Rio de Janeiro to Hamburg
Message No. 189 Date 24–7 Time 22.30

KOENIG born August 9, 1904, at UEBERLINGEN AM SEE. PRINZ born June 6, 1900, at Guntramsdorf, near Vienna. Dates OTIS to follow later.[21]

Hamburg to Rio de Janeiro
Message No. 115 Date 5–7–41 Time 01.22

Instruction about MONTE and LORENZ to follow.
HERIBERT is PRINZ
NAPP is BERKO
LOESCHNER is LORENZ

An Abwehr clerk's mania for bureaucratic detail was delivering Germany's entire South American espionage organization into the hands of her enemies. By the end of the summer, Canada was sending all such decrypts to British Security Coordination as well as to the FBI.

The only sombre note amid the Examination Unit's symphony of success was a July 5 telegram from London reporting that the Foreign Office promised full support to Canada's cryptographic experiment but wanted more details about its chief. Robertson had mentioned

Yardley by name a month earlier when informing the British authorities of the Examination Unit, but an enciphering error in his message had changed the spelling of Yardley's name to Emeley. Before "exploring the best methods of collaboration," the Foreign Office wondered whether "Emeley" was the same man as "one Colonel Yardley who also had worked in Chungking and who had written a book entitled *The Black Chamber* which was very harmful to [the] United States cryptographic organization."[22]

Robertson's original message had clearly stated that the American cryptographic expert hired by Canada had spent two years in Chungking working for the Chinese government. Encipherment error or no, the British must have been fairly sure that this was Yardley. As the U.S. military attaché had noted at the time, his activities in China were an "open secret" within the diplomatic community. Moreover, British Security Coordination had already warned the RCMP that it had heard that the notorious Yardley was working somewhere in Canada under the alias "Osborn." It would not have taken long for BSC to connect this fact with the decrypts it suddenly began receiving.

Robertson was quick to reply. Yes, it was Yardley now working in Canada and of course it was known that he was the author of *The American Black Chamber* and that it had got him into trouble with the American and British intelligence services. But he had made his peace with the United States authorities and was now working closely with them.[23]

There was a long silence after Robertson's letter. The Canadian High Commissioner in London, Vincent Massey, would have conveyed its contents to the appropriate people in the appropriate diplomatic fashion. There was still no response when Yardley and Drake pressed the British to supply a series of Hamburg–Brazil intercepts that had been missed by the Canadian monitoring stations. The Canadians were not even sure, in fact, that the Radio Security Service was actually receiving the same South American traffic. They had asked but "no reply has been received yet," Robertson complained.

Yardley continued to do an excellent job. Not only did deciphered messages flow out of the room on Montreal Road, but Yardley supplied analyses as well. He showed how internal evidence in the shipping data indicated networks of sub-agents sending information by mail, drew attention to intercepts that seemed especially important, and even did a little detective work to produce both a capsule biography and photograph of Benno Sobisch, one of the spies mentioned in Kempter's message to Hamburg. All such information was given to British Security Coordination and, separately, to the RCMP to be passed to the FBI.[24]

If the counter-espionage activities of the British Secret Intelligence Service (MI6) and the FBI in South America had so far failed, it was because looking for spies without the benefit of either censorship or wireless intercepts was like looking for needles in the proverbial haystack. The Examination Unit, however, was now giving the actual names and addresses of the spies. It is probably no coincidence that shortly after the Canadians began sending German decrypts to BSC, MI6 significantly expanded its counter-espionage activities in South America, opening several new stations.[25]

Undoubtedly, MI6 was getting a direct shove from the Admiralty. Half of all the Examination Unit decrypts dealt with merchant ship movements. Naval Intelligence in London would certainly have conveyed its concern to Captain Hastings in Washington and to BSC's Stephenson in New York. On July 16, for instance, Yardley prepared a summary showing that, in a little more than a month, German spies covering seven South American ports had radioed home the dates of 169 arrivals and sailings by eighty-five vessels. To the Admiralty, this must have seemed a far more urgent threat than the possibility of occasional dockside sabotage.[26]

It would be interesting to know how many of the ships reported by the spies were subsequently sunk by submarines. The naval intelligence officers in Britain in 1941 would have known. The Operational Intelligence Centre at the Admiralty attempted to keep track of British merchant ships throughout the world in the same way it did for enemy submarines. On a smaller scale, Canadian Naval Intelligence in Ottawa did likewise. Both centres had huge maps on which merchant ship movements were plotted. It would have been simple to correlate sinkings with the spy reports.

The Admiralty became thoroughly alarmed. Toward the end of the summer, the British asked the Coast Guard to supply the South Amer-

ican messages it was breaking. These probably also went to London
via Hastings at the British embassy.[27] Combined with what was
already coming from Yardley, the picture must have looked dismal
indeed.

In August 1941 only the Royal Navy and the Canadian Navy stood
between the German U-boats and their quarry in the Atlantic. The
sudden appearance of well-organized spy rings in South America giving up-to-date information on shipping arrivals and departures must
have caused consternation. What to do about it? MI6 had one agent in
South America and British Security Coordination had none. The only
immediate hope was the FBI.

Hoover was not a man famous for his generosity. In June, just as the
Examination Unit began producing its first decrypts on South American shipping, the Admiralty's Director of Naval Intelligence, Admiral
John Godfrey, arrived in the United States. He had come to lubricate
British–American cooperation on intelligence matters. The tour
included a visit to Hoover. Godfrey's personal assistant, a young naval
lieutenant named Ian Fleming—later to achieve world-wide fame as
the author of the James Bond spy thrillers—described it thus:

> Hoover, a chunky enigmatic man with slow eyes and a trap of a
> mouth, received us graciously, listened with close attention (and a
> witness) to our exposé of certain security problems, and expressed
> himself firmly but politely as being uninterested in our mission.…
> Hoover's negative response was as soft as a cat's paw. With the air of
> doing us a favour he had us piloted through the F.B.I. Laboratory
> and Record Department and down to the basement shooting
> range, where at that time his men had their training in the three
> basic F.B.I. weapons—pistol, automatic shotgun and sub-machine
> gun. Even now I can hear the shattering roar of the Thompsons in
> the big dark cellar as the instructor demonstrated on the trick tar-
> gets. Then with a firm, dry handclasp we were shown the door. [28]

In the United States it's called the "bum's rush," but Hoover made a
big mistake in according such treatment to Godfrey. The admiral had
one of the most important intelligence jobs in Britain, had the confi-

dence of the British Chiefs of Staff, and had only narrowly missed being chosen to head up MI6 instead of Colonel Stewart Menzies, a career army officer. He was also responsible for ensuring that adequate steps were taken when enemy intelligence activities affected the war at sea.

The British were at war with their backs to the wall. If Hoover could not help, they had to find someone who could. They needed an aggressive American spy agency that would take advantage of U.S. neutrality and carpet all Axis-occupied countries with agents.

Captain Hastings composed a letter, approved by Godfrey, to Colonel William Donovan—First World War hero, wealthy lawyer, and personal friend of the President. The letter suggested that the United States needed a proper secret service along the lines of MI6. And further: "It should be associated with but in no way controlled by the FBI who have no conception of offensive intelligence as we know it." The FBI, the letter said, simply did not have the required "strategical mentality."29

The stab at the Bureau was undeserved. The FBI was more a police organization than a secret service. The U.S. Neutrality Act forbade the kind of covert aggression the letter to Donovan proposed.

The letter further suggested that the U.S. agents be trained in Britain and directed by MI6 while operating out of American embassies. For some reason Hastings and Godfrey thought this could be accomplished with the cooperation of the State Department.

Godfrey had been drawn into a plot. Hastings cautioned in the letter that its content should not be discussed with a third party without Stephenson's approval. That was because a plan was already in motion to thrust Hoover aside. Stephenson—who had the FBI chief's confidence and trust—was the designated hit man. A few months earlier, Colonel Donovan had been approached by Stephenson with the suggestion that he try to persuade his friend, President Roosevelt, to give him the job of establishing a new U.S. secret service. Hoover was about to be the victim of the classic end run.

Donovan had become a favourite of the British as a result of a visit to Britain a year earlier when the Blitz was in full fury. Concerned by conflicting reports that England was on the verge of collapse, Roosevelt had sent Donovan to report privately on the situation. Did the British still have the will to fight? Donovan said yes. He openly admired Britain's steady calm beneath the constant drone of German aircraft and daily rain of bombs. While U.S. Ambassador Joseph Kennedy was sending home increasingly pessimistic reports, Donovan was separately assuring the President that the British people were determined to fight on and were far from beaten.

As a result, Britain's leadership—Churchill included—saw Donovan as a friend of Britain and an important ally with White House connections. Given appropriate support and advice, he was seen as someone who could bring some of America's might to bear in the fight against Germany. The trick was to get him in a position of power in the United States. That job was assigned to the forty-five-year-old Stephenson.

Even after fifty years, the Canadian director of British Security Coordination is an enigmatic figure. This was by his own choice and contrivance, for many of the accomplishments he claimed for both himself and BSC after the war have turned out to be exaggerated or false. The fact that he brazenly manipulated those who interviewed him about his experiences suggests a person who enjoyed conspiracy for its own sake.[30] He was clearly ambitious, sought the company of the powerful, and was capable of being completely unscrupulous. All this was masked by an outward show of geniality which was in sharp contrast to Hoover's stiff formality.

At London's instigation, Stephenson cultivated Donovan and vigorously urged him to try to persuade Roosevelt that the country was in desperate need of a proper secret service and Donovan should lead it. The campaign worked. On June 18, 1941, despite the opposition of Hoover and the State Department, Roosevelt gave Donovan a new, fancy title: Coordinator of Information (COI). It was the cover name of what was to be the American version of the British secret services, later better known as the Office of Strategic Services or OSS.

Before the war was over, the OSS was to employ 10,000 people engaged in all manner of espionage and sabotage. But in July 1941 Donovan began his new job with no salary, no staff, and all the existing U.S. intelligence agencies plus the State Department openly hostile to him.[31] Technically, he had an unlimited mandate for espionage and counter-espionage, but in the beginning he had no means to carry out this assignment and could expect no help, except from the British. They were prepared to go to considerable lengths to ensure he succeeded.

It was precisely at this time, in this context, that Stephenson at BSC and Captain Hastings in Washington began reading the Examination Unit's decrypts, with their chilling reports of ship movements out of South American ports.

The Canadians, of course, had no conception of the political currents swirling in British and American intelligence circles south of the border. They would not have guessed their operations could be affected by them. For Yardley it was simply the happiest of times. By the middle of August, just two months after start-up, he reported with pride that the Examination Unit was now making substantial progress against the codes of Japan and Vichy France. And the latter, to Canada, was especially important.

Some of the Vichy traffic that Yardley was attacking came from the powerful short-wave transmitter on the island of St. Pierre off the south coast of Newfoundland. When France lost Quebec to the British in the 1750s, it retained two specks of rock—the islands of St. Pierre and Miquelon—as a safe harbour for its fishing fleets operating on the Grand Banks. They had been a French possession ever since, and in 1939 a French airline company contemplating a transatlantic service had installed a powerful wireless station on St. Pierre. This transmitter was now giving the Admiralty no end of worry.

The problem was that St. Pierre and Miquelon overlooked the main shipping route out of St. John's, Newfoundland. They were an ideal vantage point from which to watch the Allied convoys gathering before venturing out onto the North Atlantic. Given that the Vichy government seemed to be leaning more toward Germany than toward neutrality, there was powerful reason to fear that the islands were being used as an intelligence outpost for the German U-boats lurking to the east. Yet there was no proof. The constant stream of messages being broadcast from the transmitter were in unreadable codes and ciphers. By November, however, Yardley had made such progress that Robertson could remark that only one code remained unreadable. [32]

Certainly, the NRC's C. J. Mackenzie was more than satisfied with what he found when he toured Yardley's operation in early August.

This is another project that is proving very successful and I think it should now be taken over by some of the Intelligence Branches of the Government. They are breaking down messages from South America to Germany, from the United States to Germany, from Japanese Embassy in Berlin to Japanese Embassy in Washington, etc. and are getting many interesting messages.

It is very interesting to see in print the amount of detail which is being transmitted. The reports clearly indicate the Germans are getting worried about the South American situation and feel that if the United States comes into the war at least the northern countries in South America will probably line up with her.[33]

Yardley had another prize to show his Canadian mentors. On August 19 the Examination Unit broke the substitution cipher used between Colombia and its embassy in London. The sixteen messages so obtained mark a milestone in Canada's diplomatic history: it was the first time Canada had intercepted, decrypted, and read the private diplomatic correspondence of a *friendly* power.

From: Bogota
To: Legacolombia Jaramillo, London

Type: CA (Cipher)

Date: June 18, 1941
Rec'd: Aug. 5, 1941

With deep regret I read your thirty-two thirty-three. Everything leads me to believe that the United States cannot do more than it is doing, as its war industries are only beginning and will not reach full production for several months. The heroism and the energy of the English are everywhere more prodigious, but I see the conclusion veiled....

        President Santos

There were more messages in the same vein. If they were not exactly exciting, they at least had some value. They showed that Colombia was genuinely sympathetic to the Allied cause and that it suspected Brazil was leaning toward the Axis. That was useful information, possibly justifying the impropriety of snooping through a friendly country's private communications. At any rate, it was an apple of temptation and External Affairs had taken its first bite.

It was not to be the last.[34]

CHAPTER FOUR

YARDLEY MUST GO

OCTOBER — DECEMBER 1941

HERBERT YARDLEY was good. There was no doubt about that. But he was not great. Despite the impression he had made on his Canadian employers, he was still in a cipher Stone Age.

Much of the Examination Unit's early success rested on the training pamphlets Yardley had received from General Mauborgne. They were a gift of diamonds. Yardley had been out of the picture for a long time, and the Signal Intelligence Service, particularly because of William Friedman's genius, had made enormous strides in analytical technique during the 1930s. Without the pamphlets, Yardley would have had to struggle.

Even more fortunately for him, the Abwehr spies in the Western Hemisphere were all using transposition ciphers. These involve scrambling the letters of a message according to a key, often based on the pages of a novel or textbook. Friedrich Kempter, for example, used the first letters of each line of a page as his key, the particular page to be determined by the date of his message. These so-called "book ciphers" could be solved using the techniques that had served Yardley so well during the First World War.[1]

Far more difficult are substitution ciphers, in which entirely different letters replace the plaintext letters of a message. This can be done by simple rules or, far more effectively, by a machine which can be programmed to replace plaintext letters by different cipher letters each time they appear. For example, a cipher machine would encipher the word Germany differently every time it was encountered: XOSTHYL, SOINTEW, PYRCVJU, and so on. The possibilities are almost endless and this was the principle behind the ENIGMA cipher machine of the Germans and the PURPLE machine of the Japanese. A message could theoretically be deciphered only by putting an identical machine on the same setting used by the original.

In 1933 Yardley had declared that machine ciphers were unbreakable. In 1941 the Germans and Japanese certainly thought so. By then, however, the British were making substantial progress against ENIGMA and the Americans had decisively broken PURPLE. The latter was an accomplishment of vast value. The Most Secret exchanges between Tokyo and its embassies abroad, including the one in Washington, were being read by President Roosevelt, the State Department, and the top brass of the Army and the Navy. The messages indicated that Japan was impressed by Hitler's easy victories in Europe, and was looking hungrily at British, French, and Dutch colonies in the Far East.

Much has been written about the breaking of ENIGMA. The machine itself consisted of a keyboard connected to a series of wheels with concealed internal wiring. When a key was pressed the wheels advanced, each time completing a different electrical circuit that illuminated the cipher letter on a panel below. The German military authorities introduced the machine before the war and the enciphered messages it produced defied British efforts to solve them for some years. Fortunately, in the late 1930s, a small group of Polish mathematicians were successful, not only in reconstructing the internal wiring of the German ENIGMA machine, but also in developing a method of recovering the settings of the cipher wheels by means of an electro-mechanical device they called a *bomba* (Polish for "ice-cream cone").

Shortly before Poland was overrun by the German armies in 1939, the Polish cipher specialists managed to deliver the results of their research to the French and British. When France fell in 1940, only Britain was left to exploit the information. This was not accomplished overnight. The German Air Force ENIGMA ciphers were penetrated in 1940, in time for the air attacks on England, followed by German Navy ENIGMA in 1941. German Army ENIGMA was not decisively broken until 1942.

The defeat of ENIGMA immensely strengthened the hand of Colonel Stewart Menzies, the new head of the Secret Intelligence Service (MI6). This post included the director-generalship of the Government Code and Cipher School, a purely administrative arrangement put in place by the Foreign Office in 1923. With the outbreak of war, code- and cipher-breaking became vastly more important and the services naturally demanded more direct control. Menzies countered the challenge by making daily visits to Churchill with the best decrypts of the day. Reading the actual messages of his enemies appealed to the Prime Minister. Menzies's hold over the Government Code and Cipher School was secure for the rest of the war.

The Americans solved the Japanese PURPLE cipher entirely on their own. In principle, the Japanese machine was similar to ENIGMA, except that it used stepped switches (as in a dial telephone) instead of cipher wheels. By an impressive feat of analysis, a member of William Friedman's cryptanalysis team deduced the nature of the Japanese machine and succeeded in reconstructing it, sight unseen. By early 1940 the Americans were regularly reading Japanese high-grade diplomatic messages.

The Americans were generous. Though the United States was still neutral, representatives from the Army and the Navy sailed for London at the end of January 1941, carrying with them two American-made PURPLE machines and details of how to use them. The British did not reciprocate on ENIGMA, despite an agreement the following month between Churchill and Roosevelt to upgrade the sharing of secret intelligence between the two countries. Soon the British Joint Staff Mission in Washington and a similar American military mission in London were established to ensure the "full and prompt exchange of pertinent information concerning war operations." This did not, however, include instructions on how to break German machine ciphers.[2]

Despite the dismissive comment in the official history, *British Intelligence in the Second World War,* that the new cooperative arrangement with the Americans "added nothing of value to the stock of British intelligence, except for the information derived from the exchange of Japanese Sigint (Signals Intelligence)," the exception cited was priceless. The British used one of the American-made PURPLE machines to break the messages of the Japanese ambassador in Berlin. These proved to be an invaluable source of German military and political thinking throughout the war. The Americans had certainly given a lot more than they had received.

To be sure, the British also welcomed the two FBI representatives to the Government Code and Cipher School a little later that spring and introduced them to the comparatively low-grade hand ciphers of the Abwehr and the Gestapo. Hand ciphers, as opposed to machine ciphers, are those which can be worked out with paper and pencil. All transposition ciphers are of this type, as well as many substitution systems. The FBI could have got identical instruction from Elizabeth Friedman of the Coast Guard. It was hand ciphers, not machine ciphers, that both the Examination Unit and the Coast Guard were working on.

Code-breaking is also essentially a paper and pencil process. Individual words or whole phrases are listed in a book beside four- or five-digit groups of numbers or letters. To prepare a message, the code clerk simply looks up the groups beside the appropriate word or phrase. For example, a message broken by Yardley from the Vichy legation in Ottawa looked like this:

From: Ristelhueber, Ottawa
To: Diplomatie, Vichy

August 18, 1941, No. 285

ICOD	OSOL	OTEI	ECIT	OHOZ	AXEL	ODIT
je vous	adresse	a	nouveau(x)	les	telegrammes	

ODUM	IKUS	YZUG	OKOG	OJIP	AHOM	YTAY
par	No.	1	65	period	le	premier

YJAD	YBUG	IYAG	OLOX	UCAT	OMOK	ESOY
	plainte?	la	date	du	23	juillet

Codes are often broken by comparing the frequency of some code groups with the frequency of common words, then working out the meaning of other code groups by the context in which they appear. It is a painstaking process and generally requires the analysis of a large number of messages.[3]

Theoretically, codes ought to be very secure. A sophisticated code usually gives several different groups for common words and phrases, thereby breaking up the frequency with which these groups appear. The codebreakers could generally achieve entry into diplomatic codes, however, by comparing the messages with information they received about the content of government discussions with foreign ministers, particularly when a formal statement was involved that an ambassador might send home verbatim. If the text of such a statement could be isolated in a message, then all the words in it could be matched to their appropriate code groups. Given a few such opportunities, and enough raw material, then someone like Yardley could lever his way into the whole code.[4]

Codes and transposition ciphers were old hat to Yardley. The methods used to break them had remained unchanged since the First World War. The help he received from the pamphlets of the U.S. Army Signal Intelligence Service that was so vital to him involved substitution ciphers. Thanks especially to Friedman, enormous mathematical progress had been made against these, making all non-machine substitution ciphers vulnerable.

What Friedman (and others) had discovered was that various statistical characteristics of a language remained in a message, so long as the letters had been substituted by fixed rules. The exceptionally high frequency with which the letter "e" appears in the English language is an example. Other languages have similar properties. By the Second World War, the danger of cipher-breaking by letter frequency was well known, and steps were taken to counter it. Friedman, however, had come up with mathematical techniques of such sophistication that the linguistic properties of a hand-enciphered message could be discerned no matter what the counter-measures.[5]

Which pamphlets Yardley received, their content, and how he used them, is still a secret in Canada. Many of them are available, however, in U.S. archives. The cipher-breaking techniques they describe are much more advanced than any that Yardley—who was not a mathematician—could have devised on his own. They probably directly contributed to his success in breaking the substitution cipher used by Colombia.

Yardley also did some of his own traffic analysis. This involved examining a message for clues to its origin and to what type of code or cipher was involved. Like any communication, code and cipher messages must have an address and be signed and dated. This information, no matter how well concealed, could usually be isolated and broken out. Sometimes, as with the South American spies, the first few cipher groups also contained the keys by which the rest of the message was read. Yardley was often able to tell at a glance whether an intercept was in code or cipher, or whether it was done by hand or machine. This must have seemed like magic to people like Colonel Murray, Lieutenant Little, and Norman Robertson.

Yardley's specialized abilities were also a great boon to Captain Drake, over at the Army's Special Wireless Station at Rockcliffe. Until the American's arrival he had been working blindly when trying to decide what he should tune his receivers to, relying mainly on the Radio Security Service in Britain to identify the traffic he was picking up. This caused much delay, because the raw material had to be sent to Britain for analysis. With Yardley's help, Drake could readily identify the specific transmissions of German agents and set up watches to copy the most promising traffic.[6]

Nevertheless, for all Yardley's show, the Examination Unit was in the foothills of code- and cipher-breaking in comparison to what was then happening at the Government Code and Cipher School in Britain and at the U.S. Army's Signal Intelligence Service. The cooperation the Canadians wanted from the Americans and British was on the lowest level of cryptanalysis, not the highest.

Enter, now, Lester Pearson. A future prime minister and the man credited with putting Canada on the map in foreign affairs after the war, he had recently returned from Britain to serve as Norman Robertson's chief assistant. Having fielded in January the original suggestion by the British that Canada do its own code- and cipher-breaking, in late August he was asked to find out why the British were not helping. He wrote to High Commissioner Vincent Massey in London:

> … we are very anxious to see a closer liaison and a fuller exchange of information between our Unit and the United Kingdom Cryptographers. We had hoped that by now the suspicion in the minds of the United Kingdom authorities regarding the Chief of our Unit would be allayed. His standing with the United States Intelligence Services is obviously good…. General Mauborgne, since Mr. Robertson's letter under reference was written, has voluntarily supplied us with several more of the United States instruction books.

Pearson went on to say that Canada was preparing to increase "substantially" the output of the Examination Unit, had already added Japanese and Spanish translators (to those speaking German and French), and would now appreciate help from the British. In particular, Canada would like the keys to the ciphers used by the Vichy French and copies of the raw traffic from Germany to South America which had been missed in Canada but which "probably" had been intercepted in Britain.

> I wonder if you could approach the United Kingdom authorities and impress upon them the high desirability of very close co-operation in this work. I know that they, like all Intelligence Branches, are loathe to give up any of the secrets of the information which they get, but I do feel that some of the old traditions of the Secret Service should perhaps be broken or at least reshaped more closely to fit the present circumstances.[7]

It is not known how promptly Massey acted on Pearson's request, but weeks passed without an answer.

All was still rosy with Yardley. His report in mid-September announced, with an air of triumph, that the Examination Unit was about to supply a daily diet of decoded Japanese and Vichy messages. Moreover, he was pleased to report a new method for breaking transposition ciphers "thought out and planned exclusively by the Examination

Unit." He was looking forward to testing the technique on the seven new enemy transmitters then being intercepted. What with a new wireless monitoring station being planned to replace the one at Rockcliffe, and better radio reception conditions expected in the fall, Yardley foresaw a "huge increase in traffic." And, he concluded with a flourish, "we feel confident in our ability."[8]

Just at this time, Britain's chief cryptographer arrived in Ottawa. This was Commander Alastair Denniston, operational chief (under Menzies) of the Government Code and Cipher School. He had been in Washington to persuade the U.S. Army and Navy to concentrate on Japanese military ciphers while the British looked after diplomatic.[9] He was on his way home when he met Pearson, and he had something special to tell him. Yardley had to go, Denniston said. Otherwise there would be no cooperation from Britain on codes and ciphers. Zero. And no help from the United States, either.

Pearson was flabbergasted. Yardley had come on the recommendation of General Mauborgne, he protested, and he had been given highly secret U.S. documents. Mauborgne's views were his own, Denniston replied. They were not shared by any other officials in the U.S. intelligence services. How he knew this with such certainty is not recorded.[10]

Then, to add to the upset, the Admiralty's intelligence liaison officer with the Joint Staff Mission in Washington, Captain E. G. Hastings, as well as William Stephenson of British Security Coordination in New York, started complaining that the Canadians were giving the Americans a bad impression because of the lax way in which decrypts from the Examination Unit were being distributed in the United States. They were blowing around "like autumn leaves" and it was jeopardizing cooperation. The system had to be tightened up. Woven into the warning was the suggestion that the best way to do this would be to send all decrypts to BSC and let BSC look after giving them to the Americans.[11]

Pearson could not figure it out. What did the British have against Yardley? The American dislike of him reported by Denniston was "in conflict with the facts" but when Britain's chief cryptographer smoothly intimated that he would be prepared to provide one of his best experts to replace Yardley, Pearson wavered. Canada was about to expand its wireless intercept facilities. The Examination Unit was "making more rapid progress along certain lines than we had hoped." Pearson, after checking with Robertson, finally agreed that Canada would not renew Yardley's six-month contract when it expired in early December. In the meantime, Yardley would not be told his job was to be terminated. That would be left to the last minute. By then, Pearson noted, the projects he had under development "should be going smoothly."[12]

Yardley was wounded, but not dead. As he blithely dispatched memos from his little office on Montreal Road, warning of new spies in the decrypts, proposing new lines of cooperation with the Americans and British, and even requesting a pay increase for himself and Edna Ramsaier, his Canadian bosses struggled with how they might do the right thing while still doing the necessary thing. Hume Wrong of the Canadian legation in Washington was asked for his theory about how Yardley could be said to be in such disfavour in the United States and yet get such excellent help.

"So far as I know, the State Department is not aware that we are using his services in Ottawa," Wrong wrote back. "I have refrained from telling them about it." Moreover, General Mauborgne had now retired and Wrong had no idea how his successor viewed Yardley.[13]

Meanwhile, the complaints from Stephenson and Hastings kept up the pressure. Canada's Director of Naval Intelligence, Captain Brand, accepted their arguments and was prepared to send all decrypts exclusively to British Security Coordination. The Army's Colonel Murray was not so sure. On a trip to the United States, he undertook his own investigation. He found that the British charge of careless distribution was groundless. The plethora of decrypts was coming from the Coast Guard, which was giving them to U.S. Army and Navy, to the Treasury Department and the State Department, and also to the FBI. Murray personally confronted Stephenson in New York and Hastings in Washington. They backed off.[14]

Stephenson, meanwhile, had asked Lieutenant Little to see if he could get Yardley to give him all the cipher-breaking keys and methodology he had developed. Yardley asked: "Who for?" Little would not tell him. Yardley said no. Little insisted. As Yardley's deputy, Gilbert Robinson, was later to recall:

... the request came to us with no name attached. I remember how
I felt at the time. We were both beginning to wonder about the evi-
dent lack of cooperation and this anonymous request for information seemed the last straw. We paid a visit to Mackenzie and
explained we could not give out the information without knowing
to whom it was going.

Little was not prepared to tell the president of the National Research
Council why he wanted the information. Mackenzie concluded that
he was dealing with a petty personal rivalry between the two men.
British Security Coordination did not get the information.[15]

It is now perfectly clear—over fifty years later—what was going on
in these manoeuvrings by British intelligence officials in the United
States. The British—Colonel Stewart Menzies, head of MI6, and
Admiral John Godfrey, head of Naval Intelligence (and therefore
William Stephenson of BSC and Captain Hastings in Washington) all
wanted to see William Donovan prosper in his new job as Coordinator
of Information. The push, perhaps, was ultimately coming from
Churchill and his Chief of Staff, General Sir Hastings Ismay, who saw
Donovan's new organization as a means "to argue the British case to
the highest authorities in the United States" and to supply "correctives
to what we may consider misinterpretations or unjust criticisms of
British [intelligence] activities."[16]

In order to achieve this entirely political aim, Donovan's new spy
agency had to be successful. It needed help, and fast. With General
Ismay's agreement, one of Donovan's men was posted to the War
Office in London, where he was to receive intelligence reports from all
three services and have access to the files of MI6. Stephenson in New
York fed Donovan his own secret service reports, plus intelligence
summaries from British Censorship in Bermuda and Trinidad. This
was not enough. If Donovan really was to succeed, then he had to be
plugged into British code- and cipher-breaking resources. In the Western Hemisphere, that meant Canada.

By mid-autumn of 1941, the Federal Communications Commission was supplying the Coast Guard with far more intercepts of secret
agent transmissions than were coming from the Examination Unit.

The FCC had eleven major and eighty subsidiary monitoring stations, as opposed to Canada's single Special Wireless Station at Rockcliffe plus ham radio operators and whatever the Navy or Department of Transport stations picked up. However, the radio skip phenomenon meant that many transmissions were heard only in Canada. Kempter's cipher, moreover, had not been broken by the Coast Guard. The decrypts in which Kempter listed merchant shipping sailings and identified other German agents in South America were exclusive to Yardley.[17]

The British had lagged behind both the Canadians and the Americans in Western Hemisphere wireless coverage. The Radio Security Service was responsible for intercepting clandestine transmissions but had concentrated first on traffic relating to spies in Britain. The Government Code and Cipher School section responsible for breaking this material (under one Oliver Strachey) had fed the resulting decrypts to MI5, and this had led to the capture of all German agents operating in Britain, some of whom were "turned" and made into double agents. It was as fine a counter-intelligence accomplishment as any during the war.

By the beginning of 1941, however, the Radio Security Service was looking for new fields to conquer. It turned its attention to clandestine transmissions emanating from neutral countries in Europe and Africa. Since overseas (non-Commonwealth) counter-espionage was under MI6's mandate, the order went out in May 1941 to take the Radio Security Service away from the War Office (MI8) and place it under MI6.[18]

This reorganization, which involved the complete overhaul of the Radio Security Service and many changes in personnel, was still in process when Drake started concentrating on South American traffic at Yardley's request. His RSS counterpart in Britain complained that they were having much trouble with reception on the Hamburg–South America wireless circuits. When Drake sent a package of raw intercepts to Britain in July 1941, the RSS could only reply that they appeared to be "almost certainly illicit." Yardley knew that already. These were messages from Kempter and he had already deciphered some of them.[19]

The British official history, *British Intelligence in the Second World War*, states that the Government Code and Cipher School had solved "the main Abwehr hand cipher" at the end of 1940. This is impossible. Transposition ciphers of the type used by the Abwehr are as variable as the rules and the cipher-books by which they are compiled. There can be no such thing as a "main" cipher, unless it refers to a single cipher of particular importance. Not only were the British unable to read Kempter's cipher throughout 1941, but Yardley had broken a number of others that also were new to them.[20] It is no wonder that Little was asked to obtain his cipher keys.

Two messages that Yardley deciphered at this time were enough to make a counter-intelligence officer's heart race. On October 14, the Examination Unit broke into an Abwehr circuit to the Near East. Among messages describing British troop dispositions and requesting explosives for sabotage was one from Hamburg to Ankara, Turkey, which said in part:

> Also find out the strength of troops and where Russian formations are placed. [Agent] 240 must bring along maps, so that they may be at the disposition of air-attack....We hope that your plan to learn something through the Turk from the British Embassy will succeed.

Clearly the Germans were trying to place a spy in the British embassy in Ankara and, in fact, they did so. A little over a year later, the ambassador's Turkish valet obtained a wax impression of the key to his safe and for months regularly photographed his Top Secret correspondence. This was CICERO, one of Germany's most famous spies. Despite the fact that this decrypt was sent directly to London, CICERO operated for more than a year and was never caught.[21]

On November 17, the Examination Unit decrypted a Kempter message that read in part:

> CLARK's daughter has been employed as a secretary in the United States Embassy at Quito, Ecuador, since November 1st.
> We cannot depend on KOENIG'S car. It is so old that it is

absolutely unreliable and has to be constantly repaired. Do you
authorize the purchase of a better car?

No doubt Yardley smiled to read of a spy's transportation problems,
but he was quick to riffle through his back file of decrypts to determine
that CLARK was the code-name of an Abwehr agent being groomed
for a mission to the United States. The Americans were immediately
alerted.[22]

Yardley's success with Abwehr hand ciphers may have been due to
something more than just hard work. His new technique for breaking
transposition ciphers had been a success. "We have discovered an original and new approach to traffic of this sort," he wrote. "To perfect this
new method we have spent approximately 2,000 hours of research."[23]

The obvious must have occurred to someone in British Intelligence. The Examination Unit was breaking South American traffic
that neither the British nor the Americans had mastered. If Yardley
could be removed so that the British could get access to his cipher keys,
and if the Canadians could be persuaded to stop giving decrypts to the
RCMP—and thence to the FBI—then British Security Coordination
could give them to Donovan. Then it would be Donovan, not the
Canadians, who doled them out to Hoover. The new Coordinator of
Information would have his own counters on the table of American
counter-espionage.

There is irony here. Even as Stephenson and Captain Hastings were
manoeuvring the Canadians into the new arrangement, Colonel Murray of the Canadian Army's wireless intelligence service was approaching the Federal Communications Commission with a proposal that
they exchange Latin American intercepts which may have been missed
in one country but received in the other. The FCC was enthusiastic
and sought approval from the FBI, but the idea was rejected. In late
October the FBI said it had its own source of wireless intercepts "direct
from Canada." It did not have to do any deals.[24]

Hoover, in fact, had shot himself in the foot. Despite what Stephenson of BSC claimed after the war, relations between Hoover and Donovan appear to have been cordial throughout the fall of 1941; so much so,
that the FBI director had regularly given Donovan copies of the Exami-

nation Unit decrypts he had received from the RCMP. Shortly after the FBI turned down Colonel Murray, however, the Canadian decrypts stopped coming.[25] By the end of the year, Hoover could only get them from Donovan.

Before any of this could happen, however, Yardley had to go. His dismissal was essential to other close ties being forged with Donovan. The British had conceived the idea of a joint attack on enemy activities in the Western Hemisphere, they to supply the expertise and Donovan to supply the manpower and the money. The first step was a decision to open a secret-warfare school in Canada "to train agents from Latin America and the United States." Next, in November, MI6 sent its counter-espionage chief, Felix Cowgill, to New York to advise Stephenson on how to set up a counter-espionage program of his own, aimed at both the United States and Latin America.[26]

These two moves represented an enormous expansion of British Security Coordination's mandate. BSC's counter-intelligence activities had so far involved cooperation with the FBI and had been confined mainly to North America. Now Stephenson was going to have the whole of the Western Hemisphere in his charge. He was going to be able to recruit, train, and run his own agents. In cooperation with the tame and grateful Donovan, he would mastermind a comprehensive counter-espionage and sabotage campaign throughout North and South America.[27]

First, however, the British had to have control over the decryption of German espionage traffic. They had to have the cipher keys to the South American intercepts that Yardley had discovered and the Government Code and Cipher School had not. When Yardley refused Little's request for the keys, and then parried a subsequent request from the War Office,[28] there was only one recourse. Persuade the Canadians to get rid of him.

The axe fell November 22, 1941. A Saturday. Lester Pearson and the head of the Examination Unit committee, Tommy Stone, were the designated butchers. Yardley was taken by surprise. He had been supplying Vichy and Japanese decodes since the beginning of October. They were only medium-grade messages, to be sure, but only the day before Robertson had considered two of them so important that he had shown them to Mackenzie King.[29] Had Yardley not lived up to Canada's every expectation? How had he failed so badly that the Canadians now wanted to fire him?

We want our own man in charge, Pearson and Stone told him. Yardley did not believe it. He asked them at least to have the decency to tell him what really was going on. They stonewalled. He accused them of bringing him to Canada and picking his brains dry. "Yardley took the news very hard," Stone later reported. He and Pearson, he added, "had a most unpleasant half hour."[30]

Fifty years later everyone present was dead. And so, too, were the emotions of that afternoon's meeting. It is probably just as well. Gilbert Robinson, Yardley's principal assistant, was still alive when contacted in 1991, but a medical condition had stolen his memory of what Yardley did after he left Pearson and Stone. Again, it is just as well. Tough man that he was, Yardley must have been devastated. Cryptography was his life; he was born to do it and did it well. Canada was his last chance. He knew it. And he had done well. He had done well.

Whatever Yardley said or did after he left the meeting, it so agitated Robinson that he sent a letter from his home to Stone that very day:

"Under his direction our bureau has shown considerable originality in attacking the problems presented to it," Robinson wrote. "Would it not be wise to encourage this originality?" After describing the enormous debt he felt Canada owed Yardley, and Miss Ramsaier who "would also leave," Robinson observed that the successful breaking of codes and ciphers is a delicate endeavour. "For this reason its organization is highly sensitive and should not be changed unless under the gravest necessity. For, like a plant, through uprooting it, it may perish."

Pearson and Stone were not unfeeling men. Yardley's dismay had upset them. Moreover, that same day, they received a long-promised official report on Yardley from the FBI which was full of innuendo and error:

Information was received from a reliable source on May 20, 1941, that Yardley was secretly representing an outside friendly power and attempting to obtain high frequency radio direction finding equipment.

Nonsense.

On June 6, 1941, information was received from a reliable source that Yardley was going to Canada in an effort to obtain one hundred short wave receivers in the interest of a friendly power.[31]

Nonsense again.

Pearson and Stone must have been struck by the fact that after five months, despite all its "reliable" sources, the FBI had failed to determine what Yardley was actually doing in Canada. This was especially ironic, considering that Hoover had been receiving the product of his genius for months. However, the "reliable sources"—cited seven times in addition to the occasional "information received"—painted an extremely damaging picture of Yardley. Pearson and Stone would have known that almost everything in the FBI report was untrue.

The Examination Unit Advisory Committee met at noon on the following Monday. It must have been a stormy meeting. The NRC's C. J. Mackenzie had already noted his disgust about the proposal to dismiss Yardley in his diary:

> I protested and don't like it. The Americans and British refuse to play ball as long as he is there. I am afraid that it may mean the crippling of our effort for a diplomatic and unreal reason.

The committee decided to reconsider the whole matter. Pearson and Little were to go to Washington to find out first hand if American opposition to Yardley was what the British said it was.[32]

It was too late. The poison against Yardley had already taken hold. On November 27 Little and Pearson began their investigation in Washington by meeting Captain Hastings, who reiterated everything that Denniston had said. As Pearson reported:

> I questioned [*Hastings*] closely as to how much of the current opin-

ion on Osborn's professional or personal qualifications was due merely to professional jealousy and … irritation at Osborn having given away secrets of the craft. [*Hastings*] said that he thought that suspicion against Osborn and the judgment on his ability held by others was an honest one.

Hastings also "strongly" suggested they be sure to get the opinion of Rear Admiral Leigh Noyes, chief of Naval Signals, "who knew the man (Yardley) and was interested in this matter." This they dutifully did the next day and Noyes condemned Yardley utterly and emphatically, saying he should be "jailed" and that he wouldn't touch him "with a ten-foot pole." Pearson apparently sensed that something was amiss. He noted pointedly in his report that Noyes had no first-hand knowledge, since Yardley had never worked for the U.S. Navy.[33]

The Army brass were equally direct but less passionate. Pearson and Little saw Major General Dawson Olmstead, the new Chief Signal Officer, and General Sherman Miles, the head of Military Intelligence (G-2). Both said they felt Yardley was "untrustworthy" and that was that. A visit to FBI headquarters elicited the same sentiment, although the Bureau was unable to produce any evidence of wrongdoing.

Finally, Pearson and Little talked with William Friedman, Yardley's old rival and head of the Army's cryptanalysis team. Friedman was kindness itself and from him the Canadians got what appears to be a candid appraisal of Yardley. Friedman said he was a man of tremendous energy and had a gift for organization and inspiring staff. His grievance over the closing of his black chamber had been legitimate, but the publication of his book had created a rift between him and the U.S. authorities that would never be healed. He was not dishonest and would not deliberately betray either the Canadian or American governments. On the other hand, while he was a good natural cryptanalyst, he was seriously out of touch with advances in the field.

Although neither Pearson nor Little then had the knowledge to appreciate it, Friedman's last observation was on target. The work Yardley had done to date in Ottawa was rudimentary. The Abwehr transposition ciphers and the Colombian substitution cipher he had broken were comparatively simple; the Japanese messages were in the easiest of their codes; and the Vichy code had been solved by cribbing from earlier material supplied by the British. Furthermore, as Friedman pointed out, Yardley had little experience with the vastly more important machine ciphers.

Friedman did not want to see Yardley fired. He had met him briefly in Washington a few weeks earlier and had "got the impression that he was very happy in Ottawa." Friedman suggested that the Canadians should keep Yardley and simply do without the cooperation of the U.S. Army and Navy. "He pointed out, for instance," Pearson wrote, "that the FBI were doing the same kind of work here that Ottawa was doing without cooperation from the Service Departments."

The next time Pearson saw Yardley, he was absolutely frank. He told him of his talks in Washington in great detail.

On Saturday December 6, 1941, Yardley made one final bid to save the job he loved. He sent a lengthy memo to Stone asking that the arrival of his replacement from Britain be delayed thirty days to give him a chance to defend himself. He enclosed a copy of a personal appeal made on his behalf to the President's wife, Eleanor Roosevelt.

There was no reprieve. The British had ruled that Yardley had to be out of town before the new man arrived. Yardley's contract had only two more days to run. Though it was a few more weeks before he actually cleared the city, it was effectively his last day on the job.

And on that day, far, far away in the north Pacific, an armada of Japanese warships awaited the dawn. The aircraft carriers turned into the wind; the exhaust flames of engines flickered in the darkness. One by one the bombers and fighters took off. The huge American naval base of Pearl Harbor was barely 230 miles to the south.

While Yardley struggled with rejection and grief, the science of cryptanalysis was to have its biggest chance—and its biggest failure.

December 7, 1941.

———————

Canada was the first to declare war on Japan. Only hours after the surprise attack that left Pearl Harbor in flames and the U.S. Pacific fleet in a shambles, Canadians glued to their radios across the country heard their government announce that a state of war existed between Canada and Japan. The United States and Britain made similar declarations the following day.

Mackenzie King had not intended to get the jump on his allies. The Canadian Prime Minister always preferred to follow rather than lead when it came to the major decisions of war. It so happened that on that Sunday—even *before* the Japanese bombers plunged out of the Hawaiian sky—all available External Affairs officers had been called in to work on the text of a war-against-Japan speech for Mackenzie King. Early that morning, undersecretary Robertson had urgently summoned them to the task.

For weeks it had been clear to the Canadians that war with Japan was imminent. From mid-November onward, the British had been sending regular bulletins on the progress of negotiations in Washington between U.S. officials and a special mission from Japan. The State Department had been keeping the British informed about the talks on a daily basis. And tough talks they were.

Japan had grown increasingly angry over sanctions imposed by the United States to curb its military ambitions in Vichy-controlled Indochina. Sympathetic to the Axis powers, and having little choice in any case, the Vichy government had allowed the Japanese to build up their military presence in the colony. From there Japan threatened to open a new front in its war against China, which the United States had pledged to support. The Americans responded by cutting off trade with Japan, particularly in vital commodities like oil and scrap steel. The Japanese mission under the distinguished diplomat Saburo Kurusu was a last-ditch effort to break this impasse. Or else.

The "or else" was war. The Japanese Navy had noted with fascination the success the British had achieved in late 1940 by launching an aircraft carrier strike against the Italian fleet in Taranto harbour. Twenty-one obsolete Fairey Swordfish biplanes from the *Illustrious* had crippled three Italian battleships and one cruiser, altering the balance of naval power in the Mediterranean in one stroke. The Japanese, with the most modern aircraft carrier force in the world, soon began to speculate on what several hundred aircraft from six aircraft carriers could do to the eight U.S. battleships and two aircraft carriers normally based at Pearl Harbor.

Historians have puzzled for decades over how the attack could have taken the Americans so completely by surprise. Japan's highest-grade diplomatic cipher (PURPLE) had been broken almost a year earlier. As Kurusu talked, Roosevelt and his top military and diplomatic advisers were reading the missives he exchanged with Tokyo. These clearly indicated that Japan was prepared to resort to military force if Kurusu could not get concessions. Instead of encouraging the Americans to try to find solutions, this made them more inflexible.

Secretary of State Cordell Hull did not mince words with the Japanese delegation. The main obstacle to any kind of settlement, he told Kurusu, was Japan's alliance with Italy and Germany. "If Japan had any different ideas on this point, he could tell them [in Tokyo] that they would not get six inches in a thousand years with the U.S. Government, who would not have anything to do with the greatest butcher in history." The "butcher," of course, was Hitler. It appears that the British had been supplying the Americans with evidence of mass executions as the German forces rolled through Poland and eastern Russia.[34]

The Canadians also were getting clear warnings of impending war, thanks to Yardley. The Examination Unit was reading a much lower grade Japanese code than the Americans, but the implication was clear. On November 21 Robertson drew Mackenzie King's attention to an Examination Unit decrypt in which Ottawa's Japanese legation exhaustively reported on a statement tabled in Parliament about Canadian armaments production. It covered everything from the number of ships and aircraft being built to the number and types of guns and ammunition being produced.[35]

Other intercepted reports from the Japanese legation in Ottawa dealt with the dispatch of Canadian troops to Hong Kong and Canadian newspaper comments on Japan's relations with Germany. Most revealing of all, though not decrypted immediately, were messages from Tokyo to Japanese consulates in the United States and Hawaii, outlining financial arrangements for the staffs and their families to return to Japan. There were six such messages, dated December 3 to December 5, but they were not actually received and decrypted by the Examination Unit until just after the Pearl Harbor attack. The delay caused Lester Pearson to complain to Military Intelligence that "had we had these decipherments earlier they would have constituted, I think, a clear indication that something was going to happen."[36]

These were circular messages, in rudimentary code, and are certain to have been intercepted and read by the Americans. The PURPLE decrypts, however, gave the United States an even more definitive insight into Japanese intentions:

- On November 28 Tokyo advised its overseas diplomatic personnel that Japan had given up on its negotiations with the United States but the Americans were not to be told;
- On November 29 Germany was warned that war was likely to come "suddenly";
- On December 1 Japanese missions in Allied countries were told to destroy their secret codes and ciphers, while consulates in the United States were ordered to take down their portraits of the Emperor, a move of tremendous symbolic significance.

All these messages and others like them were being read by Roosevelt, his Chiefs of Staff, and the Secretary of State as promptly as they were being read by the Japanese. There could be no doubt what they meant. And there can be no doubt, either, that the hint was taken.

Up until November 26, Cordell Hull had been giving serious consideration to a proposal from Kurusu that if the United States would lift its export restrictions for six months, Japan would halt its military build-up in Indochina and would undertake to make no aggressive moves elsewhere. Hull, and therefore Roosevelt, thought enough of the suggestion to consult Britain and China. Both countries reacted with alarm, fearing that the United States was softening. They need not have worried. Even as they prepared their official replies, the Americans intercepted the November 28 message indicating that the Japanese considered negotiations with the United States useless. Hull then flatly rejected the proposal. After that, both sides only went through the motions.

The Canadians, of course, knew none of this. On December 6 the Canadian legation in Washington reported back to Ottawa that Roosevelt and Hull had not missed "scarcely a day in the last ten in which they've made statements to the press of the most unyielding character." The Canadian observers in Washington noted that the American leaders had "lost no opportunity between them of educating public opinion to contemplating an early outbreak of war with Japan." Mackenzie King told his cabinet ministers that it did not appear that the United States was bargaining in good faith.[37]

Ironically, it was an intercepted German message rather than a Japanese one which prompted Robertson to believe that war with Japan might be only hours away. On December 6 the Examination Unit decrypted a startling message from the Kempter spy network operating in South America:

From: Rio de Janeiro
To: Hamburg

Dated: December 3, 1941
Rec'd: December 6, 1941

Message No. 423, 424, 425

Our navy authority learned just now from an officer of the U.S.A. Navy Mission here the following:

Firstly: The PANZERKREUZER TIRPITZ just sailed on December 2 through the Straits of Magallenes on her way to the Pacific and that the two most modern U.S.A. battleships the NORTH CAROLINA and her sistership are supposed to have orders to intercept the TIRPITZ.

Secondly: A Japanese convoy, consisting of 70 transports and convoyed by 12 cruisers, with 300,000 men on board, are supposed to be on the way to Indo-China and that it can be counted upon that this convoy will be attacked by the U.S.A. navy.

Our source of information is reliable, but we cannot count on the accuracy of this report. [38]

It was obvious immediately that the *Tirpitz* information was incorrect. Naval intelligence at both the Admiralty and in Ottawa kept close tabs on the German Navy's capital ships and knew the *Tirpitz* was still in home waters. The reference to the Japanese convoy, however, reverberated with truth. That same day Robertson had read a British dispatch from Singapore reporting that thirty-five Japanese transports, eight cruisers, and ten destroyers had been spotted off Indochina steaming to the northwest.[39] Was this the same convoy as reported by the German spy? If so, then the U.S. Navy intended to act.

The next morning, a Sunday, Robertson brought in all available External Affairs staff to work on Canada's declaration-of-war statement. They were hard at it in mid-afternoon when Robertson received a phone call: the Japanese had attacked Pearl Harbor.[40] Within a few hours the message had been confirmed. There had been heavy loss of life. When Mackenzie King decided he did not need permission from Parliament to declare war, Robertson was ready. That night, on the 11 o'clock radio news, Canadians heard that Canada was at war with Japan.

The following afternoon, G. W. Hilborn, a thirty-two-year-old third secretary of External Affairs, approached the residence of the Japanese minister on Daly Avenue in Ottawa carrying a sealed envelope. The house was already surrounded by police:

Well, then, I rang the bell and a footman came to the door dressed all in white livery and I asked if I could see the minister and he said, "Well, I'll go and see." So he said, "Come in," and ushered me into this little room, and I sat on what I suppose we would call a love seat only wide enough for two people. I had to wait about five minutes. And he had a young family and they were listening to the radio across the hall. I could hear the radio going. They were listening to *Superman*. I thought this was pretty appropriate.

Eventually, the Japanese minister, Seijiro Yoshizawa, entered the room.

Hilborn handed him the envelope, which he knew contained Canada's formal declaration of war, and informed Yoshizawa that he and his family were under house arrest until arrangements could be made to send them back to Japan.

> So the minister read all this and I watched his face and it was perfectly impassive through the whole reading. I guess it was about two pages of foolscap length. There was a lot in it. And, finally, he said, "This seems very satisfactory." And I got up to leave and he got up and said, "I guess we can still shake hands even though we are now enemies." So we shook hands.[41]

Japan was at war with the Allies. That was clear. The American Pacific Fleet had been surprised at Pearl Harbor and heavily damaged. That also was clear. What could not have been clear to the Canadians was how the U.S. Navy had been caught napping when a message from a German spy in Rio showed that the U.S. Navy had known as early as December 3—four days before the Japanese surprise attack—that a heavily escorted Japanese *invasion* convoy was on the high seas. And if a naval invasion was pending, what of Japan's main fleet?

Much has been written about the Pearl Harbor debacle in which three battleships were sunk, others damaged, and more than 2,400 U.S. servicemen killed. In the exhaustive post-mortems after the war, it was revealed that army and navy cryptographers had been decrypting messages for weeks that clearly pointed to a surprise attack on Pearl Harbor. By a series of misadventures, however, it appears that this information was overlooked until too late. As they read the intercepts, the top brass in Washington—including Navy brass—apparently never made the obvious connection between Japan's preparations for war and Tokyo's repeated requests for reports from the Japanese consul-general in Honolulu on the harbour's defences and the location of American warships. No special warning was received by Pearl Harbor authorities until after the bombs had fallen.

The Canadians were amazed that the Americans had been taken by surprise. The day after Pearl Harbor, a copy of the German message, heavily stamped "Secret," was sent to the United States via British

Security Coordination.[42] In addition, a copy was sent to the military attaché at the American legation in Ottawa. Two weeks later the military attaché wrote back:

> Ref. intercepted code message forwarded to this office Dec.8/41. Received Dec. 6.
>
> The ONI [Office of Naval Intelligence], Washington informs as follows:
>
> We know battleship was in home waters Nov. 10 so statement incorrect.
>
> With respect to paragraph 3, the statements are partly correct. A considerable number of transports near figure indicated were heading south prior to declaration of war by Japan and were accompanied by cruiser escort. However, the statement 70 transports could carry 300,000 men and equipment is not accurate.
>
> Thank you for bringing this to our attention. Sorry that we can give no more detailed information.[43]

The military attaché's Pablum reply evaded the real questions while raising a bigger one. The convoy reported by the Abwehr spy and sighted by the British had been headed northwest off the coast of Indochina. The convoy the U.S. Navy admitted knowing about was a different one. It was headed south, and it could only have been aimed, as so it turned out, at the U.S.-occupied Philippines. Yet, aside from an earlier warning on November 27, which only hinted at the possibility of an "amphibious assault" against the Philippines, the U.S. Navy leadership in Washington had done nothing.

"Indeed, on the evening of the 6th when I came in with the children for a moment, we knew that the forces (Jap) were already started for somewhere, though we did not know where," confided State Department undersecretary Adolf Berle to his diary shortly afterwards. "All this information was in the hands of the Navy—indeed, most of it had come from the Navy. But there seems to have been no effective orders sent to Pearl Harbor."[44]

Years later, as a result of lengthy inquiries into the disaster, it emerged that Roosevelt and his cabinet were indeed aware by November 27 that Japanese troop convoys were at sea. According to testimony, they considered that an attack on the Philippines was possible, along with several Dutch and British targets. Nevertheless, improbable though it seems, in the days that followed as the convoys neared their targets and as the political crisis deepened, no further alerts were issued and no special steps were taken by the leaders in Washington.

The Canadians were not the only ones mystified by the surprise that should not have occurred. The German decrypt also landed on the desk of FBI director J. Edgar Hoover, probably via British Security Coordination. He considered it of such major importance that on December 9 he wrote a covering letter marked "Personal & Confidential" and immediately sent copies of it by special messenger to the director of the Office of Naval Intelligence, to the director of U.S. Military Intelligence (G-2), and to the State Department. No documents have been found to indicate that Hoover was ever favoured with an explanation, or even a reply.[45]

On the other hand, there is little doubt about what Hoover thought. In an autobiography published long after the war, a former senior member of MI6 recalled the following:

> Our first visitor from the United States was a certain Kimball, of the FBI, who arrived shortly after Pearl Harbor. He talked with machine-gun speed, accusing the Navy, the Army, the State Department and the White House of having ignored FBI warnings of imminent Japanese attack.[46]

Whether Hoover delivered his warnings before or after the event is a moot point. In the week before the shooting started, Roosevelt and his top advisors knew very well that Japan was preparing for some kind of hostile action and they did not want to discourage it. On November 25 the Secretary of War noted in his diary that during a meeting with his cabinet the President had observed:

> … we were likely to be attacked perhaps next Monday, for the Japanese are notorious for making an attack without warning, and the question was what we should do. The question was how we

should maneuver them into the position of firing the first shot without too much danger to ourselves.[47]

If that was Roosevelt's strategy, it was 100 per cent successful. Although spectacular, the damage sustained at Pearl Harbor was not strategically significant. The injured battleships were already obsolete and were quickly repaired anyway.

That Pearl Harbor may have been deliberately left to its fate is a theory still advanced from time to time by historians. Had more urgent and timely warnings gone out from Washington, the U.S. Pacific Fleet would have been ordered to sea. Effective air and naval reconnaisance patrols would have been set up. If the Japanese aircraft carriers had been detected, or if their targets were no longer in harbour, the Japanese would certainly have called off the attack. War with Japan might have been delayed by months.[48]

The fact was, Roosevelt and his cabinet had decided that war with Japan was inevitable; the sooner it began the better.

One way or another, the United States was now in the war in earnest. "It was an immense relief to my mind," Mackenzie King noted in his diary. Churchill was much less restrained. News of Pearl Harbor gave him the "greatest joy." With the United States now on side, he had no doubt that victory was certain.

CHAPTER FIVE

MI6 REBUFFED

JANUARY — MARCH 1942

War between Japan and the United States meant a chance at the big time for Canada's fledgling wireless intelligence services.

The Examination Unit prepared to receive Yardley's replacement. Yardley was given a golden handshake of two-and-a-half months salary and a glowing letter of thanks from Norman Robertson. Edna Ramsaier received the same. Edna had decided to go with her beau.[1]

Just when Yardley was banished from cryptanalysis forever—he and Edna opened a small restaurant together—the war in the Pacific charged the airwaves with thousands of new signals, and both the Canadian Army and Navy wanted to meet the challenge. Work was urgently pushed forward on a new Special Wireless Station being built by the Army at Victoria, while the Department of Transport intercept station at Point Grey near Vancouver added three more receivers.

The Navy already had a sizeable organization. Apart from the various listening stations under its control, the Foreign Intelligence Service at Naval Headquarters had grown steadily during the previous year. By December 1941 Jock de Marbois could report that the FIS had more than two hundred personnel studying the wireless traffic of German, Italian, Vichy French, Spanish, Japanese, and Russian vessels. Most of the assignments came from the Admiralty, but there was a free exchange of direction-finding bearings and traffic analysis reports with

Royal Navy centres in Britain, Bermuda, and Singapore. Plain language messages from China and Korea were also logged and analysed.[2]

On Christmas Eve, Robertson received a formal letter from Malcolm Macdonald, the British High Commissioner in Ottawa. The British security services, he was told, were anxious to increase the interception of clandestine radio traffic between Japan and its spies in the Western Hemisphere, plus any other Japanese traffic in the Far East. Intercept stations in Britain, however, could not adequately hear Japan. Therefore the Secretary of State for Dominion Affairs "would appreciate it" if the Canadian authorities would take on this work at "first priority." In exchange, the High Commissioner wrote, Britain would look after all European and transatlantic espionage traffic, including German transmissions out of South America.

The letter included a compliment for Captain Ed Drake's small Army team at Rockcliffe "whose efficiency in intercepting enemy secret service wireless telegraph traffic is well known and highly valued." Nevertheless, the United Kingdom would be glad to send out a trained officer to help Drake set new interception priorities.[3]

The Canadians were uneasy with this proposal. After a hasty meeting in Room 123 of Parliament Hill's East Block, Tommy Stone replied on behalf of Robertson. Surely the British did not mean that Canada should drop its interception of German naval traffic? And, while Canada was prepared to stop working on German espionage traffic, which it was getting from Europe and the Middle East as well as South America, it would naturally expect to receive all the decrypts from these sources subsequently produced in Britain and the United States.[4]

Unknown to Stone, this was a condition that was unlikely to be honoured. The British move to take over German secret service interceptions in the Americas was being directed by Section V, the counterespionage division of the Secret Intelligence Service (MI6). Located at St Albans, west of London, Section V was led by former India policeman Felix Cowgill, characterized by one of his closest deputies as being "inhibited by lack of imagination, inattention to detail, and sheer ignorance of the world."[5]

The reorganization the previous year, which had resulted in the transfer of the Radio Security Service from MI8 to MI6, had put

Cowgill in charge of distributing all decrypts of German secret service traffic. This was a decision more of office politics than logic, for MI6 had thus far had little success with counter-espionage compared to MI5. By the beginning of 1942, the Security Service had pretty well stamped out all German espionage activities within Britain and the Commonwealth, whereas MI6 had no such enviable record. It had lost most of its European networks when Germany overran Europe in 1940 and was now looking to restore its fortunes—and its credibility.

The situation was further complicated by the fact that MI6 chief Stewart Menzies was an army officer. The head of the Secret Intelligence Service was traditionally drawn from the Navy, and the appointment of Menzies in 1939 had been resisted by the Admiralty, even by Churchill himself, who was then First Lord. Menzies's position was anything but secure and he spent much of the war fending off attacks on his competence. The result was a fortress mentality that pervaded MI6 and reached down to St Albans. Consequently, Cowgill routinely withheld German secret service decrypts from MI5, causing much complaint and friction.[6] What he was prepared to refuse a sister organization, he was unlikely to give the Canadians.

Stone's letter turned out to be a little too diplomatic. The High Commissioner either missed or ignored its cautious tone, and a few days later replied: "Lord Cranborne has expressed gratitude for your ready acceptance of the proposal." Of course Canada would still get the products of any traffic it was asked to discontinue. They would be supplied by the director of British Security Coordination himself. In the meantime, the Radio Security Service was providing a Lieutenant Colonel Stratton to oversee the redistribution of assignments between Britain and the United States. He would also be sent to Canada. The Canadians could very soon expect to be relieved of South American coverage, because the need to intercept Japanese secret service traffic had become both "immediate and urgent." Enemy naval interceptions by Canada were to continue.[7]

In the midst of this exchange, Robertson received an invitation from Hoover to send representatives to attend a Washington conference on the coordination of Allied intelligence activities in the Western Hemisphere. This was to take place in January, at the same time as a meeting to coordinate Allied Censorship. Robertson suggested that the question of distributing wireless intercept assignments could be settled then. He assumed that the U.S. Army and Navy were also invited. A few days later, he learned this was not the case. "It now seems the scope of this conference is not quite as broad as we thought," he commented.

Unknown to the Canadians, the initiative for this meeting was coming from the head of MI6. In an internal memorandum dated December 19, 1941, Menzies wrote:

> Examination of the material about the German Secret Service in South America which reaches us from various special sources such as the R.C.C.S. National Research Council Unit in Ottawa shows there is considerable overlapping and consequent wastage of American and Canadian skilled effort.... Attempts are being made to get the American authorities to centralize control of the various specialist units working on this material in the U.S.A. and it is to be hoped that the Canadians will take advantage of this unified control.... Arrangements have already been made to centralize in the office of the Director of Security Co-ordination in New York the handling and analysis of all material, from whatever source, about enemy espionage activity in South America. The D.S.C. will maintain close touch with London to ensure that nothing is missed and will distribute finished results to suitable Canadian and American authorities.[8]

In mid-January, the man Britain sent out to replace Yardley arrived in Canada. This was Oliver Strachey, head of the Government Code and Cipher School's team specializing in Abwehr hand ciphers. He brought with him an assistant cryptographer and the partial keys to the ciphers of Albrecht Engels, code-named ALFREDO. Engels was the leader of the other major German spy ring in Brazil, and even more important than Kempter. The U.S. Coast Guard had been reading almost all of his traffic since the preceding summer.[9]

The Canadians thought that Strachey, at sixty-seven, was a little old for work of such importance. They may have been right. The English-

man had been a member of MI-1b, the code- and cipher-breaking section of the War Office during the First World War. Like Yardley, whom
he had probably met when the latter visited Berlin in 1918, he had
gained experience during that time with various types of hand ciphers,
and it was appropriate in 1940 that he should be put in charge of breaking Abwehr traffic.[10]

Strachey had a rather odd background for a cryptographer. He had
been a minor official on the India railway system before visiting Britain
in 1911 and marrying the niece of philosopher Bertrand Russell. He
scandalized his in-laws by deciding to help his wife with the "house-
hold chores" rather than getting a job, living on her money until 1915
when the War Office opportunity came up. After the war, already in
his forties, he joined the Government Code and Cipher School and
stayed with it throughout the inter-war years, perhaps for lack of other
options.

At about the same time that Strachey arrived in Ottawa, Lieutenant
Colonel F. J. Stratton and Captain K. J. Maidment arrived in New
York. These two men were the key figures in Menzies's plan to have
British Security Coordination take charge of Western Hemisphere
counter-espionage. Stratton, a distinguished Cambridge astrophysicist
before the war but now representing the Radio Security Service, was to
coordinate the interception of enemy wireless traffic. The RSS in
Britain, Drake's Special Wireless Stations, and the Federal Communications Commission in the United States were each to take specific
assignments. Maidment, supplied by the Government Code and
Cipher School, would receive the resulting intercepts at BSC and distribute them as appropriate to the Coast Guard, the Examination
Unit, and GC&CS for decrypting. Stephenson and Donovan would
get the results.[11]

Both Stratton and Maidment first visited Ottawa. Apparently at
their direction, Drake immediately dropped coverage of Kempter's
transmissions and concentrated instead on two different Abwehr circuits, plus one believed used by Japanese spies. Even more ominously
for the future of the Examination Unit, Strachey sent Yardley's cipher
keys to Britain. From now on, the messages of Kempter's spy ring
would be broken at the Government Code and Cipher School and dis-

tributed through Section V of MI6, and thence to British Security Coordination. The British were taking no chances that the FBI—or any other American intelligence agency—would be able to get them directly from Canada.

For the next twenty-five days, from January 21 to February 14, 1942, the Examination Unit produced no German decrypts of consequence. Strachey switched the staff from working on current traffic—they had been breaking Kempter's messages within a day of receipt—to a backlog of unbroken ALFREDO messages, most of them months old. Their content was useless and already known to the Americans. There were no more lengthy shipping reports. The Examination Unit moved from the leading edge of counter-espionage to the very tail.[12]

In a final twist of the knife in the unfortunate Yardley's back, MI6 adopted the practice of labelling all decrypts derived from German hand ciphers with the acronym ISOS, standing for Intelligence Service Oliver Strachey. Even fifty years later, with publication of the official history, *British Intelligence in the Second World War*, the term ISOS continued to be used in this way.[13] Thus MI6 ensured that history would credit Strachey, not Yardley or the Examination Unit, with the breaking of the Abwehr ciphers out of South America. Yardley not only had lost his job, but had been robbed of recognition for his accomplishments.

Despite the high commissioner's promise to return decrypts of traffic taken over from the Examination Unit, the Canadians never again saw any Kempter messages. The only South American decrypts they now saw were those they solved themselves—mostly ALFREDO—with the raw material coming from Britain via Maidment at BSC or from the new circuits Drake had been assigned to. Canada had now lost what little control it had acquired over wireless intelligence and cryptanalysis.

At first, Robertson and his deputies in External Affairs did not realize what had happened. They seem to have thought the opposite: that Canada's foothold on code- and cipher-breaking was now secure. A series of meetings were held to establish the Examination Unit as part of the formal apparatus of government. Hitherto, it had only been an *ad hoc* project financed by the National Research Council with private funds. If it were to develop properly, the government had to take it over. The first question was where to put it.

After considerable debate, it was kept under the National Research Council. The NRC had a number of associate committees still engaged in non-military research, so a similar committee for the Examination Unit was a good choice for cover and for obtaining administrative services. The members of the Examination Unit Advisory Committee were Strachey, intelligence officers from the three services and the RCMP, C. J. Mackenzie as chairman, and Lester Pearson replacing Tommy Stone as the representative from External Affairs. All this and an annual budget of $100,000 was promptly approved by the Prime Minister and the Cabinet War Committee.[14] Then Mackenzie, busy with other responsibilities, stepped aside and Pearson became chairman.

In Robertson's view, the Examination Unit was to remain an External Affairs show. "We are not interested primarily in achieving immediate results but in building an organization which will gradually develop into a competent cryptographic bureau," he decreed. This was not happening. Within three weeks of Strachey's arrival, Gilbert Robinson wrote Pearson that he would be "failing in his duty" if he did not warn that Robertson's long-range plans were unlikely to be realized unless the Examination Unit's staff was given a variety of raw material to work on. "If this variety is not maintained it is possible that some may lose interest in the work," he complained.[15]

Strachey had not arrived empty-handed. He had brought with him copies of all the unenciphered French codes then in use and some keys to Japanese diplomatic traffic of higher grade than Yardley had so far broken. These expanded the ability of the Examination Unit to read Japanese and French traffic but contributed nothing toward training the staff. Codes and ciphers that are already known require clerical and translation skills, not cryptographic ones.[16]

Meanwhile, the plan for British–American cooperation on wireless intelligence in the Western Hemisphere moved forward. The FBI, British Security Coordination, and Canadian intelligence officials, including the RCMP, were to meet to discuss the matter on January 5. The conference was not actually held until January 29. In the interval, the British themselves spoiled the scheme.[17]

"I have had a free-for-all racket beginning in Francis Biddle's office," State Department undersecretary for intelligence Adolf Berle noted in his diary on January 6. "Donovan wants to take over the FBI work in S. America. At least, he does not say so, but he wants to put his own men in."

Francis Biddle was the U.S. Attorney General and, since the FBI was under the Department of Justice, he was Hoover's boss. As might be expected, both he and the FBI director objected to sharing jurisdiction over Latin American counter-espionage with Donovan's new agency, especially as the FBI now had a line on most of the German agents operating in South America, thanks to decrypts supplied by Canada and the U.S. Coast Guard. Ordinarily, the State Department might have stayed out of the issue except that, as Berle also noted in his diary that day, "Bill Donovan gets a good many of his ideas from the British" and "a British Military Attaché showed up with a plan to organize a revolution in Argentina—about the most disastrous thing anybody could have thought of at the moment."[18]

More hare-brained ideas followed, as recounted in Berle's diary. British "military intelligence"—which must be a reference to MI6—next proposed that the upcoming elections in Chile be rigged by bribery in order to ensure a new government sympathetic to the Allies. The State Department turned that down flat, despite direct representations from the British embassy's Sir Ronald Campbell. Other British proposals for Latin American "coup d'états"—specifically in Argentina—met the same fate. Nothing daunted, "the British, through Donovan and other people" made plans to intervene in Chile without State Department approval. The State Department complained to the President and Roosevelt put a stop to it.[19]

Menzies's plan to have British Security Coordination serve as the centre for counter-espionage intelligence in the Western Hemisphere was about to be dealt a body blow. While State Department officials were no great fans of the FBI, Hoover at least could be controlled. On the other hand, British "military intelligence," according to Berle, had demonstrated that it was prepared to embark on "adventures" and "wild ideas" which ran entirely contrary to American foreign policy. Since Donovan was perceived to be in thrall to the British, he became a victim of guilt by association. On January 21 Berle met with Roosevelt and suggested that the Office of the Coordinator of Information be excluded from all intelligence work in the Western Hemisphere. The President agreed. Counter-espionage work in Latin America was to be left entirely to the FBI.

A few days later, on January 29, the meeting on wireless intelligence in the Western Hemisphere convened. It must have been a disappointment to the British. The Canadian interception services were to continue to cooperate with the Americans on the coverage of clandestine traffic through the Canadian military attaché in Washington. There would be no over-all coordination by the British.[20]

This decision crippled Menzies's scheme and thwarted Stephenson's ambitions. Their intention had been that Stephenson and Donovan would mount a joint British/American assault on German activities in Latin America. It was not to be.

British Security Coordination also lost out in terms of Censorship. Throughout 1941 BSC had acted as the liaison office between the British Imperial Censorship stations in Bermuda and Trinidad and the American authorities (the FBI, U.S. Post Office, and so on) but Berle led the January meeting on Allied Censorship to an agreement whereby the British, Canadian, and American organizations would cooperate directly. There would be an exchange of requirement lists and a free sharing of both postal and telegraph intercepts. The new arrangement left British Security Coordination out in the cold.[21]

War or no war, the State Department considered Latin America the exclusive preserve of American influence. This attitude had its roots in the Monroe Doctrine of 1823, which stipulated that the United States would regard any direct European interference in the affairs of Western Hemisphere nations as an unfriendly act. The principle was reformulated at the turn of the century by President Theodore Roosevelt, to the effect that, if intervention was necessary in the affairs of Latin America, then it would be the United States that did the intervening. When Menzies planned that counter-espionage intelligence from "whatever source"—including American—be "centralized" in BSC, he obviously did not know his American history. The United States would never willingly give British Intelligence a free hand on its own back doorstep—much less tolerate clandestine interference by the British in Latin American politics.[22]

For the Americans, moreover, the issue of German espionage in South America had become one of national injury and national pride. Pearl Harbor had been a disaster, but what now was happening along the U.S. eastern seaboard was a massacre. When Germany followed Japan in declaring war against the United States, Hitler immediately ordered submarine attacks on U.S. shipping. In mid-January 1942 the U-boats closed in. It was like shooting ducks in a millpond.

> The new-moon night is black as ink
> Off Hatteras the tankers sink.
> While sadly Roosevelt counts the score
> Some fifty thousand tons—by MOHR [23]

That was the exultant message in English radioed back to Germany by Jochen Mohr, the skipper of U-124. He had just sunk his ninth ship on a single voyage.

The slaughter continued for months. At first the American ships failed to observe proper blackout procedures. Even when they did, they were clearly outlined against the lights of Miami and other coastal towns. When these communities dimmed their lights, the U-boats sank the ships by daylight. All along the Atlantic coast, Americans could look out and see plumes of smoke by day and red fires by night.

It was a matter of attitude and training. The U.S. Navy simply did not know how to protect its merchant fleet. The operational commanders disdained their own intelligence services. They did not believe in the convoy system. They told the British that they preferred to learn by their own mistakes rather than listen to suggestions. In the first six months of the year, 397 ships were sunk in U.S. Navy–controlled waters. At least 5,000 merchant seamen died.[24] The British, from Churchill downward, were appalled.

Contributing to this bloodshed was the German espionage organization in South America. The U.S. Navy, and even the Army Chief of Staff, General George Marshall, anguished over the "deadly peril" posed by their continuous shipping reports.[25] There were now at least four skilled spy rings with transmitters in Brazil and one in Chile. Between them they covered most of the major South American ports. They reported back to Germany all sailings—often to New York, Baltimore, or Philadelphia—describing cargos, presence of escorts, and so on. They even mentioned the landing of survivors as the U-boats took their toll.

Quashing this activity became the job of the State Department. Brazil was a neutral country with leanings toward the Axis powers. Thanks to the decrypts supplied by the U.S. Coast Guard plus those from Canada, the Americans knew the identities of almost all the spies. Immediately after Pearl Harbor, the State Department put fierce pressure on the Brazilian government to declare itself on the side of the Allies. If that happened, the spies could be rounded up. It was pressure few South American countries would dare resist.

Meanwhile, Lester Pearson assumed his new duties as head of the Examination Unit committee. He was also the External Affairs officer in charge of liaison with the Army and Navy intelligence organizations, making him, in effect, Canada's chief of secret intelligence. This put him in direct contact with William Stephenson.

Secret and Confidential

Ottawa, 25th February, 1942

Dear Stephenson,

I returned from Washington last Sunday. I tried to get you on Friday to tell you that my appointments were so crowded during the short time I was in Washington that I did not think I could find time to see Colonel Donovan, even if he desired to see me. However you were out of New York that day.

Since my return to Ottawa, I have discussed with those interested here the suggestions regarding centralization and exchange of information made in New York. It is felt by all concerned here that the paramount consideration in respect of the distribution of our material and reception of material from you is speed; consistent, of course, with security. For that reason we welcome arrangements which are in progress for the installation of telekrypton machines in New York and our [Examination] Unit House here.[26]

The material Pearson was referring to appears to have been German and French messages broken by the Examination Unit and raw intercepts from the South American circuits still being worked on by the Examination Unit. He went on to comment on one of the "suggestions" made by British Security Coordination:

> It may well be that under the new arrangements exchange of communications will be so speedy as to make unnecessary the establishment of a separate section of our Unit in New York. Pending a decision on this point, however, it was considered advisable to prepare the way for such a New York section by clearing the matter with U.S. authorities. I think you will agree we should not begin this work in New York without the approval and knowledge of those authorities. For that purpose, I have sent a letter to Mr. Wrong, of our Legation in Washington ... asking him to take up the matter with the appropriate people.

Stephenson was trying to get his own code- and cipher-breaking unit in New York, right under his thumb. It is a good thing Pearson reacted so cautiously. Hume Wrong in Washington was quick to sound a warning:

March 4, 1942

Dear Mr. Pearson,

> With regard to your letter of February 25th concerning the decyphering of messages between Washington and Vichy, I am rather diffident about advancing your suggestion that a section of the Canadian Examination Unit should operate in New York for this purpose. Mr. Berle, as you know, has taken rather a strong stand against the Intelligence activities conducted in the United States by the British Government.[27]

And how! American doubts as to the competence and honesty of Britain's Secret Intelligence Service—and of Stephenson in particular—were about to explode.

If British Intelligence was prepared willy-nilly to interfere in the affairs of neutral Latin American countries, what, the Department of Justice was asking itself, was it up to in the United States? One way to resolve the question—which seemed very reasonable to Biddle and Berle—was to pass legislation requiring the registration of Allied secret agents. This brought no joy in British secret service circles. As Berle noted in his diary:

> ... there has also been silent indication from the British Intelligence that they want the Act killed, because they want to protect the very considerable espionage [organization] here which they have, and they do not like to talk about. But no one has given us any effective reason why there should be a British espionage system in the United States. I believe they have gone to Colonel Donovan and that Donovan is secretly trying to get the bill stopped.

In a subsequent memo to President Roosevelt, Berle was more specific:

> There is before you for signature H. R. 6269 requiring registration of foreign agents. Colonel Donovan has written Budget requesting a veto. Colonel Stevenson [sic], head of British espionage here, has been urging this.

Arguing that there was no reason to allow free rein to "British espionage and counter-espionage in America," Berle urged the President to accept the bill as written.[28]

Stephenson reacted to Berle's intervention by ordering a BSC agent to tail the American and attempt to compile personal information that would discredit him. It was a grave mistake. Hoover's men spotted the British agent and told Berle.

If Stephenson had been hoping for a free hand at least in the United States, now he had really lost his chance. After extracting an apology from the British embassy, Berle met with Biddle, Hoover, and representatives from U.S. Military and Naval Intelligence. They compared notes and concluded that British Security Coordination was running an illicit secret service in the United States with more than 300 agents, many of them "irresponsible" and "unscrupulous." BSC was also sending out thousands of messages a month via the FBI radio station in Maryland, all of them in code. They decided to ask Roosevelt whether they could lodge a formal protest.

The next meeting was in Berle's office on March 5, 1942. Berle and Biddle faced the urbane British ambassador, Lord Halifax, and the embassy counsellor, Sir Ronald Campbell. The words exchanged were brittle.

Biddle began by saying that the President and his cabinet felt that British Security Coordination should be engaged in intelligence liaison, not operations, and that someone other than Stephenson should be in charge. Lord Halifax replied that Stephenson had assured him he was doing nothing without the approval of the FBI. The Americans said that was not what they understood and summoned Hoover. When the FBI director arrived, he explained that Stephenson's usual tactic was to make his moves first and report them afterwards. Often he did not inform the FBI at all. There were also incidents of "tapped wires and shanghaied sailors." Halifax replied that these revelations were so amazing that his "mental structure" had been altered.[29] What the Americans made of that response is not recorded.

The dispute boiled for days. After ostensibly checking with Stephenson, Halifax assured the Americans that BSC only had 137 employees and no one was doing what he shouldn't be. Berle observed in a note to file that Stephenson's spies in the United States had probably been transferred to Donovan's payroll. Biddle, who believed Stephenson was not telling Halifax the whole story, commented: "Someone has been doing some tall lying here."[30]

As for American insistence that they be told what was being sent to London via the FBI transmitter, Halifax simply said no. That was one secret the British were not prepared to share.

Berle would have been happy to run both Stephenson and British Security Coordination out of the country. He especially resented the influence Stephenson appeared to exert over Donovan.[31] However, presidential diplomacy prevailed. The spy registration bill was dropped and Roosevelt accepted British assurances that they would respect American sovereignty on secret service matters. Apparently, as a gesture of good faith, the British authorities took responsibility for running BSC's port security division away from Stephenson and placed it directly with the Security Executive in London. Stephenson would have no more opportunity to use strong-arm tactics on the seamen of neutral ships visiting American ports.[32]

The British went even further. A new approach was made to the U.S. Army's Signal Intelligence Service and to the Navy's Op-20-G, asking for a direct exchange of messages broken from German secret service traffic. The two American intelligence services agreed, provided that the exchange was made directly through Captain Maidment, the Government Code and Cipher School specialist at British Security Coordination—and without the involvement of either Stephenson or Donovan. Maidment was also to serve as liaison between the U.S. Army's intercept services and those of Canada and Britain. It hardly put the British in charge of Allied counter-espionage in the Western Hemisphere, but half a loaf was better than none.[33]

Stephenson had lost his last trump card—control over British and American decrypts coming through his office. He could no longer help Donovan and he had no hold on Hoover. His spymaster dream had vanished.

Needless to say, the daggers cut deep and the rift was absolute. For the rest of the war, it was Stephenson of British Security Coordination and Donovan's COI organization (later the Office of Strategic Services or OSS) on one side, and the State Department, the Justice Department, the FBI, and the U.S. Army and Navy intelligence services on the other. There would be no trust, little cooperation, and some outright attempts to destroy one another.

Hoover made one of the first such attempts. Until January 1942, he had always cooperated loyally with both Donovan and British Security Coordination. After the attacks led by Biddle and Berle, he became more dangerous to them than the enemy. In April, when Donovan's agents were inside the Spanish embassy in Washington, stealing its diplomatic codes at the request of MI6, FBI agents swooped in with sirens blaring and arrested the lot. It was not the way to win a war.[34]

What Robertson and Pearson knew or thought of this animosity is not known. Whatever references there are to it in Canadian archives have been withheld. Paradoxically, however, the Canadians profited. By having Donovan banned from operating in the Western Hemisphere, Berle had killed the chances of Anglo-American cooperation on Latin American counter-espionage. If Stephenson and Menzies still had ambitions in that direction—and they did—now they had to rely on Canada.

The first consequence of BSC's falling out with the State Department was that it could no longer expect to use the FBI's transmitter to send messages back to London. The answer was to build a sufficiently powerful transmitter on Canadian territory. MI6's Section V in Britain and British Security Coordination had already discussed setting up a wireless communications net to serve the needs of both Donovan's and Stephenson's agents. Now it was decided to push forward the building of an actual transmitter at Camp X, a school for sabotage that the British and Canadians had recently opened on a farm near Oshawa, Ontario, not far from Toronto.

The second consequence was an expansion of Camp X's mandate. It had been conceived in 1941 as a camp where the British sabotage organization, Special Operations Executive, could train agents from Latin America and the United States in paramilitary and secret service techniques.[35] Now that Donovan was officially out of the picture, it was to become the base from which Stephenson and MI6 intended to conduct their own counter-espionage activities in Latin America, no matter what the State Department thought.

Finally, when the Admiralty heard that BSC and MI6 were planning to build a powerful transmitter in Canada, it proposed that any spare time on the transmitter be used to send raw intercept material back to Britain for analysis. Canadian Navy and Department of Transport intercept stations had been producing an increasing amount of material, chiefly enciphered signals involving German and Italian submarines, Vichy naval units, Japanese merchant shipping, and Spanish and Portuguese vessels. There was even a smattering of traffic from the Russians and the Free French. All this had to be worked on in Britain, and the transatlantic cable charges were becoming prohibitive.[36]

Acquired from two ham radio operators in Toronto, the first Camp X transmitter went into operation in late May 1942. Its broadcast power was one kilowatt and it was linked to BSC in New York by commercial cable line. It was given the code-name HYDRA, because its several antennae brought to mind the many-headed beast of Greek mythology.[37]

Before HYDRA could be put together, however, and long before Stephenson and MI6 were able to train agents and organize their own counter-intelligence campaign for Latin America, the State Department moved. With characteristic directness and a supreme ruthlessness, the Americans set out to destroy the German spy rings. In the space of a few weeks in March, all the major German clandestine transmitters in Brazil fell silent. British Security Coordination and MI6 could only watch helplessly, through their own and the Examination Unit's diminishing decrypts, as the German stations were snuffed out like candles.

The instrument of American wrath was the U.S. ambassador in Rio, Jefferson Caffery. Hewn from the same American hardwood as his bosses, Hull and Berle, this fifty-five-year-old descendant of Irish pioneers in Louisiana was a thirty-year veteran of the State Department, with a reputation for trouble-shooting. He was aggressive, down-to-earth, and still tough physically. He took up his post in Axis-leaning Brazil in 1937, and his crude behaviour soon earned the cautious respect of that country's dictatorship. His British colleagues in Rio considered him "anti-British," "uncongenial" and possessed of a tendency "to speak freely when in his cups, though his speech becomes hard to follow." The German ambassador was more blunt: Caffery was "brutal and addicted to drink."[38]

Before American entry into the war, Caffery had been powerless to do anything about the thirty or so German spies he knew were operating in Brazil. He could not even hint that he was aware they existed. He engaged in anti-Nazi propaganda, but Brazil was in the grip of strongman Getulio Vargas, who had great sympathy for the Hitlers and Mussolinis of the world. On the other hand, Vargas was also aware that the United States was a lot closer than Germany. When Americans started dying on the high seas, the State Department warned Vargas either to break with the Axis powers or to face an economic boycott.[39] Vargas did as he was told, and Brazil severed relations with Germany and Italy on January 28, 1942. Shortly thereafter, Caffery gave the Brazilian police the names and addresses of the spies and the great roundup had begun.

Despite suggestions to the contrary in some postwar books on British Security Coordination, the British had nothing to do with the smashing of the German espionage networks in Brazil, or even elsewhere in South America. There may have been a little cooperation between MI6 and FBI agents back in late 1941, but the results were insignificant. By the beginning of February 1942, however, the State Department possessed a comprehensive collection of both Coast Guard and Examination Unit decrypts. Caffery had the names and addresses of nearly every spy in the country. It was just a matter of tipping off the Brazilian police.

"For LORENZ. Warning; Brazil very much endangered; break off contact with it," the Abwehr controller in Hamburg radioed his agent in Chile on March 23. Then, three days later: "Beware. ALFREDO arrested."[40]

They were all arrested: Kempter, Engels, and dozens of other minor agents and hangers-on. A few were captured in their homes, with their transmitters. Some had taken the precaution of destroying incriminating evidence beforehand; some had not. All the most important were soon sitting naked between bouts of questioning in the cement cubicles of Rio's police headquarters. There were beatings, and sometimes torture with pliers, cigarettes, and needles. The Brazilian authorities were now anxious to accommodate the Americans. Satisfaction at the U.S. embassy was immense.

"Under our guidance the police have so far today arrested 26 of the 30 persons we have indicated to them as connected with the four espionage rings operating [in] Rio and sending clandestine wireless messages," Caffery signalled the State Department on March 21. "That should paralyze their operations."[41]

It most definitely did. By the end of March, the FCC wireless intercept stations in the United States reported that only one transmitter was still operating from somewhere in South America (actually Chile) and that the Abwehr controllers in Germany were "sending blind" because all the others had been silenced. In mid-April Hoover attempted to present a case that German agents still represented a threat, but his thirty-five-page memo, "Axis aspirations in South America," was received with private derision by State Department officials. They felt, surely correctly, that any remaining enemy agents could safely be ignored. It was now almost impossible for these agents to communicate with Germany.[42]

Needless to say, German spy reports on ship movements in Latin America stopped abruptly. The Americans persuaded Vargas to allow them to set up direction-finding stations in Brazil but, aside from one weak station that was quickly suppressed, no further clandestine transmitters were located in that country. There was still the Abwehr agent in Chile, but he was far from the main shipping lanes and could contribute little. He, too, was soon silenced. All that remained was a nest of German agents in Argentina, irksome rather than dangerous.

Hoover was not the only one slow to see that German espionage activities in South America had been crushed. As late as June 2, a British Security Coordination report to London made extravagant claims about the dangers of enemy activity in South America, even though Stephenson had watched the destruction of the spy rings through Canadian and British decrypts. Nevertheless the memo claimed that Brazil and Argentina were "teeming with Axis agents and other enemies of the Allies," and that the common aim should be to preserve "South America as an invaluable asset to the democratic cause."[43]

While Britain has not released its wartime files on Latin American counter-espionage, the United States has. There is an extensive collection of decrypts in the National Archives in Washington, plus a large body of documents pertaining to the suppression of the enemy agent transmitters. By mid-May both Hoover and the FCC were reporting that in all of South America there was only one clandestine transmitter in Chile still operating, and possibly a short-range one in Argentina. Nothing else.[44]

The BSC memo of June 2, apparently prepared by Stephenson, can only have been deliberately deceitful. It was making a case for the continued operation of Camp X, then being considered for dismantling by the Special Operations Executive. As there was obviously not going to be any call for British-trained American saboteurs for Latin America, SOE operations chief Colin Gubbins could not see any point in keeping Camp X open. Stephenson flew to London in June to persuade him otherwise. The counter-espionage training programs at Camp X were by then in full swing.

The memo did its work. It was presumably sent to the British Joint Intelligence Committee as well as to SOE, for the day after it was written, the British JIC concluded: "Enemy power and influence in Latin America, though unlikely to be used immediately in a major attack on Allied supplies, constitute a serious danger which may at any time become critical. This danger would be greatly reduced by the destruction of enemy organizations both German and Japanese."[45] But there were no such Japanese organizations, and all of the important German ones had been destroyed.

The content of the memo also came to the attention of the British Chiefs of Staff and they reacted with understandable alarm. Instructing the military intelligence officers with the British embassy in Washington to look into the situation, the COS observed:

Donovan has been prevented from operating there [Latin America] and the only activity has been limited security control by Federal Bureau of Investigation....

Our policy in regard to secret anti-Axis activity has been one of laissez-faire, to avoid risk of upsetting Latin American states or acting against wishes of the State Department, although overt security measures to prevent sabotage to ships and cargos have been organized in all major ports by British Security Coordination.

Except for above security organization in paragraph 3, Axis have virtually had a free run.

The British Chiefs of Staff went on to urge that the American authorities be warned of the immediate need for a "counter-attack" to destroy the Axis organizations, and that the United States be offered the resources of SOE, MI6, and British Security Coordination.[46]

The very worst had occurred. The only real control a government has over its secret services is the honour and honesty of those who lead them. Yet either MI6 or BSC—probably both Cowgill and Stephenson—had deliberately deceived their bosses. There is evidence that both men knew of the mass arrests inspired by the State Department two months earlier: they had received, and continued to receive, the decrypts that told the story.[47] Four Abwehr transmitters and the spy rings they had served had been silenced in Brazil, and there had been over thirty arrests. This was hardly a situation where, except for British Security Coordination, the "Axis have virtually had a free run." In April Hoover had overstated the Axis threat that still remained in Latin America; in June his British colleagues misrepresented it.

Stephenson got his way. Camp X stayed open. The training of MI6 agents for Latin American counter-espionage duty continued.

———————

The Examination Unit mastered current ALFREDO intercepts only a month before the big collapse. This was just in time to follow one of the most dramatic efforts by the South American spies to inflict major damage on the Allies.

From: Rio de Janeiro
To: Hamburg

Intercepted: March 7, 1942
Received: March 9, 1942

QUEEN MARY, on board, Indians, Africans, Englishmen, tanks, dismantled airplanes. Came from Dutch East Indies via South Africa.

(decrypted March 9)

From: Rio de Janeiro
To: Hamburg

Intercepted: March 8, 1942
Received: March 9, 1942

QUEEN MARY sailed on March 8, 18 o'clock local time.

(decrypted March 9)

From: Rio de Janeiro
To: Hamburg

Intercepted: March 14, 1942
Received: March 14, 1942

Concerning QUEEN MARY. The troops, young people of the white race, numbering 7 to 8 thousand men. Cruiser BIRMING-HAM arrived Rio Grande on February 19th and sailed from Rio Grande on the 22nd.

(decrypted March 16)

At 80,000 tons the *Queen Mary* and her sister ship *Queen Elizabeth* were the pride of Britain. In peacetime the giant passenger liners were the greyhounds of the North Atlantic, but in 1939 they had been converted to troopships, each capable of carrying an entire army division. In wartime they always travelled singly, never in convoy, relying on their great speed to avoid U-boats. On the Admiralty plotting boards they were known as MONSTER ONE and MONSTER TWO. Because thousands of soldiers could be drowned with one torpedo, the *Queen Mary* was the ultimate target for a German submarine.

From: Rio de Janeiro
To: Hamburg

QUEEN MARY reported by Steamer CAMPKIRO on the
11th, 18 o'clock C.E. T. off Recife.

(decrypted March 13)

From: Rio de Janeiro
To: Hamburg

Intercepted: March 14, 1942
Received: March 14, 1942

No. 43. QUEEN MARY, 12 inch gun on bow and stern, as well
as 7 heavy anti-aircraft guns and 8 pom-poms. Troops 5 to 6 thousand men. Besides reported war-material, 6 inch guns.

(decrypted March 16)

The arrival of the *Queen Mary* had electrified the Abwehr spies in
Brazil. They buzzed like locusts, reporting every detail they could discover about her, and every movement, in a dozen messages intercepted
by both the British and the Americans.[48]

The Examination Unit's *Queen Mary* decrypts were sent to Washington with the greatest urgency. The Coast Guard sent additional
decrypts from other spy networks. The Americans became thoroughly
alarmed. The Germans had deduced from the accents of those on
board that the troops were principally Canadian. But they were wrong.
The *Queen Mary* was in fact carrying 9,000 *American* soldiers to the
Far East.

The *Queen Mary* was not sunk. It was one thing to report her movements, but quite another for a submarine to catch her. No torpedo
found its mark. "Had this boat been sunk with the inevitable loss of
thousands of our soldiers, the incident would have imperiled the his-

toric friendship of our two countries," Chief of Staff General George Marshall wrote the Brazilian government.[48] The Americans had had a bad scare.

On April 8 the Examination Unit decrypted one of its last messages from Brazil. It was in a batch of intercepts that had apparently gone astray, and was already nearly a month old when it arrived in Ottawa.

> From: Santos
> To: Hamburg
>
> Intercepted: March 9, 1942
> Received: April 4, 1942
>
> At 20.40, two U.S. reconnaisance planes. Source absolutely reliable. With QUEEN MARY falls Churchill. Therefore, good luck.

The Abwehr spies in Brazil were the ones who needed luck. By the time that message was decrypted, the man who had sent it was behind bars.[49]

CHAPTER SIX

WOOING
THE YANKS

MARCH − JUNE 1942

T HE CAFETERIA in the Chateau Laurier was crowded as Norman
Robertson and T. C. Davis picked their way among the tables
with their trays. The huge railway hotel next to the Parliament Buildings had its usual complement of bureaucrats for lunch that day in
March 1942. It was convenient, cheap, and had continuous background clatter that made it an ideal place to discuss the weighty issues
of government in wartime.

All the tables were occupied. Robertson and his companion chose
one with two places free, paying little attention to those already seated.
They were well into their meals and soon would be gone anyway.

Davis was an associate deputy minister in the Department of
National War Services, created to administer some of the many special
agencies that war had given birth to. Robertson wanted to discuss a
plan to amalgamate the various censorship divisions under the new
department. It made so much sense. Why have Postal Censorship
under the Postmaster General, Telegraph Censorship under the Army,
and so on, when all these activities could and should be coordinated
under one administration?

They talked animatedly between mouthfuls of chicken pot pie.

Radio Censorship was already under the National War Services, so why not the others? They tossed the idea back and forth.

Then they realized they were being overheard. A man next to them was listening. This made them uncomfortable. Even worse, the man was pretending not to be listening. They looked pointedly at him. Finally, he picked up his tray and left.

Two days later, Davis learned that the Chief Telegraph Censor, L. S. Yuill, had sent a memo to the Minister of National War Services, urging that the plan to centralize the censorship services be abandoned. Davis reacted angrily. "I did not know that the Government of Canada maintained a force of stool pigeons, spotting [sic] around local eating emporiums," he wrote Yuill, referring to the "agent of the local Gestapo who reported to you a conversation which I had a few days ago with the Undersecretary of External Affairs." Davis continued in a sarcastic vein. Was the fact that Robertson ordered chicken pot pie reported to the Commissioner of the RCMP? he asked. Wasn't it obvious to Yuill's spy that the two of them were either Communists or employees of External Affairs?

The incident also merited a full description from Robertson to the Prime Minister. It showed, Robertson concluded in a lengthy memo, "how thoroughly some of our censorship services have picked up what used to be regarded as a typical Nazi technique."[1]

Yuill had certainly blotted his copybook with Robertson. Within three months he was to be fired. Yet just over a week before the incident that provoked Robertson's memo, he had been invited to sit on the reorganized Examination Unit Advisory Committee.

Telegraph and Cable Censorship had suddenly become an especially important part of Canada's cryptographic effort. Intercepting and decrypting German clandestine messages from South America had been both gratifying and exciting, but with the wave of arrests in Brazil, the traffic had dried up. The Examination Unit had few Japanese linguists, so most Japanese traffic was sent straight to Britain. That left Vichy French. The most important source of this material, however, was telegraph interception rather than wireless.

The Canadians really thought they had a role here. In the months immediately after the Pearl Harbor attack, both Britain and the United

States feared that the Vichy government might suddenly decide to join the Axis. This meant that the still-powerful French Fleet might enter the battle against the Allies before the U.S. Navy had recovered from its losses and while the British Navy was stretched to the breaking point. Already the Japanese had sunk the *Prince of Wales* and the *Repulse*, while three other British capital ships, *Barham*, *Queen Elizabeth* and *Valiant* had recently been sunk or seriously damaged by the Germans and Italians.

It is impossible to overstate the menace posed by the French Fleet at this time. The Allied convoys on the Atlantic were protected against U-boats only by the thin screens of destroyers and corvettes that escorted them. These could not survive an attack by anything from a cruiser up. The Germans had just moved the ultra-modern battleship *Tirpitz* into Norwegian waters; the Italians had two battleships and numerous cruisers against almost no British opposition in the Mediterranean. In Toulon harbour alone, awaiting orders from Vichy, were three battleships, seven cruisers, one aircraft carrier, fifteen destroyers, and twelve submarines. There were other French Navy vessels in other harbours around the world.

The Admiralty had long been aware of the peril. The Department of Transport station at Forrest, Manitoba, had been monitoring Vichy naval frequencies for the Admiralty since mid-1940 and now was asked to step up the coverage.[2] That was only for traffic analysis. The British had not yet been able to break the Vichy fleet cipher, but if any of the French naval units prepared to put to sea, the increase in wireless activity—or even radio silence—would give the move away. Similarly, if one could tap into the exchanges between Vichy and an important post like Washington, even a medium-grade code might provide useful early warning of Vichy intentions.

The Vichy–Washington traffic was being handled by U.S. telegraph companies via the one undersea cable that did not pass through Canada or Newfoundland. Originally it went from New York to the Azores (Horta) and thence to Italy. In 1940 it had been cut by the British and then spliced into Portugal. Before American entry into the war, neither the British nor the Canadians had any way of obtaining Vichy–Washington traffic, but the three-nation Censorship agreement at the beginning of 1942 suddenly gave Canadian Telegraph Censorship direct access via American Telegraph Censorship in New York. The Canadians were quick to seize the opportunity.

At the end of January, when the Examination Unit decoded its first Vichy telegraph messages out of Washington, there was euphoria in External Affairs. Oliver Strachey, the man sent out from Britain to replace Yardley, had brought with him some reconstructed Vichy diplomatic codes and immediately set to work on the traffic. The results were sent to the Canadian legation in Washington for passing on to the U.S. authorities, and to BSC for passing on to London. Robertson believed that only Canada was in receipt of these messages and, on Strachey's suggestion, five French-speaking linguists were recruited from Postal Censorship in Vancouver to handle the expected increase in work. Three French-speaking typists were to be hired. Dispatch riders were organized to run the intercepts over to the Examination Unit as soon as they were received at the Telegraph Censor's office. Then, in mid-March, when everything was almost ready, it was learned that the U.S. Army's Signal Intelligence Service was already receiving and decoding the same material.[3]

The trouble was that four months after American entry into the war, there was still no overall coordination on wireless intelligence between the British and the Americans. Raw intercepts flowed across the Atlantic by bag or cable in fits and starts. Moreover, a wireless intelligence agreement hammered out by Denniston the previous summer with the U.S. Navy's Op-20-G simply was not working. The situation had become critical, because the Germans had made improvements to their U-boat ENIGMA machines, temporarily blinding the British to submarine movements in the Atlantic. When the Admiralty proposed an Allied wireless intelligence conference—in the midst of the catastrophic sinkings of merchant vessels off the U.S. east coast—the idea was received cordially by both the U.S. Navy and the U.S. Army.[4]

The meeting took place in Washington, April 6 to 16, 1942. It was attended by the service heads of wireless intelligence from all three countries. Captain Drake, Colonel Murray, and Commander de Marbois came for Canada. The U.S. Navy's Op-20-G and the U.S. Army's

Signal Intelligence Service sent top staffers, and Commander John Redman, vice-chief of U.S. Navy Operations, gave the conference's opening remarks. Captain Humphrey Sandwith, head of the Admiralty's wireless intercept (Y) service, led the British delegation, which also likely included Captain Roger Winn, the brilliant head of the Admiralty's U-boat tracking room. There were also representatives from the Radio Security Service and the British Foreign Office. The FBI was not invited, nor was anyone from the COI/OSS, Donovan's spy and sabotage agency.

Captain Sandwith began the formal proceedings with a lengthy summary of the wireless intelligence and cryptographic organization in Britain. The full text of his remarks is in the Canadian naval archives in Ottawa and represents one of the few contemporary descriptions of Britain's signals intelligence organization. Even in Britain, most such documents remain closed. For that reason, it is worth paraphrasing in some detail. The following, in point form, is what Sandwith told his Canadian and American listeners:

The Admiralty is responsible for reading every available intercepted and decrypted naval or naval air signal generated by Britain's enemies or potential enemies.

The War Office is responsible for the intercepted signals of enemy military organizations.

The Air Ministry is responsible for reading the intercepted signals of enemy air organizations, except those signals generated by aircraft over water.

The Foreign Office is responsible for reading intercepted and decrypted commercial and diplomatic messages.

The Radio Security Service (reporting at first to MI5 but now to MI6) is responsible for illicit wireless transmissions in the U.K., although it has recently expanded this responsibility to include illicit transmissions emanating from countries of the "Empire" and neutral countries.

Each of the five organizations cited above has its own wireless intercept or "Y service" and these are administered by a Y Committee composed of the heads of the five Y services plus certain senior intelligence officials. The head of this committee is an admiral.[5]

The cryptographic centre is "Station X" (the Government Code and Cipher School at Bletchley Park) and consists of about 2,000 people drawn from the three services and Foreign Office. It does both cryptanalysis and traffic analysis. The results are pooled.

The wireless interception program of the five Y services is determined half by the traffic needs of the cryptographers and half by the needs of the traffic analysts.

Because the cryptographic centre is in England, the main intercepting stations, Scarborough and Flowerdown, are there also. For traffic that cannot be received in Britain, there are intercept stations at Freetown, Pretoria, Durban, Colombo, Melbourne, Bermuda, Alexandria, and several in Canada.

The sixty-five receivers at Scarborough are all on German traffic whereas those at Flowerdown cover Italy, Spain, France, and any other countries heard in Britain.[6]

Sandwith went on to explain that the wireless interception network was complemented by a parallel network of direction-finding stations. There were eighteen of these in Britain, plus six in Australia, four in New Zealand, four in South Africa, and fourteen in Canada. The best of these stations were usually those operated by the Navy, which also regularly supplied bearings on transmissions of interest to the Foreign Office and the Radio Security Service.

Sandwith then undoubtedly enthralled his listeners by giving examples of the successful operation of this system.

He described the spectacular chase the previous summer which had led to the sinking of the *Bismarck*. The ultra-modern German battleship had managed to enter the North Atlantic, where it had confronted and sunk the great British battle-cruiser *Hood*, also damaging the battleship *Prince of Wales*. Immediately afterwards, it had transmitted a long message before resuming radio silence. Then, as the Admiralty rushed other battleships and an aircraft carrier to the scene, the *Bismarck* disappeared. For twenty-four agonizing hours, the British did not know where the ship was nor where it was headed. But the long message it had sent—still not yet deciphered—was on a particular frequency and directed to the great German naval base at Wilhelmshaven. Traffic analysis then revealed that stations in Occupied France as far south as Bordeaux were suddenly sending messages on the same frequency. On that basis, Sandwith said, Naval Intelligence correctly concluded the German battleship was racing for France. The *Bismark* was intercepted and destroyed.

Similarly, Sandwith described how the British had been able to detect the movement of forty U-boats to the Mediterranean because the Germans took over a wireless station at Naples and put it on U-boat frequencies.

Most fascinating of all was Sandwith's explanation of how the British had been breaking the U-boat ENIGMA ciphers. Theoretically, these were an especially difficult problem, because the cipher machine settings were changed frequently and U-boat messages were notoriously short. However, by analysing an intercepted transmission for its electronic signature and the sending characteristics of the submarine's wireless operator, the numerical identity of a U-boat usually could be determined. Since the names of the commanders of most U-boats were known (mainly from prisoner-of-war interrogations), and since they invariably signed their messages, this provided an ideal point of attack for cryptanalysis. The longer the commander's name, the more certain it was that his messages would be broken.[7]

Over the next few days, while subcommittees discussed the various issues, Sandwith proposed to the Americans that the Allies systematically divide interception responsibilities. He pointed out that on the Berlin–Tokyo diplomatic circuit, Britain was better positioned to hear the Berlin side of the traffic, while the United States was better positioned to hear the Tokyo side. Surely it made sense to assign U.S. and British intercept stations accordingly?[8]

This was probably one of the most important suggestions of the conference. The Japanese ambassador and the military attaché in Berlin regularly reported to Tokyo their conversations with top German military and political figures, including Hitler. Most of these messages were being read, and they were undoubtedly the single most valuable source of intelligence on Germany's strategic intentions throughout the war.[9]

Sandwith also recommended to the Americans that they set up a central organization like the Government Code and Cipher School to handle traffic analysis and cryptanalysis from whatever source, and to act as a "main control" on wireless intercept programs.[10] He suggested that the Americans might like to establish a central Y committee similar to the one in Britain.

The future of the Examination Unit also hung on the conference. Sandwith warned the Canadians they could not carry on with cryptanalysis if the committee studying the subject were not in favour of it. And indeed the committee concluded that it was "impractical at this stage to form a complete Canadian cryptanalysis organization." For the Canadian Navy, this meant that it would continue to be primarily a supplier of raw material, with intercepts received on the East Coast going to the Admiralty, and Japanese Navy intercepts received at Esquimalt, British Columbia, going to the American station at Bainbridge (Seattle).[11]

Jock de Marbois received a big plum, nevertheless. The conference decided to retain naval direction finding in Canada, although Britain and the United States had enough stations to do the entire job themselves. The plotting centres at Ottawa and Esquimalt were to join an American operational intelligence net centred on Washington for the western Atlantic, and on Seattle and Hawaii for the Pacific. Where Canadian and American coverage overlapped, the U.S. Navy's cryptanalysis section—Op-20-G—was to send to Ottawa the U-boat dispositions it gleaned from decrypts and traffic analysis. These moves acknowledged the vital help the Canadian Navy had given in the struggle against the U-boats in the North Atlantic.[12]

These decisions could not have made de Marbois happier. As head of the Canadian Navy's Foreign Intelligence Service, he had no interest in anything but naval operational intelligence. It had led him into increasing conflict with Lieutenant Little and others at Naval Headquarters who were fascinated by the wider possibilities of code- and cipher-breaking. De Marbois preferred to put his faith in traffic analysis and direction finding. Actual naval special intelligence—the reading of the enemy's codes and ciphers—would from now on be the responsibility of the British and the Americans.[13]

Considering that the Battle of the Atlantic was in a particularly bloody phase, especially for the Americans, naval wireless intelligence issues dominated the discussions. The British specialists in enemy clandestine traffic, Stratton and Maidment, outlined the network of listening stations—apparently single receivers operated by former amateurs—that they were setting up to monitor illicit transmissions in the Western Hemisphere. They were not required, however, to make a detailed presentation.

Of more interest was the presentation made by an official of the Foreign Office's wireless intelligence (Y) service. While it is likely he talked about the interception of enemy and neutral diplomatic traffic, he also made an appeal to the Americans to join the search for ways to break enciphered non-Morse traffic: messages sent by telephone, tele-type, or facsimile that had been electronically scrambled. This was known to be theoretically possible, and some progress had been made, but the British did not have the resources to mount major research. Would the Americans help?

Unknown to the Allies, the research division of the German Post Office had succeeded only the month before in electronically unscram-bling the very complicated system used by the radio/telephone service of AT&T in the United States. For the next two years the Germans eavesdropped on the radio/telephone conversations of high U.S. offi-cials, including the Chief of Staff, General George C. Marshall. They even intercepted the transatlantic calls of Churchill and Roosevelt. For-tunately, although the Prime Minister had great faith in the security of the system, both leaders were fairly careful in what they said. Tran-scripts of their conversations went directly to Hitler.[14]

The British also sought cooperation in the study of the ionosphere. The Admiralty had sponsored considerable scientific research into this layer of electrified gas enveloping the earth far above the normal atmo-sphere. Sandwith himself explained that the radio skip phenomenon, with which everyone was familiar, occurred because the signals bounced off the ionosphere. The trouble was that the ionosphere was subject to sunspot activity and magnetic storms, causing it to fluctuate. This affected the range of wireless transmission and direction finding. If Bomber Command was to put its aircraft on target over Germany,

Sandwith said, it was vital to have up-to-date data on the condition of
the ionosphere. In response to this need, the Canadians soon set up an
ionosphere research station under the National Research Council at
Churchill, Manitoba.

The other issue of great concern to the British was the state of communications between the U.S. wireless intelligence services and those
of the British. So far, at least between Op-20-G and Naval Intelligence
in London, it had been by one-time pad ciphers. This system, involving unique pads of random numbers, was secure but very slow. The
British asked the Americans if they would consider using a Type X
machine, the British version of the ENIGMA cipher machine used by
the Germans.[15]

There seems little doubt that the Radio Intelligence Conference, as
the Americans called it, was one of the most important Allied intelligence events of the Second World War. It ended immediately—and at
long last—the reluctance of the U.S. Navy's operational commanders
to take advantage of wireless intelligence. The U.S. Navy, indeed,
acted at once, reorganizing its operational intelligence structure on the
Admiralty model and pouring money and resources into the expansion
of Op-20-G and its wireless intercept net. Most important of all was
the admirals' change in attitude. Two months after the conference, a
U.S. fleet inflicted a decisive defeat on a superior Japanese force at
Midway Island in the Pacific, sinking four aircraft carriers, a victory
made possible by wireless intelligence.[16]

The conference gave a boost to the U.S. Army's signals intelligence
organization as well. A review ordered by the Secretary of War immediately after Pearl Harbor had revealed many deficiencies in the handling of intercepted material between U.S. Military Intelligence (G-2)
and the Signal Corps which administered the cryptographic staff of
the Signal Intelligence Service. The examples the British gave of the
value of wireless intelligence in actual operations could only have rein-
forced existing plans for reorganization and expansion. A few weeks
earlier, the U.S. Army had decided to set up a separate section of the
Military Intelligence Service, called Special Branch, to digest and distribute the products of the Signal Intelligence Service. The Signal
Intelligence Service, in turn, moved into the vastly larger premises of a

former girls' school near Washington called Arlington Hall.[17]

The conference also set the agenda for various longterm projects undertaken by Britain, the United States, and Canada. Research into ionospheric effects, and the encrypting and decrypting of non-Morse transmissions not only went on throughout the war, but continued long after it, even to the present day. Systematic cooperation among the three countries on the exchange of wireless intelligence also dates from the conference, with its discussions of the need for an international Y organization and efficient communication links. The former never came about, but within months efficient wireless and cable channels were established.[18]

The Canadian documents are incomplete. It is therefore not known what the U.S. Army representatives said, did, or gleaned from the conference. It is a safe guess, however, that they listened with especial attention to what the Foreign Office spokesman had to say. The State Department did not have its own wireless intelligence service and with the loss of the U.S. Army's intercept station in the Philippines, the U.S. Navy had a near-monopoly on Japanese traffic. The interception of diplomatic traffic, on the other hand, was up for grabs.

As the conference was winding down, and while American and British intelligence officers were tabling their decisions and recommendations, Norman Robertson and Mackenzie King arrived in Washington. They were there, the Canadian legation's military attaché noted in his diary, for discussions on intelligence. They were there, it would seem, to learn first hand of the decisions affecting Canada.

Jock de Marbois was in heaven. The decisions of the Radio Intelligence Conference gave him the ammunition he needed to urge that his wireless intelligence organization, the Foreign Intelligence Service, be reorganized on more elaborate lines, similar to the Admiralty's Operational Intelligence Centre. He wanted a wireless interception division, U-boat tracking room, direction-finding plotting section—the works. He would be in charge and answer jointly to the Director of Signals and the Director of Naval Intelligence. Most importantly, the main effort would be channeled toward the Atlantic, where he considered the real action to be.[19]

For the Canadian champions of actual code- and cipher-breaking, the future was not so rosy. The Radio Intelligence Conference had stripped the Examination Unit of any opportunity to work on enemy naval traffic. The U.S. Signal Intelligence Service was working on the same Vichy diplomatic traffic. Only the barest trickle of out-of-date South American clandestine intercepts was now arriving and, contrary to promises, the British had not returned any decrypts of German secret service messages broken elsewhere. The future did not look promising for Canada's cryptographic experiment.

Robertson, Stone, and Pearson were not prepared to give up, however. They had glimpsed first hand the potential of signals intelligence as an instrument of foreign policy. In early April, Lieutenant Little had been sent to London to confer with the intelligence authorities there. His specific task was to persuade the British to supply Canada with decrypts from the non-naval Japanese traffic being sent to Britain from Canadian listening stations on the West Coast.[20] Perhaps he could also find out what was holding up the German secret service decrypts.

In the meantime, on April 21, the Examination Unit committee met to decide what it should do. Pearson chaired the meeting. The conversation was desultory. Strachey—who announced he was soon to return to Britain—assured the committee that the British authorities still appreciated the Vichy decodes out of Washington. A new Japanese linguist had been hired to help with the low-grade Japanese traffic then being received. After further talk, someone pointed out that Vichy might recall its ambassadors from Ottawa and Washington at any time, putting an end to the telegraph intercepts. The committee finally decided it should see what it could do with Vichy wireless messages. Pearson undertook to find more French linguists to train as cryptanalysts, while orders went out to Canada's listening stations to start copying Vichy traffic.[21]

Over the next month, there were other changes. A Canadian Y Committee was set up to coordinate wireless interception along the lines suggested by the British at the Radio Intelligence Conference. The Examination Unit completed its move to a new building in downtown Ottawa, a large Victorian house on Laurier Avenue next door to the Prime Minister's residence. For the rest of the war, the dumpy figure of Mackenzie King ambling up his front walk at the end of the day was a familiar sight to those labouring over the codes and ciphers of Canada's enemies:

> He used to come home fairly late—oh, about 6 or 6:30, and the touching thing was that he would go up to the door of the house, the door would open, he would be handed out the leash of his little dog and he would take the little dog out and take him for a walk around the block before he went into the house to have his own meal. So he was very attached to this little dog. He was very courteous. He always spoke to us although he had no idea who we were. I imagine he knew we were doing something unspeakable in there but I don't even know how much he knew about that.[22]

The Americans were also busy, though on a much grander scale. The Army's Signal Intelligence Service attempted to make up for the loss of its listening station in the Philippines by using Federal Communications Commission stations on the West Coast. On March 1, 1942, the Army's ambitiously named Radio Intelligence Center began operations in the Federal Customs House in San Francisco, receiving Japanese wireless traffic and direction-finding bearings from FCC stations as far north as Fairbanks, Alaska, and as far west as Honolulu. The intention was to distribute the processed intercepts to U.S. Military Intelligence, the Navy, and the FBI.

The U.S. Navy's reaction was icy. Naval command on the West Coast deplored the Army's use of civilian wireless stations and personnel for military purposes. It claimed that the FCC had no conception of how to take bearings and accused it of "beautifully written reports on nothing." If the Army was counting on the cooperation of the Navy, it had another think coming. As the Canadians and the British were to learn, the capacity for the American services to fight among themselves was limitless.[23]

Fear of Army poaching was probably a factor when the U.S. Navy agreed in June that the Army should have sole responsibility for the interception and deciphering of diplomatic traffic. The Navy would look after enemy naval traffic, a task of no small consequence, considering that both Japanese and German naval ciphers were sophisticated and difficult to break. On June 30, 1942, communications intelligence responsibilities in the United States were divided as follows:

Diplomatic —Army
Enemy Naval—Navy
Enemy Military—Army
Western Hemisphere Clandestine—Navy and FBI
International Clandestine—Navy

President Roosevelt formally confirmed the arrangement a week later, adding that cryptographic activity was to be confined to the two services and the FBI. The FCC and William Donovan's organization, now renamed the Office of Strategic Services (OSS), were specifically excluded.[24]

The arrangement was not unreasonable. The FCC continued to provide intercept services to the Coast Guard or the Army as required or requested. While the FBI was to be allowed to operate its own cryptanalysis unit and the OSS was not, Donovan presumably (but not necessarily) continued to receive Navy and Coast Guard decrypts of enemy secret agents operating in Europe, Asia, and Africa.[25] As these were only of marginal quality that summer and fall, the head of the OSS approached Stewart Menzies of MI6 with the proposal that OSS officers be stationed at St Albans alongside Cowgill of Section V. Donovan wanted to place his own men at the fountainhead of Britain's counter-espionage effort.

Nonsense ensued. When Donovan's representative, one George Bowden, presented himself to Menzies in London the following December, Menzies pretended to be reluctant to release German clandestine decrypts to the OSS. As Bowden reported:

The chief of British SIS [Secret Intelligence Service] stated that this material had never been furnished to an ally and that it was not even sent to the field offices of SIS. Its existence was unknown to the vast majority of officials and employees of SIS. Under no circumstances would the British turn this material over unprocessed to the United States.[26]

Menzies was lying. William Stephenson of British Security Coordination had supplied Donovan with Examination Unit decrypts at least until the end of February 1942, and thereafter Captain Maidment, the GC&CS/MI6 representative in New York, had been sending British decrypts of Western Hemisphere espionage traffic to the U.S. Army and the Coast Guard. Menzies must have known this. Copies of mid-1942 German secret service decrypts in the National Archives in Washington bear notations indicating that identical messages had been received from the "SIS."[27]

Menzies was anxious to tap the considerable financial and material resources of the OSS and, after some posturing, gave everything it asked for. The OSS would be permitted to build a temporary office for clerical staff on the grounds of the Section V estate at St Albans, while OSS officers were to have access to all decrypts and biographical files on German secret agents. They were to cable interesting material to "the MI6 office in New York" which would forward it to OSS headquarters and "other authorized agencies." The latter provision was rather sly. Maidment at BSC was already distributing German clandestine decrypts to the other American intelligence services, but the OSS was given the impression that it was starting the process. It is doubtful OSS selections were ever passed on. They did not need to be.[28]

––––––––––––

In mid-May 1942, Lieutenant Little's tour of Britain brought him to St Albans where Section V of MI6 was quartered. After being shown around the office, and possibly meeting the urbane Kim Philby (who was then passing MI6's secrets to the Soviets), Little sat down with Cowgill. He put the question: Why was Canada receiving so little South American espionage traffic? Why wasn't Canada receiving any decrypts? Because Canada doesn't need to see them, Cowgill smoothly replied. But Canada had an agreement, Little protested. Not that he knew about, Cowgill answered. The head of Section V then produced Menzies's Most Secret memo of the previous December, which out-lined his plan to ask Canada to leave intercepting and decrypting German secret service traffic in the Western Hemisphere to the United States and Britain. Cowgill pointed out that Menzies specifically said that this was "to ensure that all who *need* the material will get it, while no useless copies are distributed."[29] Cowgill had interpreted this to mean that Canada should not get them.

Little was dumbfounded. Many years later he was to remember the incident vividly:

> I wanted to get this back to Captain Brand to let him know that it looked as if they were trying to cut us out of the play. That was the thing that worried me. We were going to be doing a lot of work but weren't going to get any information or benefit from it. I thought he should know that this was going on so that he would be informed when they had the next meeting of the Y Committee.[30]

He dispatched a letter to Brand by the next diplomatic pouch, enclos-ing a copy of Menzies's memo. "I can't imagine your reaction to this disclosure," he wrote. "I had never seen [this document] nor had any of us, to my knowledge." He went on to remind his boss that the British High Commissioner had promised Canada would see the American and British decrypts but that so far none had materialized. Brand passed along Little's comments and a copy of Menzies's memo to Lester Pearson.[31]

When Little returned to Canada in early June, the issue was discussed at the Examination Unit committee in the presence of Colonel Stratton, the Radio Security Service representative in North America. Stratton deftly sidestepped Cowgill's truculence and assured the Canadians that plenty of new traffic was coming from South America and that if the Canadians continued to play their part, the messages they needed "to complete their files" would be supplied.[32] This was not true. All the major South American circuits were dead, and Stratton must have known it. The Canadians received no new South American decrypts from Britain, for the simple reason that there were none to be had.

Apparently there was some effort to soothe the Canadians. The British insisted that Drake's Army intercept stations continue their search for Japanese or German clandestine transmissions from Latin America. For the next five months, Canadian Army receivers found exactly the same as the American ones—next to nothing. At the beginning of August, however, the Examination Unit finally began receiving decrypts of European Abwehr traffic from the U.S. Navy/Coast Guard and from the British, although their content was boring and inconsequential. German spies in Europe were using their radios only for the housekeeping messages of espionage.[33]

Fortunately, however, not everyone in Britain was as obsessed with secrecy as Stephenson and Cowgill. Though Little was a rather young man to be trusted with so secret a mission, and only a lieutenant in the Volunteer Navy Reserve, he had been well received by the British Intelligence authorities. It probably did not hurt that he was an Upper Canada College graduate and Rhodes scholar who had studied at Oxford, as he was toured around the Admiralty, the offices of MI5 and MI6, Censorship Headquarters, and the Government Code and Cipher School.

What Little had failed to accomplish with Cowgill he more than regained when he met Commander Denniston. In February the powers-that-be in British Intelligence had decreed that the Government Code and Cipher School had grown too large to manage. Its functions were split, with the diplomatic and commercial (business, finance, and trade) division moving to new premises on Berkeley Street in London, while strictly military code- and cipher-breaking remained at rural Bletchley Park. Denniston, who had headed the GC&CS since 1919, went with the diplomatic and commercial portion, while his former second-in-command, Commander Edward Travis, stayed with what remained.

In effect, strategic code- and cipher-breaking had been separated from the strictly tactical. For the rest of the war, Travis presided over an organization at Bletchley that steadily grew in size and ability, eventually achieving almost total mastery over German military ciphers. The story of how British decrypts of German ENIGMA ciphers contributed to British and then American operations against the German

Army is now well known: they aided Montgomery against Rommel at El Alamein and then, with increasing tempo, played a role in the battles for Sicily and Italy, and ultimately in the invasion and fighting in France. But this was almost all tactics. It was not the larger picture of enemy political intentions and long-range plans.

With the move to Berkeley Street in London, behind the facade of a storefront called "Peggy Carter's Hat Shop," Denniston withdrew into the shadows. Almost nothing has been released or written about how his division—with a staff of 500 in mid-1942—operated for the rest of the war. Its primary responsibility was to break diplomatic messages for Britain's Joint Intelligence Committee and the Foreign Office. Almost equally important, it also processed plain-language and encoded commercial traffic for MOUSETRAP, Britain's Ministry of Economic Warfare. This information, from both enemy and neutral nations and combined with that from Censorship, was used to plot the economic progress of the war and to set strategic priorities. Judging by the direct contact he subsequently had with the Canadians, Denniston appears to have had considerable autonomy.[34]

Little and Denniston hit it off. The older man took a liking to the enthusiastic Canadian naval lieutenant and toured him around his London headquarters. "I was under the impression there was a lot of people working on a great mass of material all over," Little later recalled. Denniston invited him down to his home for a weekend, and later to a pub where the pair sipped gin and talked cryptography. The result was a special gift for Canada. Denniston told Little that Britain would give Canada the decrypts of high-grade Japanese diplomatic traffic. This included the precious machine-enciphered (PURPLE) messages from the Japanese ambassador in Berlin. The decrypts would go directly to Robertson, who would read and burn them.[35]

In return, Denniston, with Menzies's approval, asked that Canada continue to monitor Japanese traffic but concentrate particularly on the Japanese diplomatic and commercial messages being received by the Point Grey station near Vancouver. The British were certainly trying to hear Tokyo themselves. The wireless intercept station at Brora, Scotland was tuned to no less than ten stations sending from Japan to Germany, but reception was incomplete. Denniston arranged through the Admiralty for the most promising traffic heard in Canada to be cabled to Britain as soon as received, while less urgent raw material—the commercial traffic—was to be packaged and sent via Ferry Command, the service set up to fly bombers built in North America to England.[36]

By coincidence, the Americans at this time made an almost identical offer. Within a few days of Little's return to Canada, a representative from the War Department told the Examination Unit committee that arrangements had been made to supply the British with "messages of special secrecy" and it was proposed to do the same for the Canadians. It appears that the Americans had taken up the suggestion made at the Radio Intelligence Conference and were now monitoring the Tokyo–Berlin half of the traffic involving Japan's diplomatic staff in Germany. The offer was so important that Robertson and Pearson immediately accompanied the Prime Minister to Washington to clinch the deal.[37]

Canada, thanks partly to Little, had managed to get a foot in the door of big-time wireless intelligence after all.

———————

Merit had its reward. Shortly after returning from Britain, Little was promoted to Lieutenant Commander and appointed Director of Naval Intelligence. Colonel Murray was made Director of Military Intelligence. There is little doubt that these moves reflected recognition by the Canadian Chiefs of Staff of the value of signals intelligence and the contribution made by these two men.

The change was easy for Murray; not so for Little. The former had no competitors; the latter inherited an organization that someone else laid jealous claim to. Little's appointment was not welcomed by Jock de Marbois.

By early summer 1942, de Marbois had his new Operational Intelligence Centre up and running. Undoubtedly influenced by visits to Ottawa by Captains Sandwith and Winn, he modelled it after the Admiralty's naval intelligence divisions, complete with sections dealing with direction finding, traffic analysis, and intelligence from "Station Z"—the group analysing wireless transmission characteristics. There were also a U-boat tracking room and several technical sections, all reporting to him, while he, in turn, reported to the Director of Naval Intelligence and the Director of the Signals Division. Then Captain Brand stepped aside and Little became one of his bosses.[38]

De Marbois could not easily subordinate himself to a man who was his junior in rank and age and who had very strong ideas of his own. Had Captain Brand stayed on as Director of Naval Intelligence, de Marbois would have had a free hand, for Brand had made no secret of his lack of interest in wireless intelligence. Little was different. De Marbois complained bitterly to the Navy brass and obtained a judgment of Solomon decision. Naval operational intelligence would be responsible only to the Director of Signals, while Little would look after all other aspects of wireless intelligence. Thus Little sat without de Marbois on the Examination Unit Advisory Committee but with de Marbois on the Y Committee. It was an awkward situation with great potential for rivalry and conflict.[39]

Colonel Murray had no such problems. Military Intelligence now assumed the structure it was to retain throughout the war, organized as follows:

MI1

This section dealt with intelligence on military operations and monitored the war situation world-wide. It relied mainly on the reports of Canadian army intelligence officers in the field and those attached to Allied commands. It was divided into five sections: Japan, Western Europe, Eastern Europe and the Middle East, Asia and Australia, and a library and map department. Because Canadian battlefield commanders were always subordinate to the British or the Americans, its usefulness was confined mainly to providing background information to the Canadian Chiefs of Staff.

MI2

By this time, this section consisted of three Special Wireless Stations (Ottawa, Point Grey, and Victoria) and a headquarters section called the Discrimination Unit, all under Captain Drake. The Discrimination Unit, first housed at the Laurier Avenue house with the Examination Unit, and later on Bank Street, received the raw intercepts from the Army's three listening stations, attempted to identify the traffic, and then passed on the raw material to the appropriate Canadian, American, or British authorities. Total staff was about 100.

MI3

This was Army Security. Set up in 1940 under Lieutenant Eric Acland, its main concern was counter-espionage and security with respect to Army personnel and classified information. It maintained close liaison with U.S. Military Intelligence (G-2), British Security Coordination, and Britain's MI5. Its primary job was to keep aggressive watch on Canadian soldiers of suspected subversive backgrounds or intentions.

MI4

This section was responsible for prisoner-of-war camps and POW mail.

MIx

This group was set up in the last year of the war to "record information" on all people in Canada, whether Canadian, British, or American, who were engaged in counter-espionage. [40]

Acland of MI3, like Colonel Murray, had come from Telegraph Censorship in 1940. With the aid of one sergeant, two corporals, and two clerks, he had undertaken to keep the Army free of undesirables. He was immeasurably helped in this endeavour when he was sent "Secret Form 125: Internal Security for HM Forces." This was the set of instructions that Britain's Security Service (MI5) had compiled on how to keep soldiers under "special observation."

MI5's system was simplicity itself. Officers (never NCOs—they were not to be trusted) were to be on the alert for any soldiers espousing "Communist, Fascist, Nazi, or IRA views" or showing any other signs of "subversion." Officers reported incidents of suspicious behaviour to their commanding officers, who passed the names of the miscreants to MI5. The Security Service then entered the names in a card-index system and kept track of them until their "cases" were brought to some kind of conclusion. [41]

Acland instituted the same system, and by mid-1942 had 500 Canadian soldiers under observation. This was done by arranging with Postal Censorship to have their mail surreptitiously opened, the contents copied, and the letters resealed without a censorship stamp. Arrangements were also made to have the RCMP shadow suspected individuals when they were on leave, and to have their telephone conversations monitored. When the numbers involved became unmanageable, Acland acquired and used his own security officers, sometimes in plain clothes and sometimes posing as soldiers posted to the target person's unit. Informers or "stool pigeons" were also employed. Presumably all these tactics were learned from Britain's MI5.[42]

MI3 was also responsible for acting on soldiers' letters routinely intercepted by Postal Censorship, another excellent means of spotting suspicious behaviour. Naturally, these sometimes involved soldiers who were not all that thrilled to be fighting for King and Country:

Letter intercepted by CPC

March 9, 1943

Hello darling,

Here's a few lines to let you know I haven't forgotten you. I'm not to bad and hope your the same. I'm still on the loose. I'm in Scotland and headed for the coast tomorrow so darling I'll be in Canada for the warm weather.... I want to see you so bad. I can't stay here any longer. This is a hel of a country. The German dropped a few bombs a couple of days ago.... I can't think of anything else to say except I love you. I hope you still love me as much as ever. Darling, I have started and can't turn back. Because there is too much time waiting for me if I go back. And they'll never get me. I'll love you always no matter what happens between us.

Your loving husband to be

The letter was unsigned but the postal censor noted that it had "numerous phrases of endearment in the margins."[43]

Subversion was a greater concern to MI3 than the occasional

deserter. Before Germany attacked Russia, and while the United States was still neutral, Acland's main concern was that Communist agents would come up from the United States and join the Canadian Forces. Early liaison was established with both the FBI and British Security Coordination to have such suspect individuals checked out. Even after the Soviet Union became an ally, Communists continued to be the focus of attention. By mid-1943 MI3 had a card file of 15,000 names, of which 400 were marked "open," which presumably meant these people were being actively spied upon.[44]

Acland's group was also responsible for making the thousands of Canadian soldiers security conscious. This was done by a continuing poster campaign, featuring slogans that would make an advertising copywriter wince:

DON'T BE A BLABOTEUR
STOP ORAL SABOTAGE
A LOOSE TONGUE WAGGLES FOR HITLER
ARE YOU A STUTTGART STOOGE?

It is hard to imagine how such literary endeavours were received by the Canadian soldiers later fighting in Italy and elsewhere.

Both Naval Intelligence and Air Force Intelligence had similar security sections—NI4 for the Navy and AMP S/A for the Air Force—but they never attained the same size or level of sophistication as Acland's operation, chiefly because they did not have the Army's sheer numbers to worry about. NI4 focused on port security at Halifax and Vancouver, two areas that because of their sensitivity were blanketed by complete censorship—all outgoing mail and telegrams, even to addresses within Canada, were intercepted and read, while Department of Transport trucks with portable receivers prowled the streets listening for signs of clandestine radio transmissions. All long-distance telephone calls were also monitored.[45]

On Little's suggestion, the directors of intelligence for the three services began to meet regularly to discuss their mutual security concerns and advise the Chiefs of Staff accordingly. They styled themselves the Joint Intelligence Committee, but had a much more restricted role

than the counterpart committee in Britain. The British JIC was
responsible for assessing intelligence from all sources; the Canadian
JIC dealt mostly with relatively routine security matters. Nevertheless—as events were subsequently to prove—the three-man Canadian
JIC was a useful inside track to the Canadian Chiefs of Staff.[46]

CHAPTER SEVEN

SPREADING
THE NET

JUNE — DECEMBER 1942

H ERBERT NORMAN was a Communist. Of that there was no doubt. It was to cost him his life.

The son of a missionary, Norman was raised in Japan and in the mid-1930s studied at Cambridge University. There he was active in various Communist student organizations—the same ones that bred the notorious British traitors, Anthony Blunt, Guy Burgess, Donald Maclean, and Kim Philby. He may not have actually joined the party, but he certainly believed in the great Soviet experiment. In 1937, while doing postgraduate work at Harvard, he sent letters to his brother extolling "the overthrow of capitalism" and the virtues of "the transitional dictatorship of the proletariat." To him, at that time anyway, Communism was "the real standard bearer for humanity."[1]

Norman was not unusual. Communism had tremendous appeal to young people in the 1930s. They had seen with their own eyes the hunger and heartbreak of the Great Depression. They blamed capitalism run amok for the soup lines and grey faces shuffling through the decade. Young people like Herbert Norman believed there had to be a better way, and Communism seemed to promise it.

Such idealism got an awful jolt at the beginning of the war. In the summer of 1939, Germany and the Soviet Union signed a mutual aid pact that shocked and disillusioned left-leaning idealists around the world. When Germany invaded and conquered Poland, Hitler and Stalin callously divided the stricken country between them. The dictatorship of the proletariat was turning out to be just a dictatorship after all. Many Communists lost faith. Norman may have been one of these.

In the summer of 1942, Norman and his wife were returning from Japan as part of an exchange of prisoners and internees. As they stood at the railing of the Swedish ship *Gripsholm* watching the glittering waters of the Indian Ocean glide by, they had no suspicion of the tragedy that awaited them in the years ahead. Their future, indeed, appeared to hold much promise.

Norman spoke fluent Japanese. He was also scholarly, brilliant, and avidly interested in the social history of Japan. A third secretary at the Canadian legation in Tokyo, he was well known for a study he had published a few years earlier, *Japan's Emergence as a Modern State*, which was remarkable (in its day) for its Marxist interpretation of Japan's swift conversion from a feudal state in the mid-nineteenth century to a twentieth-century industrial power. It was written with such authority that it received international acclaim in academic circles. Even the Japanese were impressed by Norman's grasp of their history and social organization.

Such a person, the Communism aside, was bound to be in demand. Even before Norman reached Canada, William Stephenson of British Security Coordination put in a bid for him. He was turned down. "I am afraid that we could not give Stephenson any encouragement that Norman's services would be available," Tommy Stone wrote one of Stephenson's deputies. "This Department, and in fact our whole service, is probably shorter on essential staff than B.S.C., and I am afraid there would be some pretty strong objections to giving up one of our able young juniors at this time."[2]

Lester Pearson, through whom Stephenson had made his request, observed that if External Affairs was not prepared to release Norman to BSC, then it had better make darn sure that it used his talents effectively.[3] He need not have worried. A place had been found for Norman. His future—and his fate—had been decided.

While C. H. Little was in Britain in June, Commander Denniston asked one other thing of Canada in exchange for supplying decrypts of Japanese PURPLE traffic. "As arranged," he wrote Little, "I am sending you the programme of the work undertaken here in the hope that you may be able to fit the work of your stations in Canada into this programme and thereby avoid unnecessary duplication."[4]

Attached to Denniston's letter was a Government Code and Cipher School (Berkeley Street) list of countries and call signs being monitored for their diplomatic and commercial traffic as of June 3, 1942. Britain's enemies, Germany and Japan, were well covered, but so too were many neutral countries, and at least one ally:

Afghanistan	Japan
Argentina	Portugal
Brazil	Romania
Bulgaria	Spain
Chile	Sweden
Eire	Switzerland
France	Thailand
Germany	Turkey
Hungary	Russia
Iran	Vatican
Italy	

All the countries named had some diplomatic representation from the Axis powers, including Russia and Brazil, which had broken relations with Germany and Italy but not with Japan. As most of the Axis diplomats would normally use the wireless transmitting facilities of their host countries for some of their communications, it seems safe to conclude that the main target of Denniston's cryptanalysis effort was the diplomatic traffic of Britain's enemies.

Nevertheless, in order to pick up the occasional message sent to Tokyo by the Japanese ambassador in Santiago, for example, it would have been necessary to listen to all the traffic being broadcast by Station CEA2, one of the main Chilean transmitters. The diplomatic and commercial traffic of Chile had to be copied as well.

The extent to which Britain was then decrypting the non-military traffic of neutral rather than enemy countries is unknown. Denniston's team was probably working on the codes and ciphers of Portugal, Eire, Sweden, Switzerland, Russia, and the Vatican, because the list Denniston sent Little includes the call signs of stations in these countries that were only transmitting to non-belligerents. Spain, Turkey, and Argentina were also likely targets because of the strategic consequences should the first two enter the war, and because of the openly anti-British attitude of the latter over the long-simmering Falkland Islands dispute.[5]

Canadian readers of the list in 1942 would not have missed the fact that the British were intercepting the wireless transmissions of foreign countries in much the same way that British Imperial Censorship was intercepting letters and telegrams: if they were relevant to winning the war, the communications of any country were fair game. The plain language and encoded messages of foreign banks, government agencies, trade organizations, and private companies were an invaluable source of economic information which could be passed on to Britain's Ministry of Economic Warfare. Commercial intercepts were almost as important as diplomatic ones in forming a strategic picture of a conflict that had become worldwide.

Denniston wanted Canada's help, but the man to give it was no longer Pearson. In the summer of 1942, he was posted to the Canadian Embassy in Washington. Tommy Stone took his place as the External Affairs officer in charge of secret intelligence.

Stone was an enthusiast, garrulous and rich. He had married the daughter of a wealthy plantation owner in South Carolina and when she died, married her sister. He was living a life of magnolias and mint juleps when war broke out in 1939, but he immediately hurried back to his native Canada and External Affairs, his former employer. He liked to play the piano, he liked to drink, and he liked to throw parties that were more lavish than anything his guests could afford. His career with the department was to end abruptly after the war when a new Prime Minister, John Diefenbaker, encountered him drunk at a reception, and fired him on the spot.[6]

In 1942, however, Stone was well qualified for his new responsibilities. He had been involved with the Examination Unit from its inception. He had excellent contacts in British Security Coordination. He and an assistant, University of Toronto historian George Glazebrook, had looked after the administrative arrangements of setting up Camp X—"our country estate," as the school for spies and saboteurs came to be known in the department. Most valuable of all, Stone could look back at over two years on Canada's Censorship Coordination Committee. Stone was perfectly familiar with the business of intercepting letters, telegrams, and wireless transmissions for their commercial, diplomatic, and counter-espionage content.

As an intelligence-gathering arm of government, Canadian Censorship had come of age. It had received an enormous boost earlier in the year with the reorganization of Postal and Telegraph Censorship under the Department of National War Services. This came into effect in mid-May, when Colonel O. M. Biggar was named the over-all Director of Censorship.[7]

The advantages were immense. For the first time, a single authority—a single person, really—overlooked all censorship functions. Whereas previously the Chief Postal Censor had reported to the Postmaster General, and the Chief Telegraph Censor to the Army's Information Service, now both were part of a single operation which, theoretically at least, could look out for the counter-espionage and security concerns of the military, the RCMP, and Britain's Security Service (MI5), while procuring general intelligence for any interested British or Canadian government agency.

The incentive for this change appears to have come from the Allied Censorship conference held in Washington in January. Upon U.S. entry into the war, the British were prompt to ask the Americans to join their already worldwide mail- and telegram-monitoring program, sending over the Chief British Censor himself, Sir Edwin Herbert, to explain its operation. His message was simple. He told the Americans that the real aim of Censorship was the total control of world communications.[8] Indeed, with formal American telegraph censorship established at New York on the Horta 2 cable to Portugal, the Allies achieved just such total control. Outside German-occupied Europe and the Japanese-controlled areas of the Pacific, almost all intercontinental postal and telegraph routes now passed through Allied territory.

Although Herbert certainly mentioned the counter-espionage value of postal and telegraph interceptions, the spy-chasing role of Censorship had long ago declined in importance. Neither Italy nor Japan had set up significant pre-war espionage organizations in the Allied countries, and by early 1942 most of Germany's agents had been caught by MI5, the FBI, or through the diplomatic efforts of the State Department. Those few that remained in the Western Hemisphere after the collapse in March 1942 of the major South American spy rings had no choice but to send their secret correspondence to occupied Europe via Portugal and Spain, routes that were fully covered by British Censorship stations in Bermuda and Trinidad. Similarly, once the American Telegraph Censor started reading the Horta 2 line, all overseas telegrams were being monitored. In Britain itself, of course, little escaped scrutiny if it went to or from the British Isles.

Nevertheless, the January conference in Washington led to a massive expansion of Allied Censorship. The United States, Britain, and Canada agreed that there would be a free exchange of telegraph and postal intercepts, each country giving the others lists of what to watch for.[9] From then on it was a case of supply creating demand. There were fewer and fewer spies to be caught but more and more letters were opened. Ostensibly, only war-related information was sought, but the definition of what pertained to the war became so broad that the "requirements" of the using departments lengthened enormously, covering nearly every aspect of the economic, political, and social life of the three countries and all their neighbours. By mid-1942 reading private correspondence for economic and political information became far more important than looking for signs of enemy activity. Allied Censorship had become the most elaborate and systematic invasion of privacy in world history.[10]

Canadian Censorship reflected this change. Postal Censorship, for example, became totally integrated with mail sorting. Watch lists were distributed to postal stations around the country and covered innumerable subjects. The interception of purely domestic mail was extended from the East Coast to the West Coast to counter the perceived threat of spies among people of Japanese descent in British Columbia. Something called Security Censorship was created which imitated the activity of MI5, by "examining confidentially or otherwise mail to and from persons suspected of subversive activities, espionage, and contravention of war regulations." The secretly copied contents of such letters were passed to the RCMP or the Army's security service (MI3).[11]

By far the most important aspect of Canadian Censorship's reorganization was the establishment of a new division called the Information and Records Branch. This was a direct copy of the identically named organization within British Censorship. Its function was to receive mail and telegraph intercepts, sort them, and then send them where appropriate, with marginal comments from files if warranted. Whereas the Canadians had formerly intercepted mail and telegraph messages mainly to meet the requirements of British agencies, now they began to do it especially for Canadian government departments—not only External Affairs, but also the National Research Council, the British Columbia Security Commission, the Department of Finance, the Department of Labour, the Immigration Department, and so on.

In one week in July 1943, for instance, the Information and Records Branch reviewed 88,526 overseas telegrams plus another 1,200 or so forwarded by the U.S. Telegraph Censor in New York. In the course of six years of war, Canadian Postal Censorship read the contents of more than 46 million items of correspondence. It also received copies of messages of general Canadian interest intercepted by Postal Censorship in Britain, Bermuda, and the United States.[12]

The Information and Records Branch did more than just sort and distribute. It also kept records. Files were opened on specific groups, companies, and individuals. Various watch lists were compiled, including a black list of companies with suspected Axis sympathies, and a "secret watch list" of suspected subversives. The lists took the form of card indexes with code letters in one corner indicating what agency—Canadian, British, or American—was interested in a particular person, company, or topic. MI stood for British Security Coordination, BL for the Ministry of Economic Warfare, SO for miscellaneous private correspondence, RA for Canadian confidential, etc. The lists were then sent to postal and telegraph censorship stations around the country.[13]

The range of subjects covered by Canadian Censorship was immense. The censors combed private mail for economic news, the state of national morale, technical innovations, labour unrest, financial transactions, ethnic politics, overseas communications, and even the personal exchanges of families with sons serving with the Canadian forces overseas. The telegraph censors did the same with telegrams, while the Department of Transport did it in more limited fashion with telephone conversations. For the next three years of the war, there would be no such thing as a private communication entering or leaving Canada.

Intercepted Telegram
June 24, 1942

To: J.C. Lewis
Congress of Industrial Associations,
Washington

Government commission appointed to arbitrate Dumart dispute STOP Company continues lockout of active union members STOP Decision of arbitration will be delayed by company tactics STOP Urgently require financial assistance to ensure victory STOP Local sources of help exhausted STOP

Millard
Toronto

(Sent to External Affairs, Department of Labour, RCMP)[14]

Diplomatic messages still received primary attention. The telegrams to and from the legations and consuls of all countries represented in Canada were intercepted and copied before being passed on. If they were in code or cipher, and of French- or Spanish-speaking origin, they were sent to the Examination Unit. Consular mail was surreptitiously opened, examined, and resealed. All content of interest was copied and sent to Stone, who ruled on its value and passed it along as appropriate to Norman Robertson or elsewhere within External Affairs.[15]

Even so, Canadian Censorship paled in comparison to the massive effort mounted by the United States, and especially Britain. While few Allied Censorship records have been released in Britain, a great many are available in Canadian archives. They represent an invaluable documentary history of social and economic conditions in wartime Europe. Every conceivable topic was covered, with special reports from time to time on specific subjects: morale in Russia, U.S. public opinion, opposition to the Allies in North Africa, attitude of Catholics in Europe toward the persecution of the Jews. Excerpts from specific letters or telegrams are amply scattered throughout.[16]

The British did not hesitate to intercept and copy purely personal mail between Canada and Britain, nor to pass along items of gossip so obtained. John Stevenson, a journalist with *The Globe and Mail*, probably would have been surprised to learn that his description of the romantic problems of General Andrew McNaughton's personal physician at Canadian Military Headquarters in England was the subject of a lengthy summary sent to External Affairs by British Censorship. Quoting from Stevenson's letter, the British censor wrote:

The Jewish Doctor [Israel] Rabinowitz, in the medical Headquarters of Canadian Army in England, fell in love with Lady Moira Ponsonby—greatly to the disapproval of Lord Bessborough. His Lordship "went with the story to MacNaughton [sic] and got him to remonstrate with Rabinowitz [sic] about the impossibility of marrying a Ponsonby." Rabinowitz told MacNaughton to mind his own business. Bessborough continued to rage and after a few weeks MacNaughton again sent for Rabinowitz and told him he had been transferred back to Canada. One thing is certain—that

Rabinowitz is back in Canada. "If this story is true it reflects very little credit upon MacNaughton and if Rabinowitz chose to disclose it, it would ruin him."[17]

Stevenson's name apparently made it onto one of British Censorship's watch lists, for there is another report on his correspondence which notes "his deep dislike of the English upper classes and ruling oligarchy."

It is not known what people in External Affairs thought of such nuggets, but Norman Robertson and Tommy Stone were certainly quick to take advantage of the more substantial dividends obtained from the expansion of Allied Censorship. They had understood even in the Yardley period that when it came to diplomatic and commercial intelligence, postal and telegraph intercepts were complementary to wireless intercepts. Now they proposed a special subdivision of Censorship's Information and Records Branch to marry these two sources of information for the benefit of External Affairs.[18]

In the first six months of 1942, the Examination Unit committee realized that it had too few personnel to handle Japanese messages. There were already several officers in External Affairs who spoke French and when the decision was made to expand Vichy coverage to wireless traffic, a search of the universities quickly yielded a number of French specialists. Finding people who spoke Japanese, much less anyone who knew anything about Japanese culture, was a thornier problem.

The universities and armed forces were scoured. The Navy provided Lieutenant E. R. Hope from its Foreign Intelligence Service, an eccentric self-taught linguist who had a smattering of about six other languages, including Russian. Several other people were acquired on a trial basis. The pace of decrypted Japanese messages picked up. But there was still no one sufficiently familiar with Japan and its culture to interpret their content.

External Affairs itself provided the solution. Someone remembered that the Japanese language officer with the Canadian legation in Tokyo was returning to North America on the Swedish ship *Gripsholm,* along with several hundred Allied citizens who had been interned in Japan. He was very knowledgeable about the social and political history of Japan. It was Herbert Norman.

When Pearson wrote from Washington that External Affairs needed a very good reason for denying Norman's services to British Security Coordination, Stone's answer was to offer Norman the job of running the new special section of Censorship's Information and Records Branch that he and Robertson had proposed. Shortly after he arrived in Canada, Norman accepted.

Norman and perhaps one or two other External Affairs officers were to be given space on the third floor of the Examination Unit building on Laurier Avenue. There they would be "charged with the responsibility of distributing information derived from Examination Unit intercepts instead of copies of the intercepts themselves." To make their reports as accurate and as complete as possible, they would also be sent intercepts from Postal and Telegraph Censorship and relevant secret information received from all other sources. Intelligence summaries of Japanese and Vichy French activity would be the new section's primary product.[19]

Norman's first task was to review the secret intelligence files of the Army and Navy. He was also asked to sit on the Examination Unit committee. Thus a man of strong Communist sympathies was catapulted into the centre of Canada's Most Secret wartime endeavour and, with the growing liaison between the Examination Unit and the code- and cipher-breaking organizations in Britain and the United States, into the middle of the most closely guarded Allied secret. It was already acquiring its own special code-name. Intelligence derived from cryptanalysis was coming to be known as ULTRA.

The big problem involving ULTRA intelligence in the summer of 1942 was, as usual, with the Americans. Try as they might, neither the British nor the Canadians could fathom the cut-throat rivalries among their U.S. colleagues. Dealing with one U.S. agency meant risking offence to another. Allied code- and cipher-breaking cooperation had become a diplomatic egg-walk.

The U.S. Navy jealously guarded its turf from the Army and was contemptuous of the FBI. The FBI loathed Donovan's OSS and resented the Navy and Army. The Army did not like the FBI and had given up on cooperation with the Navy. The State Department did not have anything to do with the Navy, and had a low opinion of the FBI. The OSS was ignored by all the others and went its own way.

At the Radio Intelligence Conference in early April, the British had proposed that the Americans pool their wireless intelligence organizations on the British model, with an overall Y committee to handle intercept assignments and a single agency like the Government Code and Cipher School to handle all traffic analysis and code- and cipher-breaking. By mid-summer, what with "the domestic situation surrounding the FBI" and a feeble effort by the Americans to set up a Combined Communications Board (with wireless intelligence the responsibility of the 43rd subcommittee), it was apparent that the British proposal was never going to be acted upon.[20]

If the Canadians, or the British, wanted to make any headway on cooperation with the Americans, it had to be by one-on-one deals.

The situation certainly tested Pearson's skills. He was now the senior External Affairs staffer in Washington and on the front burner of U.S.–Canada intelligence liaison. When Stone sent Pearson some important Japanese and Vichy decrypts he felt the State Department should see, Pearson held onto them until he could determine whether they had been already received from the Army's Signal Intelligence Service. If not, Pearson feared the State Department would complain to the War Department "in such a way as to embarrass the Unit in Ottawa." He solved the problem by showing the decrypts to a State Department official after extracting a promise that their source would not be given away, should it turn out that the Army was dragging its heels.[21]

The situation with the FBI was even more delicate. As a consumer of special intelligence, Hoover's organization was not a happy fit with the military. In March the Navy had won control of the Coast Guard cryptanalysis unit on which the FBI relied. That might have been bearable, except that the Navy regarded clandestine radio activity as a sideshow of little consequence. Hoover's riposte was to form his own cryptanalysis unit, although for some time he still had to depend on the Navy for translations.[22] Feelings became so bitter that the Canadian Y Committee felt it had to warn the Department of Transport against any direct liaison with the Federal Communications Commission because the "FCC is working for the FBI which in turn does not cooperate with the American services." The committee feared that a visit to the United States by a Department of Transport wireless specialist "might provoke the ire of the Army and Navy authorities."[23]

Following a tour of the West Coast later that summer, Colonel Stratton of the Radio Security Service told the Y Committee an appalling story of Navy/Army friction in the United States. The Radio Intelligence Center set up by the Army in San Francisco was successfully tracking Japanese fleet movements in the Pacific, using a network of FCC receiving stations, but the Navy at Bainbridge (Seattle) was refusing to give the Army the call signs needed to identify the traffic. Even more destructive, the Navy was refusing to use the bearings on enemy units generated by the FCC stations even when their own were incomplete.

"The curious position arose," Stratton said, "of the Navy with incomplete bearings of which they had a fuller understanding, refusing to work closely with the Army and FCC who had evidence which would likely complete the picture."[24]

Considering the excellent and successful cooperation that had existed for three years between the Canadian Navy and the civilian radio specialists of the Department of Transport, Stratton's listeners would have been amazed if they had known the extent of the vicious smear campaign the U.S. Navy was then waging to get the FCC ordered off wireless intelligence. A geyser of memos was shooting up the Navy's chain of command, complaining of FCC "encroachment," "interference," and "useless" offers of help. The Navy wanted the FCC banned from all direction finding and the Army's West Coast wireless intelligence role reduced to clandestine traffic only. It occurred to no one in the Navy, it seems, that cooperation with the Army and FCC might help win the war and even save lives.[25]

As for Canadian Navy relations with U.S. Naval Intelligence, de Marbois at Naval Service Headquarters in Ottawa got along well at first. Then he, too, felt the sting. The Radio Intelligence Conference had agreed that the Canadian Navy should continue to do direction finding on enemy submarines in the Atlantic, with responsibilty for reporting bearings west of 40 W and north of 40 N. The Admiralty was to look after everything to the east while the Americans agreed to report bearings in the "United States strategic zone," which overlapped the area covered by the Canadians. Duplication with Canadian bearings was foreseen, but it was not expected to be a problem. Then in October, when the U.S. Navy had put the finishing touches to its own plotting room in Washington and had established a direct cable link with the Admiralty, it proposed to take over sole responsibility for enemy bearings west of 40 W. The British were asked to tell the Canadians to report bearings only in their own coastal waters.

This did not make de Marbois a happy man. It would have rendered the entire Canadian naval direction-finding organization and his new Operational Intelligence Centre useless. A stiff fight ensued that continued for months.[26]

Canadian wireless intelligence cooperation with the U.S. Navy was a lost cause. From Admiral Ernest J. King at the top downward, the U.S. Navy had shown—and would continue to show—that it intended to fight its war against the Japanese and the Germans with the minimum amount of help or advice from its Allies and, preferably, none at all from other Americans. Like General U.S. Grant during the American Civil War, the Navy was content to overwhelm its enemies with men, guns, and blood, regardless of cost.

The attitude of U.S. Military Intelligence was entirely different. This may have been because, in the first six months after Pearl Harbor, the Army had no battles to fight and no operational intelligence that was urgently needed. British Intelligence, by virtue of its experience and proximity to Europe, claimed a monopoly on German Army and Air Force wireless intelligence.[27] War with Japan was still exclusively in a naval phase, so there was no room there. That left diplomatic traffic and planning for the future.

The U.S. Army's wireless intelligence service was very creative.

Apart from the ill-starred Radio Intelligence Center on the West Coast, by the summer of 1942 the Army had already attached wireless specialists to General Douglas MacArthur's headquarters in Australia capable of handling low-grade Japanese battlefield ciphers. The Army had also set up semi-mobile direction-finding units at Fort Lewis, near Tacoma, Washington, and in Alaska, in an attempt to pin-point the primary Japanese Army wireless stations. When Colonel Stratton toured Fort Lewis in August, he suggested to the commanding officer that he exchange bearings and assignments with the Canadian Army Special Wireless Station at Victoria, and the offer was readily accepted.

The Canadian Y Committee and the Examination Unit were encountering the same willingness. The spirit that had moved the U.S. Military Intelligence Service to provide Canada with the decrypts of the Tokyo–Berlin traffic was moving it still. Requests for copies of raw Vichy traffic and code information were received sympathetically and, despite the occasional hitch, acted upon promptly. The Canadians became embarrassed that they could offer so little in return. It was becoming a David and Goliath relationship, except that the giant was entirely friendly.

Part of this warmth, ironically, was fueled by the problems besetting British Security Coordination. No matter what William Stephenson told his bosses when he went over to London in June 1942, by mid-summer it must have been apparent to everyone in British Intelligence that the value of his organization in New York had vastly diminished. It was no longer an intermediary between British Censorship and the American authorities. The Security Executive had taken over direct control of BSC's dockside security functions in the United States. The intelligence services of the U.S. Army and Navy were liaising directly with their British counterparts through the British Joint Staff Mission or through the GC&CS/MI6 office run by Captain Maidment in New York. The State Department was opposed to BSC counter-espionage activities in the United States. That left Latin America. Yet there had been no significant South American clandestine transmissions in months.

If anything, British Security Coordination had become an embarrassment. In September the U.S. Joint Chiefs of Staff flatly told the

British that they had the Latin American situation entirely under control through their own organization—American Intelligence Command—and bilateral agreements with the individual countries. While they were willing to see limited liaison with Britain's Special Operations Executive on questions of potential sabotage, they did not want any "third party" intervention by British Intelligence. As the British embassy in Washington reported: "The U.S. attitude showed clearly that they consider security matters in Latin America to be a matter concerning the U.S. alone in which we should not interfere."[28]

Considering the resentment already engendered in the State Department, the British had no choice but to back off. Even worse, however, was the attitude to British Security Coordination now displayed by the FBI.

The difficulties with the FBI are best illustrated by the Bureau's experience with a British double agent named Dusko Popov. A young Yugoslav, Popov had approached the British Security Service (MI5) in early 1941, claiming to be a spy for the Abwehr who wished to work for the British as a double agent. Shortly after the FBI broke up the Sebold spy ring in June 1941, Popov claimed that his Abwehr controllers wanted him to transfer from England to the United States, where he would set up a new spy ring. The British alerted Hoover and recommended that the FBI run him as a controlled agent.

Much has been written about Popov since the Second World War, all of it from a British perspective, and all of it laudatory. The British Twenty Committee, responsible for supplying information to controlled agents, claimed at the end of the war that he was one of Britain's best double agents. Postwar British accounts of British Security Coordination have echoed this judgment and have attributed the failure of his mission to Hoover's mindless intransigence. Documents on Popov in FBI archives, however, tell an entirely different story.

In fact, following Popov's arrival in the United States in the summer of 1941, the FBI made every attempt to run him as a double agent. Because the British placed such trust in him, they gave him the freedom to roam the United States unsupervised, and even allowed him to travel to Brazil to meet Abwehr agents there. When he returned in December with a story of how he had met a spy code-named ALFREDO, the FBI showed him a photograph of Albrecht Engels. Popov said it wasn't the same man.[29]

What Popov did not know was that, thanks to Coast Guard decrypts of ALFREDO's messages, the Americans were certain that ALFREDO and Engels were the same person. That's why they had obtained his picture.[30] Popov had made a major slip.

Nevertheless, at the insistence of MI6's Section V and British Security Coordination (Stephenson personally), the FBI provided Popov with a transmitter and he began to send controlled messages back to Germany in February 1942. Despite Popov's continued promises that he would be contacted by other Abwehr agents in North America, none ever materialized. After nearly a year in the United States—during which he frequently slipped FBI traces and disappeared for weeks—Popov failed to produce any intelligence of consequence other than a few questionnaires that listed the Abwehr's alleged espionage interests. In the summer of 1942, the FBI finally got fed up and asked the British to take him back.[31]

What the FBI actually concluded from its Popov experience is not in the available records. However, the State Department's opinion is known. The dossier on Popov in State Department archives is in its file on German enemy agents.[32]

Stephenson's credit with the American authorities was approaching zero. The only friend he still had in Washington was Donovan, but the Office of Strategic Services was not allowed to operate in the Western Hemisphere and was as much on the outs with the Army, the Navy, and the State Department as BSC. In contriving to create an American secret service led by a man sympathetic to British interests, the British had hoped to get a powerful ally in Washington; instead they had created a nuisance on the one hand and an albatross—the director of British Security Coordination—on the other.

When Stephenson went to London in June 1942, he had managed to persuade the Joint Intelligence Committee and the Chiefs of Staff that there was much counter-espionage still to be done in Latin America. As the months passed, it became increasingly apparent that this was not so. By the end of the year, such intercepted messages as were being produced by the Examination Unit were of so little value that an internal report noted that even "B.S.C. have definitely admitted that they are no longer interested in what we send them."[33]

Stephenson did manage to field some Camp X agents. These were mainly amateur radio operators recruited in Canada. They were slipped into various South American countries to listen for clandestine transmitters. The Americans, on a far larger and more systematic scale, did likewise. There is no evidence that they picked up much—a little activity in Chile, a bit in Argentina. Otherwise, the South American spy rings smashed by the State Department stayed smashed, at least for the time being. As for Japanese spies, nothing.[34]

Allied Censorship also appears to have drawn a blank. The tripartite agreement of January 1942 required the British and Canadians to alert their American colleagues to any intercepts that hinted of a security threat in the Western Hemisphere. The FBI and State Department would then be notified. However, there is nothing in available records to suggest that either of these agencies had a significant counter-espionage problem in South America after 1942. And no wonder. The British Censorship reports from 1942 to 1945 are available in Canadian archives. A little bit of subversion here, some sympathy for the Axis there, but no espionage of any significance. How could there be? Short of a German U-boat touching shore, South America was completely isolated.

In his "BSC History" after the war, Stephenson made a number of extravagant claims about BSC counter-espionage accomplishments in South America. None of these after January 1942 can be separately verified, and many of those for 1941 are exaggerated or impossible.

There was no sabotage, either—not by Axis nor Allies. By November 1942, Special Operations Executive in Britain had concluded that "at this stage in the war, the usefulness of SO in Latin America is virtually at an end."[35] The continued operation of Camp X, and even British Security Coordination itself, was now in real jeopardy.

The trouble was, British Intelligence—whether MI6 or the Security Executive—could ill afford to have BSC closed down. It had become a large and important intelligence-gathering agency in the United States. It had become precisely what the State Department had feared it would be, a foreign secret service operating on American territory. Staffed mainly by Canadians with close links to the RCMP, it had

its tentacles spread widely over the continent and possessed the expertise of three years of war.[36] However, it also had powerful opponents in
the American government who dearly wanted it reduced in size or
eliminated altogether. To survive, BSC needed a role that was both
important to the war effort and acceptable to the Americans.

Somebody in British Intelligence contrived a solution. In September the Canadian Y Committee learned that a deal had been struck
with the British Y Committee. The BSC offices in New York were now
to become the major channel through which non-military wireless
intelligence would be exchanged between Britain and North America,
via a private transatlantic cable directly linking BSC in New York and
Denniston's division of the Government Code and Cipher School on
Berkeley Street in London.[37]

This made a lot of sense. Captain Maidment and his small group of
Government Code and Cipher School personnel were already established at BSC, installed at the beginning of 1942 to sort and distribute
incoming German espionage traffic. It was a logical and comparatively
simple matter to expand their activities to embrace diplomatic and
commercial traffic.

The man who was to direct the technical side of the arrangement
was Benjamin deForest Bayly, a professor of engineering from the University of Toronto. An electronics expert, it was he who had procured
the first Camp X transmitter, and he had also developed an on-line
cipher machine called the "telekrypton" that automatically scrambled
teletype messages. Now he had a new assignment. He had been
appointed the Government Code and Cipher School's technical
adviser on secret communications between Britain, Canada, and the
United States.[38]

Tommy Stone, Colonel Murray, and the new man sent out from
Britain to replace Strachey as head of the Examination Unit—F. A.
"Tony" Kendrick—went down to BSC in New York to get details of
the new plan from Commander Travis, who had arrived from Bletchley Park to sell it to the Americans. The idea, Travis explained, was to
save unnecessary transatlantic cable charges by having the raw diplomatic and commercial intercepts—those in plain language and those
still in cipher—collected from the Americans and Canadians and

screened at BSC in New York before being sent by cable to Britain using Bayly's telekrypton machine. Canadian Navy listening stations, for example, were sending their diplomatic and commercial intercepts directly to the Admiralty, whereas the Army was sending theirs to the Ministry of Economic Warfare. Everything wound up at Berkeley Street and Denniston's staff was finding many duplications. These could be avoided if the initial sorting, or "discrimination," was done in North America.

Travis stressed that the new handling procedure (which would not involve Stephenson at all) would only apply to diplomatic and commercial raw material, not decrypts. Moreover, military traffic would continue to be forwarded as quickly as possible directly to Bletchley Park. This meant that the U.S. Navy was excluded from the arrangement, because it dealt only in naval traffic and was about to establish its own direct cable link with Britain.[39]

Later Bayly appeared before the Y Committee to provide more details. While the private transatlantic cable would be the primary communications link, it had been decided it should be supplemented by the HYDRA transmitter at Camp X. This would also be used to send raw intercepts, both American and Canadian, and would also be linked to BSC by telekrypton. The enciphering machine was necessary, he explained, because the FBI had the right to tap lines. Otherwise the risk of unauthorized eavesdropping was "very small."[40]

The British proposal had considerable appeal to the U.S. Army. The Special Branch of the Military Intelligence Service (G-2) was already issuing a steady stream of summaries derived from diplomatic decrypts to the Joint Chiefs of Staff and to the State Department. Known as MAGIC summaries—dealing with the affairs of both enemy and neutral countries—these were proving to be of immense value in painting a broad picture of the political and economic aspects of the war. The Army's Special Branch was providing exactly the same type of service as envisaged by External Affairs for Herbert Norman's little unit, except on a much grander, worldwide scale. Any additional raw traffic from Britain and Canada would be appreciated.

The idea also suited the Canadians. Robertson and Stone had both been pressing hard for an expansion of work on diplomatic traffic. In fact, on the day that it heard of the British plan, the Y Committee ordered that priority be given to commercial and diplomatic traffic at all its intercept stations, second only to enemy naval traffic. Moreover, the Canadian Navy was about to open its own intercept station at Coverdale, Ontario, which would release the Department of Transport station at Point Grey. Special high-speed recorders were therefore ordered so that the Point Grey station could be dedicated to commercial and diplomatic intercepts. Herbert Norman's special intelligence section was also expanded with the addition of another young External Affairs officer, Arthur Menzies, who had been raised in China and spoke fluent Chinese as well as French. A new Spanish speaker, J. H. Parker, was hired for the Examination Unit.

When Commander Denniston made repeated requests that the Canadians concentrate mainly on Japanese commercial traffic, Stone was blunt: the monitoring of diplomatic and commercial messages was to be done "not as a service for the United Kingdom and other Governments, but for Canada." Moreover, Stone told the Y Committee, the Americans had sometimes been slow to answer requests for diplomatic raw material. It was therefore his opinion that "Canada would have to rely for the most part on her own interception of this traffic."[41]

Stone had set a course for Canada from which there would be no turning back.

The wireless intelligence territory that External Affairs hoped to carve out for itself basically consisted of any diplomatic traffic it could obtain from Japan or Vichy, with particular emphasis on the colonies and conquered territories of the Far East. This was a direct reflection of available expertise. Since it had both Herbert Norman and Arthur Menzies, his Chinese- and French-speaking assistant, Far Eastern intelligence was a logical choice. However, the Canadian wireless intercept stations were generally hearing only out-going traffic from Tokyo and Vichy. Very little was being picked up coming the other way.[42]

At the beginning of November, Norman was dispatched to New York and Washington to set up liaison with the intelligence divisions of BSC and the OSS. It was on this trip that an incident occurred which would haunt him in later years. He took a day to go over to Harvard University to obtain the papers of a Japanese citizen he had known during his Harvard postgraduate days, who had been sent back to Japan. As this man was an economist, Norman could reasonably expect to find material that would assist him in his new job. Since the man was an enemy alien, Norman had to contact the local FBI office and, after a little persuasion, he obtained the necessary permission without incident.

Unfortunately for Norman, his economist friend was a Communist, and FBI agents had already looked through the papers. Along with academic material, they contained Communist propaganda and correspondence. Although the FBI agents made no particular note of Norman's visit at the time, it would be remembered.[43]

During the autumn months of 1942, the promise of three-way cooperation on wireless intelligence drove the Canadian program forward. Norman's unit, installed on the third floor of the Laurier Avenue house, began producing its first intelligence reports. Every spare Army, Navy, or Department of Transport receiver was tuned to diplomatic or commercial traffic. Spain, Portugal, Chile, and Argentina were added to the list of Vichy and Japanese stations listened to. Decrypts flowed out of the Examination Unit at a brisk tempo.

Tony Kendrick, the new head of the Examination Unit supplied by the British, was turning out to be a great success. A shy person in his mid-thirties and partially disabled, probably by polio, he was interested in cryptanalysis for its own sake and actively encouraged his staff. The Canadians thrived under his gentle prodding as he introduced them to new systems, made suggestions, and then left them to get on with it. Morale soared as the Examination Unit began to develop genuine expertise.

The happy state of the Examination Unit, however, was not entirely due to the new man. The preceding April, while Strachey was making noises about returning to Britain, the Examination Unit's French section had made a major break-through: it had solved the Vichy French fleet cipher. For years this cipher, involving transpositions of a numerical code, had defied the Government Code and Cipher School. The Canadians immediately dispatched the solution to the U.S. Navy and to the Admiralty. Vichy French naval messages then became an open book.[44]

The accomplishment of the Canadian cryptanalysts could not have come at a better time. That summer and fall, the Americans and British were deeply engaged in planning a surprise invasion of Vichy-held North Africa. Knowing the state of readiness, location, and intentions of French fleet units could not have been more crucial. The very fact that the messages exchanged between the French admirals and the authorities in Occupied France were only routine, must have been music to the ears of those in the U.S. Navy charged with getting the invasion convoys safely across the Atlantic.

For the Examination Unit staff, the French naval messages were undoubtedly dull reading. Japanese decrypts were more interesting. Messages going from the Foreign Ministry in Tokyo to its embassies and consuls in Hanoi, Saigon, Thailand, China, Chile, Brazil, and Argentina produced the best results. Norman, Stone, Robertson, and even Mackenzie King read with their own eyes messages from Tokyo that instructed the ambassadors to get tough with the Vichy authorities in Indochina. Others spoke of Allied shipping losses in the Atlantic and disparaged American reports of successes against the Japanese Navy and in the fighting on Guadalcanal.

One message stands out as being particularly chilling:

From: Tokyo
To: Berlin, also Buenos Aires

Dated: October 19, 1942
Rec'd: October 23, 1942

(Explanatory message: Policy) After investigation of the air crews who took part in the air attack on Imperial territory on the 18th of April, and who fell into our hands, severe punishment has been meted out, in accordance with military law, for their inhumane conduct. All such cases of violent and inhumane conduct (for example, the machine-gunning of school-children and the bombing of hospitals, schools and the dwellings of the people) will be brought to trial, with the object of reducing as far as possible the ravages of war. All those who engage in this kind of criminal warfare, as common criminals, may expect to receive the same decisive treatment.[45]

The air crews referred to were the American flyers captured after the famous Doolittle Raid, named for the commander who conceived a surprise strike against Tokyo with conventional Army bombers launched from an aircraft carrier. Though it caused little damage, the raid made a mockery of the Japanese boast that Tokyo would be safe from attack. It fired the imagination of the American public at a time when the Japanese were enjoying unbroken success. But it was a one-way mission. The bombers were not designed to land on aircraft carriers. The plan had been for the crews to fly them onward to Nationalist territory in China. Some did not make it.

In American eyes the Doolittle flyers were heroes. They had volunteered for the ultimate in dangerous missions. Germany and Britain had been bombing each other's cities for over two years. The captured Doolittle flyers did not deserve to be executed as this decrypt indicated some had been. One can imagine a hardening of hearts in the American high command when this message was read.

An important theme in many of the decrypts was Japanese diplomatic attempts to encourage Chile and Argentina to remain neutral, despite strong pressure from the United States to break with the Axis powers. Argentina was decidedly anti-British but Chile was wavering. Arguments for continued neutrality presented by the Japanese ambassador in Santiago were read by Robertson and dutifully passed to Mackenzie King. The Prime Minister even reported the contents of one of these decrypts to Roosevelt during a White House meeting with the President:

> … I then showed the President the message our people had intercepted and deciphered from the Japanese minister in Chile to Japan, outlining the kind of attack on the Panama Canal, etc., when the time came…

The decrypt was not really military intelligence—just a Japanese diplomat engaged in wishful thinking. Nevertheless, it was one way for

Mackenzie King to show Roosevelt that Canada was indeed a member of the ULTRA club.[46]

The most important of the Japanese messages, however, were among the most mundane. The Japanese consuls in "The Greater East Asia Co-prosperity Sphere," as Japan dubbed its occupied territories, regularly received economic news and commercial reports from Tokyo in the simplest of codes. Frequently included were mentions of merchant shipping movements.

From: Tokyo   Dated: November 21, 1942
To: Hanoi   Rec'd: November 26, 1942

> TIKO MARU—Outward voyage—About four thousand tons general cargo for Haiphong. Return voyage—417 tons phosphate ore, 150 tons tin, 461 tons lead, 50 tons antimony, 300 tons zinc, 300 tons metal for industrial use, 500 tons hemp, 631 tons *kapok*? (All to unload Osaka and Kobe.) Ship is to leave Osaka about the 30th of November and arrive Haiphong on the 16th of December.

Such innocuous messages were actually missives of death for the ships and their crews. The Examination Unit passed them to the U.S. Army which, along with similar decodes from the Signal Intelligence Service at Arlington Hall, turned them over to the Navy. The Navy gave the information to its submarines.[47] Over the next two years, a slaughter of Japanese merchant shipping ensued on a scale only dreamed about by German U-boat commanders in the Atlantic.

Aside from the fleet cipher, Vichy traffic was of less value. By the early fall, the Examination Unit was reading a substantial number of low-grade Vichy messages involving Ottawa, Washington, and Vichy colonies in Africa and the Caribbean. Few were important. Nevertheless, External Affairs remained committed to Vichy coverage and the Examination Unit's French section grew to handle the work.[48]

Suddenly everything changed. On November 8, 1942, the Americans invaded North Africa. They landed in Vichy-controlled Algeria behind the Germans fighting in Libya. The effect on Canada's wireless intelligence program was immediate and profound.

Diplomatic relations between the Vichy government and the United States and Canada were severed. Vichy cable traffic out of Washington and Ottawa stopped. The admirals of the French fleets at Toulon and Martinique ordered their ships scuttled, so Vichy naval traffic ceased to matter. Algeria collapsed and Tunisia not long after, so Vichy messages from Africa ceased. Soon all that remained was the defunct government of Pétain in Occupied France, and the Vichy colonies of the Far East. These were of little strategic significance. Almost overnight, the interception and decrypting of Vichy messages had become of marginal importance.

Unfortunately, most of the expansion of the Examination Unit over the previous six months had been in the French section. Now there was little work to keep these people busy. Robertson had to issue an order forbidding the transfer of French-speaking staff out of the unit. He did not want to see what had been so painstakingly built up dismantled without second thought.

The British–Canadian–U.S. conference to formalize the sharing of diplomatic and commercial traffic was held at Arlington Hall in Washington on January 15, 1943. MI6 and the Government Code and Cipher School were represented by Captain Maidment and Japanese specialist Colonel J. H. Tiltman. Professor Bayly was present. Stone, Drake, Kendrick, and Colonel Murray led the Canadian delegation. The importance that the U.S. Army attached to the meeting is reflected in the fact that some of its most senior special intelligence people were there. These included Colonel Frank W. Bullock, head of the Signal Security Service (renamed from Signal Intelligence Service), Major Telford Taylor from the Military Intelligence Service (G-2), Colonel Alfred McCormack, deputy-chief of the Special Branch, and William Friedman, the U.S. Army's chief cryptanalyst. The U.S. Navy was represented by a lowly ensign.

The meeting took exactly one hour and thirty-five minutes. Eight Americans faced eight Canadians and British across a long table with Colonel Bullock at the head. Bullock came straight to the point. The meeting had been called, he said, strictly to discuss diplomatic and commercial traffic, not military. There was a brief semantic wrangle over what was meant by "commercial" and what by "diplomatic." Then

Bullock distributed some mimeographed sheets of paper. This, he explained, was a schedule of overseas stations the U.S. Army was monitoring. His Canadian and British visitors were impressed to see that it ran to many pages, covering the call signs of neutral and enemy countries alike.[49] The U.S. Army had come a long way in a year of war. Even before the conference convened, McCormack's Special Branch had been supplying MAGIC Summaries to the State Department containing the decrypted messages of the governments of Chile and Argentina, then under pressure from the Americans to break with the Axis. Spain's diplomatic codes also had been penetrated, enabling the Americans to follow with lively interest the Spanish government's attitude to the invasion of North Africa. Portugal and Brazil were being covered, too.[50]

In the absence of an immediate need to master Japanese Army and Air Force ciphers, the Military Intelligence Service (G-2) was concentrating on supplying the State Department with everything it needed in the way of decrypts. It already had under construction two enormous wireless intercept facilities dedicated to diplomatic and commercial traffic at Vint Hill, Virginia and Twin Rocks, California. The Arlington Hall cryptanalysis centre was expanding rapidly. The U.S. Army was going to make sure that Roosevelt and his policy-makers were well served.

The U.S. Army's aim, Bullock explained to his visitors, was total American "self-sufficiency" in the monitoring of diplomatic traffic worldwide. However, for one reason or another, not all stations could be heard all the time. Sometimes it was a matter of atmospheric conditions; sometimes it was a problem of geography. The Americans therefore proposed that the three Allies cooperate on their coverage. The Americans wanted to be able to ask the Canadians and the British to fill in the blanks when U.S. Army receivers were having difficulty picking up the wireless transmissions of any particular country.

After some brisk debate, it was decided that once a month the three Allies would exchange lists of what they were monitoring. If one had coverage that interested another, it could be applied for through Captain Maidment's office at British Security Coordination. A Canada–U.S. "working subcommittee" was also set up to review current wireless reception problems in North America.[51] Indeed, the Americans had already asked for Canadian help monitoring the Russian station, RUX, and later that spring the committee asked for similar assistance with another Russian station, RTZ. Canada's enormous size and northern geography was already being recognized as ideally suited for eavesdropping on Asia.

Both Canadians and British at the meeting were awed by the sheer scope of American plans. The ten-page Government Code and Cipher School list of national call-signs Denniston had given Lieutenant Little six months earlier was nothing in comparison to the blanket coverage the U.S. Army contemplated. After the meeting Maidment observed that once the Americans achieved their aim, both Britain and Canada could save themselves the trouble of intercepting their own diplomatic traffic. They could just order whatever they wanted from the United States.

The meeting was heady stuff for the Canadians. Although the discussions were confined to the sharing of diplomatic and commercial "raw material," not actual decrypts, the Canadians were at last in real partnership with their more powerful allies on wireless intelligence. The trouble was, if they wanted to read any traffic, they still had to break it themselves.[52] Yet the Examination Unit was a small operation. How could it be used to best effect? What should it concentrate on?

The Americans and the British had previously decided not to share with Canada the secrets of how to break the enemy machine ciphers: ENIGMA and PURPLE. That shut the Canadians out of German diplomatic traffic entirely and confined them to lower-grade Japanese material. With the Allied occupation of North Africa, Vichy French traffic had plummeted in both value and availability. Stone had proposed asking the Americans and British for Spanish traffic, which Canada already was gathering in some quantity,[53] but there was only one Spanish linguist in the Examination Unit. The majority of the staff spoke French. What to do? It is not known who solved the problem of how to keep the twenty or so French linguists in the Examination Unit gainfully employed. The answer was simple. Some of them were switched "to a similar French service."[54]

The Examination Unit now concentrated on attacking the codes and ciphers of the Free French.

CHAPTER EIGHT

JUNIOR PARTNER

JANUARY — DECEMBER 1943

MACKENZIE KING sat alone at his desk in the library at Laurier House. It was early January 1943. Before him was the large red leather box that travelled with him everywhere. He took a key from his watch fob chain and unlocked it. He extracted a paper and began to read. Later he dictated the contents of the document to his diary:

Conversation Ribbentrop had with Japanese Ambassador

December 12, 1942

Ribbentrop admits break through Stalingrad was a tactical victory for the Russian forces.

Thought surrounded Germans in no danger.

Thought they would smash the Soviet troops and return to position....

Rommel retreat: Bad news for us Germans.

Cause: lack of tanks and oil.

Great danger not having control of Mediterranean.

Much worried over North Africa situation....

Italy in a more precarious position than ever due to landings in North Africa....

Germany has 50 divisions watching and waiting in line from Northern Norway to Franco-Spanish border.

Thinks Germany ready for any attack by Britain and America on that line....

Soviet Union not as weak as it had been thought.

Admits Germany cannot hope to destroy Communist regime.

Germany had not changed plans to penetrate into the Caucasus.[1]

Hitler had just suffered his first major defeats. In October 1942, the British had decisively beaten the wily German general, Erwin Rommel, on the Egyptian frontier at El Alamein. A few weeks later, the Americans had invaded Vichy-held Algeria at his rear. Then the Russians had surrounded the 250,000-strong German army at Stalingrad and German attempts to relieve the beleaguered garrison had failed. The German forces at Stalingrad were doomed.

Beyond the window of Mackenzie King's study, the snow lay in white heaps along the street. Frost gnawed at the edge of the glass. And here he was, in his own inner sanctum, reading Germany's own view of its disasters.

The piece of paper that permitted him to do this was an American-supplied Berlin–Tokyo intercept, broken from the Japanese PURPLE cipher. Since mid-1942 Robertson had been receiving such messages by safe hand from Washington or London. They were to be read by the Prime Minister and burned. Mackenzie King was so impressed by the message this day, and had such a keen sense of posterity, that he dictated the decrypt into his diary.

He had good reason to be impressed. Decrypts like this one, which arrived only occasionally, were his only independent means of knowing what was really going on in the war.

It was his own fault. Canadian ships and Canadian soldiers had provided vital support to Britain in the dark days of 1940–41 when the U-boats ruled the Atlantic and German armies gathered opposite the

Strait of Dover. Nevertheless, the moment the Americans entered the war, the Prime Minister had voluntarily relinquished a place for Canada on the Combined (American and British) Chiefs of Staff, thereby yielding sole direction of the war to the United States and Britain. Canada had no voice in long-range military planning, nor any real say in how its own troops would be used.

Mackenzie King would have been an excellent subject for psychoanalysis. His wartime diary is thousands of pages long, more than half of it devoted to recording his overnight dreams and other minutiae of a lonely bachelor's life. He loved his dogs with motherly passion; he was at ease only with women; and he hungered constantly for recognition. Most of all, he indulged in lengthy self-analysis every time he was required to make a major decision. It is quite likely that he chose to deny Canada an active role in the strategic conduct of the war because he did not want to be constantly making up his mind.

The result was that Canadian military authorities were not invited to sit on even the minor committees of the Combined Chiefs of Staff. Churchill routinely ignored his Canadian ally, not bothering to inform Mackenzie King when he and Roosevelt decided on the invasion of North Africa. When Roosevelt and Churchill met at Casablanca in early 1943, the Canadian Prime Minister learned about it only after the fact. Their decision to invade Sicily filtered down to him when it was picked up a month later by Canadian military staff in London. Then, when Canadian troops were chosen for the attack, Churchill insisted they be identified as British. After much complaint and soul-searching to his diary, at the last moment Mackenzie King told reporters Canadians were involved. It was one of the few times he defied the British Prime Minister.[2]

So it was throughout the war. Even when Churchill and Roosevelt met at Quebec in 1943 and again in 1944, Mackenzie King hovered in the background like a parlour maid, fussing over issues of protocol while the other two discussed grand strategy. Churchill's personal physician, Lord Moran, was puzzled by this self-effacement:

The Canadian Prime Minister was our host at a Citadel dinner. There was apparently a proposal that Canada should take part in the Conference, but this came to nothing. As it is, Mackenzie King seems rather like a man who has lent his house for a party. The guests hardly take notice of him, but just before leaving remember he is their host and say pleasant things.[3]

As a result, Canadian defence planners, both political and military, found themselves generally in the status of observers at these great conferences, anxious to help while conscious that Canada's contributions would be by American or British invitation only.

A few days after reading the Japanese ambassador's comments, Mackenzie King reported the basic content of the decrypt to his war cabinet, telling of the fifty German divisions along the coast of Europe and warning that the war was likely to drag on to 1944 at least. His colleagues received this news soberly. The Prime Minister was primly satisfied to remind them of the weighty burden he was carrying.

———————

At the beginning of 1943, the war had decisively turned against Germany and Japan. By the end of 1943, there was little doubt the Allies would win.

The year began with the massive defeat of the German armies at Stalingrad, followed by their expulsion from North Africa. Then came the invasion of Sicily in the spring, defeat in southern Russia in the summer, and the collapse of Italian resistance in the fall. The mass bombing of Hamburg reduced the city to ruins. In the Pacific, the Japanese Navy fought fiercely but proved unable to prevent the Americans from seizing one island after another. The ships and aircraft it lost could not be replaced. American submarines prowled the seas and decimated Japan's merchant fleet.

The decisive Allied advantage, of course, was the economic and military might of the United States and Russia. Added to that, and possibly equally crucial, was the technological superiority of the British and the Americans. Germany and Japan could rely only on their own scientists and industries to come up with new weapons and defences. The Allies had a huge advantage by comparison, enabling them to develop new explosives, install radar sets in ships and aircraft, and divert enormous resources toward the development of nuclear energy and the possibility of an atomic bomb.

Here Canada did contribute. Although it did not have the industrial base to deliver much in the way of new-weapon technology, it did important research in the more arcane areas of atomic energy, and chemical and biological warfare. Under the prodding of the National Research Council, new weapons based on anthrax, botulinus toxin, and ricin were developed in laboratories at Queen's University in Kingston and at the Suffield defence research station in Alberta. Scientists at McGill University in Montreal came up with a primitive nerve gas and did pioneering research toward the building of a heavy water nuclear reactor capable of producing plutonium, the atomic explosive. These were considerable achievements, giving Canada clout with the United States and Britain in the post-war era.[4]

Nevertheless, it was men, ships, aircraft, and electronics that decided the outcome of the war. The Americans, British, and Russians had more than enough of these among them to defeat the Axis powers. Canada had been a vitally important ally of Britain at the beginning of the war; a year after Pearl Harbor she was hardly needed and rarely heeded.

The Americans made this very clear in the North Atlantic. The U.S. Navy continued to press the Canadian Navy to confine its direction-finding reports of submarines to Canadian coastal waters. Commander de Marbois objected strongly, with the result that the Canadian Navy chief, Admiral Percy Nelles, complained directly to Admiral King, Commander-in-Chief of the U.S. Fleet, pointing out that Canadian escort vessels (mostly ill-equipped corvettes) far outnumbered American escorts on the Atlantic convoy runs and were nearly as numerous as those of the British.[5] The argument see-sawed for the next five months, with the British generally siding with the Americans.

Commander Jock de Marbois was fighting a losing battle. The war at sea had changed drastically in the preceding year. The Government Code and Cipher School, in cooperation with the U.S. Navy's Op-20-G, had resumed reading the German U-boat ENIGMA cipher, giving the Allies ample warning of how and where the submarines were to be deployed. British and American escort vessels were being equipped with shipboard direction-finding equipment, enabling them to take local fixes on enemy transmissions. Even more important, they were also being fitted with high-resolution radar, capable of spotting the conning tower of a submarine or even its periscope. Life was becoming perilous for the U-boats.

De Marbois simply refused to see what was happening. He blamed his own boss, the Director of Signals, for failing to respond adequately to the Americans. He went over his superior's head and spoke of the "ignorance" of his fellow senior officers at Naval Headquarters. He demanded that all incoming correspondence dealing with wireless intelligence be referred to him, and he wrote a dozen memos arguing the superiority of shore-based direction finding. He proposed that he take sole responsibility for the Operational Intelligence Centre, reporting directly to the Vice-Chief of Naval Staff. He made himself unpopular.

In the end he got his way—sort of. In May 1943 the U.S. Navy conceded to the Canadians responsibility for shore-based direction finding for the area north of 40 N and west of 28 W. In June de Marbois was put exclusively in charge of the Operational Intelligence Centre as well as Atlantic traffic analysis and direction finding. He was master in his own house at last. It was illusion. By that time, direction finding had been almost entirely superseded by cryptanalysis and radar.[6] Had it not been that Naval Headquarters in Ottawa was receiving German naval ENIGMA decrypts from the Admiralty and the U.S. Navy, de Marbois's Operational Intelligence Centre would have been useless.[7]

To make matters even worse, the Admiralty and the U.S. Navy outfitted their own ships with new radar and ship-board direction-finding sets as fast as they could be developed and produced, leaving the Canadian Navy to rely on Canadian industry. The result was inevitable. British and American escort vessels became the U-boat hunter-killers of the Atlantic, while the poorly equipped Canadian vessels were reduced to being convoy shepherds only. This was enormously frustrating for de Marbois.[8] As one Canadian naval officer remembered:

I recall sitting down before a very tall, very thin, grim man. His thin hair was shiny black, brushed close to his head. His cheeks were hollow, skin sallow, dark rings under the bright black eyes.... Captain de Marbois wasted no time getting to the point of the interview. A short introduction on the general uselessness of the sea-going ships served to instill in him a great rage. For ten minutes he held forth on the damage done to the war-effort by the blundering, fumbling incompetence of the Halifax-based escort groups. He clearly felt that this perceived ineptitude was due not to lack of ability but to indifference. I left the office in a daze.[9]

From mid-1943 to the end of the war, the Operational Intelligence Centre's tracking room in Ottawa was redundant, wholly dependent on the intelligence handouts of the larger centres in London and in Washington. By insisting on direction finding and by giving up a role for the Canadian Navy in cryptanalysis, de Marbois had lost any say in wireless intelligence generally. Command of the war in the Atlantic passed totally under the control of the British and the Americans.

Something similar could have happened both to the Army's Special Wireless Service and the Examination Unit. Fortunately, the U.S. Army people at Arlington Hall were much easier to deal with than their U.S. Navy colleagues. Despite an overwhelming superiority in resources, the Americans at Arlington encouraged the Canadians. They did not need to do so. It was a demonstration of American generosity at its best, just as U.S. Navy intransigence represented American arrogance at its worst.

The man who most profited from this was Ed Drake, who by now had three Special Wireless Stations under his command—at Leitrim near Ottawa, at Grande Prairie in Alberta, and at Victoria, B.C.—plus a small, separate Discrimination Unit at 283 Bank Street in Ottawa that did the preliminary sorting of incoming wireless traffic. Because his Army receivers did most of the monitoring of diplomatic and commercial traffic in Canada, it was only natural that he should sit on the Joint U.S.–Canada sub-committee set up by the Arlington Hall conference of January 1943. The contacts he made and the confidence he engendered in the ensuing meetings gave him an opportunity to expand Canada's involvement in wireless intelligence in an undreamed-of way.

Throughout 1942 the U.S. Army had concentrated on building up its ability to intercept and decipher diplomatic wireless messages; in 1943 the top priority became Japanese military communications. The reason for the change was that in the first year most of the fighting had been by U.S. Navy forces or Marines. Now, as the war intensified, the U.S. Army was increasingly called into play in the island-hopping, jungle battles of the Pacific.

In mid-1942 the British had tried to persuade wireless intelligence services of both the U.S. Navy and Army to work mainly on Japanese communications and leave those of Germany and Italy, particularly ENIGMA, to the Government Code and Cipher School. The U.S. Navy flatly rejected this proposal, unilaterally building its own decrypting machines and launching its own attacks on German naval ENIGMA. By mid-1943 this rivalry had resolved into a division of effort on enemy naval ciphers between the Government Code and Cipher School (Bletchley) and the Admiralty on the one side and Op-20-G and the U.S. Navy on the other.[10]

The U.S. Army, however, had left ENIGMA mainly to the British and had concentrated primarily on diplomatic traffic. Now that American soldiers were struggling against the Japanese in New Guinea and on Guadalcanal, however, the need to master Japanese Army and Air Force traffic was more urgent. In April 1943, new negotiations between the Government Code and Cipher School and the U.S. Army's Military Intelligence Service (G-2) opened simultaneously in London and Washington.

Carter Clarke, head of the U.S. Army's Special Branch, played host in Washington to Commander Travis and his deputy, Captain Hastings, while his second-in-command, Colonel Alfred McCormack—plus William Friedman and Colonel Telford Taylor—visited Britain to be toured through Bletchley Park and Berkeley Street by Commander Denniston. Both the Americans and the British were impressed by what they saw of each other's operations.

The big pitch by the British on both sides of the Atlantic was that the Americans should have Arlington Hall concentrate primarily on Japanese Army and Air Force traffic. "For my own personal part in this matter," Denniston told McCormack, "I have urged since my visit to Washington in August 1941 that Arlington's greatest contribution to

Examination Unit staff ply paper and pencil against enemy codes and ciphers at the Montreal Road office in Ottawa, early 1942. *(Courtesy CSE)*

The telekrypton, invented by Benjamin deForest Bayly, was a punched-tape cipher machine. *(VMI, Friedman collection)*

LEFT: Commander Edward Travis, director of the Bletchley Park division of the Government Code and Cipher School.
(VMI, Friedman collection)

BELOW: Norman Robertson (left) and Prime Minister Mackenzie King pause for a photographer outside 10 Downing street in London.
(National Archives of Canada)

As head of the Canadian Navy's Foreign Intelligence Service, Jock de Marbois was responsible for setting up and directing the Navy's network of wireless intercept and direction-finding stations. *(Courtesy Nathalie de Marbois)*

LEFT: Colonel William Waldie Murray, as director of Military Intelligence, oversaw much of Canada's wartime cryptanalysis program.
(Courtesy Elspeth Boyd)

BELOW: Lieutenant C. H. (Herbie) Little copies a recording of an intercepted message at Naval Service Headquarters in 1940.
(Courtesy C. H. Little)

The Government Code and Cipher School division responsible for breaking diplomatic traffic was camouflaged behind a row of buildings on Berkeley Street in London. The arrow (drawn by William Friedman) points to the entrance beside Peggy Carter's hat shop. *(VMI, Friedman collection)*

LEFT: Captain E. G. (Eddie) Hastings, the Admiralty's liaison to the United States on code- and cipher-breaking. *(VMI, Friedman collection)*

BELOW: The leaders of Allied code- and cipher-breaking meet at Arlington on March 13, 1944. The key figures are William Friedman, front row right corner, and, beside him to the left, Carter Clarke of U.S. Military Intelligence (G-2). The other civilian in the front row is Edward Travis, head of the Government Code and Cipher School at Bletchley Park. Immediately behind him and slightly to the left is Benjamin deForest Bayly. Beside Travis to the left is W. Preston Corderman, head of the Signal Security Agency, and, immediately above and behind him, Ed Drake of Canada's Discrimination Unit. The civilian with the hat and glasses in the back row is F. A. (Tony) Kendrick, head of Canada's Examination Unit. *(VMI, Friedman collection)*

LEFT: Lester Pearson, seen in this 1945 photograph addressing a dinner in California when he was ambassador to Washington, became the chief architect of Canada's postwar signals intelligence organization.
(National Archives of Canada)

BELOW: Intelligence based on intercepted wireless messages permits staff at Naval Service Headquarters in Ottawa to plot the movements of convoys and enemy submarines during the Battle of the Atlantic.
(National Archives of Canada)

LEFT: Herbert Norman: His Communist background was an embarrassment to Canada's secret intelligence partnerships. *(Canapress)*

BELOW: William Stephenson, the man called INTREPID, exaggerated his accomplishments in secret intelligence at Canada's expense.

the war effort is the effective and operational reading of Japanese military cyphers and that G.C.&C.S. was and is prepared to fill any intelligence gap in diplomatic work which may result from a supreme effort on Japanese Military by Arlington."

The British won their point. On May 17, 1943, the U.S. Army formally agreed that Arlington would concentrate on Japanese military traffic and leave the breaking of German and Italian military ciphers primarily to the British. Each side would be responsible for seeing that the resulting intelligence got safely to the appropriate Allied battle commanders in the Pacific and European theatres.[11]

The British had a substantial edge here. The German armed forces all used ENIGMA machine ciphers, and over the previous three years the Government Code and Cipher School had acquired a great deal of experience with them, successfully breaking German Air Force ENIGMA ciphers and later those of the German Navy. By the beginning of 1943, it was already reading a great many German Army messages and distributing them to both American and British operational commanders in the Mediterranean. The Japanese Army and Air Force, on the other hand, used a hodgepodge of codes and ciphers, complicated by various forms of super-encipherments. Most of this was still unreadable. The Americans had cut themselves a daunting and massive task.

The agreement led to the exchange of small contingents of personnel between Arlington and Bletchley Park. It also led to an elaborate system for the distribution of operational decrypts to British and American commanders, which grew in sophistication as the war progressed. Of more direct value to the U.S. Army in the short term, however, was the British willingness to take primary responsibility for breaking diplomatic traffic. Theoretically, at least, this would free up personnel at Arlington.

When McCormack and Friedman went home, they left Colonel Taylor behind as the U.S. Army's liaison officer at the Government Code and Cipher School. The new agreement called for him to have full access to the work of the cryptographers at Bletchley Park and Berkeley Street, picking and choosing those decrypts he thought would be of interest to Washington. German and Italian military messages, however, were overwhelmingly abundant and of little immediate value as general intelligence. Taylor was ordered to confine himself "exclusively" to the diplomatic decrypts being produced by Denniston at Berkeley Street.[12] These ultimately made their way into the MAGIC Summaries that were sent on to the State Department and other senior American authorities.

As Yardley had observed to the Canadians two years earlier, however, nations cannot be expected to be candid with one another about sharing diplomatic intelligence. In approving the exchange of decrypts, the British Foreign Office reserved the right "to continue withholding from circulation messages which they considered too hot for general distribution." These Taylor did not see. Later, under pressure from the Americans, the Foreign Office admitted that some messages were being "unqualifiedly withheld." Taylor could only guess what these might be.[13]

Canada was not party to this latest Arlington–GC&CS accord, perhaps because of a well-intentioned but unfortunate move by Mackenzie King. Just two months earlier, the Canadian Prime Minister had received a most unusual decrypt from the Examination Unit. Somehow the Japanese embassy in Lisbon had got hold of a report filed from London by the Portuguese ambassador. It was sent to Tokyo verbatim:

From: Lisbon   Dated: March 4, 1943
To: Tokyo   Rec'd: March 8, 1943

Emergency Report. From Britain, 25th

Today, I lunched with Sir OLIVER STANLEY, the Secretary of State for Colonies. I have reported by mail what he told me in strict secrecy: however I am wiring you the following for the time being:

(A) When I stressed the seriousness of the West African question, STANLEY said that the recent abrupt expansion of U.S. power in Africa and India was the cause of grave anxiety to the British Government. Three secret Cabinet sessions had already been held to consider what to do about it....

(B) It was clear that the Americans were working on Spain with some scheme in mind and were employing deceit toward Britain when they said that they were getting Spain to give up her long cherished desire for the restoration of Gibraltar. He could not call this an honest or loyal attitude....

(D) He was savage in his censure of the recent defeat of the U.S. troops in Tunis, saying it was a demonstration of the fickleness of the U.S. Army....

There was more in the same vein, but it was the last paragraph that was dynamite.

> STANLEY, referring to the Soviet offensive, said that the strength of the Soviet Union had already passed its peak. It was possible that they might hereafter still *obtain* a position of power, but CHURCHILL's intention was to have Russia and Germany fight each other as savagely as possible and for as long a time as possible; if they fought each other to the point of emaciation, that would be for England an ideal conclusion to the war. [14]

That Churchill hoped Germany and the Soviet Union would destroy one another was no news to Mackenzie King. He had already heard the British Prime Minister say as much to President Roosevelt in private conversation. But their Communist ally was then pinning down more than 3 million German troops along a 2,000-mile battle-front. Soviet dictator Joseph Stalin was bitterly complaining that he was being left to bear the brunt of the war. It would not do for him, of all people, to learn of Churchill's remark.

As it happened, Britain's Foreign Secretary, Anthony Eden, was in Ottawa. He had stopped over in the Canadian capital to report on his talks with the State Department and Roosevelt on the problems the Allies were having with General Charles de Gaulle. When he arrived at Mackenzie King's office, the Canadian Prime Minister could hardly wait to tell him about the Lisbon intercept.

Eden had not seen the intercepted message regarding the alleged conversation between Oliver Stanley and the Portugese Ambassador in London. When I told him of it, he asked me if I could let him see it. When I showed him the message he asked me if I would let him have a copy. He agreed that it was a very serious communication; indeed, would get it off at once to Churchill.... I was careful to tell Eden that of course I could not vouch for the intercepted message and rather hesitated to bring it to his attention as appearing to be talking out of school, but I felt that if there was any chance of the Americans or Russians learning of the message he should know of it at once. He said he was extremely grateful.[15]

Eden was a man of probably even less humour than Mackenzie King, becoming in the 1950s one of Britain's stuffier prime ministers. He was also a man acutely conscious of Britain's image as a Great Power and was undoubtedly behind the Foreign Office decision a few months later to withhold from the Americans any decrypts involving "undiplomatic remarks by British representatives abroad, etc." The fact that Mackenzie King had glimpsed Churchill's inner cabinet grousing about its American ally was not likely to persuade Eden that Canada should share directly in the Anglo–American exchange of diplomatic decrypts.

In any event, Canada was excluded. Except for the limited selection of PURPLE decrypts through official channels, External Affairs and Mackenzie King had to rely on the Examination Unit for diplomatic intercepts, most of them in low-grade Japanese or Vichy codes and of marginal value. The fare became so meagre in the spring of 1943 that the Prime Minister suspected Robertson—or someone—of holding out on him. It was his "right and duty as Prime Minister" to see everything of importance, he complained. The Examination Unit, however, could not produce what it did not have.[16]

The Americans and British appear not to have told the Canadians that they had agreed to a general sharing of diplomatic decrypts. However, on his way home from Washington, Commander Travis visited Ottawa and reported on at least one aspect of the Arlington–GC&CS accord. At a meeting of the Y Committee, he explained that the U.S. Army and the British planned to set up a world-wide Most Secret wireless communication net for sharing and distributing the raw intercepts picked up by Allied listening stations. The HYDRA transmitter at Camp X was to be an integral part of the scheme, by virtue of being directly linked by a separate telekrypton line to British Security Coordination.[17]

Travis did not go into much detail. Had he done so, his Canadian listeners might have learned that another, 10,000-watt transmitter had been installed at Camp X. Cobbled together from parts acquired from a defunct radio station in the United States, it had been fitted with a huge rhombic aerial aimed at Britain and equipped with variable-frequency controls that enabled it to broadcast at five to twenty-three megahertz. Depending on which frequency was chosen, a signal following a straight line around the world—a geodesic—could be made to come down in Britain, in Egypt, or in the Indian Ocean on a broad path whose centre line passed not far from the island of Mauritius. Here the British had built another large listening post and a transmitter capable of relaying messages to either India or Australia.[18]

HYDRA's long-range capability was to be tremendously useful. Churchill and Roosevelt had agreed that the U.S. Navy would have command responsibility for fighting the Japanese in the Pacific, while the Royal Navy looked after the Indian Ocean. A ship in the Indian Ocean, however, might fail to hear a signal coming from London because of radio skip conditions, while those from the HYDRA transmitter in Canada might be perfectly clear. The same held true at Cairo, Egypt, long the location of Britain's Middle East Intelligence Centre, which operated its own intercept service and code- and cipher-breaking department. HYDRA would give Britain's military and secret service authorities the option of cabling messages across the Atlantic to British Security Coordination and having them transmitted to these distant points from Camp X. Messages from Arlington to Britain and the Far East could go out the same way.

The minutes of the Y Committee do not indicate that Travis told any of this to the Canadians. It is doubtful. He was asked, however, whether it would be necessary to install a telekrypton line between Camp X and Ottawa. No, he replied, for all raw wireless traffic intercepted in Canada would still have to be sent to BSC in New York for sorting prior to being sent on to Arlington and Britain. A telekrypton line between BSC and Camp X was all that was needed. Two weeks later Murray, Drake, and Kendrick went to Washington for their own talks with the Americans.

No documents have been released on this mid-June conference in Washington, but it is clear that its purpose was to involve Canada, India, and Australia, as well as the United States and Britain, in a systematic effort to collect as much Japanese military traffic as possible. Two weeks later Lieutenant Colonel A. W. Sandford, head of Australia's cryptanalysis centre, known as Central Bureau, appeared before the Examination Unit committee to describe the "arrangements recently concluded" whereby the Americans would supply the Australians with processed battle-zone intelligence in exchange for "certain Japanese traffic that could not be picked up elsewhere."[19]

The fact was that the area of the Far East now occupied by the Japanese was so vast that the U.S. Army, even with the benefit of its own and Federal Communications Commission receiving stations in Hawaii and Alaska, simply could not pick up all the Japanese Army and Air Force wireless transmissions it required. The June meeting was aimed at obtaining agreements whereby the United States and Canada would cover Japan and the North Pacific, Australia's Central Bureau would cover the southern East Indies (Borneo, Sumatra, etc.), and the Wireless Experimental Centre in New Delhi, India, would cover the northern East Indies, including Burma. It was only by this kind of cooperation that U.S. Army cryptographers at Arlington could get the copious amount of raw traffic needed to analyse and defeat the Japanese systems.[20]

The following day Sandford appeared before the Y Committee to describe the wireless organization in his country. Because very little has been written about Australia's wartime role in special intelligence, it is worthwhile to paraphrase his remarks:

Prior to the war there was a small Navy "Y" unit in Australia that monitored Japanese Naval traffic and did a little work on Japanese diplomatic codes. The Munich Crisis prompted attempts at an interservice organization but they fell through.

After Pearl Harbor and with the arrival the following March of

American soldiers, the Australian Army and Air Force set up a combined wireless intelligence organization called Central Bureau at Brisbane with the help of 10 officers and other ranks from the U.S. Army. The Australian Navy at Melbourne continued to work separately with the Royal Navy while the U.S. Navy soon arrived to set up a third organization.

For most of 1942, Central Bureau's primary task was the development of battlefield intercept teams for monitoring enemy combat messages. At the beginning of 1943 General Douglas MacArthur, the American theatre commander, declared Central Bureau to be the primary operation centre for wireless intelligence, leading to its rapid expansion.

As of June, 1943, Central Bureau had 15 mobile wireless receiving sections and 18 fixed stations around the country tied to it by land-line. It had a staff of about 400, half of them Americans, and combined both traffic analysis and cryptanalysis.

Almost all of Central Bureau's work was on Japanese Air Force and Army traffic, with only six people assigned to Japanese diplomatic messages.[21]

The U.S. Navy did not participate in any of the discussions that spring at Arlington. Appearing before the Y Committee a little later that year to describe his tour of the Far East, Colonel Stratton explained that attempts in Australia to set up an interservice Y Committee like those in Canada and Britain had fallen through because "Australia is fighting under an American G.H.Q. [General Douglas MacArthur] and the same reasons that prevent Washington from having a Y Committee—the lack of cooperation between the U.S. Navy and Army—acted in Australia." As a result, the Canadians were told, the exchange of vital intelligence between the Australian Navy's cryptanalysts in Melbourne and those of Central Bureau was "very poor."[22]

The Canadians received several reports from visiting Australian wireless intelligence officers during the year, and there were lessons to be learned from their Commonwealth cousins. One of the more interesting was the Australian use of women operators. Both the Canadians and the British had wondered from time to time just how much responsibility should be given to women, with Travis observing that they were at least as good as men on "repetitious tasks." The Australians, however, were training women to replace men in as many jobs as possible.

The difference between Canada and Australia was that the latter's survival had been threatened. In 1942 Darwin had been raided by Japanese aircraft and nearby New Guinea invaded. For a time it looked as though the Australians would be fighting on their own shores. As that threat receded, the Australian Army authorities promised that every able-bodied soldier would get the opportunity for a crack back at the Japanese in combat. Women were therefore being trained in wireless intelligence so that they could replace the men when the time came. They were even given a three-week course which described "the whole show" so they would appreciate what was at stake. The result was a superb state of morale at Central Bureau because "women whose men-folk are in the Services are used and the importance of the job and its secrecy is readily recognized."[23]

The Canadians also heard how the Australians had managed to plot the course of Japanese aircraft carriers by their hourly weather reports and how the Australian pearling fleet had been strung out along the coast to give advance warning of the air raids. Such stories were convincing evidence of the value of operational wireless intelligence and the Canadians became even more anxious to help the Allied effort.

During his visit to Ottawa, Travis had commented that one reason why the British wanted to have the Americans concentrate on Japanese military traffic was that the Government Code and Cipher School had not so far been able to mount an effective attack of its own. This led the Canadians to dream—and it *was* merely a dream—that the British could be persuaded to move the Government Code and Cipher School's entire Japanese cryptanalysis team to Canada, where it would be nearer the primary source of intercepts. That summer, on a visit to Bletchley, Tommy Stone actually made the proposal, arguing that it would put both the British and the Canadians in a better bargaining position with the Americans. He was told that "political pressure" made such a move impossible.[24]

Stone's vision of an expanded role for Canada in wireless intelligence nevertheless did partially materialize. The receivers at Ed Drake's three Special Wireless Stations shifted from listening to Japanese diplomatic and commercial traffic for Commander Denniston at Berkeley Street to listening for Japanese military transmissions. Soon 10,000 intercepts a week were pouring into Drake's tiny Discrimination Unit office on Bank Street for initial sorting before being sent to Arlington. The workload was enormous. In June the Chiefs of Staff gave the go-ahead to reorganize and expand the Discrimination Unit.

Because it was to use staff from the Navy and the Air Force as well as the Army, it was to be called the Joint Discrimination Unit. It would be housed in one building and would include a separate group—the Joint Machine Unit—operating ten Hollerith tabulating machines supplied by the International Business Machines company. These machines—which could mechanically crunch numbers, looking for numerical patterns—represented an enormous advance in Canada's ability to process enciphered messages.

In this fourth year of conflict, the wireless intelligence war had become much more complicated. Enemy codes and ciphers were now much less likely to be sent in their basic form; they were usually further camouflaged by the addition of what was known as a super-encipherment. This can be best understood from the point of view of the enemy code clerk. He would take the plaintext of a message and write down the numerical equivalents for each word from his code book, so that it looked something like this: 89276 17625 and so on. To make his encoded message unrecognizable, he applied a series of numerical additives by a previously agreed upon formula. For example, pi = 3141592653 ... added (without carrying) to the above numbers yields 10681 09278, etc. This is called a super-encipherment.[25]

Obviously super-encipherment creates a major hurdle for cryptanalysis. Code- and cipher-breaking cannot even begin unless the cryptanalyst is sure that the numbers before him are those that he must actually work on. Even before the war, the U.S. Signal Intelligence Service recognized the problem. Part of the answer was Hollerith machines. At the time of Pearl Harbor, the U.S. Army had thirteen of them tended by twenty-one operators. By the spring of 1945, it had 407 of them run by 1,275 operators.[26]

When the Navy and Air Force were asked to supply personnel for the new Joint Discrimination Unit, the latter cheerfully complied. The RCAF did not have a wireless intelligence organization of its own at this time—there had been little need for one—but was anxious to develop the expertise. With the Navy it was a different story.

At the beginning of the war with Japan, de Marbois had sent a group of traffic analysts to Vancouver to discriminate Japanese naval transmissions. The decision at the Radio Intelligence Conference to have the U.S. Navy do this entire job at Bainbridge (Seattle) made the Canadian team redundant, and its members were brought back to Ottawa to work under Drake. De Marbois objected, this time campaigning in vain. Bringing all Japanese traffic analysis together under one roof with a tabulating machine section was clearly a sensible approach. When the naval team arrived back in Ottawa, it remained nominally under his control but from now on worked as part of the Joint Discrimination Unit.[27]

De Marbois had officially become head of the Navy's Operational Intelligence Centre in May; by July he had lost one of its largest components to Drake.

By an odd coincidence, the Ottawa building chosen as the new home of the Joint Discrimination Unit and its tabulating machine department was the former La Salle Academy on Sussex Drive. Like the U.S. Army's Arlington Hall and Op-20-G's new headquarters on Nebraska Avenue in Washington, the large square building of cut grey limestone with a magnificent view of the Ottawa River had once been a private school. Thus for most of the war the thousands of men and women in North America who laboured over the enemy's codes and ciphers did so where once uniformed teenagers studied Latin and geometry and trained for field sports.

The Joint Discrimination Unit's cooperation with Arlington quickly blossomed. In order to help Drake as much as possible, the Americans began supplying him with intelligence reports on Japanese Army and Air Force communication systems and orders-of-battle. He was given call signs and frequencies to help his listening stations identify the correct traffic to copy. Soon Drake was sending Arlington 20,000 groups of enciphered traffic a month, and receiving a similar amount in return so that he could do his own studies. Then, as the expanded Joint Discrimination Unit got better organized, Drake asked for more. The Americans were cool at first, but when Drake's team of specialists started producing fairly sophisticated reports of their own on Japanese Army and Air Force communications systems, Arlington began duplicating to Canada all the military traffic it was sending to Britain. Before long the Americans were sending the Canadians more than they were sending the British, making Drake's Joint Discrimination Unit a larger partner than Bletchley Park in the American attack on Japanese Army and Air Force messages.[28]

Toward the end of 1943, Drake's three Special Wireless Stations and the Joint Discrimination Unit—collectively known as Military Intelligence 2 (MI2)—began to assume a role of genuine importance in the gathering of Allied ULTRA intelligence.

De Marbois's naval Operational Intelligence Centre, what was left of it, had relatively little to contribute. The Examination Unit was also a sideshow. Tony Kendrick set up a four-man section to study a handful of Japanese military codes, although it would be many months before it produced anything of value. The French section was still working on some Vichy traffic—mainly involving the colony of Indochina—but it was of slight interest. Work was proceeding on Free French intercepts, but so far little had been accomplished. Progress with Spanish messages was even more dismal, the project finally being dropped when McCormack for the Americans and Denniston for the British, after much prodding, agreed to supply whatever Spanish decodes they deemed of interest to Canada. Mackenzie King still received the occasional PURPLE decrypt, much to his satisfaction.[29]

The only real progress the Examination Unit made was on Japanese diplomatic traffic. The Canadian team was not doing anything that was not already being done more swiftly in Washington or London, but the rules of the game for Canada were that if the Canadians wanted a regular diet of Japanese diplomatic messages, they had to manage by themselves.

The Examination Unit did have modest success. After months of frustrating effort, Kendrick's team of cryptographers finally broke into a high-grade Japanese diplomatic cipher. It was used by Japanese diplomats as a Most Secret alternative to the PURPLE machines, which sometimes broke down or were unavailable. The exultant Examination Unit staff members designated it by the code-word ZERO. Unfortunately, their sense of accomplishment was short-lived. The OSS inadvertently saw to that.

In the course of the previous year, Donovan's Office of Strategic Services had expanded rapidly, and it had flooded Spain and Portugal with secret agents. In the spring of 1943, one of these managed to steal a message from the Japanese embassy in Lisbon. OSS headquarters in Washington sent a copy to General Dawson Olmstead, the U.S. Army's Chief Signal Officer, naively asking whether it would be useful to his cryptanalysts and whether he would like to be provided with more. This caused an immediate flutter of memos within the Army's Military Intelligence Service (G-2). Had the dreaded and dreadful OSS developed the means to decipher enemy messages? Had its agents stolen a Japanese code?

A few weeks later the speculation appeared to receive awful confirmation. In early July Arlington produced the following:

From: Rome
To: Tokyo

June 29, 1943

The Italian General Staff Office has conveyed to my military attaché for his most secret arcane information the following message.

"An American espionage agency in Lisbon not only knows to the minutest detail all the activities of the Japanese minister in Lisbon, but is getting Japanese code books, too."

This is very vague. I don't know what it is all about. I am making very definite inquiries through my attaché.

Rec'd 7/1/43
Trans 7/3/43

Two days later, Arlington deciphered Tokyo's reaction:

From: Tokyo (Shigemitsu)
To: Madrid

July 1, 1943

Utterly, absolutely, strictly secret. Handle with care. Extremely urgent.

Our Military Attaché in Rome has been informed by the Italian High Command that "the American Intelligence men know everything that goes on in the Japanese Ministry in Lisbon and have taken the code books." I think this is just a planted intelligence of the enemy designed to addle us but scoot a man over to Lisbon immediately to see what's the matter.

Rec'd 7/2/43
Trans 7/5/43

Army Headquarters in Washington was soon sizzling over the messages. Somehow General Marshall, the Chief of Staff, learned of them. He ordered his Military Intelligence chief (G-2), Major-General G. V. Strong, to investigate. Strong was caught by surprise, sent for copies of the messages, and was appalled by what he read. He immediately demanded an explanation from OSS headquarters. The next day he reported to General Marshall, pulling no punches:

It appears obvious that the ill-advised and amateurish efforts of OSS representatives in Lisbon have so alarmed the Japanese that it is an even money bet that the codes employed by the Japanese are in immense danger of being changed. If so, for months we will face a blank wall as far as Military and Naval Intelligence from Japanese sources is concerned … with the possibility of catastrophic results.

The following day he went even further, complaining to General Marshall that the OSS "is full of irresponsible people, who have been turned loose in neutral countries with unlimited money to squander, operating under no proper definition of their functions and subject to no proper control." He urged that the OSS be ordered to recall its agents from Spain and Portugal.

Strong was so upset by the "reprehensible activity" of the OSS that he confided in Stewart Menzies, the head of Britain's Secret Intelligence Service (MI6). "This mess is primarily an American headache and is dumped squarely in my lap," Strong cabled Menzies. He told the Englishman that he was "trying to force a radical solution."[30]

Strong's anger must have given the British Intelligence chief pause. Donovan's OSS, after all, owed its very existence to the behind-the-scenes machinations of MI6 in 1941. Menzies had fully endorsed, perhaps even planned, the secret lobbying of Roosevelt that had led to Donovan's appointment. Then he had backed Donovan's pubescent secret service with British Intelligence resources and expertise. At that very moment, OSS liaison officers in Britain were enjoying *carte blanche* at MI6's Section V, having built a temporary building for their own personnel on the grounds adjacent to the main building at St Albans.[31]

Surely, Menzies temporized, if the OSS had stolen a Japanese code book they would have turned it over to the Army by now. How did the Italians find out about the incident, anyway? Menzies suggested that perhaps the Italians had managed to get a spy on the OSS payroll. He concluded his reply to Strong by proposing that all future OSS operations in Spain and Portugal be cleared first with the local MI6 station head.[32] Anglophile that he was, there is no doubt that Donovan would have rejected that suggestion.

As it turned out, General Strong's fears were partly realized. The Japanese promptly retired the ciphers used by the Lisbon embassy. Nevertheless, they found it hard to believe that their code books had been stolen or that their messages were being systematically broken. Their security provisions were just too good, the Lisbon staff told Tokyo. The damage was confined to only three Japanese hand ciphers.[33]

In the inevitable post-mortem, the OSS claimed that the stolen messages were in a "low-level" code of little value, no great loss even if withdrawn. This was untrue. The messages involved the Japanese Military Attaché (JMA) cipher, which was probably the most important used by Japanese embassy staff after the PURPLE cipher used by the ambassador. The Japanese, fortunately, chose to retain it, but they dropped the Examination Unit's prized ZERO cipher, "the only high category diplomatic cypher being read in Canada." [34]

The incident appears to have had a major consequence. Henceforth British Intelligence was much more circumspect in dealing with the OSS. When MI6 was approached that summer to help with a wireless intercept service the OSS wanted to establish in North Africa, the response was decidedly cool. The OSS had in mind a "working arrangement" with the Radio Security Service which would involve setting up a small code- and cipher-breaking facility. Captain Maidment, from the MI6/GC&CS office in New York, countered that the British could only go along with such a scheme if the OSS could show that it had the *written* approval of Allied Headquarters in North Africa, plus promises of cooperation from the U.S. Army and Navy, and the FBI.[35] He might just as well have told Donovan's men to walk on water.

The Canadians also were affected. External Affairs could not hope to get the secret intelligence reports that were going to the State Department or the Foreign Office and Canada had no overseas espionage agency of its own. The solution was for Herbert Norman's Special Intelligence Section to exchange its wireless intelligence summaries with the Research Branch of the OSS in Washington. Donovan had hired dozens of blue-ribbon, ivy-league economists and political scientists to analyse the internal affairs of all countries to which he could send his agents. Canada could not afford that kind of extravagance. On the other hand, the OSS did not have access to any diplomatic decrypts, not even those of the relatively poor quality handled by Norman.[36]

It was a good trade for the Canadians. It was also one that as time went on would have increasing potential for embarrassment.

CHAPTER NINE

TARGET: FRANCE

JANUARY 1942 – SEPTEMBER 1944

"I RAISED HIM as a pup. Now he bites the hand that fed him." In 1943 that was Churchill's way of privately telling the American government that he did not like General Charles de Gaulle either.

A few months later, in Quebec to confer with Roosevelt on the future conduct of the war, Churchill expanded on his feelings toward the leader of the Free French movement. Mackenzie King dutifully recorded the remarks in his diary:

> [He] said that he, himself, thoroughly disliked De Gaulle, though he had many manly qualities. He went so far as to say that he was one of those Frenchmen who hated Britain and might even be prepared to join with the Germans in attacking Britain some time.[1]

Only two years previously, as France collapsed under German invasion, Churchill had welcomed with open arms this refugee general, with his long, lugubrious face and extraordinary height. De Gaulle was the man of the hour, willing to insist that Frenchmen must fight on. That was enough for Britain to recognize him as the "leader of all Free Frenchmen, wherever they may be, who rally to him in support of the Allied cause." He was put on the radio, made stirring broadcasts, and

198

was given the resources and legal status to organize a kind of Free French government-in-exile.

The love affair lasted from mid-1940 to the end of 1941. The British—through Churchill's personal intervention—set him up in London, where he gathered a staff of other refugee French soldiers and diplomats. Since the Germans and the Vichy puppet government only directly controlled France itself, it was hoped that the colonies of the far-flung French Empire would rally to the Allied cause under de Gaulle's leadership. When that failed to happen (only French Equatorial Africa and the Cameroons declared for de Gaulle), the British equipped the few French soldiers and handful of ships that were willing to serve under de Gaulle, dubbed them the Free French forces, and used them as political leverage in combined British-Free French operations aimed at wresting away those Vichy colonies of particular strategic value.

De Gaulle, however, was a specialist in tank warfare, a military man trained to strike back when struck. He was not used to the slither of diplomacy and spoke out rather too loudly when he disagreed with the policies of his British hosts. He made a nuisance of himself in mid-1941 when British and Free French forces attacked Vichy-controlled Syria, complaining openly about the armistice terms offered by the British commander and insisting that lives could have been saved had he first been allowed to appeal to his countrymen. Churchill chided him, urging him to take everything a little less personally by yielding his sole control of the Free French movement to a committee of his peers. De Gaulle softened. He formed the French National Committee in London and, although he remained chairman of the new committee, he appeared tame at last.

Then on Christmas Eve, 1941, the tiny Free French Navy seized the also tiny Vichy-loyal islands of St. Pierre and Miquelon just south of Newfoundland. In ordering the move, de Gaulle detonated the diplomatic equivalent of the hydrogen bomb. The fallout lasted for years.

If Canada had been more decisive, the incident would not have happened. In the fall of 1941, the war in the Atlantic was going badly for Britain and the islands were an ideal base for spying on the convoys assembling in Halifax. The powerful transmitter on St. Pierre was beaming a constant stream of coded messages to Europe, some of which could be read by the Examination Unit and some not. The Vichy administrator of St. Pierre and Miquelon was notoriously anti-British and married to a German. The islands were also directly connected to the then-neutral United States by an undersea cable, theoretically enabling German spies anywhere along the Atlantic to telegraph shipping reports to the wireless station for relay to Germany. It was a dangerous situation.

Tommy Stone and Norman Robertson proposed a solution. Go in with a Canadian corvette, confront the Vichy governor, and seize the transmitter. Simple. The Canadian Prime Minister, however, was scandalized.

Mackenzie King was many things, but he was not a man of action. When the Canadian War Cabinet met in early December to discuss the plan, he threw up every obstacle, especially the possibility of giving the Fascist-leaning Vichy government in France an excuse for openly siding with the Germans. Someone eventually suggested that the Free French could be asked to do the job. The idea had appeal, but the Prime Minister said the Americans and British must be consulted first.[2]

The British were quick to approve the plan, alerted de Gaulle, and suggested the Americans would agree also. Not so. The State Department said it would prefer that the Canadians seize the islands, citing the danger of the still-intact French Fleet. President Roosevelt himself had recently promised to respect French possessions in the Western Hemisphere so long as the Vichy government kept its ships in port. Even more important, it was fundamental U.S. foreign policy of long standing that the United States would not tolerate any change of territorial control in the Western Hemisphere by European military intervention.[3]

The discussions continued among the three countries for the next two weeks, while de Gaulle impatiently awaited the go-ahead. It was to be the last time he was privy to Allied planning for the rest of the war.

De Gaulle finally acted. Two weeks after Pearl Harbor plunged the United States into the war, the commander of the Free French Navy, Admiral de Muselier, sent a telegram from Ottawa saying that the

Americans still opposed Free French seizure of St. Pierre and Miquelon. De Gaulle replied that it should be done anyway:

> We have, as you requested, consulted the British and American governments. We know from a reliable source that the Canadians intend to destroy the radio station of Saint Pierre and Miquelon themselves. Under these circumstances, I recommend that you proceed.[4]

De Muselier returned to Halifax and set sail with the three corvettes and one submarine under his command, arriving off the islands on Christmas Eve, 1941. The governor was ordered to surrender in the name of the Free French Forces under General Charles de Gaulle. Mackenzie King was so disturbed when he heard the news that he cancelled his Christmas greetings to the French leader.[5]

The Americans were livid. When Churchill and Mackenzie King arrived in Washington two days later to discuss the war with Japan, they found Secretary of State Cordell Hull in an absolute rage—so much so that he blurted out to reporters that the "so-called" Free French should be turned out of the islands and the Vichy governor reinstated. That prompted interminable and passionate debate in the American media, most of it sympathetic to de Gaulle. The three leaders, gathered in Washington to discuss how to handle a conflict that had suddenly become worldwide, wound up in an interminable wrangle about two tiny islands in the Gulf of St. Lawrence. Only after four months of embarrassing publicity was the issue allowed to die.[6]

De Gaulle's decision was a personal catastrophe. Neither Roosevelt nor his senior advisors trusted him again. Indeed, over the next few years the Americans did everything that they could to block de Gaulle's claim to be the leader of French resistance. They attempted to replace him. They failed. The postwar legacy was a France under President Charles de Gaulle that decades later turned its back on military cooperation with the North Atlantic Treaty Organization (NATO) and openly expressed its dislike of the United States and its suspicion of the English-speaking world in general.

The relationship between de Gaulle and Churchill also soured, but possibly for a very different reason. A few days after the incident, the ever-alert U.S. undersecretary of state for intelligence—Adolf Berle—had a chat with Hume Wrong of the Canadian legation. He was "curious" to know how de Gaulle had sent the order for the islands to be seized, somehow communicating with the Free French Navy from London without British awareness. It was obvious to Wrong what Berle was getting at. Wrong reported to Ottawa that Berle suspected Churchill of secretly telling de Gaulle to go ahead.

"I said that I assumed that Muselier's ships were capable of trans-Atlantic radio communications and that certainly it should not be supposed that the orders had been transmitted via a British cypher or code without clear evidence," Wrong wrote.[7]

Berle's suspicions were well-founded. From his own sources he learned that, shortly before the invasion of the islands, de Gaulle had warned the British that he was withdrawing his promise not to act on his own. He then sent the crucial order to Admiral de Muselier by transatlantic cable. Documents in British archives reveal that Free French enciphering techniques had been "compromised," and that the Foreign Office was routinely reading de Gaulle's messages before they left Britain.[8]

Either de Gaulle got out an enciphered message he knew his British hosts could not break—which surely would have excited suspicion and caused it to be stopped—or the British had indeed set up the Free French leader to seize the islands and then left him to take the blame from the Americans.

One way or another, Churchill and de Gaulle were at each other's throat for the rest of the war.

The British continued to read Free French ciphers freely. While the Americans debated handing back the islands, the British wanted to know how the Free French were being received. Here the Canadians could help. The islands were in direct undersea cable contact with the United States, so Canadian Telegraph Censorship arranged with U.S. Telegraph Censorship in New York to give it copies of the messages exchanged with the Free French delegation in Washington. These were passed to the Examination Unit for breaking. Oliver Strachey, then the chief cryptographer sent out from Britain, had brought the cipher keys with him.[9]

None of the messages has been released in either Canada or France, but one can get a good idea from other documents of what they contained. Canadian Press Censorship allowed only positive newspaper reports on the takeover of the islands, but in fact there had been stiff opposition, especially from the local clergy. Monsignor Poisson was the most vocal opponent, defiantly nailing a notice on the door of his church declaring his refusal to recognize the new regime. Other priests followed suit, counselling their flocks to remain loyal to Vichy. Soon leading businessmen were openly and pointedly declaring their support for Pétain, while boys from the Catholic-run private school hurled taunts and insults at pro-Gaullists. Power lines were cut, there was minor sabotage, and the homes of Free French supporters were vandalized.[10] The situation became so tense that the Free French delegate in Washington warned of bloodshed and civil war.

Finally, the leading pro-Vichy sympathizers, including Monsignor Poisson, were warned by Admiral de Muselier that if they did not desist, they would be arrested and "given a taste of the Fascism they profess to admire." In the end some were jailed and others repatriated to Occupied France.

All this must have made the decrypted intercepts salacious reading. Norman Robertson was incensed to learn that the Canadian Telegraph Censor, L. S. Yuill, was showing them to his counterparts in U.S. Censorship. Yuill was dropped from the list of those receiving the decrypts and fired not long after.[11]

The British were prepared to take novel steps to retain their mastery of Free French secret messages. In early March 1942, de Gaulle's London headquarters warned the Foreign Office that they intended to ask the State Department to accord cipher privileges to the Free French representatives in Washington. This would enable them to send messages from the United States by wireless rather than just by cable. The Foreign Office arranged secretly to ask the Americans to turn down the request. "Please tell the State Department confidentially that we should prefer the present system to continue by which we see and transmit their telegrams," the British embassy in Washington was told.[12]

The British ambassador, Lord Halifax, objected, pointing out that the Americans might believe the British no longer trusted de Gaulle's loyalty and reliability. The Foreign Office reconsidered. It certainly did not want to fuel American hostility toward the man the British had been backing for the last two years. On the other hand, since Free French ciphers were so insecure, it was felt that the Germans would be reading them once they started going out by wireless.[13]

It was proposed to supply the Free French with British one-time pads. These were pairs of booklets containing random numbers that could be added to the numerals of an already coded or enciphered message to produce a new super-encipherment. Because each pair of one-time pads was unique, with only sender and recipient having a copy, the system was virtually unbreakable. The Foreign Office hesitated: "It has been useful to us to see the telegrams passing between De Gaulle and his representatives in Washington. If we hand over these tables, we shall no longer do so."[14]

The solution was to ask the Free French to give the British plain-language copies of all their important messages. They agreed, although Halifax doubted they would live up to their word. Ultimately, the British did not take the chance. They soon made extra copies of the one-time pads they supplied the French, and quietly resumed reading their messages.[15]

The situation was fine for the British but not for the Americans. The State Department was so angered by the St. Pierre and Miquelon incident that it, too, would have wanted access to Free French secret messages. Normally this could easily have been accomplished by the cryptanalysts at Arlington Hall, but the British one-time pads made it impossible. While Churchill could read for himself the directives issued by de Gaulle throughout 1942, Roosevelt was forced to judge the Free French leader by his actions alone. This led the Americans to be much more suspicious, as well as incorrect, in their assessments of his intentions and motives.

In May 1942 British forces landed in Madagascar. This huge island off the east coast of Africa was one of the most important of the French colonial possessions. De Gaulle was not forewarned. He was furious. When he told the Foreign Office he wanted to send a Free French official to the island to take part in peace negotiations with the Vichy governor, he was refused. This made him even angrier. He launched a stinging telegram expressing his feelings to some of the leaders of the Free French forces then in Africa. Unfortunately for him, it was intercepted by Britain's Middle East Intelligence Centre and decrypted. The Foreign Office reported on its content as follows:

> In this telegram, a copy of which fell into our hands in Cairo, he alleged that we were trying to keep Madagascar and were planning with the Americans an operation against Dakar from which the Free French would be excluded. He said that he was not disposed to remain associated with Great Britain and the United States, that the Free French should form a united front against all comers and have no relations with the Anglo Saxons, and must warn the whole world, and the French people, against Anglo-Saxon imperialist designs.[16]

An awful row ensued. It went on for months, and if the British could have dropped de Gaulle, they would have. However, he had become too identified in the public eye as the champion of French resistance. Despite his private (and secret) battles with the British government, he never failed in public appearances to refer to Britain in flattering terms and preach about a new world order shaped by Anglo–French cooperation. De Gaulle was a miserable diplomat, but he was excellent at public relations.

The British confined de Gaulle to the British Isles. He wanted to visit his Free French possessions in Africa, but the British authorities demurred. Without their approval, he had no means of transportation. He was helpless. "In the end," as a Foreign Office report of the day commented, "he was allowed to go at the beginning of August after giving a solemn promise of good behaviour."[17]

During the summer of 1942, the Free French began using a new cipher, creating more headache for the British. To make matters worse, de Gaulle's "behaviour" worsened. As the Foreign Office further reported:

> De Gaulle failed to keep his undertaking. At his first meeting with the Minister of State in Cairo he adopted an offensive and intransigent attitude over Syrian questions. When he reached Syria he renewed his old tactics of inciting his officers and officials against

the British. He indulged in a violent outburst against British methods and imperialist designs in the Middle East in conversation with
the United States Consul-General at Beirut, which caused much
uneasiness in the State Department. He dismayed the National
Committee in London by informing them that the British were
planning to obtain complete domination of Syria and Lebanon.
He also complained of British interference with Free French Forces
in the Levant and even demanded that the supreme command of
the Allied forces there should be transferred from the British to the
Free French. [18]

Now it was Churchill's turn to fume. De Gaulle was "invited" back
to London at the end of September and the two men confronted one
another. One can only imagine the diminutive, cigar-chomping British
Prime Minister in his famous one-piece zipper suit, scolding the tower-
ing and defiant Frenchman in his sky-blue uniform. Churchill was not
used to defiance; his war cabinet and the Chiefs of Staff normally
tugged forelocks and spoke to him in hushed tones.[19]

De Gaulle was grounded again. This time, however, Churchill
ordered that a special watch be put on all his communications with the
Free French authorities overseas. All his messages were to be vetted by
the Foreign Office for content of "doubtful political significance." The
trick was to do this without his knowing and sparking a new round of
confrontation.

"I suggest that we should send on those cypher telegrams which we
are in a position to read and find to be harmless," Churchill aide
Desmond Morton wrote the Foreign Office. "If I am not mistaken, we
can read quite a number of these since they will be in cyphers which we
ourselves manufactured and gave to the Free French."[20]

Morton had to admit to the Prime Minister that the ciphers now
being used by the Free French Navy could not be read. "If you wish I
will see if it is possible to work out with the Director of Naval Signals
and "C" [Stewart Menzies, MI6 chief and director-general of the Government Code and Cipher School] any method whereby suspicious
cypher telegrams may be detected so that others could be allowed to
pass."[21]

On November 10, 1942, in the midst of recriminations and outright hostility between the British Prime Minister and the "leader of all Free Frenchmen everywhere," a mainly American invasion force landed in Algeria. The German Army in Tunisia now faced British forces to the east and American forces to the west. The long process of liberating North Africa and then Europe had begun.

De Gaulle rose to the occasion. Even though once again he had not been forewarned of this major attack on French colonial territory, he broadcast an appeal to his fellow Frenchmen to lay down their arms and accept the invaders as allies. After a brief but bloody battle with Vichy army and naval forces, the Vichy authorities in Algeria surrendered.

The timing of the invasion of North Africa could not have been worse for de Gaulle. The Americans had finally broken diplomatic relations with Vichy and had occupied the most important territory outside France itself. Now, if ever, was the moment to bring forward the leader of the Free French to rally the considerable French forces in North Africa to the Allied cause. But de Gaulle had long fed American doubts and had now mortally offended Churchill. Any other choice was thought to be better. De Gaulle continued to be confined to Britain, while the Americans negotiated an armistice that kept the Vichy authorities in place in Algeria. De Gaulle, who considered all Vichy officials as "traitors," complained bitterly. The Foreign Office drafted a press statement listing all the complaints against him, as it prepared to have Britain reject him once and for all.[22]

It was at this time, with de Gaulle in the cellar of American and British official opinion, that the Canadian authorities turned the efforts of the Examination Unit away from breaking Vichy messages to attacking those of the Free French. They did not have much luck at first. With de Gaulle shut up in England, the flow of messages would have been thin and at least some would have been enciphered by British one-time pads. To take up the slack and to keep the people in the French section of the Examination Unit busy, work continued on available Vichy traffic.

The Canadian government's interest in the secret affairs of the French was directly related to its problems with Quebec. Canada's French-language province had opposed the war from the beginning, maintaining its opposition even after the collapse of France. And it was not just a matter of provincial politics. The majority of Quebeckers were firmly against the war, causing Mackenzie King to stall repeatedly on suggestions that Canada should implement conscription into the armed forces. The Prime Minister believed that any attempt to force Quebeckers to fight overseas would break up the country.

No single issue in the twentieth century has done more to divide English- and French-speaking Canada. The plebiscite of 1942 found that an overwhelming majority of English-speaking Canadians supported the war while an overwhelming majority of French-speaking Canadians were against it. Thus Canada was faced with an ironic situation in which most anglophones wanted to liberate France from Nazi and Vichy domination while most francophones, at best, could not care less.[23]

The situation was an overwhelming puzzle to Mackenzie King. He could not speak French and could not fathom what was happening inside one of Canada's most populous and important provinces. To placate antiwar sentiment in Quebec, he contrived to have compulsory military service for the protection of Canada and volunteer service for the fighting overseas. The result was that those soldiers who chose to serve only in Canada—disparagingly termed "Zombies" and perceived to be mostly French Canadians—were deeply resented by those English-speaking families whose sons dodged bullets and died on the beaches of Dieppe and Normandy. War did not unite the country—as war usually does—but had begun, by the middle of 1942, to divide it.

The national tragedy of this situation was that French Canadians did volunteer, did fight, and did die, yet failed to earn the acknowledgement and admiration of their countrymen that their sacrifices deserved. In August 1942, for example, the Fusiliers Mont Royal were cut to pieces as they attempted to reinforce other Canadian troops at Dieppe. Of the 584 Fusiliers sent to the bullet-swept beaches during the ill-conceived "raid" on the fortified French port, only 125 returned, a third of them wounded.

Dieppe was a fiasco. Faulty British planning had resulted in a massacre. Of 5,000 Canadian soldiers who embarked, 3,367 were killed, wounded, or captured. The Germans were quick to sort their prisoners into English- and French-speaking. As a result, a few weeks later, French-Canadian families with sons still missing in action could tune their short-wave radios to Vichy France and hear ...

> I would like to talk to you about our revered chief, Marshall Pétain, who was wise enough—he alone—to stop the massacre of the French in June, 1940. But I have never been so happy as I am today to have this microphone available ... I have news of your own brave soldiers. I would like to read to you the greatest possible number of their messages, as well as the addresses of those for whom they are intended, and who are in anguish. Pass the news along.... It is your mother country who is speaking to you.[24]

There were many similar propaganda broadcasts aimed at Quebec throughout the war, constantly congratulating French Canada for being loyal to the "mother country" by rejecting the "English" war. Whether these had any effect on Quebec public opinion is not known, but they certainly must have sharpened External Affairs' appetite for intelligence on French matters, whether Vichy or Gaullist.

No documents have yet been released in Canada that indicate the methods used by the Examination Unit to attack Free French ciphers in 1943. In 1990 the elderly veterans of the French section were reminded of their oaths of secrecy and forbidden to discuss anything that pertained to the Free French or even to acknowledge that Free French messages were being read. Nevertheless, documents in archives in Britain and France make it possible to reconstruct, in part, what occurred.

A few days after the landings in Algeria, the Americans seized the colony's short-wave wireless transmitter, radio station "Eucalyptus." In the ensuing months, while American and German forces battled each other in eastern Algeria and Tunisia, they added three more transmitters to the station, making it capable of broadcasting to Europe and to the entire Western Hemisphere. The Americans then turned it over to the French authorities in Algeria, on the understanding that it would be used for Allied propaganda and press reports. They were to get a nasty surprise.[25]

The cost of keeping de Gaulle out of North Africa was that someone else had to be found to replace him as leader there. At first the Americans went with the notoriously pro-Vichy Admiral Darlan. When he was assassinated on Christmas Eve, 1942, the American-backed General Henri-Honoré Giraud replaced him. The choice could not have been worse.

Giraud, then sixty-three, had been captured by the Germans in 1940 and held in the prisoner-of-war camp at Konigstein. In April 1942 he escaped. Upon arrival back in France, where he went into hiding, he told an elaborate story of braiding a rope together from the strings of prisoner-of-war parcels and sliding down on it more than one hundred feet. He told of a midnight dash through the woods, a mysterious rendezvous and a change of clothes, plus tense moments on a train chatting with a German officer and pretending to be an Alsatian. He claimed the Germans had put a price on his head and that he offered to surrender only in exchange for 400,000 French prisoners of war.

Even fifty years later, mystery surrounds Giraud's alleged escape. He was well into the autumn of his physical abilities and known to have had a very bad back, making it improbable that he could descend one hundred feet on a pencil-thin home-made rope. After the war, the German General Heinz Guderian said Giraud escaped simply by breaking parole and walking away—he was confined only on his word of honour. When he disappeared, Guderian added, the Germans did not worry much about it because they considered him a military incompetent.[26]

Nevertheless, when Giraud turned up in hiding in France, the British made the most of it in their propaganda broadcasts from the BBC. They also saw to it that Roosevelt received a description of Giraud's escape, apparently written in the general's own breathless prose. The President was impressed and the Americans began secretly to negotiate with him. On the night of November 4, 1942, a British submarine spirited Giraud away from the darkened shores of the Riviera. Just six weeks later Admiral Darlan was assassinated. His killer was caught on the spot, immediately court-martialled on Giraud's order, and executed the same night. Giraud then took over the French administration of North Africa.[27]

The whole business seems likely to have been engineered by the

British secret services. Darlan's killer, a young, fervently anti-Vichy student by the name of Fernand Bonnier de la Chapelle, had been receiving weapons training at a British-run Special Operations Executive camp in Algeria just before the attack. Also implicated—he had supplied the weapon—was an OSS instructor at the SOE camp who had received his training from the British at Camp X. The Deuxième Bureau, the French secret service, is widely believed to have engineered Giraud's escape and, although ostensibly loyal to Vichy, it is known to have maintained secret contacts with British Intelligence, especially MI6. In the few hours between his capture and execution, the young man kept insisting that his friends would intervene at any moment. He was quite surprised to die.[28]

If the plan had been to replace the Fascist Darlan with someone other than de Gaulle, then in the deepest disfavour with Churchill, it backfired spectacularly. Giraud turned out to be more Vichy than Pétain. He was also stupid.

One of the first things Giraud did when he took over as the High Commissioner for France in Africa was to give a speech in Senegal extolling the virtues of the leaders of Vichy. He also imprisoned ten people without trial, on suspicion that they were involved in the Darlan killing. He snubbed de Gaulle's overtures from London proposing cooperation.[29] Next he allowed Radio Eucalyptus to make contact with South America and with Axis-leaning Chile and Argentina. The American military authorities in North Africa forbade it. The French tried to do it anyway and a message to Chile was intercepted. Giraud was told to stop such activity *immediately.* Then a U.S. monitoring station in Cairo intercepted a French message to Argentina.[30]

This was too much.

In June 1943 the Americans and British arm-twisted Giraud into coming to terms with de Gaulle. The latter was finally allowed to go to North Africa and the two men formed the French Committee of National Liberation, more or less dividing its leadership between them. By virtue of his personality, intellect, and leadership qualities, de Gaulle soon gained the upper hand.

Both men, however, failed to pay attention to one absolute necessity in the conduct of military and diplomatic affairs. They did not look to the security of their codes and ciphers. In the brief six months that Giraud had ruled alone in Algeria he had tried to set up his own Free French organization by sending his own representatives to the United States, Britain, and other countries. For the inevitable secret communications that would be necessary, his Secrétariat des Relations Extérieurs had needed its own codes and ciphers—quickly. Expediency had outweighed security. The answer had been to utilize existing Vichy codes.

The danger of this practice was not lost on Colonel Joubert des Ouches, the head of the French Committee of National Liberation's code and cipher department. On November 4, 1943, he warned that Free French codes were not secure. In a memo to his superiors, he wrote that the art of cryptanalysis had made such enormous strides that all codes "not seriously protected by super-encipherments risk being broken." He cited as particularly vulnerable the diplomatic codes that had been adopted from Vichy: CTX and PCN9. It was absolutely urgent, he insisted, that new codes be devised.

This was easier said than done. The Free French did not have the resources to undertake a complete overhaul of the codes in use. The best that could be done was to give new super-encipherments to those Free French missions still using CTX (Europe and the Middle East) and PCN9 (South America). For the most important post of all, Washington, Colonel Joubert had less of a problem. The delegation there had been given a former Vichy naval code, HCW, camouflaged by "très nombreux additives."[31]

Inevitably, large organizations compartmentalize. At the Government Code and Cipher School, naval and military codes and ciphers were worked on at Bletchley Park and diplomatic ones at Berkeley Street. In the United States the separation was even more rigid. The U.S. Navy's Op-20-G worked exclusively on naval traffic, and the U.S. Army's Arlington Hall exclusively on military and diplomatic messages. Never the twain would meet. American and British cryptanalysts working on Free French diplomatic traffic had the former Vichy diplomatic codebooks at hand but apparently not the naval ones.

If Colonel Joubert had been able to use one-time pads like those supplied by the British to de Gaulle, he could have made Free French messages absolutely secure. But distributing one-time pads worldwide is a difficult problem of logistics. Joubert elected to do the super-encipherments on the old codes by arithmetical formulas. De Gaulle's error when he moved to Algeria as co-chairman of the French Committee of National Liberation was to accept these super-enciphered codes for his own use.

It is easy to see how the Examination Unit broke into the new generation of Free French messages. Nearly every Vichy numerical code was known. With the help of the Hollerith machines introduced to the Joint Discrimination Unit in mid-1943, the cryptanalysts were able to subtract the known code values from the cipher texts of messages to get the super-encipherment numbers. These then could be analysed for the formulas that generated them. Other code values could then be obtained by reversing the process.

In principle, it was simple. In practice, even with the help of machines, it was a laborious process. Nevertheless, by late 1943 the Canadians—and undoubtedly the Americans and the British also—were reading at least some of the diplomatic communications between the French Committee for National Liberation in Algiers and its diplomatic missions abroad.[32]

This time, being small worked to the Examination Unit's advantage. Not having had the luxury of being able to restrict itself to either Vichy naval or diplomatic codes, it had worked on both. Consequently, when the super-encipherments were stripped from Free French messages out of Washington, the code groups were recognizable. It was then simply a matter of plucking the completed Vichy naval codebook off the shelf.

The U.S. Army cryptanalysts at Arlington Hall did not have the same opportunity. In 1942 the Canadians had shared the Vichy naval code and its encipherments with the U.S. Navy, but this information apparently did not get to the Army. Arlington had no way of knowing that Free French intercepts between Washington and Algiers were based on a known code. The same appears to have held true at the Government Code and Cipher School. The Examination Unit found itself the exclusive master of one of the most important sources of Free French political intelligence.[33]

It is important to remember that Canada was not party to the Anglo–American decision to share diplomatic ULTRA that arose from the 1943 agreement between Arlington and the Government Code and Cipher School. The Canadians may not even have known about it. The Examination Unit received no diplomatic decrypts from the Americans, so there was no reason to send them any. On the other hand, some time in late 1943 or early 1944, the Canadians began regularly sending Free French decrypts to London via BSC.[34]

In the spring of 1944, de Gaulle finally managed to shunt Giraud aside to become sole chairman of the French Committee of National Liberation. By this time the FCNL had grown into a full-fledged alternative government to Vichy, complete with its own armed forces, diplomatic service, and administrative infrastructure. De Gaulle, quite reasonably, wanted it recognized as the future provisional government of France, ready to take over from Vichy the moment Allied troops landed in the invasion that was sure to come. While the British were grudgingly ready to bow to the inevitable, the Americans were not.

Upon hearing that the commander-in-chief of the pending invasion of France, General Dwight D. Eisenhower, intended to set up his own civil adminstration in France rather than allow it to be done by the Free French, de Gaulle's representative in Washington complained to the Secretary of State, Cordell Hull. He reported the conversation to Algiers in secret cipher:

Washington: June 1, 1944

> Mr. Cordell Hull ... repeated several times, with much force, that only the President could answer these questions. He added that he didn't know whether the President would reply, or whether he would reply partially or in full, or even how he might choose to convey his answers to you. All French matters are subject to the exclusive decisions of the President. Cordell Hull had absolutely nothing to tell me. [35]

"This is a very interesting telegram," Hume Wrong wrote Norman

Robertson as he sent him a copy of Examination Unit decrypt FG-2072. "It confirms, from the mouth of Mr. Hull, what we have understood to be the case. It also indicates the strain between State Department and White House on French matters."[36]

In the two months leading up to D-Day, the June 6, 1944 Allied invasion of France, both the Americans and the British treated de Gaulle and his French Committee of National Liberation shoddily. They ignored suggestions that the Free French supply administrators to supplant Vichy officials in liberated territory. They dismissed warnings that the invasion troops were being issued with too much money, which would cause serious inflation in war-wracked France. Most of all, they adamantly refused to recognize the French Committee of National Liberation as the rightful interim government to replace Vichy.

It was all very, very nasty, and descended to a personal level. Churchill once again imposed restrictions on Free French communications, this time isolating de Gaulle in Algeria from his diplomatic and military officials in London. When there was some hesitation about taking such an extreme step with an "ally," Churchill responded sharply:

> Surely we are not in this man's hands in this matter? We can stop his wireless absolutely. In my opinion, it should be stopped. I would certainly never make an appeal to him. He might possibly be invited over before the show begins in order to placate him as much as possible. Meanwhile, all means of communication out of the country with the Free French in Algiers should be prevented, unless they come under our Censorship. I thought this had been settled long ago.[37]

Cutting de Gaulle off from his staff in London enabled General Eisenhower, the Supreme Allied Commander, to discuss political questions surrounding the invasion with General Koenig, the leader of the Free French forces who had fought alongside the British in North Africa two years earlier. The hero of Bir Hacheim, it seems, was infinitely preferable to de Gaulle.

The Canadians followed all this political manoeuvring through

Free French decrypts. While there was nothing coming out of London, messages cabled out of Washington were intercepted and the Army's Special Wireless Station in Ottawa (Leitrim) monitored Radio Station Eucalyptus in Algeria.[38] The following is a sample of some of the comments made on the decrypts as they were passed through External Affairs to Norman Robertson, the undersecretary:

TOP SECRET
June 1, 1944

Re. FG-1973

The French in Washington have been informed by the United States authorities concerning financial arrangements which have been made in London governing the Allied landings in France. They are much exercised over this news but have no first-hand information. This is a good indication of the difficulties which have been caused to the French by the ban on codes and travel.

FG-1981

M. Massigli [de Gaulle's foreign minister] denies that Gen. Keonig's conversations are official in character. There would seem to be some basic misunderstanding between London, Washington and Algiers.

TOP SECRET
June 14, 1944

Re: FG-2150

M. Hoppenot has informed Dr. Stettinius concerning the change in name of the FCNL [to Provisional Government of France]. Mr. Stettinius greeted this announcement by talking of

French disunity and of American soldiers shedding their blood to liberate France. [39]

From May 19 to August 4, 1944, the Examination Unit produced 1,182 such decrypts for the benefit of those in External Affairs who were responsible for setting Canada's foreign policy.[40] Norman Robertson and Mackenzie King were able to follow the trials and tribulations of the Free French in exhaustive detail, both before and after the landings in Normandy. Thanks to the Examination Unit, Churchill and the Foreign Office were able to do so also.

The British, indeed, elaborated on the opportunity. De Gaulle was invited to England just before the cross-Channel Normandy invasion. As a condition of his coming, he insisted that he be allowed to communicate secretly with his officials back in Algiers. After arrangements were made for his messages to go by undersea cable via Gibraltar, the Foreign Office issued a further order:

> When the scheme comes into operation, it is important that copies of all of de Gaulle's incoming and outgoing cypher telegrams should be sent to Commander Denniston.... Note. Should get de Gaulle's figures in triplicate and say we need extra copy for filing in case letters scrambled, but in fact will send extra figures to Denniston automatically. [41]

Commander Denniston, of course, was the head of the diplomatic and commercial division of the Government Code and Cipher School at Berkeley Street. De Gaulle was not going to have any secrets if the British could help it.

Exactly when the Americans were permitted to dip into this cornucopia of intelligence is uncertain. The Arlington–GC&CS agreement of 1943 provided for an American liaison officer at Berkeley Street with access to all diplomatic decrypts. Almost all. The Foreign Office reserved the right to withhold what it liked. By the end of 1944, however, the British were supplying the Americans with Free French decrypts from both Canadian and British sources.[42]

The Canadians, at least, had no axes to grind as they followed the fortunes of the Free French. The Foreign Office summaries sent to External Affairs had generally condemned de Gaulle, but the information in the decrypts allowed Norman Robertson and Mackenzie King to make up their own minds about the general. If anything, they admired him. Mackenzie King generally took de Gaulle's side when his name came up, usually acrimoniously, in conversation with Churchill and Roosevelt. With the soft persistence so characteristic of him, the Canadian Prime Minister pressed them to accept de Gaulle as the proper person to lead a liberated France. On June 15, 1944, Mackenzie King noted in his diary: "I expressed my sympathy with D. G.— though he is very troublesome—as being entitled to every consideration in the light of fighting from the first for France."[43]

Roosevelt and Churchill had no choice in the end. In the weeks following D-Day, as British, American, and Canadian armies bit deeper and deeper into France, it became clear that the liberated French were enthusiastically ready to receive the French Committee of National Liberation as their provisional government. De Gaulle was no longer as easily snubbed, and in July 1944 he was invited to Washington for talks with Roosevelt. Mackenzie King was quick to ask him to stop by in Canada as well.

"If the general would accept the invitation he would be warmly welcomed by the people," the Free French representative in Ottawa reported to Algiers. "This welcome would be out of proportion to the timidity that has been shown towards us by the Canadian government in its concern never to do anything ahead of Washington."[44] Norman Robertson undoubtedly read that remark.

De Gaulle arrived in Ottawa on July 11, 1944. There were crowds, and cheering, and presentations. Mackenzie King was impressed by the general and much moved by what he saw as the historical significance of the visit. He described it in page after page of his diary, writing at length about their conversations and his perception of de Gaulle's nobility of purpose. The next day, de Gaulle presented Mackenzie King with a parting gift.

It touched me deeply that he should have handed me a framed photo of himself. I did not unwrap the picture until coming back to the library at Laurier House. We had a little talk together and I walked with him to his plane. Shook hands with him, three times holding his hand in mine and looking into his eyes and wishing him well. I told him that his visit had been a great inspiration and would do great good.

Mackenzie King, so very lonely in his personal life, believed he had found a friend.

The Examination Unit continued to decrypt Free French secret messages as before.

————————

Until the Canadian Government releases the relevant documents, or releases the Examination Unit veterans from their oaths of secrecy, it cannot be determined how completely the Canadians had penetrated the codes and ciphers of the Free French and de Gaulle's provisional government of 1944–45. What is known is that by 1944 the French section was the largest and most active group with a staff of about twenty-five. Its chief cryptanalyst was C. D. (Dana) Rouillard, after the war a professor of French at the University of Toronto. His specialty was transposition ciphers and book breaking.

The expert in French substitution systems was A. F. (Fred) Poole, after the war a high school teacher in Vancouver. Gilbert Robinson, the deputy head of the Examination Unit and later professor of mathematics at the University of Toronto, also helped with cryptanalysis. In addition, there were at least four people involved in decoding, plus others responsible for translation, filing, and editing. The finished decrypts were sent to R. G. Riddell, later a career officer in External Affairs, for commentary and distribution. Mary Oliver, Norman Robertson's sister, was in charge of office management.

By early 1945 this team had broken enough Free French codes and ciphers to compile them into a chart showing where and how they were used, and how they were related.[45]

There is no doubt the Examination Unit was freely reading the Free French HCW secret cipher. This is clearly shown by matching the decrypt summaries cited earlier with the actual messages in the archives of the Ministère des Affaires Etrangères in Paris. The forms on which the messages were written when they arrived in Algiers indicate whether they were received in Simple Code, Secret Cipher, or Top Secret Code. The summaries of Examination Unit decrypts identified in External Affairs archives match those messages received in Secret Cipher. This was the super-enciphered code cited by Colonel Joubert.[46]

Of particular interest, however, is whether the Canadians were reading the Top Secret Code. This was probably supplied by the Gaullists when the French Committee of National Liberation was formed. It was used for sending intelligence reports. If the Canadians had been able to read it, it is difficult to calculate how they would have reacted to the information contained in some of the messages.

Mackenzie King was not the only person perplexed and anxious about the lack of support for the war in French-speaking Canada. The Free French, dedicated to freeing their homeland from German occupation and Vichy domination, also wanted to know why one of the largest French-speaking populations outside France—directly descended from the French—did not share the same vision. They set about finding out.

In early 1943, the Free French arranged for a refugee Polish priest named Father Tadeusz Kotowski to tour Quebec to assess the attitude of the Catholic Church authorities toward the war. He spent over two months going around the province, ostensibly trying to drum up interest in a "Catholic plan of action." His subsequent report to the Free French in Algiers was not encouraging. From the cardinal down, he found the leadership of the Quebec clergy reluctant to take sides, and often strongly in favour of Vichy and Marshall Pétain.

Cardinal Villeneuve, the ecclesiastical head of the Catholic Church in Quebec, received Kotowski cordially enough. He suggested that the Polish priest discuss his plan with the cardinal's chief assistant, Monsignor Pelletier, who told Kotowski flatly that he was totally opposed to it. Catholics should remain the same in war or peace. Moreover, French Canadians were not at war, only supporting it. Kotowski noted that the Free French could expect no help from Pelletier and that he was very influential among the Dominicans at Laval University.

It was the same story at the University of Montreal, where the rector, Monsignor Valois, "politely" blocked Kotowski at every turn. The Church in Quebec, Kotowski observed, enjoyed a strong hold on the people and therefore preferred the rigid social stability and order exemplified by the Vichy regime. (Pétain had changed France's motto from Liberty, Equality, Fraternity to Work, Family, Fatherland.) Even more important, according to the Polish priest, was the opposition of the Jesuits. He wrote that they were very influential, especially among young French Canadians, and their anti-war stand arose from "anti-British sentiment and fear of social change which would cause them to lose their temporal influence on Quebec society." He described the Jesuits as having "une action dangereuse."

Some of this negative attitude, Kotowski concluded, was a result of lobbying by the apostolic delegate to Canada, Monsignor Antoniutti. He was having a strong effect on parish priests and congregations. He was inspired, said Kotowski, by a sense of anti-Communism, a desire to keep up the temporal power of the Catholic Church, and by the fact that he was an Italian and had an "implicit understanding with the [Fascist] regimes of Mussolini and Franco." Kotowski recommended that positive steps be taken to thwart Antoniutti's activities.[47]

It is not known whether the Free French were able to act on that suggestion. However, a year later the first two pages of Kotowski's report—minus its recommendations that the Free French take direct action to counter the Quebec clergy's support of Vichy—mysteriously began circulating in the province. It caused a flare of indignation in Parliament and the Quebec press, which rapidly fizzled a month later when newsreels showed Canadian troops dying on the beaches of Normandy. External Affairs had little doubt that it had been prepared by the Free French and deliberately released by them.[48]

Indeed, anti-war sentiment in Quebec remained a consistent preoccupation of the Free French. Throughout 1943 and 1944, de Gaulle's representative in Ottawa, Gabriel Bonneau, continued regularly to monitor pro-Vichy sentiment and activities, sending his reports back to Algiers in Top Secret Code.

The situation came to a head during de Gaulle's 1944 visit. Unnoticed by English-speaking Canada, it was marred by the pointed failure

of Cardinal Villeneuve to be on hand to greet de Gaulle. According to
Bonneau, in another Top Secret report, his informants (his spies, in
other words), had told him that the cardinal had decided not to meet
de Gaulle because of the protests he had received from within the hier-
archy of the Church.

> One can see in this attitude of the Canadian clergy a remaining
> hostility toward the general, toward Free France, and toward all
> that opposes Vichy and Marshal Pétain. This religious factor,
> which has so much contributed to fashioning [French] Canada
> and has assured its survival, will weaken the present, threaten the
> future, and strike a blow at the permanent and essential interests of
> France and the French spirit.

Because the Gaullist movement was perceived by the Quebec clergy as
a threat to social order and therefore anti-Church, Bonneau cautioned
that the Free French must be careful not to be seen as interfering in
Canadian affairs. They should also, he added, not show any more open
support for England than they could help.[49]

At the end of the summer, when Canadian newspapers were running banner headlines on the Allied pursuit of the Germans into
northern France and the liberation of Paris, Bonneau reported on the
ecstatic crowd in Montreal that gathered to cheer the release of former
Montreal mayor Camilien Houde, arrested in 1940 under the Defence
of Canada Regulations for publicly counselling Quebeckers to defy the
National Registration Act. It was an example, Bonneau noted, of continuing pro-Fascist feeling in Quebec.[50]

Bonneau's Top Secret messages were being transmitted when the
Examination Unit was reading much, if not all, of what he was sending
in his diplomatic cipher. Was the Examination Unit, and therefore
External Affairs, reading his intelligence reports as well?

De Gaulle was received in triumph in Paris, and by the end of
September 1944 he was the acknowledged leader of the *de facto* provisional government of liberated France. This time Cardinal Villeneuve,
on a visit to the Pope and to Canadian troops fighting in Europe,
wanted to call on him. De Gaulle told Bonneau that he would not see

Villeneuve unless he could explain why he had failed to receive him when he visited Ottawa two months earlier. Bonneau explained the problem to Norman Robertson, the undersecretary of state for External Affairs.

Neither the French nor the English press noticed the cardinal's absence at the time, Robertson observed. No damage was done, so why shouldn't de Gaulle let the Paris visit go ahead? Besides, Robertson smoothly added, any explanation the cardinal might give was bound to be unsatisfactory...[51]

How much did Robertson really know?

CHAPTER TEN

A HOUSE DIVIDED

JANUARY — DECEMBER 1944

A T THE BEGINNING OF 1944, the various Allied intelligence authorities knew that jet aircraft, liquid-fuelled rockets, silent submarines, and nascent nuclear reactors were emerging from the drawing boards of German science and industry. But it takes time to bring innovative ideas into production, and Germany did not have much left. Even Mackenzie King ventured cautious optimism:

> R. [Robertson] gave an interesting account of some of the intercep-
> tions being made by the British and the Americans of messages
> between Japan and Germany. One of the number was direct from
> Hitler, indicating that his intention was to wage a very heavy war
> against the Americans and the British in Italy. However, what he
> said he was going to do to Russia has not come to pass.

A few days later Canada's stodgy Prime Minister also noted in his diary:

> … no news tonight because of the hockey match—a serious reflec-
> tion on the mentality of the people at the time of a victory loan
> campaign.[1]

Mackenzie King's complacency was not shared by Tommy Stone and Canada's service directors of intelligence, especially Colonel Murray and Commander Little. The ability to decrypt and read enciphered messages was immensely gratifying, but the Examination Unit had been created in time of war; all three men wondered whether there would there be a place for code- and cipher-breaking when the shooting stopped.

The Canadian special intelligence service had evolved in a different way from that of the British. At the Government Code and Cipher School, traffic analysis and cryptanalysis were integrated at both Bletchley Park and Berkeley Street. In Ottawa, the Joint Discrimination Unit did the initial sorting and analysis of incoming intercepts in the La Salle Academy, while the Examination Unit did the code- and cipher-breaking ten blocks away in the house on Laurier Avenue.

There appears to have been little doubt in the minds of Murray, Little, and Stone that actually reading enciphered messages was more valuable than just analysing them. When Canada did only the latter, it had to rely on the British or the Americans for the finished intelligence, which usually had not been forthcoming. The British had not returned the full file of Abwehr decrypts in 1942 and cooperation on diplomatic traffic in 1943 had extended to raw material only. Colonel Murray's repeated requests to see JMA decrypts—the messages of the Japanese military attachés—had been refused outright. As far as top-grade German ENIGMA and Japanese PURPLE decrypts, only a carefully selected few reached Canada.

By the beginning of 1944, it was clear that if Canada really wanted to have the intelligence products of wireless interception, it had to do its own cryptanalysis. That meant manpower. At the Y Committee meetings, Murray and Little urged maximum expansion of the Examination Unit. Yet there was no hard argument in favour of it that could be taken to the Chiefs of Staff. Then the British offered what seemed a terrific opportunity.

Government Code and Cipher School interest in Japanese military and naval traffic had declined throughout 1943, in direct proportion to increasing American dominance of the field. The war in the Pacific, moreover, was mainly an American war. Except for Burma, the British had few troops to spare for the fighting in the Far East. But they did have the Royal Navy, whose capital ships no longer had German or Italian opponents. Once the invasion of Europe was accomplished, the Admiralty's battleships and heavy cruisers would be available for the fight against the Japanese.

Ships at sea, however, must have good weather forecasting. The British recognized that the best source for that information was the Japanese themselves. The enemy had an elaborate weather-reporting system throughout the Pacific, the information going out in its own special codes and ciphers. The British had a small team working on this traffic, and while he was on a visit to Bletchley in late 1943, Stone was asked by Commander Travis and Captain Hastings if the Canadians would like to take over the job. Stone jumped at the chance.[2]

Canada's Defence Minister, J. L. Ralston, was then in Britain and was invited to Bletchley. Captain Hastings easily persuaded him to support the idea. Back in Canada, Stone quickly obtained approval from the Y Committee and External Affairs. Norman Robertson noted that "the particular intelligence in question is not of direct interest to this department but the expansion of Canadian work in cryptography is of very considerable interest."

The plan was ambitious. The British suggested about 100 cryptographic personnel would be required, an experienced nucleus of ten supplied by the Government Code and Cipher School, and the rest provided by Canada. The whole party would be moved to Victoria, B.C., where a new listening station would be set up with twenty-five receivers. One-time pads would be distributed to those in the United States and Britain who were to receive the deciphered weather reports, which were to be re-enciphered immediately and sent out by wireless.

In utmost secrecy, the scheme rapidly went forward. Both the U.S. Army and Navy approved it. Canada's War Cabinet gave it the green light. Personnel were recruited. By the beginning of March 1944, the first advance parties were ready to be sent to Victoria. Suddenly the plan was killed.

The capture in February of some Japanese cipher tables had enabled Op-20-G to read some of the weather reports. The U.S. Navy became convinced of their operational value and decided, as so often before, that it did not need anyone's help to work on the traffic. The Navy would do the job itself, the admirals decreed. Tony Kendrick of the Examination Unit got the bad news in mid-March while in Washington attending a second U.S. Army-sponsored conference on ULTRA intelligence. The need for a Canadian "Meteorological Cryptographic Unit" evaporated.[3]

It so happened, however, that at that second Washington conference, Captain Drake's Joint Discrimination Unit gained precisely what had always eluded the Examination Unit—true partnership with the Americans and British on signals intelligence and a solid reason for expansion to the end of the war.

A veritable *Who's Who* in special intelligence met at Arlington on March 13, 1944. The nine-member Government Code and Cipher School delegation was led by Commander Travis and included senior Japanese specialists, backed up by the new GC&CS liaison officer to the United States, Colonel John Tiltman, and communications expert Benjamin deForest Bayly. Canada sent both Drake and Kendrick plus three of their top assistants. Nearly all of Arlington's top brass were there, beginning with Carter Clarke, head of Special Branch, and running down the Signal Security Agency chain of command from its new chief, Colonel W. Preston Corderman, to its top cryptanalysts, Abraham Sinkov and William Friedman. Even Australia's Central Bureau was represented and, for a change, the U.S. Navy acknowledged the importance of the meeting by sending one of its top specialists, Commander Joseph Wenger, as an observer.[4]

In the round table that followed, Arlington was given absolute suzerainty over all Japanese Army and Air Force communications. Several important Japanese military systems had been deciphered, and the Americans were keen to exploit the breakthroughs rapidly and fully. Other traffic also appeared within reach. The British, and therefore the Canadians, conceded that the Signal Security Agency should be the central coordinating headquarters for military ULTRA in the Pacific, exclusive of naval traffic. All raw traffic was to go to Arlington and all cryptanalysis assignments were to emanate from it, the results to be returned for final processing and distribution by the U.S. Army's Military Intelligence Service.[5]

The new arrangement put Bletchley Park's Japanese military section completely out of the picture and Drake's Joint Discrimination Unit in. From now to the end of the war, the work at the La Salle Academy in Ottawa became a kind of American branch-plant operation. Arlington set the tasks, distributed the raw material, and received the results.

The Examination Unit was not part of the marriage. It continued to work on its own, breaking as many Japanese diplomatic messages as it could handle, primarily for the edification of External Affairs. Cooperation with Arlington did improve, however. In exchange for Drake's Army listening stations being placed on specific Japanese military assignments, the Americans offered to supply the Examination Unit with whatever raw intercepts it wished. They also freely supplied cryptographic tips relevant to the message systems the Canadians were working on.

Arlington was so helpful that it was sometimes almost embarrassing. When Kendrick one day asked the Americans for anything they could spare that would be useful to his Japanese military section, he received a train shipment under armed guard consisting of five tons of IBM punch cards. The Canadians wound up storing the boxes of cards on the rafters in the attic of the house on Laurier Avenue. They were never used.[6]

Increased cooperation with Arlington did not, in the view of some, make up for the loss of the meteorological unit. At the Y Committee meeting following the March conference, Captain de Marbois said that as far as he was concerned the U.S. Navy intended to control all Japanese naval wireless intelligence throughout the world and that the U.S. Army was headed the same way. He informed his fellow committee members that he did not see any future for the Canadian Navy in wireless intelligence; therefore, he had offered some of his Japanese specialists to the Admiralty for use at its centre in Colombo, Ceylon.

The other committee members were taken aback, especially since the naval specialists that de Marbois was so willing to give away were with the Joint Discrimination Unit. Commander Little quickly countered by saying that they should not be too hasty. Perhaps, he suggested, they could get approval for a tri-service Joint Cryptographic

Unit to replace the failed meteorological unit.[7] It was the beginning of an open dispute between the two naval members of the Y Committee that was to last for the next year.

As the Canadian Navy's wireless intelligence chief, de Marbois certainly had reason for his views. On a trip to Washington a little later, he found out that Op-20-G had 6,500 people working on Japanese naval traffic, and that the Australian Navy wireless intelligence unit in Melbourne had been completely absorbed by the Americans. In comparison, Britain's Government Code and Cipher School then had only about fifty people working on Japanese naval communications, some of them hastily recruited from the French and Italian naval sections and devoid of even elementary training. Most were doing traffic analysis. Actual code- and cipher-breaking was minimal.

The British had little reason to try harder. A Canadian officer visiting Bletchley was told that the Admiralty received all the Japanese material it required from the U.S. Navy through "the system of 'BRUSA' (British–U.S.A.) communications"—a cable and wireless net that linked Bletchley with the U.S. Navy's intercept and cryptographic centres in Washington, Pearl Harbor, and Melbourne, Australia. (This network was entirely separate from the U.S. Army one then involving Arlington, Bletchley, Central Bureau, New Delhi, and Ottawa.) The British could not even pretend to compete against Op-20-G with a staff numbered in the thousands and over a hundred tabulating machines. The best the Admiralty could do was develop its intercept centres at Colombo and on the Cocos Islands to cover some of the gaps in American coverage. Yet even this plan was stymied, de Marbois was told, because of a "startling" shortage of trained staff.[8]

De Marbois intended to help the Admiralty and there may have been a little nationalism in the friction that followed. He was Royal Navy and Commander Little was Canadian Navy. Colonel Murray, the Y Committee chairman, was also Canadian Army through and through. He and Little saw absolutely eye-to-eye on the need for Canada to have its own signals intelligence capability in war or peace.

At the next meeting of the Y Committee, de Marbois went too far. Insisting that he should give some of his staff away, he declared that the Canadian Navy's wireless intelligence organization was "in sheer duplication" to that of the U.S. Navy. It was receiving a full range of Japanese ULTRA intelligence from Op-20-G, as was the Government Code and Cipher School, and the intelligence centres in Australia and Ceylon. Little shot back that it was unacceptable for the Canadian Navy to be "denuded" of its wireless specialists. Later, when de Marbois attempted to get the words "sheer duplication" erased from the minutes (which went to the Chiefs of Staff) Colonel Murray would not allow it. What was said, was said.[9]

When the U.S. Navy killed the proposed meteorological unit, it also caused complications for Tommy Stone and Norman Robertson. Stone had inflated the number of cryptographic personnel needed from 100 to 200, and had persuaded the undersecretary to approach the Prime Minister with a proposal calling for the amalgamation of all "highly secret intelligence"—cryptanalysis, censorship, and "the work of secret agents"—under the authority of a single, super-committee consisting of the Prime Minister, the Defence Minister, and the President of the National Research Council.

In drafting the proposal, Stone commented that "in highly secret intelligence in a small way we have nevertheless reached the point at which security considerations are equally strong as in the U.K. and the U.S." The new super-committee, he wrote, would also "avoid the confusion which now exists in the U.S."[10]

None of Stone's suggestions appear to have caused so much as a blink from Canada's Prime Minister. Mackenzie King approved the proposal just a few days before Robertson learned that the plan for the meteorological unit had been scrapped.[11]

A month or so later, Stone drew up an even more elaborate memo, calling for the amalgamation of the Examination Unit and the Joint Discrimination Unit into a Canadian equivalent of the Government Code and Cipher School, with the Y Committee being reorganized along the lines of the Signal Intelligence Board which had replaced the British Y Committee. Colonel Murray warmly supported Stone's proposal and the Canadian Y Committee unanimously approved it.[12]

Stone also sent a copy of this memo to William Stephenson, the director of British Security Coordination, who probably passed it on to MI6 chief Stewart Menzies. Although Stephenson had nothing to do with the Allied exchange of wireless traffic conducted through his office, he still dabbled in counter-espionage for MI6 in the Western Hemisphere. From October 1942 onward, BSC had supplied External Affairs with weekly Latin American intelligence reports, presumably from Stephenson's own spies and observers. They were not highly regarded. In July 1944, Hugh Keenleyside had occasion to review the entire collection and reported they were characterized "by what can only be described as a rather hysterical tone.... There have been clear misstatements of fact and in others the interpretation has been contrary to what has been accepted as reasonable in this Division." Shortly after Keenleyside's negative assessment the reports were dropped.[13]

External Affairs had a far more useful and important source of intelligence in the OSS. By mid-1944 Herbert Norman's little Special Research Section had expanded its Japanese mandate to include all of the Far East and especially Indochina and China. This inevitably led to assessments of Russian intentions in the area and Norman frequently received reports from "American secret sources" on Russian–Japanese talks (they were not yet at war), on internal dissension in the Chiang Kai-shek regime (fighting the Japanese on the one hand and the Communist Chinese on the other), and even on the assessments of the Nationalist Chinese Army made by the Russian military attaché in Chungking. These were all supplied by OSS spies.[14]

Thus, thanks to BSC and the OSS, Stone had ample reason to feel, when he made his proposals to the Prime Minister, that actual espionage as well as cryptanalysis had a place in Canadian intelligence-gathering. Then, shortly afterward, the counter-espionage value of censorship suddenly proved itself in a startling way.

For some time previously Postal Censorship had been secretly opening all diplomatic and consular mail. When "irregularities," chiefly minor disclosures of censorable information, were identified by the censors, copies of the intercepted correspondence were sent to Stone. Usually, as in the case of the Belgian Ambassador in February and the Czechoslovakian Consul-General in March, Stone simply directed that the letters be resealed and then reopened officially as if by a censorship spot check. The irregularities could then be "routinely discovered" and brought to the attention of the writers.[15]

In early May 1944, a censor opened a package from the Peruvian Consul-General in Ottawa which had been addressed to Lima. In it he found a clutch of Department of National Defence pamphlets covering everything from chemical warfare defence to artillery firing drills and the training of airborne troops. The majority were instruction manuals for soldiers on how to use new weapons or introducing them to the combat techniques of enemy or Allied forces. They bore security classifications from Restricted to Secret. Four more packages were intercepted, bringing the total to more than a hundred pamphlets.

The discovery caused consternation in the Army. Since the breach in security was substantial, Colonel Murray was anxious to know how the Peruvian Consul had got hold of the material. As the most senior bureaucrat in External Affairs, it fell to Norman Robertson to get to the bottom of the matter. He wrote an official letter to the Consul, H. F. Davila, and demanded an explanation.

Davila reacted like a man caught red-handed. He immediately replied, effusively assuring Robertson that he never dreamed the documents were confidential (despite the word Secret stamped on almost all of them). He was merely sending them to Peru for the edification of a professor at Lima's military academy. His letter was written in such haste that Davila's command of the English language somewhat failed him:

> Being Peru a Allied country, always interested in the magnificent work that Canada is doing in the war, I thought without any knowledge in the matter and only in good earnest to render a service to my country making to know how they are working here in military teaching.

Davila, nevertheless, had not answered the key question and Robertson sent another message insisting that Davila explain how he came to have the restricted material.

A few days later, a very "distressed" Davila came to Robertson's office. He explained that he had found the pamphlets in the basement of the house he had occupied at 476 Wilbrod Street. When he was preparing to move out a month earlier they had turned up by the bundle during the general house-cleaning. Because they looked interesting, he had decided to package them up and send them home. He suggested to Robertson that they had been left behind by the previous occupant of the house, Major-General L. R. La Flèche.

Possibly because of the awkward fact that General La Flèche was the Minister of National War Services, the government department responsible for Censorship, Robertson was inclined not to pursue the issue. He accepted the Peruvian's explanation. "Davila appears reliable and straightforward," Robertson wrote George Glazebrook, who had taken over the case from Stone. "I am prepared to consider the matter closed."

The Army's security service, however, had not been idle. When the pamphlets were examined, it was noted that they were all proof copies and some bore hand-written notations. When these were shown to employees at the King's Printer, they said that the writing was that of the director, Edmond Cloutier. Robertson then wrote Cloutier. How did secret documents bearing his handwriting come to be possessed by a foreign official who was not supposed to have them? There was no answer.

Six weeks passed. The matter was finally turned over to the head of the RCMP's security and counter-espionage section, Superintendent C. E. Rivett-Carnac. It took exactly one day for that veteran of wartime police work to uncover some disturbing new information: General La Flèche had moved out of the house on May 1, 1941, and Davila had lived there ever since. Most of the pamphlets were printed between 1942 and 1944.

Here, then, was an awkward problem. The RCMP commissioner himself now got involved. Perhaps, he suggested to Robertson, the Mounties should pay the King's Printer a call? Robertson agreed. Corporal B. W. Cole was given the task. One can well imagine the beads of perspiration forming on Cloutier's brow during the ensuing interview.

Yes, Cloutier admitted, he did give the pamphlets to Davila. They were his proof copies—he received one of everything that was printed—and he had amassed quite a collection. One day he happened to meet the Peruvian Consul, who asked him if he had any material on Canada. So he gave him the pamphlets. He never dreamed they would be sent out of the country. He thought that Davila wanted them "so that he could read up on Canada and Canadian ways."

How Cloutier—or Corporal Cole, for that matter—reconciled this statement with pamphlets typically entitled: "Gun drill for 75 mm Mark I Gun on Fixed Mounting," or "The Use of Wireless in Armored Formations," or "Japanese Warfare" is only to be wondered at.

Cloutier also said that he had heard, six weeks earlier, that someone from Military Intelligence had asked his employees about the pamphlets and that they had identified his handwriting. Unfortunately, he had fallen ill suddenly and had been hospitalized. Otherwise, of course, he would have replied immediately to Robertson's letter.

Even Corporal Cole, in a "disposition" which was the very model of dispassionate reporting, could not resist noting that the covers of all the pamphlets bore a warning notice that they were not to be distributed to persons not officially connected to His Majesty's Government. The RCMP Commissioner sent Cole's report to Robertson, saying that in view of the people involved he did not intend to proceed further, save to supply "general details to the Minister of Justice for his instructions, if any."

The Canadian government apparently chose to avoid a scandal. There the matter ended.

In May 1944, both the Germans and the Allies knew that the long-awaited invasion across the Channel was a matter of weeks away. Warships and landing craft choked the ports along England's south coast. Thousands of soldiers waited in hundreds of camps across the countryside. Because Canadian soldiers were to have a major role in the opening attack, Mackenzie King made a quick visit to England to review the troops. At dinner one day with Churchill and the Allied invasion commander, General Dwight D. Eisenhower, the Canadian Prime Minister—the quintessential "Invisible Man"—listened with fascination to their conversation.

There was a long talk between Churchill and Eisenhower about

Koenig. Also quite a long conversation regarding possible use of poison gas. Eisenhower was strongly against it. Churchill was for it. Eisenhower said if it would shorten the war, say get it through by July, and was absolutely necessary, he would favour its use, but otherwise would not. Churchill said that it might mean a saving of life in the end.[16]

Something dreadful had happened to Churchill's personality after nearly five years of war. He no longer saw victory in terms of the simple unconditional surrender of Germany and Japan. He wanted to punish his enemies, and that meant killing people—lots of them.

Churchill's bloodthirstiness was familiar to Mackenzie King. During his visit to Canada for the Quebec Conference the previous August, Churchill had gloated over aerial pictures of Hamburg, devastated in a massive bombing raid in which thousands of civilians died. The thought of the deaths of so many innocent women and children sickened the Canadian Prime Minister. Churchill said he wanted to do the same to Berlin.[17]

What Mackenzie King was unaware of as he listened to Eisenhower and Churchill talk, was that Churchill knew perfectly well there would be no reason to use gas against the Germans during the invasion. The Combined Chiefs of Staff had ruled earlier that year that the Allies would not use chemical or biological weapons unless attacked with them first. It was a safe strategy. ENIGMA decrypts consistently indicated, right up to D-Day and beyond, that the Germans also had decided not to use gas except in retaliation. Yet Churchill, fully aware of this, continued to urge his Chiefs of Staff to consider using gas, against civilian as well as military targets:

> I want a cold-blooded calculation made as to how it would pay us to use poison gas, by which I mean principally mustard. We will want to gain more ground in Normandy so as not to be cooped up in a small area....
>
> I quite agree it may be several weeks or even months before I shall ask you to drench Germany with poison gas, and if we do it, let's do it 100 per cent. In the meanwhile, I want the matter studied

in cold blood by sensible people and not by that particular set of psalm-singing uniformed defeatists which one runs across now here now there.[18]

At the same time, Churchill also ordered 500,000 bombs filled with anthrax from the United States. These were specifically intended for urban targets. As anthrax spores have an extremely long life, the deadly bacteria would have made German cities uninhabitable for decades.[19] Fortunately, the British Chiefs of Staff, while never actually saying no to Churchill, contrived to block him at every turn.

Canada, having its own very active research program on biological weapons, was told of the British order for anthrax bombs. At the beginning of the year it had also received OSS reports that the Germans were likely to use botulinus toxin when the Allies invaded. This toxin, derived from the anaerobic bacteria that cause food poisoning, was the most lethal substance known. The smallest speck inhaled or touching the eye could kill. The Canadians and Americans immediately launched crash programs to develop enough anti-toxin to inoculate all their invasion troops.

At first Eisenhower's headquarters (SHAEF) approved the inoculation plan. Then, when cases of anti-toxin were already on their way to England from Canada and the United States, it reversed its stand. The inoculations were not to go ahead. The U.S. Army Chemical Warfare Service tamely acquiesced to the change in orders. The Canadians did not.

There were many anxious meetings of the Canadian War Cabinet in the weeks that followed. Mackenzie King and his ministers passionately debated the need to protect Canadian soldiers no matter what the British and the Americans did. Emissaries were dispatched to Washington to pressure the Americans into changing their minds. Canadian Military Headquarters in London was ordered to talk to the British. In both countries the Canadians got the run-around. Finally, Mackenzie King and his ministers became so frustrated that they threatened to order the inoculations unilaterally. They never made good the threat for, suddenly, it was D-Day and Canadian troops were on the beaches and there was no German attack with botulinus toxin.

It was embarrassing. The Canadians appeared to have pushed the panic button needlessly.[20]

The explanation, of course, was that the British and Americans had access to intelligence derived from ENIGMA and the Canadian authorities did not. The British and Americans knew the OSS reports were exaggerated, even false. But British policy was never to supply Canada with intelligence derived from decrypts unless absolutely necessary. Thus de Marbois received German Navy ENIGMA decrypts because they were vital to the Canadian Navy's participation in the war against the U-boats. And Mackenzie King received Japanese PURPLE decrypts when they helped show him that the Allies were winning the war. German Army ENIGMA decrypts, however, were only given to Canadian field commanders and, even then, only when they were actually engaged in battle.[21]

The incident—if Mackenzie King, his ministers, and the Canadian Chiefs of Staff finally realized what had happened—was an object lesson on the need to be a full partner with one's allies on cryptanalysis.

The National Security Agency is the ultra-secret successor to the U.S. Army's wartime Signal Security Agency. Employing more than 10,000 people, for the last fifty years it has been monitoring communications worldwide from its labyrinth headquarters at Fort Meade, Maryland, using the latest technology for electronic eavesdropping and code- and cipher-breaking. It is also the repository for all still-secret documents pertaining to wartime signals intelligence. In 1991 the NSA wrote as follows to the author:

17 December, 1991

Dear Mr. Bryden,

This is in response to your Freedom of Information Act (FOIA) request of 7 June 1990 for a copy of the collection of World War II intercepts dealing with the Free French. We have determined that

the fact of the existence or non-existence of the materials you
request is a currently and properly classified matter in accordance
with Executive Order 12356. Thus, your request is denied.[22]   .

In late April 1944, Gilbert Robinson, then the Examination Unit's second-in-command, set out for Washington to offer the Americans copies
of the Free French messages being deciphered by the Canadians.[23]

Despite the U.S. Army's avowed intention to become "self-sufficient" in diplomatic intercepts, by early 1944 it had fallen far short of
that aim, even though the A-section of its Special Branch was handling
on average 1,425 diplomatic decrypts a week, plus summaries of 900
others not worth individual translation. Though these numbers seem
impressive, in fact eighty-two per cent of Arlington's cryptographic
manpower—2,110 people out of 2,574—was then devoted to Japanese
military traffic. That left only 464 people to work on diplomatic and
commercial material. If that number still appears large, it must be
measured against the need to break all Japanese diplomatic messages
and meet State Department demands for comprehensive coverage on
Latin America, especially Mexico, Chile, Argentina, and Brazil.

It may be that Arlington and the Government Code and Cipher
School had divided responsibility for diplomatic communications as
they had for military traffic: the Americans looking after the Western
Hemisphere and the Far East and the British covering Europe and the
Middle East. In any case, by the time of the Normandy landings,
Arlington was still relying heavily on the British for diplomatic intelligence. In the summer of 1944, indeed, the U.S. Army liaison officer at
Berkeley Street was required to step up the flow of diplomatic decrypts
he was sending to Washington. Roosevelt's name was also added to the
list of those receiving the Diplomatic Summary, the weekly bulletin of
diplomatic decrypts—formerly known as the MAGIC Summary—
which also went to the Joint Chiefs of Staff, the Secretary of State, the
Secretary of War, and the Secretary of the Navy.[24]

The addition of Roosevelt to those getting the Diplomatic Sum-
mary undoubtedly reflects a growing preoccupation in the White
House with the political ramifications of liberating Europe. Once the
Allied armies were established in Normandy, it was inevitable that the

Germans would be pushed out of France. That meant a new French government, with the United States finally either accepting or rejecting de Gaulle. Political intelligence on Europe, especially on France, was at a premium. Consequently, the authorities at Arlington received Robinson warmly. Yes, they were very interested in Canadian decrypts of Free French traffic.

Robinson was that same University of Toronto mathematics professor who had gone to Washington three years earlier looking for someone to head Canada's proposed cryptographic program. It was he who had anguished over Yardley's dismissal and he who, in the intervening years, had served as deputy first to Strachey and then to Kendrick. He also served as the recording secretary on the Examination Unit committee, which now consisted of Tommy Stone, George Glazebrook, and Herbert Norman, plus the three service directors of intelligence, Colonel Murray, Commander Little, and Group Captain Stewart.

The Examination Unit committee responded enthusiastically to the deal Robinson brought back from Washington. In exchange for Middle East and Far East low-grade Vichy decrypts, Arlington proposed that it receive from Canada the equivalent in low-grade Free French messages. The Americans, Robinson explained, felt that this would save them the bother of processing low-grade Free French traffic themselves.[25] The Canadians jumped at the chance. It was the first time since early 1942 that Arlington had expressed interest in any of the Examination Unit's actual products.

At first the arrangement was disappointing. The Canadians soon found that the Vichy traffic supplied by the Americans was of little value. The low-grade, unenciphered messages contained only the dross of diplomatic communications. They dealt with the movement of personnel, budgets, newspaper summaries, and the like. The material was so innocuous that External Affairs recommended most of the Vichy messages be sent only to Herbert Norman's Special Research Section, in the hope that they might be of use in his study of events in Indochina. The Americans, similarly, found the Free French low-grade traffic they received to be of little interest.

In the summer, however, the Americans proposed that the Examination Unit send them its high-grade Free French decrypts. Here the

Canadians really had something to offer. High-grade meant the secret cipher used by de Gaulle's diplomatic representatives in Washington, a cipher that Arlington had not yet broken. Considering that by then the Allied armies had decisively broken out of Normandy, and that the remnants of the German forces were fleeing beyond Paris, Roosevelt could no longer avoid recognizing the French Committee of National Liberation as the legitimate government replacing Vichy. The Americans had every reason to want to read what was being said by de Gaulle's representatives in Washington.

By August 1944, the French section of the Examination Unit was so taxed with the need to decipher everything at hand for sending to Arlington that there was no time left to work on other Free French systems. Then, toward the end of the summer, Arlington complained that the Canadians were too slow. The Americans would look after the traffic themselves. To the great disappointment of the staff, the Examination Unit was reduced to supplying only the decrypted messages of the Free French mission in Ottawa.[26]

What caused Arlington's change of heart? After fifty years the whole subject of deciphering Free French communications is still considered secret, so the available documentary clues are scarce. There are enough of them, however, to provide a plausible explanation.

There is no doubt that Arlington had not broken the HCW cipher used by the Free French delegation in Washington. The Americans would not otherwise have wanted the decrypts. It must soon have occurred to them, however, that the Examination Unit was also sending them to the British. If so, then they ought to be available to the U.S. Army liaison officer posted to Berkeley Street. The Americans had an agreement with the British on the sharing of diplomatic ULTRA; they did not with the Canadians. It would have made much better political sense to get the decrypts from London rather than Ottawa.

This, indeed, appears to have been what happened. According to a document in the National Archives in Washington, the U.S. Army liaison officer at Berkeley Street had been pressing Commander Denniston to let him see the so-called Reserved Series of diplomatic decrypts which the Foreign Office had declared was "too hot" for general distribution. The matter led to direct talks between the Foreign Office and

U.S. Military Intelligence (G-2) in Washington. In late summer, 1944, the British finally agreed to let the Americans see virtually everything. The new deal came into effect September 1.

It would be interesting to know what the Americans thought when they discovered that the British had an inside track on de Gaulle's communications, thanks to the Examination Unit. In any event, by December 1944 the U.S. Army officer at Berkeley Street was making a daily selection of available French decrypts and sending them to the newly appointed U.S. Ambassador to France, Jefferson Caffery. These dispatches were known as the Coffee Series, possibly as a play on Caffery's name.[27]

Caffery was the same man who had set the Brazilian police on the Abwehr spy rings in 1942. His appointment to Paris scandalized the Foreign Office, but that hard-nosed, hard-drinking veteran of a thousand diplomatic battles knew how to use decrypts, and use them well.[28]

George Parkin de Twenebrokes Glazebrook loved everything British. Canadian-born, he was the son of a prominent Toronto banker and was educated at the University of Toronto. He took his MA at Oxford in 1930 and returned to Toronto with a British accent to become professor of modern history. A confirmed bachelor, he had a Jimmy Stewart appearance: a long face with the hair swept back from a high forehead. His mouthful of middle names harkened back to his Norman English ancestry and to his godfather, a noted British imperialist of the turn of the century.[29]

Glazebrook had been recruited by External Affairs in 1942, and had served since then as Tommy Stone's deputy. He had been responsible for liaison with British Security Coordination and had overseen the setting up of Camp X. He had substituted for Stone from time to time on censorship matters and on the Examination Unit and Y Committees. When Stone was posted to London in mid-1944, Glazebrook was the obvious choice to take over his secret intelligence duties. The Examination Unit was almost immediately put in jeopardy.

"With Stone's departure for London there is no one left in the

Department who is nearly as intimately acquainted as he was with the operations of the Unit," assistant undersecretary Hume Wrong wrote Norman Robertson. "The chief question is whether we should seek to maintain the activities of the Unit or to contract them with a view to their elimination."

Wrong went on to disparage the usefulness of the Examination Unit to External Affairs and to urge its termination, concluding that it "is a sideshow and ought not to be much call on the time of senior Department officers."[30]

Wrong's memo set off a running struggle to determine the postwar future of Canada's involvement in cryptanalysis, pitting External Affairs against the service directors of intelligence, especially Colonel Murray and Commander Little. Ironically, External Affairs had been the chief beneficiary of the Examination Unit's product. Yet it fell to Colonel Murray and Commander Little to champion the idea of Canada continuing with code- and cipher-breaking.

At first they were unaware of the cold counter-current suddenly flowing from External Affairs. Glazebrook requested an assessment from Tony Kendrick on the work of the Examination Unit and solicited his views on what he thought its future should be. The Englishman, quite understandably, was reluctant to make a recommendation: "I do not know, for instance, the reasons for which the Unit was founded, nor what view is taken of its potential utility in peacetime. In any case I am sure the maintainance of a purely 'nuclear' staff would be useless—the organization which we now have being little more than a nucleus."[31]

On the strength of that statement, and with the expectation that Britain would be willing to supply Canada with diplomatic decrypts in exchange for raw traffic, Glazebrook recommended to Norman Robertson that steps be taken to close the Examination Unit.

> The [French] traffic might be continued at least until the spring [of 1945] since its intelligence value to this department would be considerable during the period immediately following the cessation of hostilities with Germany.
>
> The Japanese traffic should be continued at least as long as the

[*French*]. A little later we might review the situation to see whether we would like to keep it on longer than the [*French*] and, if so, whether such a move would be practical. Meanwhile we might consider building up the [*French*] section even at the expense of the Japanese section.

All the possibilities have been examined in the last few weeks and it does not seem that we can entertain the idea of maintaining a Canadian Examination Unit.[32]

All the possibilities had definitely *not* been examined. The three service directors of intelligence—Murray, Little, and Group Captain H. R. (Ronnie) Stewart—had not been consulted. Y Committee meetings were still blissfully discussing a postwar Canadian Code and Cipher School along the lines proposed earlier by Stone. They had no idea the debate in External Affairs was leaning the opposite way. When Gilbert Robinson learned of the situation from Kendrick, he promptly dispatched his own memo to Glazebrook warning that if the department "did not maintain a Unit for diplomatic work, interception will be taken over by one or more of the Services."[33]

That forced Glazebrook to bring up the matter at the next meeting of the Examination Unit committee. Murray and Little were aghast. Murray argued at great length for the continuance of the unit, pointing out that nearly all its decrypts had been done to provide intelligence for External Affairs. The unit had only been of incidental value to the services, he said, and if External withdrew its support, the Chiefs of Staff would never agree to continue it. As Robinson noted in the minutes:

Both Colonel Murray and Commander Little were emphatic that, in their opinion, Canada's position in world affairs required the existence of a cryptographic organization. They felt that Canada could not expect to obtain information on this level from the U.K. or elsewhere without making some effort in the field itself. Not only would it be undignified to attempt to follow such a course, but it might well mean she would be excluded from such intelligence in the very critical period following the war.

Murray suggested that External Affairs nominate some single person to be in charge of all secret intelligence, including all signals intelligence and cryptanalysis. The services could provide the manpower and facilities, he offered, but External Affairs could run the whole show.[34]

Incredibly, despite Murray's remarks, Glazebrook said they should get the views of Britain's Director of Military Intelligence, General John Sinclair, who was expected to stop by in Ottawa for talks with Norman Robertson on his way to Washington. Murray and Little both made strong representations to the undersecretary before the meeting. It was Glazebrook, however, who prepared the memo that was to be given General Sinclair summarizing the issues. It was full of loaded questions designed to prompt negative answers. During the meeting with Robertson, however, Sinclair refused to be drawn into making a suggestion either way. Afterwards, Glazebrook still insisted that "it be decided not to maintain a cryptographic unit in peace time."[35]

Now Gilbert Robinson tried again. He bypassed Kendrick, Glazebrook, and Wrong with a direct appeal to Robertson. He was eloquent:

> Through the Unit and all that has come with it, Canada has been led to a window on world diplomacy which otherwise she may never have looked through. Whatever is decided concerning this office, most countries of the world will continue doing cryptographic work after the war is over and I cannot agree that Canada will improve her position in world affairs by renouncing all activity in this work.

And further:

> This is not to foresee another war, but the world will be a troubled place for a long time to come and there will undoubtedly be countries in whose activities we will be particularly interested.

And finally:

> I have wondered sometimes whether certain quarters could wish for the closing of the Examination Unit on the larger ground that,

being in the cryptographic field, Canada might sometimes have access to information of significance which might or might not concern her.[36]

At the very least, Robinson made Robertson pause. The undersecretary deferred final decision for the time being.

Robinson was correct in guessing that there were some who did not want Canada to continue with code- and cipher-breaking. While Robertson pondered the future of the Examination Unit, Glazebrook asked Stone, then in England, to solicit the views of the British Intelligence authorities. Stone went directly to Stewart Menzies, the overall head of the Government Code and Cipher School and chief of the Secret Intelligence Service (MI6). Menzies told him the Examination Unit should be closed.

Menzies, Stone reported, offered much in return. He suggested that Canada maintain its wireless intercept facilities and send all the raw traffic to Britain. In exchange, the Government Code and Cipher School would take Canada's top cryptographers, one of whom "should be specially nominated as liaison between [C] and the Under-Secretary of State for External Affairs." He would be shown everything, thereby supplying Canada with all the signals intelligence it needed.[37]

Stone's discussions with Menzies were quickly dubbed the "UK/Canada plan." When the Examination Unit committee again met, Glazebrook asked Kendrick to draft a paper on how the plan would work, for formal presentation to External Affairs. A few days later, Kendrick submitted the following for discussion:

> Under the [UK/Canada plan] Canada would receive intelligence in return for providing [the U.K.] with raw material....
>
> The [French] section produces intelligence which is of interest almost exclusively to the Department of External Affairs, and there seems no reason why its work should continue after the [UK/Canada plan] comes into operation; but if the Department maintains its interest in this material, it may wish to be assured of access to decodes of traffic at present intercepted by the cable censors in Ottawa [and in the United States and Britain].

Moreover, it is desirable that [*SSA*] should be notified as soon as possible of future developments in Canada. They [the Americans] have in part shown a tendency to be ruffled when not informed of arrangements between [*the U.K.*] and Canadian "Y" authorities.[38]

At a subsequent meeting of the Examination Unit committee, Murray, Little, and Stewart continued to oppose dropping code- and cipher-breaking. Murray argued heatedly that if External Affairs no longer wanted to break French traffic, that was its own affair, but "he would have something to say" if it was decided to discontinue Japanese work. He also said that in his opinion the cost of sending raw material by cable to Britain "would be almost as great as supporting a cryptographic unit." Little backed him up, adding that he would hate to see Canada return to its former state of "cryptographic ignorance."

Then Murray brought up a new issue—"the possible importance of [*Russian traffic*] following the close of the European war."[39]

All to no avail.

CHAPTER ELEVEN

MESSAGE
FOR STALIN

JANUARY — AUGUST 1945

To cambridge university professor Desmond Bernal, playing scientific lackey to Churchill was a big joke. The NRC's C. J. Mackenzie had encountered Bernal at the Quebec Conference in August 1943. He remembered Bernal as "quite the humorist" about being at the Prime Minister's beck and call.

Churchill and Roosevelt, with their top staffs, had met in the Citadel of Quebec City to discuss grand strategy against Japan and Germany. Up for debate, behind the cannons and ramparts of another age, was the prospect of a cross-Channel invasion of Europe in 1944. Even more important, the two leaders were to discuss nuclear research and the possibility of developing the ultimate in war-winning weapons—an atomic bomb. The meeting at Quebec was the most important Anglo–American conference of the war.

Normally, Churchill would have come to Quebec accompanied by his personal scientific adviser, Lord Cherwell, but Cherwell had become ill just before the projected trip. The Combined Operations chief, Lord Louis Mountbatten, helpfully suggested one of his own staff take his place: Bernal, who had been pestering Mountbatten about going to Quebec for some time.

Bernal was a Communist, through and through. Irish-born and contemptuous of the English Establishment, Bernal had been an outspoken proponent of Marxism at Cambridge during the 1930s. He had visited Russia on several occasions and submitted articles to Communist periodicals calling for the overthrow of capitalism. He publicly decried the tyranny of Britain's middle class and advocated that the workers take power by violence. He worshipped everything Soviet, and was, as one senior British scientist put it, "as Red as the flames of hell." He was a well-known security risk.[1]

Mountbatten, however, was apparently ignorant of Bernal's background when another Marxist scientist, P. M. S. Blackett, recommended him to Combined Operations. Mountbatten was one of Churchill's most fawning favourites and the Communist-hating Prime Minister never questioned Mountbatten's choice of scientist to accompany him to Quebec. The result was that Bernal was at Churchill's elbow during the super-secret discussions on atomic bomb development. How much he actually learned is unknown, but he delighted in telling C. J. Mackenzie what it was like to work for the Great Man himself:

> Bernal would report to Churchill at 9 or 10 o'clock. Churchill didn't get up but he worked. He said he sat in bed with all these papers in front of him and he would say, "Give me that paper. Give me this." And he would kick the right foot out. "This one down here." Then the left foot out.[2]

The irony here is that, only a few months later, Churchill put out a general reminder to the effect that "we are purging all our secret establishments of Communists because we know they owe no allegiance to us or to our cause and will always betray secrets to the Soviets."[3]

In fact there were many Communists at the heart of Britain's Most Secret endeavours. MI5 had done an excellent job of rounding up German spies and kept a good eye on subversives below officer rank in the armed forces, but it could do little with those of Communist sympathies who were part of Britain's intelligentsia, or who moved in the world of gentlemen's clubs and privilege. One of Bernal's colleagues at

Cambridge, for instance, the distinguished biochemist, J. B. S. Haldane, was discovered after the war to have been passing Admiralty research secrets to the Soviets.[4] The postwar atomic spies—Klaus Fuchs, Allan Nunn May, and Bruno Pontecorvo—were all British-sponsored scientists whose various Communist affiliations somehow escaped MI5. The book has yet to be written on the real extent of spying by British scientists.

Bernal had two great good friends whose flat in London he visited from time to time. They were Guy Burgess and Anthony Blunt, both then spying for the Soviets. Blunt worked for MI5, the Security Service. He had been assigned to section B1(b), responsible for assessing Abwehr and Sicherheitdienst (the Nazi Party's secret intelligence service) intentions.[5] His opposite number in Section V of MI6 was Kim Philby, also spying for the Soviets and also responsible for monitoring the activities of Germany's espionage organizations. Both regularly received and read wireless decrypts. Combined with information supplied from other turncoat spies in the Foreign Office and the Government Code and Cipher School, the clandestine reports of Blunt and Philby meant that the ULTRA secret was no secret to Stalin.

Of the two now-infamous British traitors, Blunt was better placed than Philby during wartime. Apart from decrypts, he also had access to MI5's files of suspect individuals. The dossier on Bernal must have been bulky, for the Security Service had kept track of the Communists at British universities before the war and Bernal had made no secret of his loyalty to the Soviet Union. A missing or misplaced dossier would certainly explain how Bernal managed to survive the inevitable security checks that would have been conducted for the conference at Quebec.

MI5, it should be remembered, was quartered at the former prison of Wormwood Scrubs during the war. This also was the operational home of British Imperial Censorship. Blunt would have had ample opportunity—and legitimate occasion—to acquaint himself with Britain's elaborate program of mail and telegraph interception.

One way or another, by late 1944 the Soviet Union was well aware of the intelligence-gathering capabilities of its English-speaking allies. While Americans, Canadians, and British battled in France, Stalin had become arrogant and difficult to deal with. At all levels of liaison, the Soviets were becoming more secretive, asking their allies for much technical information and giving nothing in return. In November 1944, U.S. Censorship warned the RCMP that censorable mail was being deliberately smuggled aboard Russian merchant ships in Vancouver. U.S. Navy Intelligence in Washington, meanwhile, was puzzling over the fact that it had suddenly become impossible to intercept the wireless traffic of Russian merchant vessels. They all seemed to be observing radio silence.[6]

While the likelihood of victory in Europe beamed brightly, a new shadow was spreading across the world.

———————

By the beginning of 1945, both the U.S. Navy and the U.S. Army had built up two huge but separate cryptographic organizations for the war in the Pacific, each linked to separate wireless monitoring networks in Alaska, Canada, the continental United States, Britain, Hawaii, New Zealand, Australia, Ceylon, and India. For the Far East, the British, even more so than the Canadians, were mainly limited to supplying raw material, with the Americans doing the lion's share of traffic analysis and code- and cipher-breaking. This led to the creation in Washington of the U.S. Army's Joint Intelligence Center for the Pacific War, which took charge of the processing and distribution of all Japanese military and diplomatic traffic, regardless of source.[7]

The result was that the Examination Unit no longer had to rely on Japanese traffic intercepted in Canada. Now it worked on assigned diplomatic circuits, with the raw material being supplied by the Americans. The decrypted results were sent to the "common pool" in Washington. The Government Code and Cipher School had a similar arrangement.[8]

The Canadians were also now receiving decrypts broken from the Japanese Military Attaché (JMA) cipher. This traffic was considered especially important because it dealt with military subjects. Colonel Murray had been trying to get it for two years. Now JMA decrypts were being sent to Herbert Norman, as the result of an unusual agreement.

When the British Director of Military Intelligence, General Sinclair, visited Ottawa in the fall of 1944, he told Norman Robertson that Canada should discontinue its intelligence-sharing arrangement with the OSS. Relations between it and U.S. Military Intelligence (G-2) had deteriorated so badly, warned Sinclair, that G-2 was likely to pull the plug on all cooperation on signals intelligence if it found out the Canadians were dealing with Donovan's much-loathed espionage agency. Robertson replied that neither the U.S. Army nor Navy had shown much interest in a close working liaison with Canada, whereas the OSS was supplying "one type of Intelligence we could hardly have asked for." By that he presumably meant the reports of OSS spies.

General Sinclair replied that if the U.S. Army stopped sending traffic to Canada, the British would have to do the same. On the other hand, if the Canadians did break with the OSS, Sinclair was confident that he could persuade the Americans to send them JMA decrypts. Robertson did not have much choice. Herbert Norman stopped sending his diplomatic summaries to the OSS and began receiving JMA messages on November 27, 1944. He was under orders to read and burn them, reporting their contents only to Norman Robertson. Not even Colonel Murray was to see them.[9]

The deal also led to the apparent closing of Norman's Special Intelligence Section. Lester Pearson had been instructed to tell OSS headquarters in Washington that it would not be receiving any more intelligence reports from Canada because they were no longer available. This excuse was given an aura of truth by closing Norman's little office; however, he simply moved over to the main offices of External Affairs and continued to read Far East decrypts and write summaries as before. The OSS, faithful to an agreement that it did not know had been abrogated, continued to supply Norman with its reports.[10]

As 1945 unfolded, with its expectation of victory, the signals intelligence services of the three English-speaking nations began to scramble for new tasks. With Japanese shipping obliterated and the Battle of the Atlantic essentially won, the U.S. Navy was able to turn its attention to the interception of merchant shipping traffic, especially Portuguese, Spanish, Swiss, Swedish, and Russian. Naval Operations (OpNav)

staffers in Washington suggested informally to their Canadian colleagues that such work continue in peacetime "either as a sort of silent
policing or to maintain a proper basis for any future war work." The
resulting intelligence could go to appropriate government departments. The Canadians were also praised for their initiative in compiling monthly reports on Russian shipping and were asked to send
OpNav "all addresses and signatures of personal messages, and details
related to [merchant] ships' personnel, whenever intercepted." [11]

U.S. Army cryptographers at Arlington also found themselves less
taxed. By the beginning of 1945, most of the major Japanese military
ciphers had been broken, freeing up hundreds of cryptographic personnel. Japanese diplomats in Eastern Europe were being forced to
burn many of their code books as they withdrew with the retreating
German armies. Changes in cipher keys were consequently less fre-
quent, while increasing reliance was placed on emergency codes that
were already known to the Allies. Arlington turned to more comprehensive coverage of Japanese commercial traffic, though it was of
much lower intelligence value.

The British likewise found themselves with a large cryptographic
organization handling diminishing tasks. German Army, Air Force,
and Navy ciphers had all been overpowered. Moreover, the intelligence
obtained from ENIGMA decrypts was not half so vital now that
Hitler's armies had been chased back to Germany's frontiers and were
obviously on their last gasp. The Government Code and Cipher
School's emphasis shifted from operational traffic at Bletchley Park to
diplomatic and commercial traffic at Berkeley Street. Commander
Denniston was supplying the Foreign Office with decrypts pertaining
to France, Belgium, and Holland. He was also able to report that the
ciphers of the nationalist Chinese had been broken. [12]

These changes were mirrored in Canada. De Marbois released some
of his Department of Transport stations to general listening assignments. This enabled the Y Committee, at long last, to resume supplying Commander Denniston with Japanese commercial traffic, only to
be told that the British did not need it any more. They were getting all
they required from the new intercept station they had built on the
island of Mauritius in the Indian Ocean. [13]

Meanwhile, Commander Little and Colonel Murray awaited Robertson's decision on the future of the Examination Unit. They were not idle. They had an ally in Herbert Norman.

Norman did not share the view of his colleagues in External Affairs that Canada should leave cryptanalysis to Britain and become only a producer of raw intercepts after the war. In a formal report to the Y Committee in early January 1945, he proposed a "Canadian Signal Intelligence Centre" which would fuse the functions of both the Examination Unit and the Joint Discrimination Unit. It would have a special intelligence section which would evaluate the resulting decrypts for passing on to the appropriate authorities—"keeping in mind," he wrote, "the special security regulations which pertain to ULTRA reports." The Y Committee roundly endorsed the plan and put his name forward as director of the proposed agency.[14]

This incident is all the more interesting in the light of the postwar scandal involving Norman and his Communist background. Had the plan gone through, he would have become Canada's chief of secret intelligence.

By the time Norman wrote his formal report, however, Robertson had made up his mind. He had decided—undoubtedly after discussions with the Prime Minister—that there would be no formal agreement with the British because of "the larger political questions," and the Examination Unit would be discontinued "because the size and expense of a modern cryptographic unit made it impossible for one to be set up in Canada." In mid-February Glazebrook helpfully suggested that the French section could be closed by July and all staff released, except for a few from the Japanese section who could be turned over to Drake's organization for any remaining cryptographic tasks.

"Any arrangement to carry this plan into effect would presumably be arranged by you with the departments concerned," Glazebrook wrote Robertson. He also proposed making these moves without consulting the service directors of intelligence. "I think that any previous discussion by the Y Committee would have no useful purpose and might cause awkwardness."[15]

Murray and Little did not find out about the decision until nearly a month later. They were appalled. By then, however, the necessary paperwork was already on its way up to the Chiefs of Staff. A desperate rearguard action was now waged by the three service directors of intelligence. External Affairs had not reckoned on the fact that Murray, Little, and Stewart comprised the entire Canadian Joint Intelligence Committee, reporting directly to the Chiefs of Staff. They had their own trump cards to play.

At first it went badly for them. De Marbois announced that the Navy was pulling its staff out of the Joint Discrimination Unit and he was resigning from the Y Committee. Intemperate as ever, he coupled this announcement with a sweeping denunciation of the Y Committee, informing the Assistant Chief of the Naval Staff that it had completely failed in its purpose because of "its lack of expertise." Murray, Little, and Stewart, with justifiable bitterness, had no choice but to let him have his way. The Navy withdrew its personnel from the Discrimination Unit.[16]

External Affairs also made haste to dismantle the Examination Unit. The Americans were still receiving decrypts of the traffic between Paris and the French delegation in Ottawa, and one of the "more delicate problems" was how to explain to them that these would no longer be forthcoming. Pearson, at the Canadian embassy in Washington, was carefully coached on what to say. Glazebrook, under Robertson's signature, wrote a 500-word essay of proposed excuses, concluding: "From your knowledge of the Examination Unit, other ideas might occur to you. If so, perhaps you would suggest them to us."[17]

The French section of the Examination Unit was again running along smartly when those words were written in mid-March 1945. By then the Allied armies had crossed the Rhine and the Germans were fighting on their own territory. De Gaulle had had more than six months to restore the machinery of government in Paris and his diplomatic service was now in order. Already his representatives in Washington were looking to the United States to bankroll France's recovery, while trying to side-step American pressure to revise France's prewar colonial policy. Offering more independence to French overseas possessions did not fit well with de Gaulle's vision of restoring the country to its former glory, so there was much to be read between Paris and Washington. The "IBM room"—the Joint Machine Unit under

Drake—was kept busy crunching the numbers out of the French diplomatic ciphers.[18]

Nevertheless, once Germany collapsed in early May, the dismantling of the Examination Unit quickly proceeded. Kendrick left for Britain to rejoin the Government Code and Cipher School, and Robinson took his place to wrap things up. The French staff was let go. Arlington was offered the Examination Unit's collection of French decrypts, and both the British and Americans received copies of the French code books reconstructed by the Canadians.[19] The house on Laurier Avenue was closed and the Japanese section was transferred to the Discrimination Unit so that it could continue to cover its Arlington-assigned diplomatic circuits until Japan surrendered.

Indeed, the Japanese decrypts now being broken by the Canadians were taking on a desperate tone:

From: Tokyo

Between 10:00 p.m. and 2:00 p.m. on May 25th 300 B29s concentrated their attack on the centre of the capital with incendiary and high explosive bombs, and as a result it is estimated that within the area bounded by KOJI-MACHI, AKASAKA and AZABU wards, 130,000 houses were burnt to the ground and 510,000 people were afflicted.

With parts of the Imperial Palace, the OMIYA Palace, the palaces of the Prince CHICHIBU and Prince KAN'IN heading the list of establishments completely destroyed by fire, the foreign, navy and war ministries were also razed.

From: Nanking

… the above is connected with measures now being considered by the army to mobilize Japanese residents in China for the decisive battle, and is based on the policy of progressively enlisting suitable male Japanese 14 years of age and over for the prosecution of total war.

From: Kaifeng

Although the collapse of Germany has been expected since
about the autumn of last year and we knew it was only a matter of
time, one feels somewhat sorry now that it has come. However,
with reference to the future of Europe, in view of the national feeling of the three countries—England, America and the Soviet—
and also of their political philosophies, continued mutual
agreement is unthinkable. They are just like three stray dogs fighting for a piece of meat, and in the near future a new conflict will
break out.

It is regrettable that Japan and China, and Japan and America
are fighting each other.[20]

On May 30, 1945, while the Examination Unit was being dismantled, Murray, Little, and Stewart made their move. They proposed to
the Chiefs of Staff that their Joint Intelligence Committee be enlarged
to include a member from the RCMP and one from External Affairs.
That would justify it becoming responsible for general intelligence
rather than just security. It could also encompass signals intelligence:
the intercept stations, the Discrimination Unit, and whatever was left
of the Examination Unit's staff.[21]

Glazebrook was quick to recognize the danger. "I am getting more
and more despondent about the possibility of reaching any agreement
with National Defence and am now mentally designing a continuing
Examination Unit," he wrote Stone. "My feeling is that we must do
the work and we cannot be bothered with J.I.C. control."[22]

It was too late. Ten days later the Chiefs of Staff announced that
they had approved in principle a plan by which an expanded Joint
Intelligence Committee would take over all administrative responsibility for signals intelligence, including cryptanalysis. External Affairs
was invited to name *one* official to the new committee.[23]

Glazebrook, again under Robertson's signature, attempted to sal-
vage the situation. In July, though the Examination Unit was now
closed and its entire French staff dispersed, he submitted a counter-
proposal whereby "cryptographic activities in the diplomatic and com-

mercial fields" would be subject to direction by a subcommittee of the Joint Intelligence Committee chaired by a person from External Affairs. This proposal was flatly rejected. The Chiefs of Staff were prepared to entertain a submission for postwar wireless intelligence and cryptography, but direction would come from the entire membership of the Canadian JIC. External Affairs had lost its chance.[24]

Behind all this manoeuvring lurked the figure of General Maurice Pope, then acting as advisor to the War Cabinet and Chiefs of Staff. All the memos from both sides had gone through him. Probably unknown to Glazebrook, it was he who had first proposed that Canada get involved in cryptanalysis back in 1939. He was the person who first appreciated the potential of the Army's tiny wireless experimental station at Rockcliffe Airport in 1940. It was he who had backed the hiring of Yardley in 1941.[25]

Pope was also a man who had few illusions about peace. The defeat of Germany had been costly in an unexpected way: millions of Soviet troops were spread across the countries of eastern Europe, and it was going to be difficult, if not impossible, to pry them out. Pope glimpsed the future in an entry in his diary:

> Surely, if range ourselves we must, it should be against Russia. At a time when they are enslaving their contiguous European neighbours, it is eminently reasonable for us to make a straight forward defensive pact with the Western Nations and that should Joe Stalin object to this course of action, we should tell him politely, though none the less firmly, to go to hell.[26]

In a very real way, Stalin was soon to receive just such a message.

––––––––––––

Roosevelt had died suddenly in April, just short of witnessing the final destruction of the Nazi regime. It was left to his former vice-president, Harry Truman, to pick up the reins of war.

The new U.S. President met in mid-July with Stalin and Churchill amid the ruins of Berlin. The Potsdam Conference, which took its name from the nearby Palace of the Princes of Potsdam, was held to discuss what to do with defeated Germany, and to negotiate the Soviet Union's entry into the war against Japan. The talks soon soured, however, over American and British complaints that the countries liberated by the Russians in eastern Europe were being treated like conquered territories. Communist regimes were being imposed in all of them. Churchill and Truman protested. Stalin ignored them. He also began making unreasonable territorial demands as a condition of declaring war on Japan. The Soviet dictator said he would be ready to strike in the Far East by mid-August.

Then, in the midst of this frustrating debate with an arrogant and obdurate Stalin, Truman and Churchill secretly received news that the test-firing of the atomic bomb had been successful. Two were now ready. The United States and Great Britain issued an ultimatum, calling for Japan's immediate and unconditional surrender. The Japanese demurred. Eleven days later the first atomic bomb exploded over Hiroshima. Next came Nagasaki.

When the news reached the Examination Unit, Lieutenant Commander Earl Hope, the head of the Japanese diplomatic section, put his head down on his desk and wept.[27]

———

There has been much speculation over the years about the motive for dropping the atomic bombs. The standard explanation—apparently backed up by contemporary documents—has been that it was to save the American lives that would be lost if Japan were invaded. Yet by July 1945 the Japanese Air Force and Navy had been completely destroyed, leaving the Americans with a total stranglehold on the home islands. Japanese decrypts spoke of a nation absolutely stripped of its powers of resistance. The debate about invasion was only theoretical. Within a few months the Japanese could have been starved into surrender.

The statement that Japan was already defeated in every real sense is not speculation. Japan's home islands were not self-sufficient and were already being crippled by blockade. Yet, as late as 1992, at least one American historian has cited the fact that the U.S. Joint Chiefs of Staff allowed preparations for the invasion of Japan to go ahead as proof that invasion was necessary.[28] This is to misunderstand the military mentality. As long as invasion was an option left open by the political leadership, the military authorities had to make a 100 per cent effort to be ready.

Invasion was not necessary. The Diplomatic Summaries of Japanese intercepts then being received by General Marshall, Secretary of War Henry Stimson, and President Truman at Potsdam revealed that the Japanese themselves knew the situation was hopeless. Excerpts from a July 22 message to Tokyo from the Japanese ambassador in Moscow spoke of the total "paralysis" of the Japanese armed forces. It pointed out that the Americans needed only to destroy the rice harvest in the home islands to reduce the country to "absolute famine." Indeed, the U.S. Army's Chemical Warfare Service had just such a plan in hand.[29]

They all knew—Truman, the State Department, the Chiefs of Staff—that the Japanese were still fighting only because they were afraid the victorious Americans would remove the Emperor, a revered institution absolutely essential to Japan's sense of national identity. Consequently, in June 1945, when Stimson drafted the ultimatum demanding Japan's surrender, he included the assurance that afterwards "the Japanese might choose a constitutional monarchy under the present dynasty." The wording of the ultimatum received tacit approval from Truman on July 2. On July 12 the wisdom of the assurance was explicitly confirmed by decrypts which revealed that the sole stumbling block to Japanese surrender was American insistence on "unconditional surrender." The Emperor himself had dispatched a special envoy to Moscow with personal instructions to clarify the point and seek peace with the United States through the Soviets.[30]

Bearing in mind that the Japanese intercepts described above and below are from Diplomatic Summaries and were therefore being read by Truman, Stimson, the U.S. Joint Chiefs of Staff, and the Secretary of State, the actual sequence of events that unfolded at Potsdam is as follows:[31]

July 16: The talks between Truman, Stalin, and Churchill open. On that day the President, Stimson, and the U.S. Joint Chiefs of Staff—the latter also at Potsdam—receive news that the first test explosion of an atomic bomb has been successful.

July 17: Churchill is told of the test. An intercepted message from Tokyo to its embassy in Moscow again discloses to the Americans that Japan cannot accept "unconditional surrender." It will give up, however, "if … the Anglo–Americans were to have regard for Japan's honor and national existence." Yet, on this same day, the U.S. Joint Chiefs of Staff review the text of the ultimatum proposed by Stimson and recommend dropping the clause guaranteeing that Japan's monarchy will be retained.

July 18: Stalin tells Truman that Japan has made peace overtures through its embassy in Moscow. Truman suggests Stalin give an "unspecific" answer. The President also secretly learns that the test-firing of the atomic bomb shows it to be even more destructive than forecast. He and Churchill lunch together privately.

July 20: Stimson reverses his stand on the ultimatum and decides to go along with the recommendation of the Joint Chiefs of Staff to drop the promise to retain the "constitutional monarchy under the present dynasty." Truman also agrees.

July 22: A Diplomatic Summary, also received at Potsdam, contains a message from Tokyo authorizing the Japanese ambassador in Switzerland to approach the local OSS chief to ascertain "American intentions toward the Imperial Family and the national structure."

July 23: Churchill tells his own Chiefs of Staff that the atomic bomb is ready, stating that "we now had something in our hands which would redress the balance with the Russians."[32]

July 24: Truman hints to Stalin that the Americans have a powerful new weapon. He gives no details. Stalin asks for none.

July 26: Without prior consultation with the Russians, the ultimatum is finally issued in the name of the United States, Great Britain, and China. It calls for Japan's "unconditional surrender." There is no mention of the monarchy. Before this day is out, Truman and all the other top American officals read an intercepted message in which the Japanese Foreign Ministry tells its ambassador in Moscow that Japan is prepared to accept peace on the basis of the "Atlantic Charter"—a statement of war aims issued in 1941 by Roosevelt and Churchill which says that the people of defeated Germany and Japan will have the right to choose their own form of government.

July 27: Japan makes no official reply to the ultimatum. Meanwhile, the Americans read from intercepts that Japanese embassy officials in Switzerland are urging immediate surrender and that the Emperor himself is pressing for an end to the war.

July 28: Stalin reports to Truman more peace proposals from the Japanese in Moscow. In addition, the Americans receive more intercepts between Tokyo and Moscow, revealing that Japan wants to accept the ultimatum but is still concerned that there has been no assurance its national institutions will be preserved.

July 29: The Japanese government issues a press statement simply saying it will ignore the ultimatum. This, in diplomatic parlance, is far short of official rejection. Intercepts between Tokyo and Switzerland reveal that the Japanese government does not know how it should respond.

August 2: As Truman and his staff return by ship from Europe, the OSS in Switzerland reports that the Japanese Navy in Tokyo is urging surrender pending clarification of the Emperor's future. The OSS also says that it has been told that surrender could come, regardless, in about a week. This report is marked to go directly to Truman, the Joint Chiefs of Staff, and the Secretary of State.[33]

August 6: Hiroshima destroyed.

August 9: Nagasaki destroyed.

August 10: The Japanese Government officially declares it is willing to surrender, provided this does not prejudice the Emperor's position as sovereign.

August 11: In reply, the United States says that after surrender the Emperor will derive his authority from the Supreme Commander of the Allied Powers. Three days later the war ends.

The conclusion is irresistible: Truman and all his top political and military advisors knew that there was no need to use the atomic bomb. To end the war, all they had to do was tell the Japanese, even in the vaguest terms, that they would be allowed to keep their Emperor as the head of state. Yet this assurance was withdrawn and then withheld.

Indeed, Americans knew that the Japanese themselves were aware that an atomic bomb was being developed. As former Examination Unit cryptanalyst Victor Graham later recalled:

We were aware of machine ciphers and were also aware through Japanese communications of the existence of an atomic bomb before it was set off. From the point of view of the Japanese it was simply what they called the "Big Bomb." They had heard of its existence, didn't know anything about it and were very fearful. They had heard incredible stories about what it might be and what it might produce and so forth.[34]

The collection of wartime Japanese decrypts released by the Canadian authorities is incomplete. In a numbered sequence of 4,911 decrypts that is otherwise unbroken, sixty-three messages from June 6 to July 16, 1945, are missing. The collection also abruptly ends on this latter date, even though other documents reveal that the Canadians continued to decrypt Japanese diplomatic traffic for some months afterwards. There are also deletions in the otherwise declassified Diplomatic Summary for July 29, 1945, in the National Archives in Washington. Here the available Diplomatic Summaries end also.[35]

It should be noted that the Japanese section of the former Examination Unit—by then merged with the Discrimination Unit at the La Salle Academy—was breaking "assigned" diplomatic circuits for the Americans. One of these was the Moscow–Tokyo link. It is a safe bet that at least some of the missing decrypts dealt with the instructions from Tokyo to the Japanese ambassador regarding peace overtures to the United States. Perhaps one also mentioned the "Big Bomb."

In any event, four days after the OSS had reported that the Japanese would surrender in about a week no matter what, a huge fireball rose into the sky over Hiroshima.

Why?

———————————

A month after the bombs had fallen, with 105,000 people incinerated in two mighty flashes, Mackenzie King dictated the following entry into his diary:

... the most appalling statement which Robertson gave me this morning was that at Potsdam, when the 3 Great Powers were assembled there, Churchill brought up the question of the Balkan States and what was developing, and said they would have to thrash this out by process of argument and reasoning. Stalin had replied: they would be settled by power. This caused Churchill to speak to Truman about the necessity of letting the Russians see where power really lay. The atomic bomb had been brought sooner into action on this account than otherwise would have happened.[36]

Whatever the source of Robertson's information, it is lent support from the wartime diary of Churchill's personal physician, Lord Moran, who recorded Churchill telling him at Potsdam on July 23 that it had been decided to use the atomic bomb "in Japan, on cities, not armies." That statement was made after the acrimonious debates with Stalin and before the release of the ultimatum with its crucial deletion.

Churchill further told his doctor: "We thought it would be indecent to use it in Japan without telling the Russians, so they are to be told today. It has just come in time to save the world."[37]

It wasn't Japan that was the perceived threat to the world when Churchill said those words. It was Stalin. *Political necessity*, not military, had dictated the need for the ultimate demonstration of military might.

In the final count—allowing for subsequent death through injuries and radiation poisoning—199,000 men, women, and children died.

CHAPTER TWELVE

THE NEW ENEMY

SEPTEMBER — DECEMBER 1945

THE LIGHTS came on around the world. As news of Japan's surrender spread throughout the Pacific, soldiers put up their weapons, American bomber crews stood down, warships at sea turned on their navigation lights. Those at home involved in secret intelligence, particularly the many thousands recruited for the duration only, began to cease the activities most believed had no place in peacetime.

In the United States, the OSS, under assault in the press as William Donovan's secret empire, was quickly declawed and within a month dispatched altogether. Legalized interception of telegrams and cables in Canada and the United States stopped almost immediately. In Canada the Director of Censorship informed all the government agencies that censorship had ceased and that they were to "destroy by fire" all copies of intercepted correspondence. They were to report back formally by letter when they had done so.

Most of the departments did as they were told, but External Affairs and the new Department of Veterans' Affairs dragged their heels. The latter wanted to retain its collection of soldiers' correspondence because letters which mentioned illness or injury could be used as the basis to settle future pension claims. In a sharply worded exchange, the Director of Censorship reminded officials in Veterans' Affairs of the "inviolability of the mails," stressing that private messages were copied only because of the wartime emergency. Now they were to be destroyed. The dispute became quite furious and eventually was referred to the Department of Justice for arbitration; Veterans' Affairs won the right to retain the excerpted letters. External Affairs also kept much of what it had.[1]

As for wireless interception, there was great reluctance to call a halt. By the middle of 1945, the special intelligence programs of the United States, Britain, Canada, Australia, and India had become largely integrated, centring on the Government Code and Cipher School for Europe and the Middle East and on the U.S. Navy and U.S. Army for the Far East. These vast, overlapping networks were made possible by the direct telekrypton cable links between Ottawa, Washington, and London, backed by HYDRA, the British Security Coordination transmitter at Camp X, plus similar American and British transmitters in the Pacific. There was no hurry to shut these systems down.

The U.S. Army's Joint Intelligence Center in Washington managed to survive for a time by continuing to monitor Japanese transmissions. The Japanese had fought with such fanaticism that there was concern not everyone in the far-flung Pacific Empire would obey the call from Tokyo to surrender. Military Intelligence (G-2) consequently recommended that the interception of Japanese communications should continue. Canada was asked to carry on with certain diplomatic traffic "essential for the occupation and control of Japan."[2]

When the Americans later asked for a specialist from Canada to advise on the social and political reorganization of the vanquished country, Herbert Norman's name was immediately put forward. No one else in External Affairs had the requisite knowledge or had been as involved in the receipt of secret intelligence and the study of Japanese decrypts. By the end of the war, Norman had emerged as Canada's top expert in the handling of Japanese ULTRA. He was sent to Japan in October as liaison officer to the U.S. Army's Counter Intelligence Corps attached to General MacArthur's headquarters. Here he continued to assess Japanese attitudes and intentions by analysing their intercepted communications.[3]

Meanwhile, Canada's three service directors of intelligence—Murray, Brand (replacing Little), and Stewart—used the new assignment from Arlington to deflect any immediate move to cut back on the staff of the Discrimination Unit and its supporting intercept stations. Nine days after the war ended, they sent a memo to the Chiefs of Staff saying that both the Americans and the British were counting on the Canadians to continue with the Japanese intercepts, and that it was vital "to the prestige and good faith of Canada" that the work not be disrupted. They promised a full outline of their postwar proposals as soon as possible.[4]

They met three days later—August 27, 1945—the last meeting of the Canadian Joint Intelligence Committee (CJIC) in its wartime form. George Glazebrook attended as the External Affairs nominee to the soon-to-be expanded committee. He came armed with a series of "hypothetical" questions challenging the appropriateness of carrying on with cryptanalysis, but the three directors of intelligence remained unmoved.[5]

It fell to Colonel Murray to prepare the formal plea to the Chiefs of Staff to retain a peacetime cryptanalysis and intercept organization. He wrote a lengthy Top Secret paper which outlined the history of Canada's wireless intelligence program from its prewar beginning to the present. He described how it had begun as a simple adjunct of the British worldwide Y network, and how it had grown to become by 1945 a full-fledged signals intelligence service, complete with intercept stations, traffic analysis, and code- and cipher-breaking. He also mentioned the HYDRA communications channel run by British Security Coordination, the sharing of assignments among the three countries, and the exchange of raw intercepts and decrypts between Ottawa, the Government Code and Cipher School, and the U.S. Army's "Special Security Agency" in Washington.

After explaining that collaboration with Britain and the United States on a *quid pro quo* basis had given Canada access to "Intelligence which bears a higher security than TOP SECRET" (ULTRA SECRET, in other words)[6] Murray went on to observe:

The advantage of this approach was clearly impressed during the early war years. When our contribution was nil, we received nothing from either Bletchley or Washington. When, in agreement with them, our contribution became substantial, we received ample return—a seat in their counsels and a regular budget of valuable Intelligence. If we contribute to the pool we shall draw something from it in the form of finished products; if we fail to contribute, we shall receive nothing.

On that ringing note, coupled with the statement that cryptanalysis was "a short, straight road into the opponent's mind," Murray pitched for a postwar signals intelligence organization that retained the Army and Navy intercept stations and a Discrimination/Examination Unit.7 The Americans and the British were going to continue the activity; Canada must also.

Murray's proposal was to be discussed by the Chiefs of Staff at their meeting on September 7, 1945. On September 5 an event occurred which would make the debate academic. A young Russian cipher clerk named Igor Gouzenko rifled the message files in the code room of the Soviet embassy in Ottawa. Then, his shirt bulging with the plaintexts of over one hundred messages, he walked out into the evening darkness. His action changed everything.

Norman Robertson was one of the first to hear. As the deputy minister in charge of both foreign affairs and foreign intelligence, he was the obvious person to be notified when Gouzenko presented himself early the next morning, September 6, at the offices of the Justice Department and asked for asylum. Robertson immediately set off to find the Prime Minister. Mackenzie King captured the drama of their meeting in his diary:

Robertson said to me a most terrible thing had happened. It was like a bomb on top of everything. He then told me that this morning, just a half an hour or so earlier, a man had turned up with his wife at the office of the Minister of Justice. He asked to see the Minister. That he was threatened with deportation and once he was deported, it would mean certain death. That the Russian democracy was different than ours.

He went on to say that he had in his possession documents that he had taken from the Embassy and was prepared to give them to the Government. They would be seen to disclose that Russia had her spies and secret service people in Canada and in the U.S. That some of these men were around Stettinius in the States, and that one was in our own Research Laboratories here (assumingly seeking to get secret information with regard to the atomic bomb). He indicated that he had to do with the cyphering of messages. Robertson was not sure that he did not have the cypher code book with him....[8]

As the number-one Canadian consumer of wartime intelligence gained by cryptanalysis, Robertson could barely contain his anxiety to see the documents Gouzenko had. The undersecretary of state for External Affairs would certainly have been aware that Soviet high-grade ciphers were about the only ones that had consistently defied Allied cryptanalysis. Soviet diplomatic traffic had been collected by the Allies, but it had remained impregnable.

The Prime Minister said they should do nothing. Russia was a "trusted" ally and Canada could not afford a breach in relations. The man must be rejected. He might "only be a crank trying to preserve his own life," Mackenzie King said. Robertson pleaded. As the Prime Minister noted on September 6 in his diary, "Robertson seemed to feel that the information [the documents] might be so important to the States and to ourselves and to Britain that it would be in their interests to seize it no matter how it was obtained."

Mackenzie King prevailed. The seventy-year-old Prime Minister returned to the afternoon session of Parliament and points of order; the twenty-six-year-old Russian cipher clerk returned to his apartment vowing suicide. When Mackenzie King later that day learned of Gouzenko's despair, he suggested to Robertson "that a Secret Service man in plain clothes watch the premises. If suicide took place let the city police take charge and this man to follow in and secure what there was in the way of documents...." And Mackenzie King was a man who kissed his dog goodnight every evening and wrote page after page in eulogy whenever one of his pets died.

Robertson pointed out that if they did not help Gouzenko, they would be "a party to suicide on the one hand ... and murder on the other." Mackenzie King remained unmoved. "For us to come into possession of a secret code book—of a Russian secret code book—would be a source of major complications."

Support for Robertson was nearby. As Mackenzie King recorded in the special, separate section of his diary:

> The head of the British Secret Service arrived at the Seignory [sic] Club today. Robertson was going down to see him tonight. I told him he should stay and make this individual come to Ottawa to talk with him. This was finally arranged.[9]

This quotation was omitted from the *Mackenzie King Record*, the 1970 published version of the Prime Minister's 1945–46 diary. As a result, historians have time and time again erroneously reported on who this person was and what influence he may have had on the Gouzenko affair.

However, the following passage in the diary, from the next day (September 7), was quoted in the *Mackenzie King Record*. The identification in parenthesis was inserted by the editors.

> Someone at the head of British Secret Intelligence had come to the Seigniory Club yesterday [Sir William Stephenson, head of British Security Coordination in New York]. He came up and saw Robertson last night. Robertson will a little later tell me of his talks with him on the whole situation. This man returned to the Seigniory Club at night.[10]

The insertion of William Stephenson's name in this quotation is incorrect, because later that same day Mackenzie King also wrote:

> [Robertson] said he thought he would try to get in touch with Stevenson [sic] in New York, along with the FBI men from the United States.... I authorized R. to phone Stevenson.[11]

Obviously Stephenson could not be at the Seigniory Club across the Ottawa River at Montebello and in New York at the same time.

How has such an obvious error had such a long life? The original text of Mackenzie King's journal is unambiguous. On the other hand, eight years before the 1945–46 volume of the *Mackenzie King Record* was published, Montgomery Hyde's biography of Stephenson came out. In it Hyde reported the following:

> Late on the night of September 6, 1945, William Stephenson, who happened to be on a routine official visit to Ottawa, called on Mr. Norman Robertson, Under-Secretary of State in the Canadian Department of External Affairs, at his private residence. With him he found Mr. Thomas Archibald Stone, Counsellor in the Canadian Embassy in Washington. Earlier that day Stephenson had heard a story to the effect that an employee of the Soviet Embassy had been in touch with the Department of Justice through the R.C.M.P., offering to furnish information, and he wanted to know whether Robertson knew anything about it. As a matter of fact Robertson did. He told Stephenson that the head of the Intelligence Branch of the R.C.M.P. had informed him that a man....[12]

Mackenzie King's original, unpublished journal contradicts this account in every particular. Gouzenko had been in RCMP custody at least sixteen to eighteen hours before Robertson sought the Prime Minister's permission on September 7 to phone Stephenson. Moreover, Mackenzie King noted the following day (September 8) that "Robertson said that Stevenson and the F.B.I. representatives would be here tonight." Then, later that same day, he added that "two on the British side will be coming up tonight and F.B.I. men will be here in Ottawa on Monday morning," as though Stephenson was not coming after all.

It appears that the situation was too important to be entrusted to Stephenson or to British Security Coordination. On September 10 Mackenzie King wrote:

> R. told me that the head of the British Secret Service had sent two of his men to Ottawa. They had been given particulars and one at least was leaving by plane [for London] to give the information to Cadogan, the Under-Secretary of the Foreign Office.

It is now known that the senior of these two men was Secret Intelligence Service (MI6) officer Peter Dwyer, sent from Washington rather than New York, and sending his reports back to London (to Kim Philby) rather than to BSC.[13] The "head of the British Secret Service" and the "head of British Intelligence" must therefore refer to the person who really did occupy that post: Stewart Menzies, the man known as "C" in British Intelligence circles. Indeed, only Menzies, the chief of the Secret Intelligence Service, could have authorized a direct briefing of a deputy minister.

All of the above makes nonsense or fabrication of the picture of Stephenson visiting Robertson at his home on September 6 and then, as Hyde also described, going over with Stone to Gouzenko's apartment building and huddling in the bushes outside trying to assess the situation. As Stone was then serving with the Canadian Embassy in Washington, was there even any reason for him to be in Ottawa on that particular night?

Just to muddy the waters even further, George Glazebrook, then Stone's successor in charge of secret intelligence, recalled the following:

> Stephenson was coming to Ottawa for another reason. I don't remember what it was and the case broke later that day. A dinner was already arranged for Stephenson at the country club. That went through its normal course, but I have a photographic memory of Robertson and Stephenson sitting on a sofa and Stephenson having this story told to him for the first time. Later on he went and hid behind the bushes, watching the building where Gouzenko was hiding.[14]

Again this does not jibe with Mackenzie King's diary, which has Robertson phoning Stephenson the day *after* he had talked with the person from the Seigniory Club and *after* Gouzenko had been taken into custody.

Armchair intelligence analysts might like to ask themselves what is happening here. Hyde said that his book was based on interviews with Stephenson, and his personal papers. In later interviews Stephenson certainly did claim the role Hyde assigned him. Why would Stephenson lie and Glazebrook also? Why would two senior intelligence officers engage in deliberate deception?

There is also the so-called "BSC History" on which author William Stevenson based much of his 1976 biography of Stephenson, *A Man Called Intrepid.* According to the people who worked on it in 1945, Stephenson himself directed the writing of this wartime history of BSC and it was revised many times before he was satisfied. Stephenson then destroyed all BSC documents he could lay his hands on.[15]

No copies of the "BSC History" have ever been released to the public. Author William Stevenson has continued to keep his copy private since publication of *Intrepid,* allowing only the occasional journalist to see it. Qualified historians have therefore assessed the content of the "BSC History" only by what he and Hyde wrote. However, in 1991 after lengthy negotiations, Stevenson allowed me to examine the "BSC History" in the form Stephenson gave it to him. It consists of almost 400 pages of printed text with index. Having promised not to quote from it without permission, I examined it while sitting at the dining room table in Stevenson's Toronto home.

Compared to the actual documentary record of British Security Coordination activities uncovered during research for this book, it is full of errors, misdirections, and exaggerations. It appears to have been written from someone's faulty memory. The sequence of events is often hopelessly confused and there are elementary errors of fact. There is little acknowledgement of the central role played by the Examination Unit and the U.S. Coast Guard in identifying German spies through cryptanalysis. One can only conclude that the information in it was deliberately cooked to cast BSC in the best possible light at the expense of both the Americans and the Canadians.[16]

Stephenson's later description, with elaborate details, of being present the night Gouzenko defected is consistent with the claim in the "BSC History" that BSC was a major force in defeating German espionage activities in the Western Hemisphere. Both claims are untrue.

Who, then, was it who came to Ottawa from the Seigniory Club that night of September 6, 1945, to talk to Robertson? It certainly was not Stephenson, but was it really Menzies? Could Mackenzie King have mistaken someone else for the "head of the British Secret Service?" Why should Menzies be in Canada at this particular point in time?

The answer is quite simple.

In the 1940s the Seigniory Club was one of the most exclusive private resorts in North America. Established in 1931, it consisted of a huge log building at the centre of a 65,000-acre sportsman's paradise extending back from the Ottawa River into the Quebec hinterland. There were seven private lakes for fishing, guides for hunting, plus stables, tennis courts, ski jumps, and a bobsled run. Charter members were assigned permanent rooms in the lodge with their privacy guaranteed by the club's own police force. Only the very wealthy or influential were allowed such suites, and the list of members included names like Rockefeller, Sir Harry Oakes, and Southam. Ordinary member No. 145, however, was one "H. Stuart Menzies."

The first initial is different and it is "Stuart" instead of Stewart on the Seigniory Club membership list, but there seems little doubt that this is the Stewart Menzies who was the head of Britain's Secret Intelligence Service. His membership card is even partly filled out in bright green ink—a Menzies hallmark. He applied to join the club September 22, 1940, and gave as his address the Ritz-Carlton Hotel in Montreal.[17] This date corresponds with the presence of the Tizard mission in North America, a high-powered delegation from Britain sent by Churchill to divulge the secrets of radar and atomic energy to the Americans and Canadians. It would have been entirely appropriate for Menzies to have come along.

Menzies was an avid hunter, and it appears that he was a guest at the Seigniory Club sometime during his 1940 visit to Canada and liked what he saw. He became a member and on that fateful September night in 1945 was back at the Seigniory Club enjoying a little rest and relaxation. And what had brought him to Ottawa? That, too, can be explained. Two days before Gouzenko's defection, Glazebrook received the following letter from Tommy Stone:

Washington

September 3rd, 1945

My Dear George,

Another thing which might come up in our conference with

[*Stuart Menzies*] is the future of [*HYDRA*] which, as you know, is the communication centre [*for GC&CS*]. This is apparently an excellent radio station and I think we considered once before whether the Department of Transport or the military might take it over but we never came to any definite conclusion. [*Blank*] tells me at the moment it is paying for itself once a week. It now sends, I believe, about 80,000 groups a day to the [*Blank*]. I am going down this afternoon, as I told you, to see [*Stephenson in New York*]. When I see you on Thursday, therefore, I ought to be able to give you the latest [*BSC*] news.[18]

Stone had good reason to be in Ottawa that fateful night of September 6. He was there to meet Menzies. When Norman Robertson contacted "the head of the British Secret Service" at the Seigniory Club, that was exactly who it was.

As for the lies Glazebrook and Stephenson told, they can also be explained. The British government has always, until very recently, been paranoid about even admitting it has a secret service. The head of the Secret Intelligence Service was not supposed to exist, much less ever be named. Hence the code-letter "C" and the tradition of his writing in a special green ink which is difficult to photograph. Glazebrook had been on very intimate terms with the British intelligence authorities in London and New York throughout the war, and he undoubtedly would have felt he had to go along with the charade if Menzies did not want it known he had been in Ottawa. As for Stephenson, it appears he simply took advantage of Menzies's shyness to add lustre to his own reputation.

The morning following the meeting between Menzies and Robertson, Gouzenko was taken into RCMP protective custody, despite Mackenzie King's misgivings. After that there was no stopping the flow of events. His stolen messages revealed an extensive spy ring in Canada, which included a member of Parliament, a cipher clerk in External Affairs, and several scientists connected with military and atomic research. While the Russian embassy made repeated demands that he be surrendered, Gouzenko and his wife were taken away under heavy guard to a secret location for extensive questioning.

Although thousands of documents on the Gouzenko case have been released in Canada, almost none of them pertain to the actions of Canadian security and intelligence authorities. Nevertheless, one can piece together at least a partial picture of how the situation was handled.

After the first round of interrogation, Gouzenko was taken to Camp X near Oshawa for further debriefing. Not only was it still guarded by the military, but the HYDRA transmitter was still in operation, as was the telekrypton line linking Camp X to British Security Coordination and thence to Arlington and the Government Code and Cipher School in Britain. Gouzenko was a Russian cipher clerk. The secure communications facilities at Camp X meant that cryptanalysts in Britain along with those in the United States could be kept continuously informed as he was questioned about the Soviet code and cipher systems.[19]

For the cryptanalysts, Gouzenko's information must have been riveting. The baffling Russian cipher was actually a combination code and cipher system, backed by one-time pads. Gouzenko couldn't help much with the cipher side of the problem, but he could with the codes.

The procedure used by the Russians was approximately as follows. A Russian cipher clerk worked from two code systems. The first took plain language words and rendered them into code words. These in turn were rendered into five-digit code numbers, as were individual letters of the alphabet. Thus:

Plain Language	Code Word	Code Number
hiding place	dubok	93616
the KGB	neighbours	86521
Canada	Lesovia	34625
Soviet Embassy	Metro	80192
passport	shoe	12864
passport forger	shoemaker	04512
Communist Party	corporation	21075
front for espionage	roof	60051
MP Fred Rose	Debouz	99431

Alphabet Letter	*Code Number*
A	75901
A	32286
A	21664
B	44896
B	99642

Where the clerk did not have a specific word or codeword in his book, he could spell it out with the numerical equivalents of the letters. To confuse possible codebreakers, there were many different numbers for each letter. The resulting message might look like this:

54287   92737   98357   61420   76849   17364   19927 ....

The cipher clerk then turned to his one-time pad. This consisted of sheets of paper with randomly generated five-digit numbers. Choosing a page that had been previously agreed upon and was possessed by the recipient, he would add numbers from it (without carrying) to those of his message. The sums obtained would represent the final encipherment.[20]

Such a system—similar to that which the British supplied the Free French in 1942—is impregnable as long as the original codes are unknown, and as long as only sender and receiver have identical pads and they are used only once. Its weakness, however, is that it is slow and clumsy. Every embassy, every spy, every user of the system has to be provided with unique pairs of number pads. If a high volume of traffic is involved, this is difficult to manage. It can mean thousands of pads, with the logistical problem of getting each pair matched to the correct two users. The Soviets ultimately succumbed to the temptation of producing multiple sets of the same one-time pads and of using the same pages more than once.[21]

In 1944 the OSS acquired a partially burned Russian code book from the Finns. It contained the numbers that matched the various letters and a few common codewords used in Soviet messages. When this was turned over to the U.S. Army, an enterprising cryptanalyst at

Arlington soon realized that he could sometimes identify the original code words whenever one-time pads had been used more than once. This meant that the U.S. cryptanalysts could now at least partially unlock some of the enciphered Russian messages the Allies had been intercepting throughout the war. Many of the words recovered, of course, were still unknown codewords. It was here that Gouzenko's information must have been priceless.[22]

Matching the repeated one-time pads and the damaged code book with the mountain of Soviet messages that had been collected was a monumental task. Codenamed VENONA, the project dragged on for decades in tight secrecy. One early dividend was evidence in the decrypts that led to the 1952 arrest and subsequent execution in the United States of the spies Ethel and Julius Rosenberg. VENONA decrypts also contributed to the identification of spies such as Donald Maclean in the British embassy in Washington and atomic scientist Klaus Fuchs.[23]

Few documents have been released on the code-breaking aspect of Gouzenko's defection, although Mackenzie King did report in his diary that Gouzenko was believed to have taken a code book. If so, then his defection was vitally important to the VENONA solutions.[24] However, Canadian involvement in the processing of Gouzenko's disclosures is unknown. In September 1945, the Discrimination Unit was still decrypting Japanese messages with a staff of twenty-five from the former Examination Unit. There were Russian linguists like Earl Hope and Captain de Marbois available, but no records on their possible involvement are acknowledged or available from either External Affairs or the Department of National Defence.

One thing is certain: Gouzenko's defection had far-reaching consequences. The news that the Soviets had been spying spread like a shock wave through those at the centre of government in Ottawa. Mackenzie King was appalled. His war diary contains numerous admiring comments about the Soviet embassy staff. He'd had the ambassador's wife to tea at Laurier House several times. He had often publicly supported Canada/Russia friendship societies. Now he found himself noting in his journal: "If there is another war, it will come against America by way of Canada from Russia."

It was decided, likely by Mackenzie King, to keep Gouzenko's defection out of the public eye for the present. It was to be life as usual. Most Cabinet members were told nothing, or very little. Knowledge of Gouzenko's disclosures was confined to those at the centre of the government's security and intelligence establishment: senior staff in External Affairs, the Chiefs of Staff, the RCMP, and the appropriate military authorities. It profoundly affected all of them. Before Gouzenko, they had been considering how to put Canada's wartime security and intelligence apparatus on a peacetime footing; after Gouzenko, they considered only how to make it ready for war.

The biggest turnaround occurred within External Affairs. There was no more thought of giving up cryptanalysis. Gilbert Robinson, who had presided over the dismantling of the Examination Unit, was now asked to draft a "blueprint" for a revived code- and cipher-breaking team with all the bells and whistles. This he did, in four tightly typed pages of foolscap, calling for renewed agreements on the exchange of raw traffic such that "intercepts in a given language" could be obtained as desired. He suggested they should start up the French section again under Sonya Morawetz, a twenty-two-year-old Czechoslovakian-born woman who had shown a flair for cipher-breaking. "Canada should stand on her own feet with regard to personnel from now on," Robinson stressed, underlining the words. "There is ample cryptographic talent and experience available here."[25]

Robinson also insisted that the work had to have the full support of External Affairs. He need not have worried. Robertson, Wrong, and Glazebrook were now fully on side, and the three service directors of intelligence generously swung behind them, agreeing to revise their proposal to the Chiefs of Staff to recommend that External Affairs, not the military, should set policy on wireless intelligence and cryptanalysis. The bureaucratic wrangling of the previous months was completely set aside.

On September 20, two weeks after Gouzenko's defection, the newly expanded Canadian Joint Intelligence Committee held its first meeting. The membership now consisted of the three service directors of intelligence—Murray, Brand, and Stewart—plus Glazebrook of External Affairs and Superintendent Rivett-Carnac of the RCMP's security division. Colonel Acland of the Army's security service also attended. All would have known about Gouzenko.

The meeting first agreed that Colonel Murray's memo to the Chiefs of Staff on wireless intelligence should be amended to make External Affairs responsible for cryptanalysis policy. Then discussion turned to the complete overhaul of Canada's procedures for handling secret intelligence. The result was another elaborate memo from Murray entitled, "Foreign Intelligence in Peacetime." After describing in detail how cryptanalysis, general intelligence, security, and counter-espionage had been the scattered responsibility of various government departments during the war, it proposed the creation of a new body— a Joint Coordination Bureau for Intelligence—which would receive and digest all secret intelligence from whatever source. The Army, Navy, and Air Force plus External Affairs and the RCMP would all contribute. Non-military intelligence would also have to be gathered, and special security precautions were called for, as during the war, to protect the "ULTRA" secret.[26]

Now the Chiefs of Staff had two major proposals before them and they invited Norman Robertson's comments. The undersecretary immediately approved in principle carrying on with signals intelligence, but asked that further discussion be deferred. Mackenzie King had become so alarmed by the Gouzenko revelations and the implicit threat of war with the Soviet Union that he had decided to go to Washington and warn President Truman personally. Then he intended to go on to London to warn the new British Prime Minister, Clement Attlee. Robertson was to go with him.

Robertson and the Chiefs of Staff wrote the Canadian Joint Intelligence Committee to say that they supported retention of the wireless intercept stations and the Discrimination Unit, details to be worked out later. That was all for now.[27]

Three weeks passed. The interrogation of Gouzenko at Camp X continued. There were no arrests. The Prime Minister had given orders that the whole matter was to be treated with the greatest discretion. He would get the views of Truman and the new British Prime Minister, Clement Attlee, first; then he would decide what to do.

On October 22, 1945, while Robertson and the Prime Minister were in England, the Canadian Joint Intelligence Committee received a visitor. Newly knighted Sir Edward Travis, operational head of the Government Code and Cipher School (Bletchley), had arrived in Ottawa on his way to Washington to follow up on earlier discussions regarding the postwar management of ULTRA and other forms of special intelligence.

Documents in Britain pertaining to the decisions discussed in the following pages are still considered secret and have never been released.

The United Kingdom, Travis told the Canadians, was looking for a peacetime agreement with Canada and the United States which would involve full cooperation in the sharing of wireless traffic. Because Britain alone could not cover the entire world, the interchange would be on a *quid pro quo* basis, with the three powers dividing up areas of responsibility in much the same way they had during the war. The focus would be on military and clandestine traffic, and would involve checking "as many countries as possible from time to time." The sharing of diplomatic intelligence would not be included.

In Britain, Travis explained, the wireless intelligence organization was being completely overhauled. The Government Code and Cipher School was being absorbed into a new body called the General Signal Intelligence Centre (later named the Government Communications Headquarters)[28] which would manage the product of all intercepts. It was to be divided into five divisions: 1) Technical; 2) Traffic analysis; 3) Cryptanalysis; 4) Intelligence; 5) Cipher security. About 1,150 people would be employed, most of them civilians.

The British Treasury Board also had given approval for a postwar wireless intercept service consisting of 800 receivers, with the Army, Navy, Air Force, and Foreign Office financing 200 each. Around 5,000 people would be involved, which was about the same number that the U.S. Army and U.S. Navy wireless service each employed. An equivalent number for Canada, the Canadians were told, would be about 800. Furthermore, any agreements between wireless intelligence agencies would be on a national basis, not departmental. In other words, Travis said, the Admiralty was not going to have the independent management of its own wireless intercepts that it had enjoyed during the war.

Travis encouraged the Canadians to carry on with their own code- and cipher-breaking. He hinted, however, that it would be preferable if only Britain dealt with the United States on any exchange of actual decrypts. He also asked that he be informed should the Americans make their own approaches on cooperation. To this his listeners agreed.

There was even something for the RCMP. Travis, obviously thinking of the Soviet Union, told Superintendent Rivett-Carnac that there was much of police value to be gained by intercepting the enciphered transmissions of a foreign country to its secret agents abroad. As the minutes of the meeting noted:

> In the United Kingdom the police have been concerned with this form of Signal Intelligence ever since the General Strike of 1926, and the RCMP though concerned with *internal* radio traffic will find this form of service of value in tracing 'personalities.' From learning who is transmitting into a country it is possible to track down the partners in the country, and if care is taken not too readily to shut down illicit traffic, a great deal can be learned. Sir Edward Travis is of the opinion that it is preferable for the RCMP to join the larger setup rather than attempt to maintain a service independently.

In conclusion, Travis said that commercial codes and ciphers—those of business and industry—were not seen as the legitimate targets of peacetime wireless intelligence, despite the interest of Britain's Board of Trade. They would not be covered—"probably."[29]

It was a vitally important meeting. It is remarkable in retrospect that Travis should have been authorized to make such proposals to another country at a level lower than that between the War Office and the Department of National Defence or between the Foreign Office and External Affairs. It was probably a case of testing the waters: if so, they were warm indeed. The Canadian Joint Intelligence Committee formally thanked Travis for his information. Then they all went to dinner.

Given the heavy secrecy in Britain that still surrounds the subject of intelligence, and the fact that few, if any, British documents are available which mention the above-described reorganization, a number of comments should be made. From what Travis told the Canadians, it appears that at the end of the war there was a palace revolution in British Intelligence. And the big loser was Menzies.

From 1940 onward, when the Government Code and Cipher School began to decrypt German ENIGMA traffic with increasing success, Churchill had insisted that he receive the results daily. That task fell to Menzies, then the newly appointed chief of MI6 and overall head of the Government Code and Cipher School. Menzies also sat on the Y Board and, after the reorganization of 1943, was chairman of the Signals Intelligence Board. As a result, he had sweeping power over all signals intelligence, military as well as diplomatic and clandestine.

Churchill was constantly interfering with military operations, usually wrong-headedly. He insisted on receiving decrypts from Menzies in their raw form and refused the commentaries from his own Joint Intelligence Committee which put them in the larger context of the war. As a result, like Hitler, he constantly badgered his military and political advisers, insisting on courses of action that often turned out to be dismal failures.[30]

The resentment and discontent this caused within the British military leadership was profound. Churchill was fighting one war and his generals another. The British Joint Intelligence Committee, consisting of the three service directors of intelligence, as well as representatives from the Foreign Office and the Ministry of Economic Warfare, had evolved by 1942 into an effective management centre for intelligence from all sources. Yet Churchill repeatedly discarded its reasoned assessments and made his own judgment calls based on the decrypts Menzies selected and supplied. Thus, the link between Menzies and Churchill short-circuited the entire British intelligence apparatus.

The War Office and the Admiralty repeatedly tried to solve the problem by bringing the Government Code and Cipher School under the control of the Joint Intelligence Committee. These attempts were usually spearheaded by whoever was Director of Military Intelligence—especially General John Sinclair. The final attempt, which involved all three service directors of intelligence, occurred in the spring of 1945. All failed.[31] As long as Churchill continued to get his daily dispatch box of decrypts, Menzies was safe.

To everyone's surprise, however, Churchill was voted out of office in the general election of July 26, 1945. Clement Attlee became Prime Minister. With Churchill gone and the war nearly over, it appears that Menzies's enemies lost no time in severing his control over ULTRA and returning the Government Code and Cipher School to more orthodox control.

One of the first acts was to amalgamate the wireless intercept organizations of the three services and the Foreign Office. Group Captain Claude Daubeny was appointed head of the new organization and was given the job of finding a new postwar home for the Government Code and Cipher School. The end of the war had brought a massive release of staff from Bletchley Park, and it was proposed to recombine what remained with the diplomatic section at Berkeley Street. Eventually both divisions, on Daubeny's recommendation, were moved to new headquarters at Cheltenham.[32]

Secondly, in September a committee was set up to review the overall organization and operation of MI6. Its members included an outsider, Captain Hastings, the long-time deputy to Commander Travis and the newly appointed head of the Berkeley Street division of the Government Code and Cipher School, replacing Commander Denniston. Hastings and another senior member of GC&CS, Eric Jones, had long been critical of MI6's management of decrypts. No details are available on the recommendations of this committee.

Thirdly, with the endorsement of the Minister of Defence and the Foreign Secretary, the British Joint Intelligence Committee's mandate was greatly strengthened. Its "charter" is worth paraphrasing:

> Under the chairmanship of a senior member of the Foreign Office, the JIC's new responsibilities were:
>
> 1. to give higher direction to defence-related intelligence and security operations and to keep these under constant review;
> 2. to assemble and analyse secret and non-secret intelligence and to write reports for the Chiefs of Staff as required;

3. to keep the entire British Intelligence organization under constant review to ensure efficiency, economy, and responsiveness to changing demands;

4. to coordinate the general policy of overseas JICs, both those under British command and those of the Commonwealth.[33]

This move hobbled MI6 generally and Menzies specifically. Almost all of his power during the war had sprung from his control over wireless intelligence and the distribution of decrypts. Now the British JIC was to set code- and cipher-breaking policy and assess the product. Menzies would merely occupy a chair at the committee table, an equal among equals that included a Foreign Office chairman, the service directors of intelligence, and the head of MI6's wartime rival, MI5.

Finally, Menzies's most determined critic, the wartime Director of Military Intelligence, General Sinclair, was appointed his deputy and successor-designate.[34] An overhaul of MI6 itself was about to begin.

It was too late. Soviet mole Kim Philby had bored into the very heart of the Secret Intelligence Service. He had been promoted. He was now head of Section IX, the MI6 division responsible for Communist counter-espionage.

———

On October 23, 1945, the day after Travis left for Washington, the Canadian Joint Intelligence Committee sent a summary of his proposals to the Chiefs of Staff. Again action was deferred. Robertson and Mackenzie King were still out of the country.[35]

There was no lack of will on the part of Canada's military chiefs, but on intelligence matters they were committed to full consultation with External Affairs. On other defence issues they were free to act. The new Army Chief of Staff, General Charles Foulkes, was especially keen to revamp Canada's defence organizations to meet the Soviet threat. Foulkes was a fighting general; he had distinguished himself leading Canadian troops against the Germans in Italy and was ready to do battle again. And he had an excellent ally: C. J. Mackenzie, the president of the National Research Council.

Mackenzie was one of the first to learn of Gouzenko's defection. During the war, he had steered Canada through a remarkable program of military research. Starting with the seed money provided in 1940 by Canadian industrialists, he had overseen research that touched upon all manner of new weapons and processes. Canadian scientists had contributed significantly toward new explosives, the proximity fuse, high-altitude aviation, anti-submarine devices, chemical and biological weapons and, most important of all, the development of atomic energy.[36]

In 1943 Britain had moved what little it had of a nuclear research program to Canada. Work began in laboratories in Montreal and was soon almost completely administered and financed by Canada through the National Research Council. While the Americans pressed toward the production of a uranium-fueled atomic weapon, the Canadian program concentrated on building a special type of nuclear reactor that used heavy water and produced the alternative atomic explosive—plutonium. All this was done in deep secrecy in both Canada and the United States. The very day that Canada started up its first nuclear reactor, code-named ZEEP—to become the second country in the world after the United States to achieve nuclear capability—Mackenzie learned that one of the British scientists on the project was a spy.

> Well, then, ZEEP goes critical and that night we drove down [to Ottawa].... We got home about 7 o'clock and I got a phone message from Norman Robertson. He said, "I would like to have a word with you."
>
> I said, "Well, I have just got in from Chalk River and I am just having dinner. Is it important?"
>
> And he said, "I think it is rather important. You better come over."
>
> So I went over and he gave me a cocktail and he told me about this Gouzenko business. And, of course, this was very top secret then. They weren't spilling this at all. And then he told me about the number of people at the NRC that were involved and about Allan Nunn May. And we had just left Nunn May up at Chalk River.[37]

For Mackenzie and Foulkes one war was over and another looming. Both knew that technology could be decisive. With Mackenzie's support, Foulkes proposed to radically redesign the way in which military research would be conducted in Canada. It had formerly been done mainly under the auspices of the National Research Council. Now NRC personnel were clamouring to be allowed to return to peacetime science. If operational research were left to the three services, there would be rivalry, waste, and duplication. Foulkes proposed that all military research be gathered into one organization headed by a civilian scientist. To give this new organization financial and political clout, he suggested that its director be made a fourth chief of staff.

It was a terrific idea. It led within two years to the creation of the Defence Research Board, which assumed a mandate for military research that crossed all service boundaries and during the Cold War ranged into areas like missile development, chemical and biological warfare, new aircraft, anti-submarine weaponry, and Arctic warfare. Because it eliminated duplication among the services, Canada's defence research program was far more productive than might be expected of a country Canada's size. It was truly a twentieth-century approach to hi-tech warfare and much more efficient than the fragmented, though much larger, research programs in Britain and the United States.

In October 1945, however, Foulkes and Mackenzie were still only at the early stages of the plan. The concept had been formulated; now they had to lobby the other Chiefs of Staff and the politicians. The Gouzenko disclosures must have lent haste and cogency to their arguments.

Meanwhile, during that month, Mackenzie King and Robertson visited first the United States and then Britain with their story of Soviet spying. At first, Truman and Attlee were inclined to minimize the importance of what they were told but as time passed and their own intelligence staffs had a chance to assess Gouzenko's evidence, their attitudes changed. There was a growing sense of alarm, particularly in the United States. The three leaders planned a conference the following month in Washington, when they would then discuss how far they should go in releasing information on atomic energy, and decide what they should do about the Soviet Union.

November 10 to December 31, 1945. This is the period of the vanished pages. Mackenzie King kept a daily record for almost fifty years. When his diaries were assembled in the 1960s, it was found that one loose-leaf binder was missing. Repeated searches have failed to locate it. The gap it creates could not be more crucial. It covers the meeting in Washington of the three leaders. What was decided publicly is known; what was decided secretly is not. Mackenzie King would have confided those secrets to his diary; it is hard to believe that the disappearance of these key pages is accidental.[38]

While what the three leaders decided to do about the Soviet threat remains unclear, there was one definite result. Truman moved to rename and resurrect the defunct Office of Strategic Services under a new National Intelligence Authority although, thanks to the usual inter-service rivalries, it took more than a year before this plan led to the creation of an effective agency for gathering foreign intelligence. This was the Central Intelligence Agency, later better known as the CIA.

Canadian reorganization also had problems. The friction between External Affairs and the military had not entirely vanished. In November Glazebrook wrote a memo which considerably watered down Murray's proposal for a Joint Coordination Bureau for Intelligence. Such a body, Glazebrook suggested, should have a small staff and be concerned only with collecting intelligence "connected with war plans and indications of preparations of war by foreign states." Its director would be a senior officer from External Affairs with access to ULTRA intelligence. Glazebrook also noted that an agreement between Canada and Britain on sharing ULTRA intelligence had been drafted, and that a Commonwealth conference on the subject was scheduled for February in London. Glazebrook's proposals, in their implicit reliance on Britain for secret intelligence, fell far short of what Murray and the Canadian Joint Intelligence Committee had wanted.[39]

Meanwhile, despite the continued absence of Robertson and the Prime Minister, the strengthening of the Discrimination Unit gathered momentum. Mackenzie promised that the NRC would financially underwrite an increase in the number of cryptanalysts. The British were asked to supply a chief cryptographer for two to three years, and to start sending some enciphered traffic for the Canadian team to work on. Existing staff was to be assured they had permanent jobs, while the Americans were to be told that, for the time being, Canada would not accept any new Japanese assignments from Arlington.

In mid-December 1945, Foulkes won approval for the appointment of a Director-General for Defence Research. The new man was to start in a couple of months and help draft the details of the new organization. He was O. M. Solandt, a Canadian scientist who had been caught at Cambridge at the outbreak of the war and had stayed on in Britain for the duration, eventually taking charge of the British Army's Operational Research Group. He was in Japan touring the ruins of Hiroshima and Nagasaki when he received the offer to return to Canada and head up the new defence research program, thereby becoming a fourth Chief of Staff. He was only thirty-six.

Once the idea of a separate military research division had been formulated and its first director chosen, Foulkes turned to the equally pressing issue of how Canada should go about gathering foreign intelligence while safeguarding its own secrets. He still had before him the original proposal for a Joint Coordination Bureau for Intelligence and Glazebrook's subsequent suggestions. In December 1945, he took the plan and proceeded to rewrite it.

Entitled "Proposal for the Establishment of a National Intelligence Organization," Foulkes's lengthy memo was distributed only to his fellow Chiefs of Staff and to Robertson. It began by setting out a position that was diametrically opposed to that of Glazebrook:

> To be most effective, the appraisal of international affairs, in relation to its political and economic influence, must be from a national viewpoint. Any system whereby the appraisal is made from incomplete intelligence acquired from other countries, or acceptance of another nation's appraisal insofar as it relates to itself, cannot possibly satisfy the Canadian requirement. Such a system would presuppose a degree of political, economic and military dependence incommensurate with the national outlook.

In other words, Canada's sovereignty was intimately tied to developing its own sources of intelligence. Other countries—even great allies—could not be trusted to supply Canada with the kind of information it needed to make its own decisions. Foulkes was again arguing for independence against the willingness of External Affairs to rely on others.

The reason for this division in attitudes is clear. Canada's top military leaders had ended the war deeply dissatisfied with the way in which Mackenzie King—as Secretary of State for External Affairs—had yielded all strategic decision-making to Britain and the United States. Canadian soldiers had fought and died in Hong Kong, Sicily, Italy, France, and Holland. Their fighting prowess had earned the admiration of their enemies. Yet the Canadian Chiefs of Staff had been without a real say in how they were deployed; Canada's top military leaders had been shut out of the deliberations of the Combined (U.S.–U.K.) Chiefs of Staff. When it came to decisions about how Canadian soldiers, sailors, and airmen were to be used, they were often the last to know.

For the coming struggle with Russia, Foulkes wanted a comprehensive Canadian organization that independently managed intelligence from all sources, including that from other countries and from ULTRA. He did not exclude espionage:

> The question of whether or not, or to what degree, Canada should enter the field of active secret intelligence is a matter of high policy which is not dealt with in this paper. It is to be noted, however, that a secret intelligence organization could be added, if required, to the [Joint Coordination] bureau suggested above.

The centrepiece of Foulkes's lengthy memo is a flow chart, blue ink representing TOP SECRET information, red ink ABOVE TOP SECRET. On a corner in red are the words: "Part of chart in red not to be shown on future charts."

First the blue ink. The Joint Coordination Bureau for Intelligence would receive special intelligence (ULTRA) from a Signal Intelligence Unit and political, economic, and scientific intelligence from a special Foreign Intelligence Unit. Domestic and foreign topographical data would come from a Topographic Unit. All this would be digested and summarized for the benefit of External Affairs, although relevant information would also be sent sideways to the Canadian Joint Intelligence Committee for passing on to the appropriate Army, Navy, and Air Force intelligence staffs. So far, so good.

Next the red ink. The Director of the Joint Coordination Bureau for Intelligence would have a shadow Co-director of Counter-intelligence whose identity and very existence was "to be kept secret." This person would be in charge of shadow counter-intelligence units linked to the RCMP and to each of the three service intelligence organizations. He would also maintain secret liaison with the FBI in the United States and with both MI5 and MI6 in Britain.

Foulkes was proposing the creation in Canada of a totally secret counter-espionage agency. It would be headed by a man whose very name would be Above Top Secret. The ultimate spy-chaser.

Here's the catch: there is no easy way of knowing whether this aspect of Foulkes's plan was ever adopted. Not only are the minutes of the Chiefs of Staff Committee still withheld in Canadian archives, the counter-espionage aspect of his memo was probably never discussed in open session. Foulkes intended that there would be no record in the formal files of his Above Top Secret proposal. It was mere accident that his blue-ink/red-ink flow chart found its way into an obscure file that was declassified long before passage of Canada's Access to Information Act.

To work at their best, Foulkes believed that Canada's counter-espionage chief and his men had to be officially invisible.[40]

CHAPTER THIRTEEN

THREE
SECRET FRIENDS

DECEMBER 1945 – DECEMBER 1947

Lester Pearson had a problem: how to hide from Parliament and the people of Canada the cost of a major expansion of Canada's ability to eavesdrop on international communications—the building of three new wireless intercept stations.

"The purpose of these stations," the new undersecretary of state for External Affairs wrote, "is to intercept traffic upon which the cryptographers here, in London and Washington work." It was February 18, 1947. Pearson was trying to persuade the president of the National Research Council, C. J. Mackenzie, to hide the needed $3 million—at least $50 million in 1993 terms—within the NRC's budget.

"The general opinion," Pearson continued, "is that the clearness of reception and the amount of traffic which can be taken is far greater in the Arctic areas than elsewhere. From the point of view, therefore, of the United States and the United Kingdom, the setting up of the Whitehorse and the Churchill stations will be extremely important."[1]

Thus did Canada become partner with the United States and Britain in the biggest secret of the immediate postwar years. In 1947 the world knew about the atomic bomb. It did not know about ULTRA. It did not know that throughout the war the English-speaking Allies had been intercepting and deciphering foreign military and diplomatic messages on a massive scale. It also did not know that they intended to continue to do so.

―――――――

The possibility that Canada's sub-Arctic areas might be especially good for radio reception had been raised by Colonel Drake in January 1946. In casting around for an excuse to maintain a postwar wireless intercept service, he suggested that the Air Force might want to build a station of its own. There had been no operational reason for RCAF intercept stations during the war and the Air Force authorities responded warmly to the idea of a ten-position facility at Whitehorse in the Yukon. According to Drake, the location should be good for picking up parts of Asia not heard elsewhere.

The Canadian Joint Intelligence Committee liked the proposal and tried to expand upon it. G. G. Crean, the new member from External Affairs, declared that his department put the highest value on wireless intelligence and that it was "paramount that Canada should make an adequate contribution to the common pool." It was also vital, Crean added, to decide at least in principle what Canada would offer at the Commonwealth Communications Conference coming up the next month in London.[2]

The thirty-five-year-old Crean was a postwar addition to the staff of External Affairs. The G.G. of his initials stood for Gordon Gale but for some reason he always preferred to be called "Bill." A graduate of the University of Toronto, he had served in the war as an intelligence officer with the British Army.

The result was an even more aggressive memo to the Chiefs of Staff, on top of the two they had already received from Murray plus the master-plan for secret intelligence submitted by Foulkes. They were told that if Canada was to participate in the postwar sharing of wireless intelligence, then it needed to equip and operate 100 new high-speed monitoring positions "distributed so as to cover the gaps in the coverage by other Empire and U.S. positions." A quick decision was necessary to get "Canadian interception underway as soon as practical." Just as this missive was launched, the Gouzenko story broke.[3]

MOSCOW STEALS NUKE SECRETS the *Toronto Daily Star* front-page headline howled. **OTTAWA SPY RING** echoed *The Globe and Mail*. Similar headlines—big, black, and bold—reverberated in newspapers around the country and, in the next few weeks, rang the changes in the American and British press as well, and then around the world. It was Canada's big story—bigger news than anything involving the country during the war. Bigger than the catastrophes of Hong Kong or Dieppe. It even rated a character assassination of Mackenzie King in the Moscow press (a "vile item" the Canadian chargé d'affaires wrote), and the accusation that the Gouzenko defection was a contrivance of the Canadian government similar to the Reichstag fire set by the Nazis in 1933 and blamed on the Communists.[4]

It went on and on, all spring and into the summer of 1946. Headline after headline: **MOSCOW PIPELINE** and **MAY CHARGE TREASON IN SPY CASE.** When reporters had the chance to see those arrested, there was a kind of lower-case sympathy: **Spy ring folk unassuming** and **First four accused were average wage-earners.**

The media hullaballoo prompted an earnest debate at the Canadian Joint Intelligence Committee about whether "D notices" should be used to muzzle the press. These were secret self-censorship guidelines issued to publishers by the British government. The Admiralty had helpfully suggested the idea and furnished a sample "D notice" that forbade publication of information relating to the Special Air Service, methods of enciphering messages, British secret intelligence, and British counter-intelligence.

The concept was new to Canadian directors of intelligence and they were intrigued. They were not sure, however, that journalists in Canada would react as tamely as their British counterparts to restrictions on what they could report. Besides, the Canadian public was not even aware that Canada was involved in secret intelligence. The committee concluded that it "would be bad security to advise all publishers that there exist such items of information to conceal." The idea was rejected.[5]

Meanwhile, at the end of March, with Soviet espionage stories still ringing through the press, the Chiefs of Staff and Norman Robertson not only approved the expansion of the wireless intercept program as formulated by the Joint Intelligence Committee, but endorsed a proposal from External Affairs that the Discrimination Unit and its cryptanalysis section be reorganized into a new civilian agency to be called the Communications Research Centre. The first director would be Colonel Drake; there would be 179 staff; and it would work on ciphermaking as well as cipher-breaking. Robertson steered the plan directly to cabinet for signature.[6]

The Chiefs of Staff decision was prompted by the favourable response at the Commonwealth Communications Conference to Canada's offer to contribute 100 intercept positions. Further details of this February 1946 meeting are unavailable, but it presumably involved wireless intelligence representatives from Australia, New Zealand, and India.[7]

On September 1, 1946, after a minor name change, the forerunner of Canada's Communications Security Establishment formally came into being. It was called the Communications Branch, National Research Council, and was ostensibly set up to police the security of government ciphers.[8] Its real job—its ULTRA task—was to analyse and break the enciphered traffic of foreign governments. It was the Canadian equivalent of the Army's Signal Security Agency in the United States and the Government Code and Cipher School in Britain.

These decisions were a victory for Colonel Murray and Commander Little. They had fought long and hard to ensure that the special intelligence expertise developed during wartime would be preserved. Now, thanks to Gouzenko and the onset of the Cold War, they had won. Canada was set firmly on a road that guaranteed her a place in the secret deliberations of her two more powerful English-speaking allies. Considering the emerging tendency of Americans to see their country as the unqualified leader in international affairs, it was an achievement of great consequence for Canada in the decades to come.

Colonel Murray now retired to civilian life. Little had left the year before. It was time for the professionals to take over. Murray was replaced as Director of Military Intelligence by Colonel W. A. B. Anderson, who had served as General Staff Officer with the Canadian troops fighting in Europe.

Canada, it should be said, managed for over fifty years to keep its signals intelligence activities cloaked in secrecy. In the United States and Britain, rumours of government agencies engaged in gathering electronic intelligence gradually leaked out, despite tight security and "D notices." Not so in Canada. The Communications Branch was generally accepted as just another research division of the National Research Council. The arrays of aerials at the major intercept stations at Ottawa (Leitrim) and elsewhere elicited little public speculation or comment. That trait of the Canadian national character which assumes Canadians are incapable of originality—and certainly incapable of deviousness—proved to be superlative camouflage.

The man responsible for deciding on the final shape of Canada's security and intelligence organizations—and the ultimate beneficiary of them—was Lester Pearson. By the summer of 1946, it was obvious to Mackenzie King that Norman Robertson was failing in health. The man had carried an enormous burden throughout the war, followed immediately by the Gouzenko emergency. Robertson desperately needed a rest. The Prime Minister advised him to take the newly vacated post of High Commissioner in London, while Pearson would be brought up from Washington to be his successor. The Prime Minister also decided to give up the External Affairs portfolio.

In September 1946 Louis St. Laurent became the new Secretary of State for External Affairs and Pearson the new undersecretary. St. Laurent was sixty-six years old, Pearson forty-nine.

One of the new undersecretary's first tasks was to figure out how to hide the cost of the 100 new intercept positions that had been approved. It was decided to retain forty-two positions spread among the existing Army/Navy stations at Ottawa (Leitrim), Coverdale, and Prince Rupert. The balance would be made up by building three new stations at Whitehorse, Vancouver, and Churchill. The total capital cost would be $1,050,954.[9]

The estimated outlay quickly escalated to almost $3 million and Pearson asked C. J. Mackenzie if the money could be hidden in the National Research Council budget. The NRC was already funding the Communications Branch, so what could be more logical? The NRC, Pearson argued, would also be able to insulate the intercept stations from the "inevitable" cuts in defence spending that were sure to come.

Mackenzie was cool to Pearson's request. In peacetime the National Research Council was supposed to be a civilian agency doing civilian research. It would be difficult to hide such a huge sum of money. On the other hand, the Defence Research Board then taking shape under O. M. Solandt might be an ideal alternative. "Parliament would naturally expect Defence Research to be concerned with secret matters," Mackenzie observed. He suggested that if the money was concealed in the DRB financial vote, there would be much less likelihood of "embarrassing questions." Exactly that was done. The troublesome $3 million vanished from public view.[10]

Meanwhile, details of the postwar signals intelligence-sharing arrangements were still being worked out. Further talks in London were scheduled for October 1946, this time involving the Americans. Colonel Drake, as the head of the new Communications Branch, represented Canada. The other major parties were the Government Code and Cipher School—now reorganized as the Government Communications Headquarters (GCHQ)—and the U.S. Army's Signal Security Agency, now renamed the Army Security Agency. The extent of FBI and U.S. Navy participation is unknown. It was probably non-existent. The U.S. Navy dealt separately with the Government Communications Headquarters at least until the early 1950s.[11]

The purpose of the October talks was to divide responsibility for wireless interception. Canada's promise of 100 positions was modest in comparison to the 800 apiece pledged by the U.S. Army and the British. Travis's statements on his visit to Canada the year before probably provide an accurate picture of the arrangement the participants arrived at: the intention was to aim all this listening power at the Communist Bloc under the same basic rules that existed toward the end of the war. Each party was assigned a particular area to concentrate on. Canada's target was Soviet Siberia.[12]

That assignment alone would have been enough to guarantee Canada's full partnership in what would come to be known as the BRUSA and CANUSA agreements.[13] Pearson made the tie almost unbreakable. Immediately after the London conference he proposed to Travis that Canada take over the running of the HYDRA transmitter at Oshawa and that it be used once again as the main channel for sending signals intelligence traffic from Canada and the United States to Britain. Pearson also promised to upgrade the equipment. As the post-war British government was strapped for cash, Travis readily agreed.[14]

Pearson's later explanation to C. J. Mackenzie is worth quoting at length:

> The chief purpose of the link is for trans-Atlantic communication, which will link the London Signal Intelligence authorities with the United States Communications authorities and ourselves. Its chief purpose is to carry traffic from the intercept stations in its raw form and to make for ease of handling and speed at the various centres. In addition, it will carry Foreign Office traffic to Washington and External Affairs traffic to the U.K. The Oshawa station is, therefore, an important link in the general signals intelligence network and is of vital importance to the United Kingdom and the United States, as for political reasons they do not want to pass the traffic direct.[15]

The "political reasons" presumably related to the propriety of the United States intercepting foreign communications and then giving them to Britain. Having Canada serve as middleman permitted "deniability"—a time-honoured ploy of democratic governments whereby an embarrassing question is answered literally. Was the United States sending the intercepted messages of foreign governments to the United Kingdom? The answer would be no, since they were being sent to Canada.

The political importance of the HYDRA transmitter is further underlined by the fact that some of the raw traffic it handled definitely was illegal. Cable and telegraph interception had been a vital source of raw traffic during the war, especially for diplomatic and commercial messages, but U.S. Telegraph Censorship was no more. Nevertheless, U.S. Military Intelligence (G-2) officials managed to persuade the major American telegraph companies to supply them with copies of their daily messages. These went to Arlington. This was against the law and amounted to outright espionage against Americans and foreigners alike. The FBI made similar arrangements, and the British likewise.[16]

It is not known whether Canada was privy to these illegal activities—or whether it was a party to them—but the Anglo–American agreements on signals intelligence certainly put it in step in terms of the coming struggle against the Soviet Union. What still remained to be settled was: how should Canada's Cold War security and intelligence organization be structured?

General Foulkes presented his memo calling for a "National Intelligence Organization"—the proposed Joint Coordination Bureau for Intelligence—to the cabinet Defence Committee in early March 1946. Discussion was deferred. Glazebrook had accompanied Drake to the Commonwealth Communications Conference in London the previous month and Robertson wanted to wait for his report on "British arrangements for intelligence and security." Ultimately this report caused the Foulkes plan to be shelved.[17]

British Intelligence could do no wrong in Glazebrook's eyes, and he managed to persuade Robertson, and then Pearson, to model Canada's secret intelligence services along British lines. This meant that the Canadian Joint Intelligence Committee—like its British counterpart—would have overall charge of intelligence policy under an External Affairs chairman. Signals intelligence policy was to put under a separate committee—the Communications Research Committee—which had overlapping membership with the CJIC, minus the Defence Research Board representative.

Next came the problem of what to do about gathering information of a more general nature. Much of the Allied intelligence effort during the war had been directed toward collecting data on the economic, trade, and industrial activities of the Axis powers. In Britain the Ministry for Economic Warfare had been created to give vital assistance in estimating the enemy's strategic intentions and for deciding what targets to bomb.

The Dieppe raid of 1942, so costly in Canadian lives, had also taught a valuable lesson. When planning the raid, the British discovered that they did not have even the most elementary knowledge of the beaches where the Canadians were to land. They were forced to rely on aerial photographs and prewar holiday snapshots in trying to determine shoreline gradients and ground conditions. They badly miscalculated: the Canadian tanks that landed became stuck in the soft shingle on the beaches and were leisurely destroyed by German shore batteries. The Normandy invasion in 1944 was similarly bedevilled by the lack of elementary terrain information that could easily have been gathered on location or from public sources before the war. The British were determined not to suffer again from this deficiency.

The British postwar solution was to set up a secret agency manned by civilians called the Joint Intelligence Bureau (JIB). Its mandate was the collection of information from designated foreign countries dealing with their economies, topography, communications, ports, and airfields. It divided the world into western, central, and eastern divisions (JIB2, JIB3, JIB4). It also had a rather interesting subdepartment:

> The Procurement Sub-Division is responsible for the systematic collection of intelligence from both secret and open sources. This responsibility involves: (a) direct liaison with establishments engaged in obtaining intelligence by secret means, including photographic as well as agents' reports ... (c) the maintenance of a photographic library and appropriate registers of personalities, contacts, and captured documents.

For scientific and technological innovations, the Joint Intelligence Bureau relied on liaison with the scientific intelligence departments of the air force, army, and navy.[18]

The British JIB could hardly expect to cover the entire world on its own, so not surprisingly it asked for help from the Commonwealth. London would look after Europe, and satellite JIBs would handle the Middle East and India. Australia was then asked to set up its own JIB to cover southeast Asia—Japan, Burma, Korea, Indochina, Malaya, and the Pacific islands east of 180 degrees longitude. Canada was asked to take on Siberia, Greenland, the Pacific coast of Mexico, Central America, and its own vast Arctic territories. Australian agreement came quickly; Canada, with the Chiefs of Staff still dreaming of a single central intelligence organization, held back. The hesitation vanished, however, when Glazebrook returned with Drake from the Commonwealth conference on wireless intelligence. Apparently the discussions had included the setting up of JIBs.[19]

In one of his last acts as undersecretary of state for External Affairs, Robertson approved formation of a Canadian Joint Intelligence Bureau. He endorsed the British concept entirely, including the use of "secret sources." The Chiefs of Staff still were doubtful, but the new undersecretary, Lester Pearson, appeared before them and argued that the American concept of a central intelligence agency (later the CIA) still had not proved itself, was too expensive, and would not fit in with Commonwealth intelligence organizations. The Chiefs of Staff had little choice. Pearson had the ear of Mackenzie King and the new prime minister-designate, Louis St. Laurent. They gave in.[20]

The next step was to find someone to head the new agency. The process took months. After exhaustive biographical reviews of about twenty potential candidates, the Canadian Joint Intelligence Committee narrowed the choice down to an air marshall and Captain de Marbois, with the latter especially favoured. Aside from the fact that he had set up the Navy's Foreign Intelligence Service during the war—which was essentially the same idea as a JIB—and was entirely familiar with all forms of secret intelligence, de Marbois spoke and read Russian, Spanish, French, and German fluently and was conversant in Arabic, Turkish, and the Scandanavian languages. He appeared ideally qualified. Then External Affairs intervened.

It was Glazebrook who wielded the dagger. "De Marbois would not, repeat not, be at all suitable," he wrote Crean. "There is a very long and involved story about his position during the war...." A few days later a formal note was issued from External Affairs which objected to him on the grounds that at fifty-eight he was too old. The Chiefs of Staff inevitably agreed.[21]

It was a sad reversal for the Navy's wartime head of operational intelligence. Upon discharge at the end of the war, de Marbois found that his former post at Upper Canada College had been filled. After desperately trying to find other employment, he pleaded for any job in government. Finally, he resorted to farming. It was too much for a man nearly sixty. He spent the rest of his life in near-poverty.

Subsequent events make one wonder whether Glazebrook had a

hidden agenda. Fault was also found with the other candidate. An interim director was appointed and after six months Glazebrook himself was named to the post. He served for six months and then asked to step down. Another lengthy candidate search ensued and again External Affairs rejected everyone. Glazebrook then suggested the liaison officer who had been sent to Canada from the British Joint Intelligence Bureau.

In comparison to the Canadian candidates who had already been considered—former intelligence officers, academics of high standing, war heroes, multilinguists and so on—the credentials of Glazebrook's nominee were pale indeed. Ivor Bowen was thirty-five years old, had spent most of the war in the Royal Artillery, a little time in the Army's Topographical Department, a few months in the British JIB, and that was that. Despite the fact that the Chiefs of Staff had repeatedly said that the new director should be a Canadian who could better manage liaison with the Americans, especially the newly formed CIA, they grew tired of the interminable prevarication of External Affairs. Bowen, an Englishman, got the job.[22]

The creation of the Joint Intelligence Bureau enabled Canada's intelligence authorities to keep a promise to the British to maintain Canada's "contact register." This was another ingenious and closely guarded wartime idea. It consisted of a list of security-cleared individuals who had lived abroad, including refugees and immigrants, who could help with the interpretation of pictures obtained by photo reconnaissance. Even the sharpest aerial photograph could not disclose all the vital features of an area being surveyed. How deep was a river or pond? How firm was the soil? How strong was a bridge? These were vital questions to military planners responsible for selecting the best routes for columns of tanks and armoured vehicles, or for advising generals in the field on how best to deploy their forces.

By the fourth year of the war, photo reconnaissance had reached a high degree of sophistication, with specially modified high-altitude Spitfires ranging over much of Occupied Europe. The resulting photographs were examined at Britain's Central Interpretation Unit at Medmenham, and here people from the contact registers were brought to help with their interpretation.

The contact registers were also used to obtain first-hand knowledge of political, social, and economic conditions in foreign locales, valuable in the planning of both military and intelligence operations. By late 1943 the British contact register—suitably indexed, alphabetized, and cross-referenced—consisted of more than 70,000 names. These became the responsibility of the British and the Canadian JIBs, and of the CIA also.[23]

The Allied development of contact registers explains why the Communist countries kept such repressive restrictions on travel and emigration throughout the Cold War. High-altitude photo reconnaissance could not easily be stopped, but supplementary information from people could. With "moles" in many of the major departments of British Intelligence by the end of the war, the Soviet Union could not have failed to learn about this method of gathering intelligence. The answer was to build a wall around the Communist Bloc—literally the Berlin Wall, figuratively the Iron Curtain. For the next forty-five years, Communist countries generally refused to allow emigration.

People tried to escape to the West nevertheless, especially over the wall that divided East and West Germany. The Communist border guards had orders to shoot to kill. The most enduring legacy of those in Britain who spied for the Soviets in the early 1940s was the concrete and barbed wire of the Berlin Wall, and the blood-soaked ground along one side of it.[24]

Glazebrook's ideas prevailed. The Canadian Joint Intelligence Committee became Canada's central coordinating authority for secret intelligence, each member of the committee speaking for the agency or department he represented. Intelligence responsibilities were divided as follows:

Chairman, External Affairs	political
Director, Naval Intelligence	naval
Director, Military Intelligence	military
Director, Air Intelligence	air

Director General, Defence Research   scientific

RCMP   counter-intelligence

Joint Intelligence Bureau   topographical

    and economic

Each department also contributed personnel to a small permanent staff (the Joint Intelligence Staff) charged with writing up intelligence appreciations as required.[25]

This structure mirrored that which existed in Britain, with two significant exceptions. The British Joint Intelligence Committee was chaired by a Foreign Office official of deputy-minister rank and it lacked a representative from an agency that specialized in scientific intelligence—a yawning omission, considering that one of the biggest lessons of the war had been that a country's survival depended on staying abreast (if not ahead) of the technological innovations of its potential enemies. Recent advances in guided missiles, electronics, atomic energy, biological warfare, and jet propulsion were now making scientific intelligence even more crucial. Yet the British failed to provide for it. Had the Soviets scored again?

Another Marxist scientist who had penetrated the inner sanctum of Britain's wartime intelligence establishment was physicist P. M. S. Blackett. He had not made as much of a prewar show of his Communist sympathies as Desmond Bernal, but nevertheless was regarded as a security risk. As he had done particularly good work with the Admiralty, toward the end of the war his background seemed to have been forgotten. It fell to him in 1946 to plan the postwar reorganization of Britain's scientific intelligence effort. Much to the chagrin of R. V. Jones, who had brilliantly led the wartime counterattack against German electronic developments, Blackett all but destroyed it.

According to *Most Secret War*, Jones's autobiography, Blackett was able to convince the authorities to dismantle the close cooperation that had developed on scientific research both within and among the three services. Their scientific intelligence departments were separated from one another and from their own operational staffs. Jones resigned in disgust, and defence research in Britain languished right up until the Korean War. The British Joint Intelligence Committee did not get a scientific intelligence representative until 1952, after Churchill returned to power and Jones was appointed Director of Scientific Intelligence.

It took years for the damage caused by the Blackett reorganization to be undone and it is certainly perplexing that someone of Blackett's left-leaning background should have been given so much influence.

While Canada followed Britain's lead in many things, in this instance it did not. Right from the outset, there was a Defence Research Board representative on the postwar Canadian Joint Intelligence Committee. Before long, a Directorate of Scientific Intelligence was formed within the DRB to advise the Chiefs of Staff and External Affairs on "the progress of intelligence and technology, and the development of new weapons and new methods of warfare in potential enemy countries." This it did by studying Russian periodicals and evaluating material obtained from Canada's military attachés, by "interrogations," and by material obtained from "special" sources.[26]

Scientific intelligence-gathering in the United States came under the newly formed Central Intelligence Agency, which established liaison with Canada by 1950. The CIA sent the Canadians a constant stream of memoranda dealing with estimated Soviet advances in nuclear, chemical, and biological warfare, missile development and so on, coupled with proposals for U.S.–Canada cooperation on various military research projects. When the CIA expressed disappointment in the quality of intelligence it was getting in return, the Canadians responded by outfitting Canada's military attachés with miniature tape recorders and wrist microphones so that they could record the sounds of aircraft engines for later analysis. It is not known how well this program worked.[27]

Canada's military attachés certainly had their work cut out for them. As early as January 1948, an elaborate memo was prepared for those assigned to Europe detailing information they should try to collect about East Germany. Topics included the Soviet order-of-battle, scientific research centres, supply bases, secret police (activities and personalities), anti-Soviet resistance groups, anti-West groups, harbours, steel production, specific details on the new Joseph Stalin Mark-3 heavy tank, and identification and specifications for an unknown artillery piece, photographs attached. It is hard to see how military attachés could fill such a shopping list without resorting to clandestine contacts.[28]

These are among the few examples (in available documents up to 1955) of active espionage in other countries undertaken by Canada. It has long been believed that the Canadian government has never been involved in collecting foreign intelligence by clandestine means in the same sense as MI6 and the CIA (or the KGB, for that matter). The only agency perceived by the Canadian public to be involved in secret service work has been the RCMP's security service which, in the 1950s, undertook to bug the Soviet embassy in Ottawa. Its mandate, and that of its successor organization, the Canadian Security Intelligence Service (CSIS), has always been limited to Canada's national boundaries. During the war, Canada had relied principally on the OSS for foreign intelligence obtained by espionage. It did not continue to do so.[29]

In March 1949, G. G. Crean, then chairman of the Canadian Joint Intelligence Committee, made the following curious remark in answer to the CIA's request for closer relations. Having told CIA director Henry Hillenkoetter that Canada's Joint Intelligence Bureau and Directorate of Scientific Intelligence would welcome direct contact, Crean added:

> There is also the possibility of establishing liaison with my own department on the foreign secret intelligence side, but this is a matter I should like to discuss further.[30]

At about the same time, Glazebrook reported on the progress he was making with the Joint Intelligence Bureau:

> Particular attention is now being given to the Canadian field which is being explored both for covert and overt intelligence. The Department of External Affairs has already offered to put at our disposal the relevant material and to secure from its missions abroad information for which we might ask.[31]

If these comments mean what they seem, External Affairs was also preparing to try its hand at gathering intelligence by clandestine means.

At this time External Affairs was in the process of developing a new division within the ministry to handle secret intelligence from all sources. This was Defence Liaison Two (DL2), which Glazebrook took charge of at the end of 1949. Housed in the East Block of the Parliament buildings, it was to act as a distribution centre for decrypts and other intelligence coming from the Communications Branch. It had secure cable links directly with Britain's Government Communications Headquarters and with the National Security Agency, the giant successor organization that finally emerged in 1952 from the U.S. Army's wartime Signal Security Agency.

DL2—it was always known by the acronym—was a child of Herbert Norman's wartime Special Intelligence Branch, and for much of the Cold War it was one of the most secret branches of government. It had much the same function as Norman's tiny group, though on a larger scale. In the 1950s decrypts from the Communications Branch —by that time in larger premises in a former convent on Alta Vista Drive—arrived by special vehicle under a two-man guard. Staff in DL2 filed and collated them with other sources of intelligence and sent the results to the appropriate diplomatic branches of External Affairs—the European division, the Far East division, the Latin American division—and to the Privy Council Office. Truly urgent or significant decrypts went directly to the undersecretary or to the Secretary of State for External Affairs himself—Lester Pearson.[32]

DL2's other function is obscure. The need-to-know rule was followed absolutely, with staff subgroups compartmentalized behind closed doors. The other section dealt with security, both within External Affairs in Ottawa and by means of "security officers" in Canada's missions abroad. While it is possible that these individuals were strictly confined to issues of diplomatic confidentiality, it is worth noting that the "security" or "passport control officers" that Britain assigned to its embassies were usually MI6 personnel, with area responsibility for both counter-espionage and espionage. Whether in this case External Affairs followed the British pattern—as it so often had done—is unknown. With George Glazebrook as the first director of DL2, and considering his statement that he was developing covert sources of intelligence within External Affairs, it seems likely.[33]

Glazebrook was succeeded as director of DL2 in the late 1950s by Crean, who was followed in the 1960s by Hamilton Southam, best known for his later role in setting up Canada's National Arts Centre. The DL2 directors' comparatively brief periods in office, and the fact that none were truly professional intelligence officers, suggests that the overall coordination of secret intelligence from all branches of government may have been managed elsewhere. But where? That can only be answered definitively when Canada releases the appropriate secret files. However, there is one clue.

Confirmation that Canada was at least considering ways to get into the espionage game comes from an unlikely source. In 1949 British traitor Kim Philby, then a high-ranking counter-intelligence officer in MI6, was posted to Washington. In the memoir he wrote after he fled to Moscow, he recalled that his new duties involved dealing with the RCMP and with "individuals in the Department of External Affairs who were dickering with the idea of setting up an independent Canadian secret service." Philby also reported that the senior MI6 officer he was replacing, Peter Dwyer, was going on to Canada where a "congenial government post" awaited him.[34]

Dwyer was one of the bright lights of MI6. He had served much of the war as liaison officer in Washington and was one of the MI6 operatives sent to Ottawa to interview Gouzenko shortly after his defection. It was also he who in 1949 put the final finger on British scientist Klaus Fuchs as the spy inside U.S. atomic bomb research, thereby winning the absolute confidence of the FBI and the CIA. This would have made him an excellent candidate to oversee Canada's counter-espionage activities while liaising with his opposite numbers in the United States and Britain.

In 1952 Dwyer was given a job in the Privy Council Office, where he remained until 1957.[35] This put him right at the centre of government, next to the Prime Minister and out of reach of normal departmental curiosity. If Dwyer was also charged with coordinating the covert activities of the Directorate of Scientific Intelligence, the RCMP, External Affairs, and the various military attachés, it was the perfect place to be. Perhaps General Foulkes got his wish for a secret service chief whose identity, staff, and very existence would remain

Above Top Secret. Perhaps there was another blue ink/red ink flow chart leading to a single person responsible for coordinating espionage as well as counter-espionage.

Unfortunately, since Philby knew about Dwyer and Canada's plans for a secret service, the Soviets did also.

Keeping secrets is just as important as acquiring them. After the Gouzenko disclosures, it became a major preoccupation in all government departments. During the war only the armed forces had their own security branches, while other departments merely liaised with the RCMP in hit-or-miss fashion.[36] Gouzenko revealed that the Soviets were interested in more than military matters and that External Affairs and the National Research Council were especially promising targets for penetration. It was decided (apparently again on Glazebrook's recommendation) to set up a separate committee—the Security Panel—to take care of the problem. Modelled after an identically named committee in Britain, it was to be chaired by a senior member of the Privy Council, with representatives from Defence, External Affairs, and the RCMP.[37]

There was an immediate objection. Colonel Eric Acland, head of the Army's security service (MI3), pointed out that the British Security Panel system was based on its link to Britain's Security Service (MI5), which looked after both military and civilian counter-espionage. The closest parallel in Canada was the RCMP, but it had never been directly responsible for keeping tabs on military personnel. That had been Acland's job. This time the Chiefs of Staff dug in their heels. They created a Joint Security Committee that would oversee the security concerns of the Army, Navy, Air Force, and Defence Research Board. The Security Panel was left with jurisdiction over everything else.

The withdrawal of the military meant that the Security Panel began as a comparatively low-level committee with no executive power. Chaired first by Arnold Heeny of the Privy Council Office, and then by Peter Dwyer when he arrived, it was charged with drafting security regulations, securing public buildings, improving Canada's own ciphers, and upgrading the terms of the Official Secrets Act. Except through liaison with the RCMP, it did not have its own staff for identifying and keeping track of potential subversives. James Angleton, the head of the CIA's counter-espionage division, apparently found the Security Panel so inadequately conceived when he visited Ottawa in 1949 that he advised against CIA cooperation with it. Liaison was established a few years later, however, after the arrival of Dwyer.[38]

The Security Panel did have one rather interesting responsibility: censorship. This had proved to be a most important security and intelligence tool during the war and the Americans, British, and Canadians wanted to be ready to impose it again, should a warlike emergency arise. To do this the three countries set up shadow censorship organizations, complete with skeleton staffs and directors of censorship who held secret conferences from time to time, at least until the late 1950s, to discuss the mechanisms of tripartite cooperation.[39]

There is evidence, at least in Canada, that there was substance as well as theory to the postwar shadow censorship organizations. During the war, Security Censorship had been a subdepartment of Postal Censorship. It dealt with letters plucked from the mails and secretly copied to the RCMP according to the names on a watch list of suspected subversives. In 1950 RCMP assistant commissioner L.H. Nicholson was able to supply the CIA with extracts from a private letter exchanged between two members of the Labour Progressive Party as part of an overall report on the "Communist Peace Offensive" in Canada. It is hard to see how the RCMP could have got such information other than by mail interception. Security Censorship, it appears, was still alive and well.[40]

By late 1950 reorganization of security and intelligence in Canada was complete. External Affairs had opted to imitate the British in almost every particular. There were almost exact Canadian counterparts to the British Joint Intelligence Committee, the British Joint Intelligence Bureau, and the British Security Panel. Even DL2 was probably an imitation of a similar division with similar functions in the Foreign Office. The Communications Branch and the Communications Research Committee were analogous to the Government

Communications Headquarters and the Signals Intelligence Board in Britain. All these bodies had essentially the same roles. Only the Defence Research Board and the armed forces Joint Security Committee could lay claim to having been conceived in Canada.

Significantly—surely significantly—most of the intelligence agencies under External Affairs were directly controlled by former British Intelligence officers. By 1950 Crean chaired both the Canadian Joint Intelligence Committee and the Communications Research Committee. The chief cryptographer at the Communications Branch (name unknown) was supplied from Britain. Ivor Bowen headed the Joint Intelligence Bureau. The Privy Council Office had hired Dwyer. As for Glazebrook at DL2, he was considered by his contemporaries to be "more British than the British." Thanks to him, indeed, External Affairs had ignored the Army's vision of an independent Canadian central intelligence organization and had created a British clone instead.

Presiding over all this was Lester Pearson. Prime Minister St. Laurent had no experience in such matters. He had been parachuted into government in 1941 from private law practice in Quebec in an attempt to curry favour with his home province. He had had little direct involvement with secret intelligence during the war and, in comparison to Pearson, knew nothing about how to negotiate the minefields of Canada–U.S.–U.K. cooperation on secret matters. He had no choice but to rely on his deputy minister.[41]

It is testimony to Mackenzie King's peculiar approach to politics and international affairs that he should see someone as untested as St. Laurent as his successor. But so it was. On announcing his retirement in 1948, Mackenzie King gave a last demonstration of his uncanny grasp on the Liberal Party by managing to have St. Laurent named the new leader. The prime minister-designate then made one of the best decisions of his political career. He asked Pearson to replace him as Secretary of State for External Affairs. The choice could not have been better.

Pearson did one thing which may have helped to nationalize the intelligence agencies under him. Complaining that control of the Communications Branch was a little too remote from senior policy makers for his liking, he was instrumental in creating the so-called Senior Committee consisting of himself, the Chiefs of Staff, and C. J. Mackenzie of the National Research Council. It sat several times a year to hear the reports of the Communications Research Committee (the "junior" committee) and to discuss "matters of high policy"—presumably the setting of targets and priorities for signals intelligence. This function has remained essentially the same over the years, although the Senior Committee has undergone a number of name changes: Communications Security Board (1953–1960); Intelligence Policy Committee (1960–1972); Interdepartmental Committee on Security and Intelligence (1972–).[42]

The change from Senior Committee to Communications Security Board in 1953 also immensely strengthened the control that Defence Liaison Two exerted over the Communications Branch and Canada's signals intelligence program in general. The director of DL2 (then still George Glazebrook) also became the Director of Communications Security which, despite the misleading term "security" in the title, actually involved overall supervision of signals intelligence. Glazebrook, in other words, became Drake's boss at the Communications Branch and was answerable only to the Senior Committee/Communications Security Board to which he was attached as its permanent "executive agent," responsible for keeping it informed and for carrying out its instructions. He also chaired the Communications Research Committee, which now was reduced to a purely advisory role, chiefly on technical matters. This arrangement remained in force until 1972.[43]

By the early 1950s, Canada's intelligence organizations were functioning smoothly. At the behest of the Americans, who were concerned about a possible Soviet attack over the Arctic, the Joint Intelligence Bureau gave priority to topographical studies of northern Canada while receiving an ample diet of unclassified, Secret and Top Secret reports from its British counterpart. These covered subjects such as rubber purchases by the Soviet Union, its oil needs, the condition of roads and bridges in Poland, lines of defence in west Russia, the building of a railroad in Saudi Arabia, and secret negotiations between the Czechoslovakian Government and Oerlikon, the Swiss arms manufacturer.[44] The CIA and the Pentagon suppied the same kind of information.

It is not known what the targets of the Communications Branch were at this time. It retained some of the wartime Japanese specialists and rehired some of those who had served with the Examination Unit's French section. During the war Herbert Norman's Special Intelligence Section had built up a considerable file and expertise on French Indochina. The new station at Whitehorse was designed to intercept traffic from Asia. Indeed, in the late 1940s there seemed to be trouble everywhere in the Far East: India clamouring for independence, the Communist Chinese crushing the nationalists, Korea divided, and Communist insurgents threatening Malaya. In the midst of this, France, which was still struggling to recover from the Second World War, faced a determined independence movement in Indochina led by an obscure Vietnamese politician named Ho Chi Minh.

There was much to listen to. Canada had its *quid pro quo*.

CHAPTER FOURTEEN

STILL IN THE GAME

AFTERMATH

THE BEST-KEPT SECRET of the Cold War has not been a secret for some time. In 1960 two National Security Agency analysts disappeared, only to resurface later in Moscow. When Bernon Mitchell and William Martin were paraded before the international media, they told an elaborate tale of how their former employer was engaged in "unethical" intelligence-gathering practices involving high-altitude overflights of the Soviet Union. Near the end of the press conference, almost as an afterthought, the two traitors also mentioned that the United States was "intercepting and deciphering the secret communications of its own allies." They said more than forty countries were targets, specifically naming France, Italy, and Turkey, all of which were members of the North Atlantic Treaty Organization (NATO).

It was the latter statement—not the information about spy planes—that did the greatest damage to U.S. interests, justifying one Pentagon official's estimate that it was "possibly the worst security breach since Klaus Fuchs gave the Russians the secret of the atomic bomb." Former President Truman said of the pair that "they ought to be shot."[1]

Because of the spies the Soviets had in place during the Second World War, ULTRA was known to Stalin and his successors.[2] As a result, the really important communications of the U.S.S.R. and its Communist allies were impregnable during the early days of the Cold War. The Anglo–American communications conference in London in October 1946 had been aimed at sharing signals intelligence on the Soviets but actually breaking the traffic was easier said than done. The American, British, and Canadian signals intelligence organizations had to work their miracles against the Communists more by plain language intercepts and traffic analysis than by cryptanalysis.[3]

Other countries posed less of a problem. Immediately after the war, most countries continued to use antiquated codes and book ciphers. Later, with British encouragement, many adopted versions of the ENIGMA machine (called "Hagelins") which produced ciphers that were breakable, given that the cryptanalysis attack was backed by sufficient resources.[4] All relied mainly on wireless or telegraph to send their messages. Suddenly, thanks to the two American traitors, they learned that they—not just the Communists—were the targets of American code- and cipher-breaking. It is a safe bet that non-Communist countries around the world scrambled to improve cipher security.

Obviously, the National Security Agency henceforth had a much harder time of it, but the Soviets may have been hurt as well. Being in the know about ULTRA probably meant that they, too, were taking advantage of the cipher ignorance of less powerful nations. The Soviets had orchestrated the press conference to make additional propaganda points about the shooting down a few months earlier of an American U-2 spy plane piloted by Gary Powers. It is only speculation, but there is a good chance that the comments made by Martin and Mitchell about diplomatic code- and cipher-breaking was an unrehearsed disclosure that took their Soviet hosts by surprise.

In his 1987 autobiography, *Spycatcher*, former MI5 employee Peter Wright confirmed that Britain and the United States were exchanging intelligence on diplomatic communications in the 1950s. It is likely that this was limited to requested raw traffic and cryptographic information, as it had been during the war. It is doubtful that the State Department and the Foreign Office (and Canada's External Affairs, for that matter) were on such intimate terms that they freely exchanged diplomatic decrypts. This probably only happened when they had a mutual interest in specific world trouble spots.

At least until 1960, however, all the diplomatic communications of the non-Communist world were potentially vulnerable to the Americans, British, and Canadians. While it was well known that the United States and Britain had dabbled in diplomatic interception before the Second World War—Herbert Yardley's book *The American Black Chamber* had revealed it, for example—the difference later was a matter of scale. Yardley and Commander Denniston had worked with just a handful of people; by the mid-1950s the staffs of the Communications Branch, the Government Communications Headquarters, and the National Security Agency were counted in the hundreds, the thousands, and the tens of thousands, backed up by early computers and a world-wide interlocking network of interception facilities.

One must hand it to the British and American security authorities. The interception of diplomatic traffic—both during the Second World War and after—was an extremely well-kept secret. Colonel Alfred McCormack, head of the U.S. Army's Special Branch, perfectly expressed the principle in 1943 when he wrote: "Not present secrecy, not merely secrecy until the battle is over, but permanent secrecy of this operation is what we should strive for."[5] Until 1960, American intelligence authorities went a long way toward achieving this aim.

The Canadians had an easier time of it. Even though ninety per cent of the Examination Unit's cryptanalysis effort was directed at diplomatic traffic, and much of that against an ally—Charles de Gaulle—the Canadian public had no inkling that Canada was involved in signals intelligence. Security was relatively simple. When the Prime Minister's 1939–44 wartime diaries, *The Mackenzie King Record*, were edited for publication in 1960, the many references to Mackenzie King reading decrypts were deleted. When the full diaries were released by External Affairs, few scholars took the time to read them through and those who did apparently failed to note the significance of the passages referring to intercepted messages.

It was more difficult for the Americans. After the war there was an exhaustive inquiry into the Pearl Harbor disaster, making it impossible to hide the existence of the U.S. cipher-breaking programs. The Americans confronted the problem head on, releasing tens of thousands of documents over the years. Most related to the interception of German, Japanese, or Vichy French traffic. Material pertaining to non-belligerent countries was withheld. Nevertheless, because of the sheer volume of what has been released, there are many useful clues in American archives to the other side of the story.

The British have been far more restrictive. Having no freedom of information legislation to trouble them, they have been able to withhold their wartime intelligence files in highly selective fashion. They have manipulated the signals intelligence story by releasing only wartime material pertaining to Bletchley Park, with the result that British historians rarely make any mention of the diplomatic branch of the Government Code and Cipher School that Commander Denniston ran in London. Yet it was here that the decrypts of strategic rather than tactical consequence were handled. Across Denniston's desk flowed the messages of the German Foreign Ministry, the Japanese military attaché in Berlin, and Japanese diplomats in neutral countries around the world. In addition, Denniston's group was reading the ciphers of Spain, nationalist China, the Free French, and probably many other non-belligerents. There was also the commercial traffic processed for the Ministry of Economic Warfare. Denniston's contribution to the war effort was at least equal to that of Travis at Bletchley.

Denniston, like Herbert Yardley, is a rather sad figure in the history of cryptography. He had overseen the development of Britain's Government Code and Cipher School from its beginning shortly after the First World War through to the first few years of the Second, when he took over the diplomatic branch. Yet when it came time to hand out the honours toward the end of the war, Travis received a knighthood and Denniston nothing.

It may be that Denniston was denied the reward he so richly deserved because his work was considered far too secret. A knighthood might have drawn unwelcome attention to a department of the Government Code and Cipher School that the British Government still prefers to pretend never existed. But it did, and surely still does. Its staff at Berkeley Street made the move to the new centre at Cheltenham at the same time as the people from Bletchley.[6] Peter Wright in *Spycatcher* confirms that the Government Communication Headquarters was working on non-Communist diplomatic traffic—Egyptian, French, and Greek at least—in the 1950s and 1960s.[7]

The same continuity of effort surely existed in the United States. The Signal Security Agency went through a number of reorganizations in the late 1940s, as various attempts were made to integrate the rival Navy and Army organizations into what finally came to be known in 1952 as the National Security Agency. There is no reason to suppose that these bureaucratic vicissitudes stopped the work on diplomatic traffic. There were no mass firings at Arlington Hall and the State Department certainly remained the Army's top priority client. The illegal interception of telegrams in the United States which began immediately at the end of the war is ample indication that diplomatic traffic remained of high interest.

In any event, in 1960 the great secret was out: the United States was using its vast capacity for collecting communications intelligence against friends as well as foes.

Just as the revelation a decade later that the Allies had been reading ENIGMA and PURPLE forced a historical reassessment of how the Second World War had been fought, so too will the foreign policies of the United States, Britain, Canada, and Australia during the Cold War someday have to be re-examined when the appropriate documents become available. It has to be assumed that at least until 1960 the four countries were capable of—and likely to have been—reading the secret communications of at least some of the nations they were dealing with. In the case of the State Department—whose advantages included the far superior resources of the National Security Agency and the New York location of the United Nations headquarters—this probably involved most of the non-Communist world.

Indochina appears to have been an early target. Thanks to the success of Canada's Examination Unit, France began its postwar recovery with the Americans, Canadians, and British all able to read its codes and ciphers. It immediately became embroiled in revolution in Indochina. When France first appealed for aid from the United States, it was given. Then the French made some bad decisions and the military situation worsened, leading to the encirclement of French forces at Dien Bien Phu. France again appealed for help but this time was refused. The question now must be posed: had the Americans read enough intercepted traffic to conclude that the French were handling the situation incompetently and they could do better?

Dien Bien Phu fell in 1954 and France lost Indochina. The Americans moved in, setting the stage for the Vietnam War, the most unpopular and disastrous conflict in U.S. history.

Canada seems to have been involved also. It is not known on what countries the Communications Branch focused in the late 1940s and the 1950s, but Herbert Norman and the Examination Unit had specialized in Indochina during the war. French linguists were acquired in the postwar reorganization, and the newly built receivers at Whitehorse were aimed at Asia. External Affairs files for the 1950s on Indochina and Vietnam in the National Archives are at least three times as extensive as those on any other country except for Britain and the United States. Why all this political and economic data on a corner of the world of such little consequence to Canada's national interests?

France, indeed, had reason to feel annoyed with its English-speaking NATO allies. If France did tighten cipher security after the disclosures of 1960, the attempt was immediately frustrated. Peter Wright describes in *Spycatcher* how he obtained the plaintext of a French high-grade cipher by tapping the telex cables in the French embassy. "Every move made by the French during our abortive attempt to enter the Common Market was monitored," he wrote. "The intelligence was avidly devoured by the Foreign Office, and verbatim copies of De Gaulle's cables were regularly passed to the Foreign Secretary in his red box." The operation lasted until 1963.[8]

France obviously found out about this and other attacks on its diplomatic communications, but it did not go public with its chagrin. Anger was better expressed in less embarrassing ways, including withdrawal from military participation in NATO. To Charles de Gaulle, who then was President of France, it must have seemed like a vast English-speaking plot.

Gaulish sour grapes may also have led to the General's notorious "Vive le Québec libre" speech in 1967. By then, unless the French secret service was totally incompetent, he must have known that Canada had a long history of intercepting and reading French government communications, his own in particular. Since Pearson had been involved in this activity from the very beginning, and was now Prime Minister, it was a nice shot that wounded Pearson specifically and Canada generally. It is a pity that de Gaulle did not realize that, because the Examination Unit was able to read his messages in 1944, Canada had championed his cause against the opposition of both Churchill and Roosevelt.

What of Lester Pearson? No assessment of his career can possibly come near the truth without evaluating his knowledge and use of secret intelligence. He gained great respect for Canada—and the 1957 Nobel Peace Prize—by urging the intervention of Canadian-led United Nations troops during the Suez Crisis. How different his diplomacy seems, however, when it is assessed against the fact that Defence Liaison Two was then feeding him decrypts from Syria, Saudi Arabia, and other Arab states.[9] The risks are somewhat lessened when, as Colonel Murray had observed more than a decade earlier, you have "a short, straight road into the opponent's mind."

The Suez Crisis arose from Egyptian president Gamal Nasser's seizure of the Suez Canal, then under ninety-nine-year lease to Britain. Britain reacted by plotting with France and Israel a joint invasion of Egypt to topple Nasser from power, despite adamant opposition from both Canada and the United States. The crisis in Anglo–American relations which followed the attack by the Israelis on October 29, 1956, and British air attacks a few days later, extended to more than diplomacy. "The difficulties between our two countries on the Middle East are rather marring my trip home," complained Eric M. Jones, head of Britain's Government Communications Headquarters. He had been on a visit to the National Security Agency, which was then reading the ciphers of most of the Arab states. GCHQ was reading Nasser's.[10]

Pearson was then Secretary of State for External Affairs and the ultimate consumer of the Middle East intelligence reports coming in through Defence Liaison Two. It seems likely, too, that the Americans were the ultimate source of the Middle East decrypts coming from the Communications Branch. Such close cooperation on both secret intelligence and diplomacy suggests that Pearson's proposal of a United Nations peace-keeping force may have arisen from something more than personal inspiration. Was this an occasion when Canada and the United States jointly contrived a diplomatic strategem based on shared intelligence? Were there others?

It must have been a daunting responsibility for Pearson, this access to the deepest secrets of Canada's two more powerful English-speaking allies. Mackenzie King had believed at the outset of the Cold War that the Americans would stop at nothing to protect themselves against the Soviets, even if it meant marching troops into Canada. The choice he saw was either to cooperate fully with the United States and maintain some sovereignty, or to be subjugated absolutely. He may have been over-simplifying, but there is little doubt that the America of Senator Joseph McCarthy and the great Red Scare was in no mood to scruple over its northern neighbour's sensibilities. By 1952 there had been the Berlin blockade, the fall of nationalist China, the drubbing of American forces in Korea, and the first Soviet atomic bomb tests. The United States was preparing for a war that everyone thought would be fought over Canada. By being privy and party to America's greatest secrets—especially communications intelligence—Canada had at least some voice in the decisions that could have led to mushroom clouds across the Prairies.

Some Canadian historians have criticized Pearson for falling easily in step with the Americans over the Soviet peril, accusing him of anti-Communist rhetoric when he wrote in 1948 of "a cold-blooded, calculating, victoriously powerful Slav empire" which would stop at nothing. Pearson was even more specific in an earlier note to Mackenzie King in which he said that "without some fundamental change in the Soviet state system and in the policies and views of its leaders, the U.S.S.R is ultimately bound to come into open conflict with western democracy." He was right. There was plenty of conflict and the Cold War did not end until the most sweeping and fundamental changes had occurred in Russia.

The point is that leaders like Pearson and Louis St. Laurent, who became Prime Minister after Mackenzie King, did not simply rely on current events and the reports of diplomats to make their assessments of Soviet intentions. They had the benefit of secret intelligence. In late 1945, for example, the Canadian Joint Intelligence Committee presented a paper which stated that the Soviet Union was forced to keep its armies in Eastern Europe because it did not have enough food at home to feed them. Given Stalin's ambitious and ruthless character, it would have been foolish for Canada's military and political leaders to take such a report lightly, or to think that three million armed and hungry Soviet soldiers represented anything less than a serious threat to peace.[11]

Similarly, in a secret speech in 1947, the new head of Canada's Defence Research Board, O. M. Solandt, described how advances in biological warfare research had created agents that were a million times more toxic than poison gas, and how the high-speed submarines and V-2 rockets invented by the Germans would soon be developed into unstoppable delivery systems for atomic bombs and biological warfare weapons. How right he was.[12]

Added to the Canadian intelligence estimates were those from Britain and the United States. While cryptanalysis may have provided few insights into Soviet intentions, there was ample flow from other sources. Canada received a steady stream of reports from the British Joint Intelligence Committee, the Commonwealth Joint Intelligence Bureaus, the CIA, the Pentagon, and so on. Only a small percentage of these have so far been made available in Canadian archives, but those that have deal with massive Soviet defence spending, arms to Yugoslavia, intervention in Malaya, and estimates of military strength which concluded that the Soviets had the most powerful army in the world. One 1949 summary was especially chilling. It was addressed to the U.S. Joint Chiefs of Staff and copied to the Canadians. Its preamble stated:

> The probability of war will increase with the ratio of Soviet capability to United States capability in the delivery of atomic weapons, and will become critical after 1955.

The document went on to warn of surprise attack using atomic, chemical, and biological weapons which would be used ruthlessly "unless deterred by overwhelming retaliation." These last words enunciated the fundamental principle behind an arms race that lasted for the next forty years.[13] It would have been foolish of Pearson and St. Laurent to shrug off such warnings.

Historians who make light of the Soviet threat of the 1940s and 1950s are perhaps remembering the Cold War of their undergraduate days. By the 1960s submarine-launched missiles and stockpiles of hydrogen bombs had made nuclear war impractical. There was much posturing by both East and West, but surely no desire on either side for all-out conflict. A decade earlier, however, the rival arsenals had consisted mostly of atomic bombs loaded on aircraft. The Americans urged and principally financed belts of radar stations across Canada's northern territories so that incoming Soviet bombers could be intercepted and shot down. The Soviets made similar preparations in Siberia. As long as either side believed it could defend itself and survive, nuclear war was a viable option.

Having several hundred atomic bombs exploding in the sub-Arctic as the price of alliance with the United States hardly seems much of a bargain for Canada, but surely there was little choice. Canada was in precisely the same situation as Belgium before the two World Wars in Europe. It was caught between rival powers. Belgium tried neutrality but Germany, Britain, and France made plans to fight on her territory anyway, and Belgium became a battleground twice in twenty-five years.

Canada opted to take sides. It would not have made much difference had a nuclear clash occurred, but at least it provided opportunity to see the international dangers as they unfolded, and to counsel calm to the Americans when calm was urgently needed. If the United States may be said to have had its hand upon the trigger during the early days of the Cold War, then Canada at least had a restraining hand on its shoulder.

The key was mutual trust. This was achieved more by the sharing of intimate secrets than by the formal alliance expressed in various Canada–United States mutual defence plans drafted in those years. Signals intelligence was just one example. In 1947 Canada, Britain, and the United States came to a number of secret agreements leading to the continuous exchange of Top Secret information on atomic energy, chemical and biological warfare, guided missiles, and electronics.[14] The great 1,000 square-mile armed forces proving ground near Suffield, Alberta, became in the 1950s the principal testing site for the chemical and biological warfare weapons of all three countries. The consequence of all this was that thousands of Americans, Britons, and Canadians worked together on secret projects. The trust was not confined to diplomats and politicians; it included scientists, intelligence personnel, and soldiers at every level, from the humblest courier to the exalted chiefs of staff.

Undoubtedly, the most direct benefit of this sharing of secrets was that it gave Canadians a voice in American and British defence planning, and the ability to take informed diplomatic initiatives. While it was important to be aware of the dangers posed by the Soviet foe, it was of even more practical use to Canada to know the attitudes, the thinking, and the intentions of its friends.

When Herbert Norman was fingered as a possible Communist spy by the Americans in 1950, it could not have come at a worse time.

The United Nations police action in Korea had turned into fanatical and bloody war with the Chinese Communists. Klaus Fuchs had just confessed to being a spy in the U.S. atomic energy project. Julius and Ethel Rosenberg were under arrest and on their way to the electric chair for helping him. Donald Maclean, a top official at the British embassy in Washington, was soon to flee to Russia. He had been privy to Anglo–American policy planning on the Korean War and on atomic energy. Guy Burgess, another Foreign Office official in Washington, went with him. Kim Philby, MI6's liaison officer in Washington, came under suspicion as another likely spy. The great Communist hunt in the United States had begun.

Norman's name came up during a routine check by the FBI of Far Eastern experts, apparently inspired by security concerns arising from the Korean War. In the probe which followed, MI5 helpfully supplied its file covering Norman's Cambridge days and his links to the Communists. The FBI reviewed Norman's 1942 visit to Harvard and rediscovered that the Japanese economist whose papers he had collected was a Communist. The name "Norman" was noted to have cropped up in a notebook seized during the Gouzenko arrests. Norman was called back from Japan to answer the charges.

George Glazebrook, then head of Defence Liaison Two and therefore responsible for security and counter-espionage in External Affairs, conducted the interrogation. He was assisted by a senior investigator from the RCMP. It must have been terribly awkward for Glazebrook. He, Tommy Stone, and Norman had been the three External Affairs officers most involved in secret intelligence during the war. Norman knew everything. He had been involved in ULTRA since 1943; he was aware of the breaking of ENIGMA and the agreements to share wireless intelligence; he had regularly received American and British espionage reports; he had written intelligence estimates on Communist intentions in the Far East; he had served with General MacArthur's counter-espionage team in Japan; he knew the order-of-battle of most of the secret intelligence organizations in the United States and Britain as well as in Canada. He also knew that Glazebrook, the man doing the questioning, was currently the director of Canada's signals intelligence program. In other words, if Herbert Norman was a spy, he was a stellar one.

Norman told Glazebrook that he had been attracted to Communism in his student days, but that his interest had long since ceased. He denied ever being a member of the Communist Party and denied spying for the Soviets. Since it was not unusual for young men in the 1930s to flirt with Communism, Glazebrook accepted the explanation. Norman was given a clean bill and allowed to keep his Above Top Secret security clearance. The official External Affairs statement clearing him, however, sidestepped confirmation of his Communist past.[15]

Historians have criticized External Affairs for accepting Norman's explanations too easily. Yet it has to be remembered that the accusations against him had come before the Kim Philby scandal exploded. Although suspicions had surfaced about Philby, MI6 was convinced of his innocence. A spy at the heart of British Intelligence was too huge a disaster to contemplate, for the Canadians as well as the British. Not so for the Americans, who were then actively on the lookout for rotten apples. Accusations and innuendo continued to flow out of Washington from the Senate Subcommittee on Internal Security, even after confidence in Norman had been reaffirmed. After a brief stint with the American and Far East Division of External Affairs—responsible for

China, Indochina, and Japan—Norman was posted as ambassador to New Zealand. If only External Affairs had kept him there.

In 1956, just at the outset of the Suez Crisis, Norman was recalled from New Zealand and sent to the Middle East. His diplomatic responsibilities included Egypt and Lebanon, and he did admirable service in the difficult months that followed by winning the confidence of the fiery Egyptian president, Gamal Nasser. Then, in the midst of this success, his name again came up in the United States as a possible spy. This time, however, the pursuit was deadly.

The problem this time was certainly Philby. By then both the CIA and MI5 were convinced Philby was working for the Soviets, though MI6 still refused to believe it. When rumours began circulating about him among British journalists, MI6 staged an "interrogation" which led to a public statement from the British government exonerating him. The FBI and CIA were scandalized. Perhaps they saw Norman as another Soviet mole likely to get off scot-free. When his name again came up at the Senate Subcommittee on Internal Security, its deliberations and the contents of secret FBI reports about Norman were leaked to the press, probably deliberately. There was furor in Canada. Parliament, Pearson, and the Canadian news media sprang to his defence.

On April 4, 1957, Norman jumped to his death from the ninth floor of a Cairo apartment building.

Was Norman a spy? None of his contemporaries in External Affairs believed so. He certainly does not fit the profile of known American and British traitors. He was moderate in his tastes and actions, happily married, comparatively modest, and highly idealistic. The known traitors were exactly the opposite in at least three out of four of these respects. It is hard to see Norman sticking to the likes of Stalin as he read intelligence reports on the Soviet takeover of Eastern Europe. But one can never be sure.

The fact remains, however, that Norman caused excruciating embarrassment to the Department of External Affairs. The Burgess–Maclean–Philby episodes shredded the confidence of the American authorities in British Intelligence. As one CIA agent later commented: "The wartime alliance that I had always considered as strong as the Rock of Gibraltar was full of suspicions and bitterness and worry and concern." The doubts extended up to the U.S. Joint Chiefs of Staff and lingered more than a decade. Even under the best of circumstances, the Canadians would have suffered guilt by association.[16] Canada's intelligence agencies had been modelled closely on those of the British, and former British intelligence officers occupied key posts. The accusations against Norman made matters infinitely worse. They put the precious secrecy-sharing arrangements with the United States in jeopardy.

It was probably fortunate for Canada that two years later Martin and Mitchell fled to the Soviet Union gushing with National Security Agency secrets. They were a confirmed security disaster; Norman only a suspected one.

In one of four suicide notes he left, Norman said that he had never knowingly done any harm but that he regretted the trouble he caused External Affairs.

> Illusion has been my besetting weakness, naivete my chief flaw....
> I thought innocence against any act against security was enough—
> how naive! The department is too well aware of my error—but
> crime no—that I have not committed.

Perhaps these words mean that he realized that it had been foolish for someone of his Communist background to stay in secret intelligence once the Soviet Union had been identified as the new enemy. If so, he was right.

———————

The rest of the story is quickly told. Documents on Canadian Intelligence agencies after 1955 are scarce, but some broad trends can be perceived.

The Communications Branch gradually got out of serious cryptanalysis. Worldwide improvements in cipher security made it too expensive. Cipher construction became extremely complicated and, though all ciphers are theoretically breakable, the good ones require sophisticated mathematics and very powerful computers. It was probably hard enough for the Americans to keep up.

Technology changed everything, anyway. Satellites made photo reconnaissance and traffic analysis king and queen instead. A country could restrict emigration and muddle its ciphers, but it still had to use radio and telephone communications. It also could not hide from digital imaging from outer space or from radar and infrared scanners that pierced clouds and even the ground. This was especially valuable for topographical and economic intelligence. There was no need for contact registers when satellites could probe the depths of harbours, map road networks, and measure the lengths of airfields. There was no concealing crop failures, inefficient heavy industry, railway traffic, pollution, fossil fuel consumption, and a host of other indicators of national health. The Soviets, by means of their own satellites, must have been appalled to see the steady economic and industrial growth of the West, even as they knew that the Americans were seeing their increasing feebleness. The great Communist experiment died in the comparison.

The Cold War was a struggle involving espionage, propaganda, political opportunism, military adventures, and the arms race, but it was economic intelligence from satellites which declared the winners.

The United States has not needed Britain and Canada for a long time. The signals intelligence-sharing agreements of the 1940s arose because listening stations on U.S. territory could not by themselves intercept all traffic of interest. Satellites can. Both Argentina during the Falklands War and Iraq during the Persian Gulf War have painful, first-hand experience of how hard it is to hide from prying eyes and ears in the sky.

Despite overwhelming American capability, Britain and Canada have not dismantled their intelligence organizations. They still monitor the airwaves and cooperate with the United States. One of the great lessons learned since the beginning of the Second World War is that if a country wants to obtain secret intelligence from others, it must bring something to the table.

The other great lesson is that a country must maintain a viable and up-to-date intelligence establishment of its own. Espionage is something practised against a nation's friends as well as its foes, embracing diplomatic and commercial interests as much as military. To be able to monitor the Portuguese and Spanish fishing fleets off the Grand

Banks, for example, is to protect a Canadian resource. To collect the traffic of foreign corporations and industries is to ensure that international trade agreements are honoured and deals honestly conducted. To probe for French attitudes to Canada's internal problems with Quebec is to ward off interference. To do all this is to know that others are doing the same to you. The example set for Canada by the Americans and the British over the past fifty years is clear: nations unable to gather their own quality intelligence are easy prey for those that can.

The names have been changed, but Canada in 1993 still has essentially the same intelligence agencies and committee structure it had in the 1950s:

1. The Examination Unit/Communications Branch is now the Communications Security Establishment (CSE) on Heron Road in Ottawa. It is only administratively responsible to the Department of National Defence.

2. The signals intelligence programs of the CSE are directed by the Intelligence Advisory Committee, consisting of the service directors of intelligence and others, and replacing both the original Joint Intelligence Committee and the Communications Research Committee.

3. Signals intelligence policy is set by the Interdepartmental Committee on Security and Intelligence, consisting of the appropriate deputy ministers, and replacing the former Senior Committee and Communications Security Committee.

3. The authority for signals intelligence policy is derived from the Cabinet Committee on Security and Intelligence, an echo of the supercommittee proposed by Tommy Stone in 1944. Its membership includes the Minister of National Defence and the Secretary of State for External Affairs. It is chaired by the Prime Minister.

4. The intercept stations, which now include one at Alert as well as at Ottawa (Leitrim) and elsewhere, are organized as the Canadian Forces Supplementary Radio System.

5. Defence Liaison Two has become the Political and International Security Affairs Branch of External Affairs. DL2's original functions have been split between two main sub-departments: the Security Division for overseas counter-espionage (and espionage?) and the Intelligence Services Division for receiving, collating, and distribution of overt and covert intelligence from other agencies and from the Communications Security Establishment.

6. The former Joint Intelligence Bureau has become the Economic Intelligence and Political Intelligence Divisions of External Affairs.

7. Military, scientific, and topographic intelligence (maps and charts) come under various divisions of the Department of National Defence.

8. The permanent staff supporting the Intelligence Advisory Committee, the Committee on Security and Intelligence, and the Cabinet Committee on Security and Intelligence is in the Privy Council Office.

10. Domestic counter-espionage (Canada only) is with the Canadian Security Intelligence Service rather than the RCMP and answerable to the Security Operations section, also in the Privy Council Office.

11. The successor to both Peter Dwyer and George Glazebrook as Canada's over-all coordinator of counter-espionage and secret intelligence from all sources is the Deputy Clerk (Security and Intelligence, and Counsel), Privy Council Office, in 1991 a person named Ward P. D. Elcock.

12. Elcock's operational deputy is the assistant Secretary to the Cabinet (Security and Intelligence)—at the time of writing N. Jauvin—who oversees the three main intelligence divisions in the Privy Council Office: Policy, Security Operations, and the Intelligence Advisory Committee Secretariat.[17]

13. The ultimate beneficiary of all secret intelligence, and the only person who can authorize statements regarding the responsibilities and

accountability of the various intelligence committees and agencies, is the Prime Minister.[18]

However one might shuffle names and responsibilities, the requirements for overt and covert foreign intelligence-gathering and counterespionage always remain the same. Far from being a neophyte in the business, Canada has long had a fully mature intelligence organization, reporting, just as in Britain and the United States, to the head of government. If there is anything missing in comparison to the two other countries, it is the apparent lack of an agency like MI6 independently responsible for running secret agents abroad. This is hardly a deficiency. Intelligence-gathering is now handmaiden to science. James Bond is obsolete.

There is another corollary. Sophisticated intelligence-gathering is the province of large, wealthy nations, not small ones. An independent Quebec would be the inevitable victim of the vast resources of its English-speaking neighbours rather than, as now, their beneficiary. It is something to think about.

The Communications Security Establishment fell on hard times during the 1970s and early 1980s. Cryptanalysis all but disappeared. In 1985, however, the CSE acquired an $8.5-million CRAY super-computer which has been continuously upgraded. A new team of cipher-breakers has been hired. The CSE now has a staff of about 1,000 and spends about $36 million on salaries. It still has liaison with the National Security Agency in the United States and the Government Communications Headquarters in Britain. A huge fortress-like, electronically secure annex has just been completed behind the CSE building on Heron Road. It has much concrete and few windows.[19]

The Cold War is over, but signals intelligence continues to be collected. The reason for doing so, according to a 1990 statement by Privy Council Deputy Clerk (Security and Intelligence) Ward P. D. Elcock, is "to provide the government with foreign intelligence on the diplomatic, military, economic, and commercial activities, intentions, and capabilities of foreign governments, individuals, and corporations."[20]

Canada is still in the game.

SOURCES

M OST OF THE STORY in this book has been told from primary
sources, mainly documents in the National Archives of Canada
(NAC) or held by the Communications Security Establishment (CSE)
while being processed for transfer to the NAC. I have also used valuable records from collections of the National Archives and Research
Administration (NARA) in Washington and Les Archives de la Ministère des Affaires Étrangères (AMAE) in Paris. To a much lesser extent,
because of excessive restrictions, I also located useful documents at the
Public Record Office (PRO) in London.

The Comunciations Security Establishment released photocopies
of thousands of documents, many containing extensive deletions of
text according to the rules of Canada's Access to Information Act. The
Act also forbids access to most intelligence documents that have been
transferred to the National Archives. However, the intelligence records
of the RCAF were declassified at the National Archives before the
Access to Information Act became law. Consequently, I was able to
obtain the Air Force records on the Canadian Joint Intelligence Committee and Joint Intelligence Bureau from this source while identical
documents were being denied me by External Affairs. I was never able
to locate the parallel collections of the Army or Navy.

Equally important, the National Archives Access Department
released the Navy's collection of Y Committee minutes in 1990. This
was fortuitous for the collection was complementary to those documents received from the CSE, enabling me to fill in many of the gaps

and blanks in the latter. I suddenly found myself with the "whole story."

Another very useful documentary source has been the unpublished version of Mackenzie King's wartime diary (WLMK diary) which contained many references to signals intelligence that had been deleted from the published version, *The Mackenzie King Record*. Indeed, if ever there was justification for book-burning, then the four-volume *Mackenzie King Record* should be consigned to the flames. Even though its editors warned that nothing would be reproduced that the former Prime Minister would not have approved of, it has been slavishly relied upon by Canadian historians who could not be bothered to plough through the lengthy and sometimes boring originals. Consequently, many of the really valuable insights Mackenzie King had to offer on the characters and actions of Churchill, Roosevelt, Eisenhower and de Gaulle—not to mention signals intelligence—have so far been lost to history.

I spent many an afternoon at University of Toronto Library scanning a microfiche copy of the original diary and once I got used to skipping over the lengthy passages of dream analysis and soliloquies to pets, I found the reading fascinating. Mackenzie King was an intelligent observer and excellent reporter, often quoting the conversations he overheard almost verbatim. When these show negative sides to the Allied leaders, they are either omitted from the *Record* or completely emasculated. This is a pity, for the original wartime diary is a priceless historical record.

In 1990, I also located several key documents pertaining to Canada's wartime secret intelligence activities at the Directorate of History (DHist), the historical division of the Department of National Defence. Two years later, when I again called the file (193.009,D48) in which I had found them, they had been removed. Fortunately, I had been allowed to photocopy them the first time around. They are identified in the endnotes which follow.

Finally, I made good use of the diaries of Adolf Berle at the Franklin Delano Roosevelt Library (FDRL) at Hyde Park, New York, and William and Elizabeth Friedman's private papers at the Virginia Military Institute (VMI) in Lexington, Virginia. The latter comprise the

Friedmans' library of books and papers on cryptography gathered over their lifetimes. The hours flew by as I sifted through these treasures.

I conducted a number of interviews with former Canadian intelligence personnel but as I felt obligated to warn them that the government still considered them bound by their oaths of secrecy and regarded their wartime activities as sensitive—even after fifty years— few were forthcoming. There were some exceptions, and they made valuable contributions, but no one told me anything of significance that I had not already obtained from documents.

Finally, the CSE documents were released in several numbered collections which I presume will be sorted into separate files at the National Achives. In the Endnotes which follow I cite the CSE documents by these numbers so there are inevitable duplications. Those wishing to find a particular document should be prepared to search for it by date as well as number in every file. The "Examination Unit history" and the "Sigint history" are also at CSE.

SECONDARY SOURCES

To read through the many books written on Allied secret intelligence is to negotiate a minefield of half-truths and myth. I early decided to reject all secondary sources which were not either autobiographical or backed up by archival records. Other than those dealing with wartime operational intelligence, that eliminated most British books on the subject. Even Christopher Andrew's *Secret Service* (1985) is poorly documented, though this is surely a reflection of the lack of available material rather than any shortcoming of scholarship. All records pertaining to MI6, MI5 and the Security Executive are still closed in Britain and there is very little pertaining to the various intelligence committees and censorship. Serious writers in Britain have little to go on. One must also be mindful of Peter Wright's observation in Malcolm Turner's *The Spycatcher Trial*, (1989), p. 31, that MI5 (and MI6, presumably) "used to leak stuff into the newspapers and into books all the time." British Intelligence, it seems, has been very much in control over what has been written about the secret services.

Hinsley's *British Intelligence in the Second World War* Volumes 1-4 (1979-1990) also has many shortcomings. This is strictly an official history, written by a former intelligence officer, and based on many still-secret documents the public cannot check. It appears to be the story of British Intelligence as British Intelligence would wish it to be told, and has coloured much subsequent writing on the subject. Documents in Canadian archives, however, reveal its many omissions and some errors which I have recorded in endnotes as I encountered them. As an authority on non-operational signals intelligence and the activities of the British secret services, it should used with caution.

The best book on the British secret services is *Spycatcher* (1987) by former MI5 operative Peter Wright. I have used it freely because the British Government, in seeking to block its publication in Australia, presented an affidavit before the courts asserting that "everything in the book was true" (*Spycatcher Trial*, pp. 51, 55). As it is inconceivable that Her Majesty's Government would perjure itself, and since many of the incidents Wright describes fit with my own documented discoveries, I feel that Wright's narrative is as accurate as one can expect of an autobiography.

There is a much greater selection of American books on secret intelligence, although few really go into any depth on signals intelligence. The exception is James Bamfield's *Puzzle Palace* (1982), which I found useful but incomplete. David Kahn's *The Codebreakers* (1967) is a classic, and still required reading after 25 years. Michael Gannon's *Operation Drumbeat* (1990) and Robert Lamphere's *The FBI-KGB War* (1986) are both excellent and authoritative.

Because Canada's involvement in secret intelligence has been little known, there are few Canadian books worth serious consultation. Two exceptions are John Sawatsky, *Gouzenko: The Untold Story* (1984) and David Stafford, *Camp X* (1986), both of which are well done and provide much useful information. Bill Robinson's article in *Cryptologia* (January 1992), "The Fall and Rise of Cryptanalysis in Canada," is an excellent example of what can be achieved by determined sleuthing through public documents. There was not much else of value to choose from.

Of all the secondary sources I consulted, the most valuable was Stanley Hilton's *Hitler's Secret War in South America* (1981). Without the benefit of his work, I would never have appreciated just what it was that Yardley was up against in the first year of the Examination Unit, or have been led to appropriate files in U.S. archives. Hilton made some errors with respect to the various intelligence organizations in the United States, and the involvement of British Security Coordination in South America, but he did wonderful service in bringing to light one of the most important episodes of German espionage during the Second World War.

The downside of the research for this book was the discovery that certain sources, especially William Stephenson's "BSC History," have muddied our understanding of wartime secret intelligence. Stephenson's warped version of events has directly or indirectly influenced dozens of histories, many of them by very competent writers. From first to last, however, Stephenson was a liar.

The only known copy of the "BSC History" is held by author William Stevenson. I am sure that he would be willing to release it to a suitable archive if he were asked to do so. A detailed study of it by qualified historians would certainly separate a lot of chaff from a handful of wheat.

NOTES

The following are the acronyms for the archives cited in the Endnotes:

AMAE   Archives de la Ministère des Affaires Étrangères (Paris)

CSE   Communications Security Establishment (Ottawa)

DHist   Directorate of History (Ottawa)

FDRL   Franklin Delano Roosevelt Library (Hyde Park, N.Y.)

NAC   National Archives of Canada (Ottawa)

NARA   National Archives and Records Administration (Washington)

NRCA   National Research Council Archives (Ottawa)

PRO   Public Record Office (London)

VMI   Virginia Military Institute, George Marshall Library (Lexington, Virginia)

Also consulted were files at the Federal Bureau of Investigation (FBI) headquarters in Washington. Copies of the "History of the Examination Unit" are available at CSE and NAC.

CHAPTER ONE

1 Col. W. W. Murray, "Foreign Intelligence in Peacetime," Appendix E, 26 Sept. 1945, NAC, RG24, HQ-22-1-43. However, Canada had cooperated with Britain on secret intelligence during the First World War.

2 The correct title for MI6 is Special Intelligence Service but popular usage has changed this to Secret Intelligence Service. To avoid confusion with special intelligence as cryptanalysis, I have used Secret Intelligence Service for MI6 throughout.

3 Nigel West, *The SIGINT Secrets: The Signals Intelligence War 1900 to Today* (New York: William Morrow, 1988), p. 20.

4 Later in the war the Admiralty adopted a more formal nomenclature by which **Y** intelligence meant information derived from simple codes and ciphers, **Y** inference meant traffic analysis, and special intelligence meant information obtained from high-grade codes and ciphers, usually by cryptanalysis or other sophisticated techniques. See E. G. N. Rushbrooks (DNI), "Secret Terminology," 20 March 1943, NAC, RG24, 3807, NSS-1008-75-44(2). Thus, depending on the source and time period of a document, the term "wireless intelligence" might be used in a general or specific sense.

5 "History and Activities of the Operational Intelligence Unit, NSHQ - 1939-45," DHist, S1440-18.

6 Herbert Yardley, *The American Black Chamber* (Indianapolis: Bobbs-Merrill, 1931), pp. 368-69. Canadian Telegraph Censorship memo, 25 Oct. 1940, NAC, RG2(14), 5760, TC26/(1). War Office 1938 map of undersea cables of the world, PRO, WO193/211.

7 Memorandum of Edwin Herbert, British Censor, 31 Jan. 1942, NARA, RG26, E92, Box 8, 54.

8 Documents on the beginning of censorship are widely scattered in various collections and files, but see especially the summary "Development of Canadian Postal Censorship," 8 June 1945, NAC, RG2, 5753, No. 206 and passim, NAC, RG12, 2355, 11-38-12(5) and 11-38-15.

9 Report of postal censors, March 1939, PRO, DEFE 1/5. This is opposite to what is reported in F. H. Hinsley, *British Intelligence in the Second World War*, Vol. 4 (London: Her Majesty's Stationary Office, 1990), p. 185. This official four-volume government history (1979-1990) is unreliable on this subject for, with the occasional exception like the document cited here, Britain's Second World War censorship records are still secret.

10 See passim NAC, RG12, 2355, 11-38-12. Also Hinsley, *British Intelligence*, Vol. 4, p. 25.

11 "Historical Outline of Canadian Telecommunications Censorship," 29 June 1945, NAC, RG2, 5760, TC25. This document gives much detail about the telegraph companies involved.

12 NAC, RG2(14), 5760, TC26/(1). It is not clear why this was done, since all the British cables passed through Newfoundlandand or Bermuda, enabling the British to use their own telegraph censors on these lines. Presumably they did so.

13 "History of the Activities of the Operational Intelligence Centre, 1939-45," DHist. Because there was no intelligence staff with the pre-war Canadian Navy, the Director of Naval Intelligence had always been a Royal Navy appointee of the Admiralty.

14 De Marbois resumé circa 1946, NAC, RG24, 6178, HQ-22-1-43, plus his personal papers, DHist. He was born in the Mascarene Islands.

15 De Marbois monograph courtesy of his daughter, Natalie de Marbois. This is a fascinating record of the last days of sail. De Marbois was an avid photographer as a youth and his photo album, also in possession of his daughter, is proof of his adventures.

16 The first two HF/DF DOT stations to go over to the navy were at Shediac, N.B. and Saint Hubert, P.Q. The British Air Ministry also agreed to put the DF station at Gander (Botwood), Nfld., at the disposal of the Canadian Navy. "History of the Activities of the Operational Intelligence Centre, 1939-45," DHist. See also NAC, RG24, 3807, NSS-1008-75-44(1). Subsequent descriptions are from this file until otherwise stated.

17 C. H. Little, *Salty Dips*, Vol. 2 (Ottawa: Naval Officers' Association of Canada, 1985), pp. 112-13.

18 "Historical Narrative of MI2," 1945, CSE doc. 614-619.

19 W. W. Murray to Payne, 16 Jan. 1940; Memorandum from Maurice Pope (DMO&I), 1 Nov. 1939, NAC, RG2, 5760, TC26/(1). S. R. Elliot, *Scarlet to Green: a History of Intelligence in the Canadian Army, 1904-1963* (Toronto: Canadian Intelligence and Security Association, 1981), does not list Pope as one of Canada's wartime directors of military intelligence so he may have been serving only in an acting capacity. The telegraph censors were reading the cable "slips."

20 For the above exchanges, see CGS to War Office (for Capt. Wethey), 5 Dec. 1939; CanMilitary to Defensor, 19 Dec. 1939; Pope (DMO&I) to Crerar, 29 Nov. 1939, NAC, RG24, 12,324, s.4/cipher/4D.

21 Col. D. A. Butler (MI8) to DDMI(O), 27 Dec. 1939, ibid. regarding remarks by Denniston.

22 Notes by Major Wethey of meeting at GC&CS, undated; Crerar to Pope, 29 Dec. 1939; NAC, RG24, 12,324, s.4/cipher/4D. Also see Historical narrative of MI2, CSE doc. 614-617. For the composition of the RSS, see Hinsley, *British Intelligence*, Vol. 4, p. 72. In peacetime Britain's General Post Office had been responsible for monitoring and administering domestic and international communications in the same way as the Department of Transport in Canada and the Federal Communications Commission in the United States.

23 Chronological entry for January, 1940, in "History and Activities of the Operational Intelligence Centre, 1939-45," DHist. See also passim, NAC, RG24, 12,341, 4/INT/2/2.

24 Memorandum of 3 Sept. 1939, NAC, RG12, 2355, 11-38-15. Also "Development of Canadian Postal Censorship," 8 June 1945, NAC, RG2, 5753, 206.

25 Report of F. E. Jolliffe, 8 March 1940, NAC, RG2(14), 5750, 152. MC2 was permit issuing, located in Liverpool. British Censorship was put under the Ministry of Information the following May and became a separate department in April 1943.

26 For MI5 at Wormwood Scrubs see Bruce Page et al, *The Philby Conspiracy* (New York: Doubleday & Company, 1968), pp. 132-134. See also "Ministerial Requirements" cited below for details on the collection of information on subversives.

27 Report on British Censorship by Major W. L. Stephenson, January 1940, PRO,

DEFE 1/5. British Censorship trade and general intelligence reports from early 1940 on are to be found in NAC, RG25, 2841 and 2842. They are not available in Britain.

28 Coolican to Underwood, 8 April 1940, NAC, RG2(14), 5750, 154. Also "Development of Postal Censorship," ibid, 5753, 206. It is not clear from these documents whether this incoming mail was openly or covertly examined.

29 This was Major O. T. Raynor, code-named CHESOR. Canadian Censorship was code-named DEPICTION. See passim NAC, RG25, 5753, 206 and NAC, RG24, 12,344, 4/INT/3.

30 For 1941 "Ministerial Requirements," see NAC, RG2(14), 5751, 157-163.

31 By late 1941 the committee was still interested mainly in companies on British-supplied blacklists and in diplomatic or consular correspondence. Postal Censorship memo, 22 Dec. 1941, NAC, RG2(14), 5758, 78.

32 "Following (are) Italian troop movements from cashed remittances in U.S.," CHESOR (Rayner) to BLANKETING (British Imperial Censorship), 24 May, 1940; also memos of 27 May, 14 June 8 Aug., NAC, RG24, 12,341, 4/INT/2. See also description in minutes of meeting, 18 Aug. 1942, NAC, RG12, 11-38-12(13).

33 Obituary, 2 Aug. 1956, from Canadian Press files. Also interview with family members.

34 W. W. Murray, "How we tricked the Nazi Spies," *Maclean's*, 15 Sept. 1949.

35 In the midst of Murray's success, the British severed the Horta 2 cable in the Atlantic, cutting off his source of intelligence. They realized their mistake, however, and soon spliced it into Portugal, enabling the censors at Canso to resume their interceptions.

36 Sir Edwin Herbert, "Censorship Planning," 25 July 1946, NAC, RG25, 2686, 11229/40. Hinsley, *British Intelligence*, Vol. 1 (1979), pp. 207-08.

37 Passim, NAC, RG25, T1807, 540. See also WLMK diary, 18-22 June 1940.

38 For details of DF procedures, see passim, NAC, RG12, 2158, 11-30-1(2).

39 For this controversy, see various items of correspondence from 1 April 1940 to June 1941 in NAC, RG24, 3807, NSS-1008-75-44(1) and 3805, NSS-1008-75-10.

40 For Long Island references, see Special Wireless Section Daily Journal, 30 Aug. 1940, CSE unnumbered release. CanMilitary to Defensor (RSS to Drake), 13 Oct. 1940 and passim, NAC, RG24, 12,341, 4/INT/2/2. This was German agent William Sebold. See below Chapter 2, p. 46 and Chapter 3, p. 57.

41 Drake to MI8, announcing that four-month study of EAN, EAX, and EAM2 reveals "disposition of Spanish troops," 24 Feb. 1941, plus subsequent correspondence in this file, NAC, RG24, 12,341, 4/INT/2/2.

42 DMO&I (Murchie) to CSC, 29 Nov. 29 1940; DPD(Naval) to DNI, 2 Dec. 1940; CSC to DMO&I, 12 Dec. 1940, NAC, RG24, Acc83-84/167, 189, S-1310-6. Drake visited Washington Nov. 10-23, 1940. His conversation with General Mauborgne is fully described in "A History of the Examination Unit, 1941-1945," pp. 4-9, which also fills in the Access to Information deletions in CSC to DMO&I, 29 Nov. 1940.

CHAPTER TWO

1   Hoover to Miles, 14 Feb. 1941, NARA, RG165, 10039-299. Some previous writers might have treated Yardley with a little more sympathy had they discovered this file and the documents it contains.

2   FBI report on Edna Hackenberg who "now resides with Yardley," 5 Dec. 1940, NARA, RG165, 10039-299; E. P. Coffy to D. M. Ladd, 28 Jan. 1941, FBI files, cited by Louis Kruh in *Cryptologia*, Vol. 13, no. 4, p. 348. The subjective morality of Hoover's note smacks more of the police than the press.

3   Yardley, *The American Black Chamber*, pp. 250-317.

4   For the sequence of events see Lt.-Col. O. S. Albright to Col. A. T. Smith, 24 March and 5 June 1931, NARA, RG457, SRH-038. Interestingly, my conclusion from the documentary evidence is the opposite to that of Louis Kruh, *Cryptologia*, vol. 13, no. 4, pp. 336-38 who states that Stimson played the "principal role in determining Yardley's fate." Kruh's analysis relies mainly on the 1946 U.S. Army history, "Historical Background of the Signal Security Agency" and William Friedman's description of the incident. Neither source can be expected to be candid.

5   Judge Advocate-General to Col. O. S. Albright and Col. A. T. Smith, 28 March 1929, and correspondence 13-23 Sept. 1932, NARA, RG457, SRH-038.

6   Correspondence 13-23 Sept. 1932, NARA, RG457, SRH-038.

7   For a description of the debate surrounding the legislation see David Kahn, *The Codebreakers* (London: Weidenfeld and Nicolson, 1967), pp. 365-68.

8   Herbert Yardley, *The Chinese Black Chamber* (Boston: Houghton Mifflin, 1983), p. 38. He wrote this book about his years in China shortly after the Second World War but, fearful of government reaction, never submitted it for publication. It was printed twenty-five years after his death.

9   Yardley to General Tai, 11 March 1940, NARA, RG165, 10039-299. It would be interesting to know how this private letter from Yardley came to be in a Military Intelligence (G-2) file.

10 Military attachés to Assistant Chief of Staff, G-2, 11 March and 10 May, 1940, ibid.

11 See NARA, RG457, SRH-222, 318 and 320. The U.S. Government has never acknowledged that it was intercepting Russian wireless traffic before the war and the declassified text of Commander Laurence Safford's description of the prewar operations of Op-20-G in SRH-000 contains a number of deletions when reference is made to a country other than Japan. That this other country is Russia comes from a British document in the Canadian archives in which it is specifically stated that Op-20-G was covering Russia as well as Japan. See Sir Charles Kennedy-Purvis to Admiralty, 28 March 1941, NAC, RG24, 3805, 1008-75-12(1)

12 Notes by Yardley, 6 Dec. 1941, CSE doc. 000250.

13 Pearson to Robertson, 1 Feb. 1941, CSE doc. 000175. The quoted suggestion from the War Office is blanked out under the Access to Information Act but appears in the

partially declassified departmental "Sigint History," 5, p. 2. CSE doc. 000412.

14 Hinsley, *British Intelligence*, Vol. 1, p. 273 says that the GC&CS had increased four-fold in the first sixteen months of the war and was "poorly organized." An American visiting GC&CS in early 1941 reported a total staff of 800 consisting of army, navy, air force, and Foreign Office personnel, the majority of whom would have been working on traffic analysis, plain language intercepts, translation, and clerical tasks. Considering the military situation, the number of code-breakers available for diplomatic tasks would have been quite small. Abraham Sinkov to G-2, 11 April 1941, NARA, RG457, SRH-145.

15 Winston Churchill, *The Second World War* (Boston: Houghton Mifflin, 1949), Vol. 2, pp. 488-92.

16 Memorandum signed by the three Chiefs of Staff, 28 May 1941, DHist, 193.009(D2).

17 Churchill, *Second World War*, Vol. 2, p. 508. Also WLMK diary 13 Feb. 1941.

18 The other was the 52nd (Lowland) Division. All other British Army units were either disorganized or without much of their equipment. C. P. Stacey, *Six Years of War* (Ottawa: Queen's Printer, 1957), pp. 274-5.

19 For details and documentation of these events, see John Bryden, *Deadly Allies: Canada's Secret War, 1937-1947* (Toronto: McClelland & Stewart, 1989), pp. 40-42.

20 Fifth meeting of the WTSDC, 14 Jan. 1941, NAC, MG30, B122, Vol. 2. Then see note referring to Keenleyside on margin of Brand to DMI, 20 Jan. 1941, NAC, Acc 83-84/167, box 189, S-1310-6. Also, Brand to Keenleyside, 21 Jan. 1941; Keenleyside's reply, 27 Jan. 1941; Brand to Keenleyside, 29 Jan. 1941; CSE docs. 000001-3.

21 Brand to Rush, 20 Jan. 1941, NAC, RG12, 2158, 11-30-1(3).

22 The Admiralty repeatedly asked for coverage of station KYU, an American call sign, until well into 1942. De Marbois to Bennett, 12 March and 23 April 1941, NAC, RG12, 2158, 11-30-1(3). Naval Service to DOT, 16 Feb. and Nov. 1942, ibid, 11-30-1(4). KYU appears to have been aimed at Russia.

23 "Examination Unit History," p. 2, CSE. This was the German spy, William Sebold. For Sebold see above Chapter 1, p. 26, and below, Chapter 3, p. 57.

24 Little, *Salty Dips*, Vol. 2, p. 115. De Marbois to DNI (Brand), 31 Dec. 1940, 20 Feb and 6 March 1941, NAC, RG24, 3807, NSS-1008-75-44(1).

25 The minutes of the seventh meeting of the WTSDC and C. J. Mackenzie's 1941 appointment book are both in NAC, MG30, B122, Vol. 2. Mackenzie's correspondence regarding the search for specialists in codes and ciphers is at CSE. Little's name appears in marginal notes on documents of 13 Feb., 9 April and 16 April 1941, CSE docs. 131, 132, 136. For mention of the new station see Rush to Halifax requesting coverage, 11 May and 5 June 1941, NAC, RG12, 2158, 11-30-1(3).

26 Reference to an earlier meeting in minutes of 12 May 1941, CSE doc. 000193-97. This document also mentions the lack of progress by Little's group.

27 S. Beatty to C. J. Mackenzie, 9 April 1941 and Mackenzie to Robertson, 24 April 1941, CSE docs. 132, 137. Sinkov's name has been blanked out of both these documents but appears in "Sigint History," 5, p. 3, CSE doc. 000413.

28 DND (Army) circular, 3 April 1941, NAC, RG17, 2684, N-3-19.

29 See correspondence for this period in NAC, RG12, 2158, 11-30-1(3) and NAC, RG24, 3807, NSS-1008-75-44(1). For mention of Russian wireless interception see DHist, Naval Weekly Reports, no. 14, 21 Dec. 1939, NSS-1000-5-7.

30 For foregoing and the following see Report to the National Research Council by Coxeter and Robinson, 3 May 1941 and Canadian legation, Washington, to External Affairs, 3 May 1941, CSE docs. 000177-84.

CHAPTER THREE

1 The description in the foregoing paragraphs is based on Stanley Hilton, *Hitler's Secret War in South America: 1939-1945* (Baton Rouge: Louisiana State University Press, 1981) p. 70, and the transmission data on Examination Unit decrypt GA-33, CSE. This decrypt, missing from the main German decrypt collection, turned up in a small unnumbered file. The German text of the message was sent to the Americans for it is quoted in slightly different translation in U.S. embassy (Rio) to State Department, 9 Sept. 1941, NARA, RG59, 862.20210/721. Why the original text of this version is likely to have been supplied by Canada is explained below.

2 T. A. Stone to R. M. Macdonnell, 23 June 1941, CSE doc. 000088.

3 Report to the National Research Council by Coxeter and Robinson, 3 May 1941, CSE doc. 000182-84. Canadian legation to External Affairs, 3 May 1941, CSE doc. 000177-80.

4 For all of the foregoing discussion and the quotation from Yardley see, "Report of a Conference of the Interdepartmental Committee on Cryptography," 12 May 1941, CSE doc. 000193-97. Only two copies of this report and one the following day were made. It is fortunate they survived.

5 The 5 Dec. 1940 FBI report on Edna Hackenberg, nee Ramsaier, is to be found in the G-2 file on Yardley, NARA, RG165, 10039-299.

6 Minutes of meetings, 12 and 13 May, 1941, CSE docs. 000188-97. Coxeter declined the invitation to join the cryptanalysis unit.

7 Various documents from 20 May to 9 June 1941, especially Minutes of meeting, 11 June 1941, CSE doc. 000084-86; "Examination Unit history," pp. 15-16, and decrypts GA-6 to GA-12, CSE. Also, Brand to Robertson, 16 June 1941, NAC, RG24, Acc83-84/167, 169, S-1310-6 and Herbert Osborn (Yardley) report, 30 June 1941, CSE doc. 000089-90.

8 To grasp the sequence of events in this paragraph it was necessary to consult widely scattered sources. See Hilton, *Hitler's Secret War*, p. 217, n. 58 for FCC documentation in NARA, RG172. Then see NARA, RG457, SRIC, 1793 *et seq.* for the first Coast Guard decrypts beginning in October 1940 and switching to South America on 10 June 1941. For the FBI as the initial beneficiary of Coast Guard decrypts see NARA, RG457, SRH-270 and for a third "independent" cipher-breaking service see

William Friedman's remark to Lester Pearson in Memorandum of Visit to Washington, 26 Nov. 1941, CSE doc. 000235-43.

9 Kahn, *Codebreakers*, pp. 802-14. Elizabeth Friedman's little group was funded by Treasury but because it worked so closely with the Coast Guard, it is usually referred to in documents as the Coast Guard cryptanalysis unit. The occasional reference to Treasury Department cryptanalysts has led some historians to think there were two code- and cipher-breaking units where there was only one.

10 Hinsley, *British Intelligence*, vol. 4, pp. 142-144. BSC passed 75,000 postal intercepts to the Americans during 1941.

11 Ibid, p. 142. MI6 twice sent missions to South America, in September 1940 and April 1941, in attempts to organize intelligence coverage. NARA, RG59, 841.20210/18.

12 C. H. Little, taped interview, 1992. The FBI has not released the files on the Sebold case and the State Department file on him is missing (NARA, RG59, 862.20211/2414). However, the Long Island (Centerport) station's relay role between Mexico and Germany from 10 Jan. to 21 June 1941 is mentioned in a State Department memo on F. J. Duquesne, 21 June 1941, NARA, RG59, 862.20211/3082. See also NARA, RG165, "Microscopic Dot Case," pp. 24, 26, 37.

13 Hinsley, *British Intelligence*, Vol. 1, p. 313. This was a visit only. The FBI representatives did not become "pupils" as Hinsley suggests.

14 Hilton, *Hitler's Secret War*, passim. Compare also Examination Unit decrypts GA-series at CSE with those of the Coast Guard in NARA, RG457, SRIC. The GA-series is the source of the German decrypts cited below.

15 Examination Unit Committee minutes, 2 July 1941; Stone to Osborn, 2 July 1941; Robertson to Wrong, 18 July 1941; CSE docs. 000201-05, 000026, 000207-08.

16 "Examination Unit history," p. 17. See, for example, German decrypt No. 233, CSE.

17 Robertson to L. F. Jackson, 18 July 1941; Jackson to Robertson, 22 July 1941; CSE docs. 000028, 000099.

18 Robertson to Wrong, 24 July 1941, CSE doc. 00210-11.

19 Evidence cited below indicates that the Government Code and Cipher School was not reading either Kempter's messages or those of ALFREDO at this time. Hastings was attached to the British Admiralty Delegation (BAD) in Washington. One of his jobs was to supply Japanese naval traffic intercepted by Canadian listening stations to the cryptanalysts at the U.S. Navy's Op-20-G. See Point Grey and Esquimalt report, May 1941, and British embassy to DNI (Ottawa), 15 Dec. 1941, NAC, RG24, 3805, NSS-1008-75-12(1). Also see William Friedman's description of Hastings as "the 1st liaison officer between Great Britain and U.S. (GCHQ & SSA)" on the back of a photograph, VMI, William Friedman papers, photo 574. In 1941 the Admiralty ran its own show at GC&CS.

20 German decrypts GA-34, 63, 64 at CSE. Stone to Jolliffe, 12 July, 1941, CSE doc. 000096. Robertson to Wrong, 18 July 1941, CSE docs. 000207-11. Shipping decrypts were being sent by the Director of Naval Intelligence "direct to Washington," undoubtedly to Captain Hastings along with the Japanese naval traffic.

21 German decrypts GA-62, 84, 86 at CSE.

22 Robertson to High Commissioner in London, 5 June 1941; High Commissioner in London to Robertson, 5 July 5 1941, CSE docs. 000083, 000091. The error was a numerical transposition: Eme 6972, ley 0602 instead of Yard 6792, ley 0602; "Sigint history," part 5, p. 7, CSE doc. 000417.

23 For "open secret" see U.S. Military Attaché in Chungking to Military Intelligence (G-2), 10 May 1940, NARA, RG165, 10039-299. Then Robertson to the High Commissioner, 7 July 1941, CSE doc. 000092. The warning of the "Secret Service ... from New York" is definitely BSC because it was then cooperating with Canadian Military Intelligence and the RCMP. See Murray to DMO&I, 11 March 1942, NAC, RG24, 2750, S-6403(3). Moreover, FBI headquarters was in Washington and it did not get onto Yardley until October 1941. See FBI report 22 Nov. 1941, CSE doc. 000035-40.

24 Osborn to Drake, 10 July 1941; Robertson to Wrong, 19 July 1941; Report by Osborn, 5 Aug. 1941, CSE docs. 000095, 000209, 000212-13.

25 Hinsley, *British Intelligence*, vol. 4, p. 146.

26 See sixteen-page summaries by Yardley, 16-17 July 1941, CSE unnumbered file. These were based mainly on Kempter's traffic, which the Government Code and Cipher School was not yet able to decipher.

27 Historical summary in NARA, RG457, SRH-270. The single document in this sanitized file says the arrangement was made through the British Joint Intelligence Committee in Washington, but this appears to be an error since the British JIC in Washington had not yet been set up. The writer probably intends the British Joint Staff Mission.

28 John Pearson, *The Life of Ian Fleming* (London: Jonathan Cape, 1966), p. 114.

29 Memo on behalf of Godfrey to Col. William Donovan, 9 June 1941, NARA, RG226, E92, box 1, 32. It is unsigned, but the writer assures the reader that Godfrey approved of its content in every particular.

30 I believe I am the only trained historian to have examined the "BSC History" prepared by Stephenson after the war and still held by his biographer, William Stevenson, author of *A Man Called Intrepid* (1976). Tested against the documents encountered in research for this book, it is full of distortions, exaggerations, and falsehoods. Stephenson was not above deceiving his subordinates, for his earlier biographer, H. Montgomery Hyde, author of *The Quiet Canadian* (1962), worked for him during the war and reports similar errors of fact.

31 The machinations surrounding Donovan's appointment are well described in Anthony Cave Brown, *Wild Bill Donovan: The Last Hero* (New York: Times Books, 1982) pp. 162-64 and *"C" The Secret Life of Sir Stewart Graham Menzies* (New York: Macmillan, 1987), pp. 354-59. The formal order setting up the Office of the Coordinator of Information is dated 11 July 1941. See NARA, RG226, E180, A3304, reel 12.

32 Notes on conversations with Norman Robertson, 8 July and 3 Nov. 1941, Harvard University Library, Moffat papers. Cited in Douglas Anglin, *The St. Pierre and Miquelon "affaire" of 1941* (Toronto: University of Toronto Press, 1966), p. 133.

33 NRCA, C. J. Mackenzie diary, 6 Aug. 1941. The messages referred to were in the LA code, the lowest grade and easiest to solve of the Japanese codes. Yardley was not

reading highly secret material. See Examination Unit report No. 5, para. 1, 15 Sept. 1941, CSE doc. 000105.

34 Examination Unit report No. 4, para. 2, 15 Aug. 1941, CSE doc. 313-14. The relevant information has been deleted from this paragraph under Section 15 (national security) of the Access to Information Act but in fact the blanked out portion reads: *The ciphers used between President Santos of Colombia and his representative in London have been broken....* See also Examination Unit decrypts GA 113-29, CSE.

CHAPTER FOUR

1 Yardley was helped considerably in these solutions when Hamburg radioed a new set of letter codes for the dates, stipulating that they should inserted in the fifth group of five letters in the message. See unnumbered German decrypt, Hamburg to Rio, 27 Nov. 1941, CSE.

2 Abraham Sinkov to G-2 regarding visit to GC&CS, 11 April 1941, NARA, RG457, SRH-145. Also Brown, *"C"* (New York: MacMillan, *1983*), pp. 325-29 citing the diaries of Rex Benson but note that Brown errs on p. 329 if he means that the ENIGMA secret was disclosed when he says Benson supplied "technical data on Enigma and Ultra." There may have been an exchange of "technical data" but the fact that the British were able to break the ENIGMA ciphers was not disclosed to American intelligence authorities until after Pearl Harbor. Hinsley, *British Intelligence*, vol. 2, p. 55.

3 Osborn (Yardley) memorandum, 15 Aug. 1941, CSE doc. 313. In the message quoted, two four-letter groups remain unbroken. Spelling and missing words are exactly copied from the document.

4 Advice on breaking diplomatic codes given to Captain Drake by General Mauborgne, "Examination Unit history," p. 6.

5 For a full description of Friedman's techniques, see Kahn, *Codebreakers*, passim.

6 Correspondence Drake to RSS(MI8), Jan.-June 1942, NAC, RG24, 12,341, 4/INT/2/2.

7 Pearson to Massey, 22 Aug. 1941, CSE doc. 000216-17. The Spanish translations were done by a Dr. Peter Brieger. The names deleted in this document are *Charles des Graz* (of British Censorship) and *Col. Stratton*.

8 Yardley memo, 18 Sept. 1941, CSE doc. 000105-06. He writes "beginning Nov. 1" for the Japanese and Vichy decodes but he probably meant Oct. 1, for that is when they (the D series) actually started.

9 For Denniston's mission to the United States see Denniston memo of May, 1943, in VMI, William Friedman papers, 110, SRH-153. Denniston also held talks with Op-20-G on the exchange of naval wireless intelligence. See Sandwith to Brand regarding 1941 Y mission to U.S., 19 Feb. 1942, NAC, RG24, 3805, NSS-1008-75-10(1).

10 Pearson to Massey, 23 Sept. 1941, CSE doc. 000221-22.

11 Because of deletions in text by CSE declassifiers, the following documents must be compared to get the sense of what was going on and who was involved: Brand to Stone, 23 Sept. 1941, CSE doc. 000219; Stone to Brand, 29 Sept. 1941, CSE doc. 000225; Robinson's recollection in "Examination Unit history," p. 19; Murray to Stone, 14 Oct. 1941, CSE doc. 000226 and the declassifying error on CSE doc. 000424 cited below in note 33.

12 Pearson to Massey, 23 Sept. 1941, CSE doc. 000221-22. Also, Stone to Wrong, 23 Sept. 1941, CSE doc. 000223.

13 Stone to Wrong, 23 Sept. 1941; Wrong to Stone, 8 Oct. 1941; CSE docs. 000223 and 000110.

14 Murray to Stone, 14 Oct. 1941, CSE doc. 000226. The name blanked out on this document is *Captain Hastings*. His name is consistently deleted when it appears in CSE documents, presumably in accordance with Britain's policy of withholding the name of anyone who later became involved with MI5, MI6, or the postwar Government Communications Headquarters (GCHQ). See also declassifying error cited below in note 33. For Coast Guard distribution of decrypts as of 17 June 1941, see NARA, RG457, SRH-270 and as of 9 Dec. 1941, see NARA, RG59, 862.20210.

15 "Examination Unit history," p. 22. NRCA, Mackenzie diary, 10 Oct. 1941. Little conveyed the request from BSC in Little to Stone, 25 Sept. 1941, CSE doc. 000224.

16 Ismay to Churchill, 18 Nov. 1941, NARA, RG26, 180, A3304, reel 12.

17 This conclusion is drawn from an examination of the wartime Coast Guard decrypts in NARA, RG457, SRIC. Those of the latter half of 1941 mostly involve the ALFREDO spy network which was not then producing comprehensive shipping intelligence.

18 Hinsley, *British Intelligence*, vol. 4, pp. 72-73. The changeover took some time. Drake continued to address his correspondence to RSS/MI8, with occasional references to MI6, until the end of the year. NAC, RG24, 12,341, 4/INT/2/2.

19 RSS to Drake, 29 June 1941; RSS to Drake, 19 July 1941, citing message 18-1-3, NAC, RG24, 12,341, 4/INT/2/2. Message 18-1-3 is also cited on Examination Unit decrypt GA-56 of 12 July 1941. A cross-reference in this decrypt to GA-46 which mentions "Loeschner" proves this to be a message from Kempter, since Loeschner was one of Kempter's sub-agents according to Hilton, *Hitler's Secret War*, p. 168. Hinsley, *British Intelligence*, vols. 1-4, makes no mention of the RSS intercepting South American traffic or the Government Code and Cipher School breaking it; nor is there mention of the vital problem of South American spies reporting merchant shipping movements.

20 "Examination Unit history," p. 24. Yardley had broken three South American Abwehr ciphers by this time, of which Kempter's—Group 32—was the most important. Osborn to External Affairs, 14 Oct. 1941, CSE doc. 000111.

21 Reference to Group 42, Near East, in Osborn memo, 14 Oct. 1941, CSE doc. 000111. Examination Unit German decrypt 233 of 22 Oct. 1941, CSE. Defensor to TROOPERS (MI8) with text of decrypt, 23 Oct. 1941, NAC, RG24, 12,341, 4/INT/2/2.

22 Yardley to Stone, 17 Nov. 1943, CSE doc. 000233-4. Examination Unit German decrypt 264 of the same date, CSE.

23 Yardley to External Affairs, 25 Sept. 1941, unnumbered from microfilm L-117-4, CSE.

24 H. F. G. Letson (then military attaché in Washington) to DMO&I, 7 Oct. and 22 Oct. 1941, NAC, RG24, C-5258, 8706(2).

25 Hoover to Donovan form letters re. decrypts with dates from 11 Sept. to 13 Dec. 1941, NARA, RG226, 180, 1, 4, reel 36 and 2, 7, reel 61. The actual decrypts are not in the file but deletions on the letters citing Freedom of Information section (s)(b)(1) indicate that the decrypts were from a foreign government. For Canadian decrypts received by Hoover from Donovan see, NARA, RG59, 862.20210/1152. Donovan also was on the distribution list for Coast Guard decrypts. See memo 9 Dec. 1941, NARA, RG59, 862.20210/681.

26 Hinsley, *British Intelligence*, vol. 4, p. 146. War Office memo of 30 Oct. 1941, PRO/WO/193/631. Its official name was Special Training School 103, later known as Camp X. See also original documents cited by David Stafford, *Camp X* (Toronto: Lester & Orpen Dennys, 1986), p. 31.

27 Stephenson apparently began his counter-espionage campaign immediately, specifically with a forged letter to the Brazian government designed to discredit LATI, the Italian transatlantic air service. His claim in the "BSC History"—repeated in William Stevenson, *A Man Called Intrepid: The Secret War* (New York: Harcourt Brace Jovanovich, 1976)—to have been successful, is false. Brazil dropped LATI only when the United States entered the war and demanded it do so. FDRL, Adolf Berle diary, 30 Dec. 1941.

28 Osborn to Stone, 14 Nov. and 17 Nov. 1941, CSE docs. 000232 and 000234.

29 Memorandum to Prime Minister regarding Vichy "dossiers" on Frenchmen in Canada and Japanese report of Canadian arms production, 21 Nov. 1941, NAC, RG25, T1807 (microfilm). The actual messages are in the Examination Unit's D series.

30 Stone to Wrong, 22 Nov. 1941, CSE doc. 000120-1.

31 Robinson to Stone, 22 Nov. 1941 and FBI Memorandum regarding Herbert Osborn Yardley, 22 Nov. 1941, CSE docs. 000119 and 000036-40.

32 NRCA, C. J. Mackenzie diary, 17 and 24 Nov. 1941.

33 "Memorandum on Visit to Washington," 26 Nov. 1941, CSE doc. 000235-243. Captain Hastings name (in italics) has been deleted from this document but in the description of this incident in "Sigint History," it appears at the top of p. 14 on CSE doc. 000424 prior to the same quoted passage. This was a slip by CSE declassifiers, for on other duplicated versions of doc. 000424 the name is blanked out. Little also remembered that it was "Eddie" Hastings whom he and Pearson met. C. H. Little taped interview, 1992.

34 See reports from the Secretary of State for Dominion Affairs to the Secretary of State for External Affairs for November and December 1941, NAC, RG25, Acc89-90/029, box 30, 28-C(s). Descriptions of U.S.-Japan talks are from this source unless otherwise cited.

35 See above note 29.

36 Pearson to Murray, 23 Dec. 1942, referring to Examination Unit decrypts D-288 to D-292, CSE doc. 000127.

37 Canadian legation in Washington to Robertson, 6 Dec. 1941, NAC, RG25, Acc89-90/029, box 30, 28-C(s). Also WLMK diary, 6 Dec. 1941.

38 Examination Unit German decrypt 295, CSE. This is an SWS Group 32 decrypt which means it was sent by Kempter's transmitter. It was actually sent Dec. 5.

39 Admiralty sighting report relayed to External Affairs, 6 Dec. 1941, NAC, RG25, Acc89-90/029, box 30, 28-c(s).

40 The connection between the Japanese convoy sightings and Robertson's decision to prepare the text of a declaration of war is established in Escott Reid, *Radical Mandarin: The Memoirs of Escott Reid* (Toronto: University of Toronto Press, 1989), pp. 160-61. Reid's memory may be faulty, however, in that he says External Affairs had known for a week about "a Japanese expeditionary force of fifty to seventy ships." The available documents suggest that External Affairs only learned of the convoys on Dec. 6.

41 G.W. Hilborn, taped interview, 1991.

42 Little to Stone, with list of decrypts sent to William Stephenson as of 9 Dec. 1941, CSE doc. unnumbered. The Kempter decrypt on the list about the Japanese convoys is No. 295.

43 Major Francis Graling, assistant military attaché at U.S. legation, to Major P. W. Cooke, 22 Dec. 1941, NAC, RG24, C-5258, 8706(2).

44 FDRL, Adolf Berle diary, 18 Dec. 1941.

45 Hoover to Berle, 9 Dec. 1941, NARA, RG59, 862.20210/718. The text is worded differently from the Examination Unit version, but considering the date Hoover handled it and the fact that the Coast Guard was not decrypting Kempter's messages, it was undoubtedly an American or BSC translation of the Canadian decrypt. BSC required that the Canadians send decrypts in their original languages so that it could do its own translations. C. H. Little, taped interview, 1992.

46 Kim Philby, *My Silent War* (London: MacGibbon & Kee, 1968), pp. 54-55.

47 Henry L. Stimson diary entry cited in Russell Buchanan, *The United States and World War II*, vol. 1, (1962), p. 51.

48 The commander of the Japanese armada had orders to cancel the attack if his force was detected. Much has been written about the inadequacy of the U.S. air reconnaissance before the attack but had the naval authorities at Pearl Harbor received warning of imminent danger, they would surely have put out picket boats. It is puzzling that they were not out already.

CHAPTER FIVE

1 Yardley's Canadian employers were generous. To give him and Edna their parting bonus, they put in an expense claim in conection with assigning the pair to fictitious "special duty" in Washington. Unsigned letter to Mackenzie, 12 Jan. 1942, CSE doc. 136.

2   Outline of organization of FIS for Capt. E. G. Hastings, British Admiralty Delegation, Washington, 2 Dec. 1941, NAC, RG24, 3807, NSS-1008-75-44(1). The "200 people" de Marbois mentions probably included DOT personnel.

3   MacDonald to Robertson, 24 Dec. 1941, NAC, RG25(G1), 1930, 724-AU39c. See also NAC, RG12, 2158, 11-30-1(3).

4   Stone to MacDonald, 27 Dec. 1941, NAC, RG25(G1), 1930, 724-AU39c.

5   Philby, *My Silent War*, p. 32. Note that Philby's assessment of Cowgill is confirmed by another former MI6 intelligence officer, Graham Greene, in the Foreword to Philby's book.

6   Brown, *"C"*, pp. 221-23; Hinsley, *British Intelligence*, vol. 4, pp. 131-37; Philby, *My Silent War*, p. 33. The Royal Navy may have continued to regard Menzies as only temporarily in the job as late as early 1942. See the reference to "an admiral" as head of GC&CS in discussion paper of Captain H. R. Sandwith, 6 April 1942, NAC, RG24, 3806, NSS1008-75-20(1).

7   Macdonald to Robertson, undated 1942, NAC, RG12, 2158, 11-30-1(3).

8   British Most Secret and Personal memorandum (addressee and addressor missing), 19 Dec. 1941, attached to Brand to Pearson, 13 May 1942, CSE docs. 303 and 304. The document was given by Cowgill to Lieut. Little, who forwarded it to Brand from Britain. It is almost certainly from Stewart Menzies, because MI6 chiefs traditionally addressed and signed their correspondence in green ink, apparently so that the writing could not be photocopied. See example cited below p. 274 and Philby, *My Silent War*, p. 47. CSE confirmed that there had been no Access to Information deletions from it.

9   "Examination Unit history," p. 24. Strachey and Margaret Rogerson arrived 15 Jan. The ALFREDO (and HUMBERTO, his assistant) decrypts begin 21 Jan. 1942, as Group 40. To conform to RSS nomenclature, they are relabelled Group 1/49/A. See Examination Unit German decrypts beginning at 378. Strachey had only partial keys because the Examination Unit experienced considerable delays in breaking ALFREDO messages over the next two months, whereas the Coast Guard was deciphering them promptly. This conclusion is based on an analysis of the Canadian and American decrypts.

10 Hinsley, *British Intelligence*, vol. 4, p. 44.

11 Macdonald to Robertson, undated 1942, NAC, RG12, 2158, 11-30-1(3). Drake to [*blank*] (probably Captain Maidment at BSC), 23 Feb. to 12 March 1942, CSE docs. 034-44. One of Drake's assignments was coverage of 1/49, the ALFREDO circuit.

12 Group 32 and 35 decrypts disappear from the Examination Unit collection of German decrypts on 20 Jan. 1942 and the ALFREDO messages begin the next day. The next 199 decrypts are months old. The Examination Unit did not finally start reading ALFREDO's ciphers currently until 16 Feb. 1942. See Examination Unit German decrypts, CSE.

13 Hinsley, *British Intelligence*, vol. 4, pp. 44, 108. Then see, Bowden to Donovan describing "British ISOS", 23 March 1943, NARA, RG226, 180, 3, 9, reel 73. This document, incorrectly interpreted by previous historians, has contributed much to

the myth of MI6 accomplishments with respect to German secret service traffic. Bowden—presumably because of "need to know" restrictions—was unaware that the U.S. Navy, U.S. Army, Coast Guard, FBI and the Examination Unit had been receiving or deciphering German secret service traffic for more than two years, and thus was susceptible to the extravagant suggestion from Menzies that its mastery was entirely a British achievement. Hence the erroneous statements about ISOS in Anthony Cave Brown, *The Last Hero: Wild Bill Donovan* (New York, Times Books, 1982), pp. 181-83.

14 The detailed proposal was prepared by Pearson 26 Jan. 1942 and approved by the Cabinet War Committee two days later. Most Secret Memorandum, 26 Jan. 1942; Pearson to Mackenzie, 28 Jan. 1942; Stone to file, 28 Jan. 1942; Mackenzie to Robertson, 26 Feb. 26 1942, CSE docs. 000267-71, 461, 000051.

15 Robinson to Pearson, 5 Feb. 1942, CSE doc. 000047.

16 "Examination Unit history," pp. 24, 26.

17 For the expected attendance at the conference see, Pearson (for Robertson) to Des Rosiers, 31 Dec. 1941 and Robertson to Wrong, 31 Dec. 1941, NAC, RG25(G-1), 1930, 724-AU39c. Montgomery Hyde, *Secret Intelligence Agent* (London: Constable, 1982), p. 182 describes a conference involving Hoover, BSC, and the RCMP that occurred New Year's Eve but this is almost certain to have been a meeting of the Standing Committee on Western Hemisphere Security. Hyde's report of friction between Adolf Berle and BSC at this meeting may be hearsay. Berle makes no mention of a conference on this date in his diary.

18 FDRL, Berle diary, 6 Jan. 1941.

19 "Sir Ronald Campbell proposes to rig the elections in Chile...," FDRL, Berle diary, 21 Jan. 1942. For "military intelligence" and "coup d'etats", see ibid, 24 Jan. 1942. The letters MI in MI6 stand for Military Intelligence, even though it was a civilian organization.

20 Hoover to Berle, 30 Jan. 1942, FDRL, Berle papers. Also, FDRL, Berle diary, 30 Jan. 1942. Note, too, the numerous exchanges between DMO&I(Ottawa) and FCC on illicit intercepts from 26 Jan. to October 1942, all through Letson and Drury of the Canadian legation, NAC, RG24, C5258, 8706(2).

21 Memorandum on Censorship signed by Edwin Herbert (U.K.), Byron Price (U.S.) and Hume Wrong (Can.), 21 Jan. 1942, NAC, RG25, 2686, 11229/40.

22 For evidence that the Munroe Doctrine was still State Department policy at this time, see Hume Wrong's report of conversations with Berle about "no change in territorial control in the Western Hemisphere by force." Wrong to External Affairs, 1 Jan. 1942, NAC, RG25, 2938, 2984-40.

23 This quote and the summary of German U-boat successes is from Thomas Parrish, *The Ultra Americans: The U.S. Role in Breaking the Nazi Codes* (New York: Stein and Day, 1986), pp. 141-146. Mohr apparently wrote English fluently.

24 Michael Gannon, *Operation Drumbeat: The Dramatic True Story of Germany's First U-Boat Attacks along the American Coast in World War II* (New York: Harper & Row, 1990, pp. 163-65, p. 389 and passim. This is an authoritative and excellently written

account of the German U-boat victory and the U.S. Navy lapses that led to it. See also Patrick Beesly, *Very Special Intelligence: The Story of the Admiralty's Operational Intelligence Centre* (London: Hamish Hamilton, 1977), pp. 107-15.

25 Hilton, *Hitler's Secret War*, p. 240. During the last half of 1941 U.S. shipping accounted for over half of all foreign sailings out of Rio, 312 to 598. See list in Rio to Hamburg, 15 March 1942, Examination Unit German decrypt 744, CSE.

26 Pearson to Stephenson, 25 Feb. 1942, CSE doc. 000286-87.

27 Wrong to Pearson, 4 March 1942 and Pearson to Wrong, 25 Feb. 1942, CSE docs. 000290, 000882. Pearson hoped to be able to offer the Americans Vichy decrypts in exchange for Japanese ones.

28 FDRL, Berle diary, 30 Jan. and 5 Feb. 1942.

29 All of the foregoing is from FDRL, Berle diary, 5 Feb. to 5 March, 1942. See also Berle memo of meeting, 5 March 1944, NARA, RG59, 841.20211/36.

30 Biddle memo, 10 March 1942, NARA, RG59, 841.20211/36.

31 DeWitt Poole to Donovan regarding conversation with Berle, 20 March 1942, NARA, RG226, E92, 9, 85.

32 Hinsley, *British Intelligence*, vol. 4, p. 144. The Security Executive was a committee responsible for coordinating the secret services. It took over BSC's security division in March, 1942. The coincidence of dates suggests its actions were in response to Stephenson's clash with Berle.

33 The new approach was made in March, presumably after the flare-up involving Biddle and Berle; NARA, RG457, SRH-270. Direct liaison began almost immediately because messages with an SIS designation (for Secret Intelligence Service) suddenly appear in the American numbered collection of German secret service decrypts at NARA beginning 9 March 1942. See, NARA, RG457, SRIC beginning with decrypt 3724. C. H. Little, telephone interview, 20 April 1993, confirmed that Maidment was answerable to GC&CS/MI6 in London rather than to BSC. See also mention of direct liaison with Maidment in Y Committee minutes, 15 Nov. 1942, NAC, RG24, 8125, NSS-1282-85(1). Also, Drake to BSC, 20 July 1942, CSE doc. 000347; Robertson to Stone, 11 July 1942, CSE doc. 000332. Drake continued to deal with the FCC through the Canadian legation.

34 Harris Smith, *OSS: The Secret History of America's First Central Intelligence Agency* (Berkeley: University of California Press), p. 20. Harris gives no source for this incident.

35 War Office memo of 30 Oct. 1941, PRO/WO/193/631. Stafford, *Camp X*, passim.

36 There are numerous references to what was being intercepted for the Admiralty at this time but see especially FIS to DNI, 12 March 1942, NAC, RG24, 3805, NSS-1008-75-10(1); NSHQ to Edwards (DOT), 16 Feb. 1942, NAC, RG12, 2158, 11-20-1(4); Drake to Examination Unit (Japanese Navy and merchant vessels), 22 Jan. 1942, CSE doc. 000044 and note on margin of Admiralty to NSHQ (Free French naval), 15 June 1942, NAC, RG24, 8125, NSS-1282-85(1).

37 Stafford, *Camp X*, p. 161. Bernie Sandbrook, taped interview, 1992. Mr. Sandbrook

was one of the original operators of the transmitter and remained with the HYDRA station for the next twenty years.

38 Foreign Office memo regarding Caffery in Rio, 20 Sept. 1944, PRO/FO371/4/1959. He is also described in the same file as being openly hostile to members of the British embassy and so vain that he had "nearly a dozen photographs of him in his own study." For the German view see Hilton, *Hitler's Secret War*, p. 208.

39 Hilton, *Hitler's Secret War*, p. 156. Original documents cited. It was probably Caffery who delivered this threat.

40 Examination Unit German decrypts 781 and 776, CSE. The LORENZ message was deciphered April 2 and sent to the Americans as SIS 31760. An "ALFREDO arrested" message also appears in the Coast Guard file with the notation that it is the same as SIS 31818. As SIS stands for Secret Intelligence Service (MI6), this is conclusive evidence that MI6 was aware of the collapse of the South American spy rings. See NARA, RG457, SRIC-3806, 3809.

41 Hilton, *Hitler's Secret War*, pp. 256-57, 238.

42 State Department to Rio Embassy, 27 March and 20 April 1942, NARA, RG59, 862.20210/1211. Hoover's April 10 assessment was described as having its "emphasis misplaced" and containing "wild reports poorly evaluated." It was condemned by all State Department officials who saw it. See, ibid, 862.20210/1329.

43 Stafford, *Camp X*, p. 244, citing a document in SOE archives, London.

44 For Coast Guard decrypts see NARA, RG457, SRIC. For FBI, FCC and State Department reports on the remaining clandestine transmitters, see NARA, RG59, 862.20210/1211-1469.

45 Stafford, *Camp X*, pp. 243-44, 188.

46 Air Ministry to Britman (Washington), 9 June 1942, PRO/193/634.

47 See above, notes 33 and 40.

48 Examination Unit German decrypts 704, 708, 727, 718, 734, at CSE. There were six others in similar vein, with decrypt 726 appearing in the Coast Guard collection as SIS 31213, indicating it had been supplied by Britain's Secret Intelligence Service (MI6). The American/British collection of Queen Mary decrypts is in NARA, RG457, SRIC beginning with number 3738.

49 Hilton, *Hitler's Secret War*, p. 240.

CHAPTER SIX

1 Davis to Yuill, 14 March 1942, and Robertson to Mackenzie King, 16 March 1942, NAC, RG25, 2961, 35.

2 The Admiralty asked the Canadian Navy to monitor all French naval frequencies when France fell in 1940. "History and Activities of Operational Intelligence Centre," DHist. For Allied fears about the Vichy fleet see WLMK diary 3 June, 10 Dec. 1941. "The Vichy situation is very acute. They want ten extra men to handle that."

14 Feb. 1942, NRCA, C. J. Mackenzie diary. Naval Service to Edwards (DOT), 16 Feb. 1942, NAC, RG12, 2158, 11-30-1(4). This is a full summary of DOT intercept assignments and includes Italian, Spanish and Portuguese. Also NSHQ to Admiralty, 12 June 1942, NAC, RG24, 8125, NSS 1282-85(1). Forrest could hear Vichy naval traffic not heard elsewhere.

3   Various documents from 27 Jan. to 19 March 1942 ending with CSE doc. 000295.

4   Sandwith to Brand regarding proposed Y mission to U.S. 19 Feb. 1942, NAC, RG24, 3805, NSS-1008-75-10(1).

5   The Royal Navy team at GC&CS enjoyed considerable autonomy and Sandwith's reference to "an admiral" as director rather than to an army officer, may reflect a situation in which navy cryptanalysts reported preferentially to the Admiralty's Director of Naval Intelligence rather than to Stewart Menzies.

6   Discussion paper presented by Captain H. R. Sandwith, 6 April 1942, NAC, RG24, 3806, NSS-1008-75-20.

7   Ibid. The importance of cribs in solving machine ciphers is excellently explained in David Kahn, *Seizing Enigma: The Race to Break the German U-Boat Codes* (Boston: Houghton Mifflin, 1991), although this author's research apparently did not turn up this example involving the names of U-boat commanders. It would have been a precious secret at the time and shows the British were being candid at this conference.

8   Extracts from U.S.-British Radio Intelligence Conference, 6-16 April 1942, NAC, RG24, 3806, 1008-75-20. This is the source of much that follows. The entire conference is covered in a single sentence in Hinsley, *British Intelligence*, vol. 2, p. 56.

9   Patrick Howarth, *Intelligence Chief Extraordinary: The Life of the Ninth Duke of Portland* (London: Bodley Head, 1986), pp. 160-61. This is a biography of William Cavendish-Bentinck, head of Britain's Joint Intelligence Committee during the war.

10 The American response to this suggestion is dealt with later, but it is worth noting that it was not finally acted upon until after the war with the creation of the present National Security Agency.

11 Recommendations of chief of Y mission, 25 June 1942, NAC, RG24, 3806, 1008-75-20. "Principle Recommendations of April Conference," 15 Nov. 1942, NAC, RG24, 8125, NSS-1282-85(1).

12 Report of British/Canadian/U.S. radio intelligence discussions, 6-17 April 1942, NAC, RG24, 3807, NSS-1008-75-44(1). See also 3 May 1942 note regarding "sub dispositions" received from Op-20-G, and traffic to the Admiralty in "Outline of Y organization," 17 July 1942, ibid.

13 I am now using British terminology here as defined by E. G. N. Rushbrooks, U.K. DNI, in "Secret Terminology," 20 March 1943, NAC, RG24, 3807, NSS1008-75-44(2). Y=wireless; Y raw material=intercepted foreign messages; Y inference=traffic analysis and direction finding; Y intelligence=results of cryptanalysis on low-grade codes and ciphers; special intelligence=results of cryptanalysis on high-grade codes and ciphers.

14 David Kahn, *The Codebreakers*, pp. 555-556.

15 Most of the foregoing is taken from conference documents in NAC, RG24, 3806, NSS-1008-20. If some of the facts should appear in conflict with other sources, the reader should remember this represents what the British *chose* to tell the Americans at this time.

16 The Americans identified the code-letters for the place the Japanese were preparing to attack by having the garrison at Midway broadcast a plain-language message indicating a shortage of fresh water. This message was picked up by a Japanese intercept station and relayed back to Tokyo using the same code-letters. The Americans in turn intercepted this transmission.

17 NARA, RG457, SRH-035.

18 "Principle recommendations of the April conference," 15 Nov. 1942, NAC, RG24, 8125, NSS-1282-85(1) and passim, NAC, RG24, 3807, NSS-1008-75-44(1).

19 Correspondence, April-May 1942, NAC, RG24, 3807, NSS-1008-75-44(1).

20 Little to Denniston, 18 April 1942, CSE doc. 300.

21 Examination Unit committee minutes, 21 April 1942, CSE doc. 000301-02. In attendance were: Pearson, Brand (Navy), Murray (Army), McBurney (RCAF), Perlson (RCMP), Strachey, Yuill and G. de B. Robinson as recording secretary. The Department of Transport intercept stations at Ottawa and Winnipeg (Forrest) were put on Vichy diplomatic and naval assignments. Sandwith Y Mission Report, 19 May 1942, NAC, RG24, 3806, NSS-1008-75-20.

22 David Hayne, taped interview, 1990. Mackenzie King knew perfectly well what they were doing.

23 See correspondence from Jan. 1942 until Walker to Lt.-Cmdr. John Cross, 18 May 1942, in NARA, RG457, SRMN-007. The Walker memo is very nasty.

24 NARA, RG457, SRH-270. See also ibid, SRH-041. The U.S. Navy took over responsibility for the Coast Guard cryptanalysis unit from the Treasury Department in March 1942, which is the reason why it thereafter shared responsibility for clandestine traffic with the FBI.

25 While it might seem incredible that the OSS was not given access to Navy/Coast Guard decrypts of German secret service traffic, I found no evidence that it did get them. In any case, the OSS did not begin receiving such decrypts from the U.S. Army until the following year. Shepardson to Donovan, Aug. 5, 1943, NARA, RG226, 180, 3, 10 (reel 92).

26 Bowden to Donovan, March 23, 1943, NARA, RG226, 180, 3, 9 (reel 75). Most of the deletions in this document were released 10 March 1977, as the result of a Freedom of Information request by the author.

27 See the series of decrypts beginning in March 1942 with number 3723 in NARA, RG457, SRIC. Note especially SRIC 3966, which bears a U.S. Army and Coast Guard serial numbers and is noted to be a "Dupe of SIS 35533."

28 Bowden to Donovan, March 23, 1943, NARA, RG226, 180, 3, 9 (reel 75). Menzies, aware of the low opinion of the OSS held by other American intelligence agencies, appears to have been trying to hide the extent of his cooperation with Donovan by

separately housing the OSS staff at St Albans and by using MI6 channels for the delivery and distribution of the information they selected.

29 British "Most Secret" memo unsigned and unaddressed but likely from Stewart Menzies, head of MI6, 12 Dec. 1941, CSE doc. 000304. See above Chapter 5, note 8.

30 C. H. Little, taped interview, 1992.

31 Brand to Pearson quoting letter from Little, 15 May 1942, with "Most Secret" enclosure dated 19 Dec. 1941, CSE docs. 303, 304.

32 Examination Unit committee minutes, 18 June 1942, CSE doc. 333-34 and 312-314. This document was released in duplicate by CSE declassifiers with different deletions. By comparing them, one can deduce that the omitted names are *Colonel Stratton* and *Captain Maidment.*

33 These messages, which run from August to November, 1942, can be identified in the declassified CSE files as those designated by the prefix CG2 for Coast Guard series 2 and by the RSS Group notation that always includes a number-slash-number. An examination of the parallel Coast Guard collection in the National Archives in Washington reveals that the missing numbers in the Canadian CG2 collection are decrypts of controlled agents—German agents who had been turned and were working for the FBI. See NARA, RG457, SRIC-2632 to 2741.

34 Denniston's link to the Ministry of Economic Warfare can be inferred from a number of Canadian documents but most notably from the diplomatic and commercial distribution list prepared by Col. Murray, 15 Nov. 1942, NAC, RG24, 8125, NSS-1282-85(1). MOUSETRAP is identified 23 Oct. 1942, p. 2, ibid. The size of Denniston's division is given by Drake in Y Committee minutes, ibid. Menzies, as director-general of the Government Code and Cipher School, remained in charge of both divisions while Travis and Denniston became deputy-directors. Hinsley, *British Intelligence,* vol. 2, pp. 26-27.

35 Little to Pearson, 7 June 1942 (contents deleted); Pearson to Little, 8 June 1942, CSE docs. 000524, 000308. The "Japanese messages" to be "burnt" mentioned by Pearson are certainly Japanese diplomatic because that was Denniston's baileywick. That they included the Berlin-Tokyo circuit is confirmed by C. H. Little, taped interview, 1992. The PURPLE cipher machine was used in important embassies like the one in Berlin.

36 Denniston to Little, 6 June 1942, NAC, RG24, 8125, NSS-1282-85(1). The "director" mentioned in this message can only be Menzies, because both Travis and Denniston were made deputy-directors of their respective divisions in the reorganization. Brora was a British Post Office intercept station in Scotland.

37 Despite extensive deletions by CSE declassifiers, the nature of the messages of "special secrecy" is deduced from Examination Unit committee minutes, 18 and 26 June 1942, CSE docs. 334-36. WLMK diary 25 June 1942, 7 Jan. 1943 (page 17a) and 27 Feb. 1944 (page 405d). For mention of Germany-Japan intercepts from both the British and the Americans see WLMK diary, 31 Oct. 1943.

38 De Marbois FIS reorganization proposal 4 May 1942, and Outline of Y organization, 17 July 1942, NAC, RG24, 3807, NSS-1008-75-44(1).

39 De Marbois correspondence 4 May (proposed reorganization), 15 May (approved), 30 July (to Naval Board) 1942, NAC, RG24, 3807, NSS-1008-75-44(1). The documents in this file do not make clear whether de Marbois was officially allowed to report only to the DSD. See also C. H. Little, taped interview, 1992.

40 Murray to DMO&I, 11 March 1942 and Military Intelligence operations chart, 3 May 1943, NAC, RG24, 2750, S6402(3). For MIx see DDMI(s) to GSO2, 20 Feb 1945, NAC, 2748, S6265(3).

41 NAC, RG24, 2750, 6403(1); ibid, 2748, S6265(1-2) and S6265-14(1).

42 Acland reports on MI3, 1 Nov. 1941, 27 July, 1942, NAC, RG24, 2748, S6265(1). Acland claimed in the first document that in cooperation with the wireless station at Rockcliffe he was monitoring the activities of fifty-two enemy agents in Central and South America. This was an exaggeration.

43 Ibid. MI3 investigators identified the writer but it is not known whether he was ever caught.

44 Memo of 3 March 1943, NAC, RG24, 2748, S6265-14(2).

45 Reference in NAC, RG2(14), 5753, 206.

46 Passim, NAC, RG24, 2469, S715-10-16-1-3(1-4).

CHAPTER SEVEN

1 Peyton Lyon, "The Loyalties of E. Herbert Norman," External Affairs monograph, 1990, p. 15.

2 Stone to Pleydell-Bouverie, 31 July 1942, CSE doc. 000354.

3 Pearson to Stone, 6 Aug. 1942, CSE doc. 000358.

4 Denniston to Little with list attached, 6 June 1942, NAC, RG24, 8125, NSS-1282-85(1).

5 For instance, on Denniston's list, Vatican station HVJ on 15095 cycles was broadcasting to the Belgian Congo, Eire, and the United States. In sounding out the possibility of Argentina's joining the Allies, the British ambassador was flatly told that "Argentinian blood should be reserved for the reconquest of the Falklands." Report to the Foreign Office, 2 May 1942, PRO, FO118/708.

6 James Gibson, taped interview, 1991.

7 Memo to Mackenzie King regarding Censorship, 5 March 1942, NAC, RG25, Acc89-90/029, 69, 300-Bs. Also, PC4012 of 13 May 1942, NAC, RG12, 2355, 11-38-18 and passim NAC, RG2, 5760, T/26(2).

8 Stone to Macdonald, 27 Dec. 1941; Pearson to Des Rossiers, 31 Dec. 1941, NAC, RG25, 1930, 724-AU-39c. Hinsley, *British Intelligence*, vol. 4, p. 144, incorrectly says that this conference occurred in December 1941 rather than January 1942. See also Herbert memo apparently prepared for the OSS, 31 Jan. 1942, NARA, RG226, E92, 8, 54.

9   Memo on history of Censorship, 28 July 1945, NAC, RG2(14), 5752, 194.

10 See the hundreds of British Imperial Censorship reports (still secret in Britain) and U.S. Censorship reports in NAC, RG25, 2846 and 2847.

11 NAC, RG2(14), 5753, 206.

12 NAC, RG2(14), 5758, DC135.

13 E. A. Martin memo, 8 Feb. 1944, *et seq.*, NAC, RG2(14), 5760, TC/4(2-3).

14 NAC, RG25(G1), 1930, 724-AS-39. There are similar postal intercepts in this file dealing with the elections of the United Mineworkers and comments of a representative of the International Brotherhood of Boilermakers, Iron Shipbuilders, Welders and Helpers of America on an illegal strike at the Midland and Kingston shipyards believed to be Communist inspired. Copies went to External Affairs, the RCMP, and the Departments of Labour, Justice, and Munitions & Supply.

15 Intercepted consular telegrams as of January 1942 involved, among others, those of Norway, Thailand, Sweden, Guatemala, Belgium, Mexico, Chile, Spain. NAC, RG25, 1930, 724-AT-39. This file also contains examples of secretly opened consular mail.

16 NAC, RG25, 2841, 1484-40(2-4) and 2842, passim. The files in the latter box run to thousands of pages.

17 Letter intercepted in Liverpool, NAC, RG25, 1989-90/029, 40, 73-A(s). Rabinowitch was General Andrew McNaughton's personal physician at Canadian Military Headquarters. Stevenson, the journalist, spelled the names of both men incorrectly.

18 Stone to Robertson, 15 July 1942, CSE doc. 000338-40.

19 Robertson to Biggar, 18 Aug. and 29 Aug. 1942 and Examination Unit minutes, 23 Sept. 1942, CSE docs. 000066, 000159, 347.

20 Y Committee minutes, 3 July and 28 Aug 1942, NAC, RG24, 8125, NSS-1282-85(1). Joint Combined Communications Committees were set up but the British Chiefs of Staff had no faith in them either. PRO, WO193/211.

21 Pearson to Stone, 30 June and Stone to Pearson, 2 July 1942, CSE docs. 016 and 017. The deletions are *State Department, Hickerson* and some variation of the U.S. Army's Special Branch or Signal Corps.

22 NARA RG457, SRH-270. FBI decrypts of clandestine traffic begin in May, 1942; NARA, RG457, SRIC-3993. For the U.S. Navy's negative attitude see Stafford to Op-20-E, 5 Feb. 1941, NARA, RG457, SRMN-007.

23 Y Committee minutes, 10 July 1942, NAC, RG24, 8125, NSS-1282-85(1).

24 Paper presented to the Y Committee, 14 Aug. 1942, ibid.

25 See U.S. Navy correspondence from January 1941, to April 1943, in NARA, RG457, SRMN-007. For sheer nastiness, it is quite amazing.

26 See month-long correspondence beginning British Admiralty Delegation (BAD) to NSHQ, 19 Nov. 1942, NAC, RG24, 3807, NSS-1008-75-44(1). The U.S. Navy began exchanging bearings with the Admiralty by direct cable link on 23 Oct. 1942, ibid. See also passim, NAC, RG24, 3806, NSS-1008-75-29.

27 On disclosing their success with ENIGMA on a visit to the U.S. after the Radio

Intelligence Conference, GC&CS representatives proposed to the Americans that they leave the deciphering of this traffic to the British. Both the U.S. Navy and U.S. Army insisted that they wanted at least to acquire the ability to break this traffic themselves. Hinsley, *British Intelligence*, vol. 2, p. 56.

28 Joint Staff Mission (Washington) to Chiefs of Staff, 21 Sept. 1942, PRO, WO/193/634.

29 "Report on the CEL espionage ring," 15 Sept. 1942, NARA, RG59, 862.20210/1816. Otherwise the description of Popov's activities is taken from the Dusan [sic] Popov file at FBI headquarters in Washington.

30 On Dec. 8 1941, the Americans deduced from decrypts that Engels was ALFREDO. On Dec. 11 the FBI reported further decrypts from ALFREDO to Germany on his meetings with IVAN, which was Popov's Abwehr code name. "Report on the CEL espionage ring," 15 Sept. 1942, NARA, RG59, 862.20210/1816.

31 FBI, Dusan Popov file. Popov's controlled messages are Coast Guard Group 3-G and 2-D in NARA, RG457, SRIC. He was replaced at this time by another German agent who arrived in the United States and surrendered to the FBI. He also came under "control." The British monitored their progress with the FBI by having the Examination Unit decrypt their messages. In the 1942 German decrypts at CSE, Popov's messages (matching ones in the "controlled agent" file in NARA, SRIC) are those of SWS Group 56 and the other agent's those of SWS Group 1/53. These were sent only to External Affairs and BSC. See, decrypt distribution list, 15 July 1942, CSE doc. 000342.

32 NARA, RG59, 861.20211 (Popov, Duchau). Most of the contents of this file are missing. Neither the FBI or the State Department seems to have been able to get his first name straight.

33 "Report on the Clandestine Situation," 18 Dec. 1942, CSE doc. 403-04. This report also notes that there had been nothing of interest "since the closing down of the big South American circuits...."

34 Other than the occasional ones from Chile and Argentina, most of the Latin American decrypts after the summer of 1942 involve FBI-run controlled agents. There was still a major German espionage presence somewhere in the Western Hemisphere, however, for in February, 1943, a German controller in Cologne asked South America for information on Hollerith machines, biological warfare and "atom splitting and isotope separation." See NARA, RG457, SRIC passim and especially SRIC-2577.

35 Stafford, *Camp X*, p. 191, citing SOE documents. In summarizing the accomplishments of Camp X when it was finally closed in 1944, Stephenson said agents were sent to Yugoslavia, France, Hungary, Romania, Italy, and Bulgaria but made no mention of Latin America. Stephenson to Murchie, NAC, MG26(N1), 72, special training school.

36 The files on BSC in Canadian archives remain closed but it appears that one major function after 1942 was to gather intelligence from expatriates living in the United States. See comments on BSC report on Chinese informant, Robertson to Mackenzie King, 11 Aug. 1944, NAC, RG25, Acc90-91/008, 69, 50055-40(1). The stealing of

telegrams from the Vichy Embassy in Washington, mentioned in "Examination Unit history," p. 81, also was probably a BSC espionage operation.

37 Various reports from Benjamin Bayly in Y Committee minutes, 25 Sept., 20 Nov. and 4 Dec. 1942, NAC, RG24, 8125, NSS 1282-85(1). A "private TK [telekrypton] line" and a "commercial TK line" were envisaged, the latter to handle the "overflow." It is not clear whether this means that a new transatlantic cable had somehow been laid. More likely, the cable between the United States and France which had been cut in 1940 was patched from the English Channel into Britain in the same way as the Italian Horta cable had been patched into Portugal after being cut at Gibraltar. In any event, Op-20-G also got a direct cable link with London at this time. Y committee minutes, 23 Oct. 1942, ibid.

38 Ibid. Bayly had originally been recruited by Stephenson, but the setting up of a separate wireless intelligence department at BSC under Maidment put Bayly directly under GC&CS/MI6. Bayly is so identified in the caption to a photograph of the second JAC conference 13 March 1944, VMI, William Friedman papers. See also Stafford, Camp X, pp. 158-165.

39 Reports of Captain Maidment in Y Committee minutes, 9 Oct. and 25 Oct. 1942, NAC, RG24, 8125, NSS-1282-85(1). See also Stone memo undated 1942, CSE doc. 000571-72. One of the tasks Stone set for himself on this trip was to mollify Stephenson over the fact that he was getting only some of the decrypts—likely just clandestine—from the Examination Unit. Stone to Pearson, 2 Oct. 1942, CSE doc. 000372.

40 Y Committee minutes, 8 Jan. 1943, NAC, RG24, 8125, NSS-1282-85(1). The private cable to Britain was to be ready in March. Two of Britain's cable ships, the *Faraday* and *Retriever*, were sunk at this time, making it "imperative" to obtain the services of the U.S. cable ship, *John W. Mackay*. Chiefs of Staff Committee memorandum, 2 Feb. 1942, PRO, WO193/211.

41 Y Committee minutes, 23 Oct. 1942, NAC, RG24, 8123, NSS 1282-85(1). "While the Department of External Affairs is very interested in meeting United Kingdom requests for commercial traffic (principally for economic warfare purposes here and in the U.K.) we are equally, if not more interested in the expansion of our facilities for intercepting diplomatic traffic." Stone (for Robertson) to DOT, 26 Oct. 1942, NAC, RG12, 2158, 11-30-1(4).

42 Memo on French diplomatic traffic, June 1942, CSE doc. 000323. Robinson to Stone, 21 Sept. 1942; Stone to Kendrick, 29 Sept. 1942, CSE docs. 000163, 000371. By the end of the year 18 Vichy stations were being monitored. Army assignment list, 15 Dec. 1942, NAC, RG12, 2158, 11-30-1(4).

43 For the setting up of this trip, see Stone to Stephenson, 21 Oct. 1942 and Robertson to Pearson, 31 Oct. 1942, CSE docs. 000382-83 and 000385. Despite the sinister motives that were later imputed to Norman concerning the visit to Harvard, it was entirely consistent with his new responsibilities.

44 "... to the United States Navy Department, we gave a description of the French Naval Cypher System A1," Naval Section memorandum, 9 July 1942, CSE doc. 000526-28. This "cypher" was a code in which the numbers were scrambled using a

stepped grid system fully described in this document. The Examination Unit first broke it in April, 1942, and then broke its replacement grid the following June. The code itself was apparently obtained from photographs taken by an allied spy who had penetrated the French embassy in Washington, probably CYNTHIA. "Examination Unit history," p. 91.

45 Examination Unit decrypt, J-708, CSE.

46 WLMK diary, 5 Dec. 1942.

47 Examination Unit decrypt J-815, CSE. Mention that the U.S. Army was supplying shipping intelligence to the U.S. Navy is in NARA, RG457, SRH-041. The Examination Unit later specialized in breaking shipping movement traffic. See Victor Graham, taped interview, 1991.

48 The collection of decoded Vichy messages after December 1941 were not released by CSE save a sampling; CSE docs. 1076-81. Also see, "Examination Unit history," pp. 60-62, 90, and Naval Section memorandum, 9 July 1942, CSE doc. 000526-528.

49 Minutes of meeting in Washington, 15 Jan. 1943, NAC, RG24, 8125, NSS-1282-85(1). This document would ordinarily have been withheld under the provisions of Canada's Access to Information Act. It appears to have wound up in this file due to wartime clerical error. The description of the meeting is from this document unless otherwise cited.

50 NARA, RG457, SRH-116, SRH-035. See also Signal Corps language letter-frequency tables for German, Italian, French, Spanish, and Portuguese as of August 1942 for an indication of what diplomatic traffic was being worked on. VMI, Friedman library, 905.

51 Y Committee minutes, 26 Jan. 1943, NAC, RG24, 8125, NSS-1282-85(1). The members of this subcommittee were Drake, Kendrick, and E. G. Bennett (DOT) for Canada and Lt.-Col. H. McDonald Brown and Lieutenant W. F. Drees for the United States. Also, 7 May 1943, ibid.

52 Robertson summarizes the arrangement to share wireless "raw material" with GC&CS and Arlington through BSC in Robertson to Massey, 10 June 1943, NAC, RG25, 2116, AR418/2. For the American request for coverage of RTZ (Kuibyshev) see "Report of working sub-committee," 7 March 1943, RG24, 8125, NSS-1282-85-1. The Americans complained that even with three stations monitoring RTZ, they could only get 75 per cent of the traffic.

53 Stone to BSC, 11 Jan. 1943, CSE doc. 1215. The word *Spanish* is deleted from this document but the tops of the letters S, i and h are visible.

54 Examination Unit committee minutes, October 1942, CSE doc. 347.

CHAPTER EIGHT

1 WLMK diary, 7 Jan. 1943 (page 17a). Ribbentrop was the Nazi Foreign Minister. Mackenzie King's "red leather box" is from James Gibson, taped interview, 1992.

2   "Canada had no control over its own soldiers whatsoever." Quoted from "Canada and the Higher Direction of the War," a report prepared by Canadian Army Headquarters, 5 March 1952, NAC, RG25, Acc89-90/029, 69, 300-Bs. When noting in his diary that 25,000 Canadian soldiers were to go into action that week, Mackenzie King could only write: "I gather the attack will be on Sicily." WLMK diary, 3 July 1943. For Churchill's insistence that they be called British see WLMK diary, 18-19 July 1943.

3   Lord Moran, *Churchill Taken from the Diaries of Lord Moran* (Boston: Houghton Mifflin, 1966), p. 116.

4   John Bryden, *Deadly Allies: Canada's Secret War 1937-1947* (Toronto: McClelland & Stewart, 1989), passim. These assertions are all derived from documentary sources.

5   Nelles to King, 1 Dec. 1942, NAC, RG24, 3806, NSS-1008-75-29. This document summarizes the division of naval responsibilities in the Atlantic throughout 1942. See also ibid, NSS-1008-75/24.

6   For the foregoing see passim NAC, RG24, 3807, NSS-1008-75-44(1-2); ibid, 3806, NSS-1008-75-29, NSS-1008-75/24.

7   Hinsley, *British Intelligence*, vol. 2, p. 551. Also for "ULTRA" being received from Op-20-G see historical summary of OIC in de Marbois to ACNS, 29 March 1945, NAC, RG24, 8125, NSS-1282-85(1).

8   David Zimmerman, *The Great Naval Battle of Ottawa* (Toronto: University of Toronto Press, 1989), passim but especially pp. 109, 116.

9   Postwar recollection of W. H. Wilson in de Marbois papers, DHist.

10 Hinsley, *British Intelligence*, vol. 2, p. 57.

11 "History of MIS," NARA, RG457, SRH-035. Also Denniston to McCormack, May 1943, VMI, William Friedman papers, 110, SRH-153, and ibid, passim, SRH-110.

12 These arrangements are described in detail in NARA, RG457, SRH-110. This file was read, however, at VMI, William Friedman papers, box 110.

13 Postwar history of U.S.-U.K. liaison on diplomatic traffic in VMI, William Friedman papers, 110, SRH-153. The deletion in the "Coffee Series" paragraph is *Berkeley Street*.

14 Examination Unit decrypt J-1355 on Reel L-117-1, CSE.

15 WLMK diary, 31 March 1943. This passage was omitted from the published version of Mackenzie King's diary, J. W. Pickersgill, ed., *The Mackenzie King Record* (Toronto: University of Toronto Press, 1960), vol. 1. The relevant External Affairs file on this incident—NAC, RG25, Acc89-90/029, 36, 60s—is still closed under Section 15 of Canada's Access to Information Act.

16 "I also spoke of communications that were intercepted ... if they contained information which it was at all likely the P.M. would wish to have." WLMK diary, 14 May 1943. Omitted from *The Mackenzie King Record*.

17 Y Committee minutes, 28 May 1943, NAC, RG24, 8125, NSS-1282-85(2).

18 Details about this second transmitter and the effect of variable frequency on radio skip were obtained from Bernie Sandbrook, taped interview, 1992. From Oshawa a bearing with a heading of 54.7 degrees passes through Ottawa, central England,

Cairo and the central Indian Ocean. *DXCC Country List and Great Circle Computa-tions from Toronto* (Guelph: Hammond Manufacturing Company: 1991), passim. For references to the British intercept station at Mauritius see Y Committee minutes, 5 November 1943, 8 September 1944, NAC, RG24, 8125, NSS-1282-85(2).

19 "[*Blank*] described arrangements recently concluded [*blank*] which would make available [*blank*] all intelligence concerning the East India battle zone in exchange for certain Japanese traffic which could not be picked up elsewhere." Examination Unit Committee minutes, 23 June 1943, CSE doc. 287-88. The CSE declassifiers omitted removing Sandford's name from the list of attendees, enabling one to fill in the blanks by context and letter-count (each 14 characters counting spaces) as *Col. Sandford, at Arlington* and *to Australia*. For Travis speaking to the Y Committee, see Y Committee minutes, 28 May 1943, NAC, RG24, 8125, NSS-1282-85(2).

20 Comments by Col. Stratton, Y Committee minutes, 18 Oct. 1943, NAC, RG24, 8125, NSS-1282-85(2). New Zealand was excluded because the few Post Office wireless receiving stations it had were under the control of the U.S. Navy.

21 Y Committee minutes, 24 June 1943, ibid.

22 Stratton, "Report ... on a visit to Australia, New Zealand and India," 18 Oct. 1943, ibid. This lengthy document deals mainly with developing counter-measures to pos-sible Japanese clandestine activities in the Pacific.

23 Wing Commander V. E. Marshall, RAAF Director of Signals, to Y Committee, 26 Jan. 1943, ibid.

24 Kendrick to Stone, 15 July 1943; Stone to (blank), 5 Aug. 1943; Stone to Kendrick, 29 Sept. 1943, CSE docs. 1390, 1397, 1439-40.

25 "Without carrying" produces random numbers, but the Japanese may not have used the Fibonacci system for super-encipherment. See Examination Unit decrypt JC-58, 6 April 1945, for a Japanese example of an additive constructed by means of a grid with a transposition key on one coordinate. Such systems seem very complicated to their creators but still can be expressed algebraically and therefore broken. For an even simpler arithmetic additive used by the Japanese see Budapest to Vatican, 14 Feb. 1944. Both on CSE microfilm L-117-4(2).

26 Kahn, *Codebreakers*, p. 318.

27 Chiefs of Staff authorization, 22 June 1943 and subsequent correspondence, NAC, RG24, 3807, NSS-1008-75-44(2). Also de Marbois to ACNS, 7 July 1943, NAC, RG24, 8125, NSS-1282-85(2). The original suggestion came from Col. Murray a year earlier and was vigorously resisted by de Marbois. See Y Committee minutes, June-July 1942, ibid, NSS-1282-85(1).

28 Y Committee minutes, 14 July, 23 July 1943; "Memorandum on Japanese Commer-cial (KANA)," ca. September, 1944, NAC, RG24, 8125, NSS-1282-85(1).

29 Kendrick to Denniston, 27 July 1943, and "The work of the Examination Unit," 8 Sept. 1943, CSE docs. 1398, 1417-21. The word *Spanish* is blanked out in these docu-ments but is obvious from the context. Also see Kendrick to Stone, 18 Nov. 1943, CSE doc. 1489. The deleted words in this document are: *Denniston, New York, Spanish, Taylor, McCormack, Spanish* and unknown. For Mackenzie King reading

another PURPLE decrypt, see WLMK diary 29 Oct. 1943.

30 All of the foregoing is from NARA, RG457, SRH-113.

31 Bowden to Donovan, 23 March 1943, NARA, RG226, 180, 3, 9 (reel 75). Philby, *My Silent War*, p. 55.

32 Menzies to Strong, 13 July 1943, NARA, RG457, SRH-113.

33 OSS report, July, 1943, NARA, RG226, 180, 1, 3 (reel 29). Strong to Marshall, 7 July 1943, NARA, RG457, SRH-113.

34 "Examination Unit history," p. 153, and J-series decrypts with a Z notation (for Zero) which cease in August, 1943, CSE. Anthony Cave Brown errs badly in his decription of this incident by erroneously placing it in mid-1942 rather than 1943 and by accepting only the OSS version of events. Brown, *Wild Bill Donovan*, pp. 305-06.

35 Mero to Donovan, 16 June 1943; McDonough to Donovan, 2 Aug. 1943, NARA, RG226, 180, A3304 (reel 6).

36 "The purpose of the trip [by Norman] had been to arrange a liaison on intelligence work, and in this he had been notably successful as far as the O.S.S. was concerned." Examination Unit committee minutes, 11 Nov. 1942, CSE doc. 000391-92. "OSS carefully excluded from all ULTRA" (except Abwehr and Sicherheitdienst traffic), NARA, RG457, SRH-153. For the withholding of Army decrypts see also Whitney Shepardson to DirOSS, 5 Aug. 1943, NARA, RG226, 180, 3, 10 (reel 92).

CHAPTER NINE

1 WLMK diary, 19 May, 10 Aug. 1943. The first quotation was omitted from the *Mackenzie King Record* and only the first sentence of the second was used.

2 WLMK diary, 1-3 Dec. 1941.

3 For a contemporary expression of this "long-standing U.S. policy" see report of conversation with Adolf Berle, Wrong to External Affairs, 1 Jan. 1942, NAC, RG25, 2938, 2984-40. This U.S. position is known as the Monroe Doctrine.

4 Robert Mengin, *De Gaulle à Londres: Vu par un français libre* (Paris, La Table Rond, 1965), p. 233. My translation.

5 Mackenzie King to High Commissioner, 24 Dec. 1941, NAC, RG25, 2938, 2984-40.

6 WLMK diary, 27-28 Dec. 1944. Winston Churchill, *The Second World War: The Grand Alliance* (Cambridge: Houghton Mifflin, 1950), vol. 3, pp. 665-67. Also passim, NAC, RG25, 2938, 2984-40.

7 Hume Wrong to External Affairs, 1 Jan., 9 Jan. 1942, NAC, RG25, 2938, 2984-40. Berle would have been aware that all messages between de Gaulle in London and his representatives abroad had to pass through British Telegraph Censorship or go out via Admiralty wireless.

8 "… he withdrew that assurance some days ago—which is another way of saying that the British knew about this and were perfectly agreeable to it…." FDRL, Berle diary, 26 Dec. 1941. For the British ability to read Free French ciphers see Foreign Office

correspondence of 9 March and 16 April 1942, PRO, FO371/32070. Also quoted and cited below.

9 "St. Pierre and Miquelon ... decypherments." Stone to Pearson, 13 July 1942, CSE doc. 334. The Free French were likely using a comparatively primitive hand cipher that they had devised themselves. This document also enables one to read others where the words *St. Pierre and Miquelon* have been blanked out. See, for example, Robertson to Stone, 11 July 1942, CSE doc. 332-33.

10 Various reports from the Canadian consul and intercepted letters January to June, 1942, in NAC, RG25, 2984-40. Although the messages from the Free French administrator are still withheld in the Paris archives, a summary of their content in the relevant finding aid mentions Monsignor Poisson, political problems, and the repatriation of Vichy sympathizers. AMAE, Guerre 1939-45, 116, finding aid.

11 Pearson to Stone, 9 July 1942, CSE doc. 331. Stone to Pearson, 13 July 1942, CSE doc. 334. Also, passim NAC, RG2, 5758, DC4/2. Yuill was replaced by Wilfred Eggleston in August.

12 Foreign Office to embassy in Washington, 9 March 1942, PRO, FO371/32070.

13 Halifax to Foreign Office, 12 March 1942, ibid.

14 Foreign Office memo, 15 April 1942, PRO, FO371/32070. See also Willoughby to Foreign Office regarding cipher pads for Free French, 23 June 1942; also memo 27 July 1942, regarding more cipher pads, ibid.

15 Halifax to Foreign Office, 18 March 1942; Desmond Morton to Foreign Office, 1 Oct. 1942, PRO, FO371/32070. Also cited below. The Free French continued to use the one-time pads for much of the year.

16 Foreign Office memo, "Relations with Charles de Gaulle," August, 1943, NAC, RG25, Acc89-90/029, 1, 1-A(s)(3). See also similar Foreign Office memo, July 1943, PRO, FO371/36064. The Middle East Intelligence Centre in Cairo operated its own intercept and code- and cipher-breaking service.

17 Foreign Office memo, "Relations with Charles de Gaulle," August, 1943, NAC, RG25, Acc89-90/029, 1, 1-A(s)(3).

18 Ibid.

19 For "tugging forelocks" see C. J. Mackenzie's view of Churchill's War Cabinet in Bryden, *Deadly Allies*, pp. 153-54.

20 Morton to Foreign Office, 1 Oct. 1942, PRO, FO371/32070. Morton was also the chairman of the War Cabinet Committee on French Resistance.

21 Morton to Prime Minister, 2 Oct. 1942, ibid.

22 Foreign Office memo, 10 March 1943, PAC, FO371/36064. Churchill consistently understated his problems with de Gaulle in his memoirs, *The Second World War*. These were published in the 1950s when de Gaulle was out of power but still influential.

23 English-speaking provinces voted on average 83 per cent for conscription in comparison to Quebec's 27.1 per cent. As English-speaking areas in Quebec voted overwhelmingly "Yes" the latter figure for French Canadians in Quebec would be

considerably lower. French Canadians outside Quebec also voted "No." J. L. Granat-stein, *Canada's War: The Politics of the Mackenzie King Government, 1938-1945* (Toronto: Oxford University Press, 1975), p. 227.

24 Vichy propaganda broadcast, the "Parisian Chronicle," 9 Sept. 1942, NAC, RG24, C-5258.

25 The description of the activities of Radio Station Eucalyptus both here and below are from PRO, WO204/6575.

26 Nerin Gun, *Les secrets des archives américaines: Pétain, Laval, De Gaulle* (Paris: Albin Michel, 1979), pp. 319-23. This author's analysis of Giraud's "escape" is devastating.

27 R. G. Nobécourt, *Les secrets de la propagande en France occupée* (Paris: Fayard, 1962), pp. 165-72. If Giraud really had wanted to know who was behind the assassination, he certainly made finding out difficult.

28 Nobécourt, *Les secrets*, passim. Stafford, *Camp X*, p. 3. Brown, *Wild Bill Donovan*, pp. 266-69. Michele and Jean-Paul Cointet, *La France à Londres* (Brusselles, Editions Complexes, 1990), p. 214.

29 Robert Aron, *Histoire des Années 40* (Paris: Jules Tallandie, 1976), 4, pp. 64-73.

30 Correspondence 14 Feb. to 9 April 1943, PRO, WO204/6572. Giraud or his staff seemed not to appreciate the efficiency of the Allied wireless interception and decrypting services. General Eisenhower shortly afterwards forbade direct wireless contact by the Algerian stations with South America.

31 Memorandum from Colonel Joubert, 4 November 1943 (and other documents), AMAE, Guerre 1939-45, 1511.

32 Evidence that the Americans and British had broken French codes CTX (Europe and the Middle East) and PCN9 (South America) is in PRO, WO204/6572, cited above in note 30. It is not known whether the Examination Unit mastered these systems but others it did master are described below.

33 This is established by comparing twenty-four descriptions of Free French decrypted messages discovered in External Affairs files with the texts of messages in AMAE—Archives de la Ministère des Affaires Étrangères (Paris)—Guerre 1939-45. Eight descriptions and the actual telegrams from the Washington embassy were conclusively matched. See examples cited below. For the sources pertaining to the breaking of the French naval cipher, see Chapter 7, note 44.

34 "Examination Unit history," p. 78. This does not make it clear that all French decodes were going to BSC. As for the Anglo-American agreement on exchanging diplomatic ULTRA, see detailed descriptions in Chapters 7 and 10.

35 The French-language text of this message with the words "beaucoup de force" is reprinted in Charles de Gaulle, *Mémoires de Guerre: L'unité 1942-1944* (Paris: Librairie Plon, 1956), p. 639. Compare it to the description of decrypt FG-2072 which reads: "Mr. Hull has told Mr. Hoppenot 'avec beaucoup de force' that it is the President alone who decides on French policy." NAC, RG25, Acc89-90/029, 1, 1-A(s)(5).

36 Note in margin. Ibid. For direct evidence that the Examination Unit was breaking FG-series messages see Glazebrook to Kendrick with reference to FG-2140, 15 June

1944, CSE doc. 1927. The failure to delete FG-2140 from this document appears to have been a slip-up by the CSE declassifiers.

37 Churchill to Foreign Office, 4 April 1944, PRO, FO371/41980. The French were told that their telegrams were being halted because it was feared they were being intercepted by the Germans, an explanation that made them suspicious, since the messages went by undersea cable via Gibraltar. Hoppenot to Diplofrance, 16 May 1944, copy to de Gaulle, AMAE, Guerre 1939-45, P2245.

38 Y Committee assignments sub-committee report on coverage, June 1944, NAC, RG24, 8125, 1282-85-1. As well as Algiers (THA), the Army receivers were monitoring Martinique, Papete, Dakar, Cayenne, and Rabat, all colonies then controlled by the Free French.

39 All in NAC, RG25, Acc89-90/029, 1, 1-A(s)(5). FG-1981 matches Massigli to Washington, 25 May 1944, AMAE, Guerre 1939-45, 1634, no. 473. Because of time constraints and the fact that the hundreds of wartime telegrams are scattered through almost 2,000 files, I was unable to match the other two descriptions.

40 As the May 19 description is noted as being from FG-1793 and the Aug. 4, 1944, description from FG-2975, the total received is obtained by simple subtraction. FG probably stands for "French Gaullist."

41 Foreign Office internal memo from R. L. Speaight, 5 June 1944, PAC, FO371/41980.

42 See SRH-110 and SRH-132 in VMI, William Friedman papers, 110.

43 WLMK diary, 15 June 1944. Mackenzie King made this remark to the British High Commissioner to Canada during a private discussion about Churchill's problems with de Gaulle.

44 Bonneau to Diplofrance, 29 June 1944, AMAE, Guerre 1939-45, 1615, no.237. By this time the Examination Unit had also broken Bonneau's messages out of Ottawa.

45 This very brief summary of who in the Examination Unit was responsible for Free French messages is taken from manuscript notes written by G. de B. Robinson and found among his personal papers by his daughter, Nancy Hill. Now in Robinson's file in the archives of University of Toronto. Shortly after the war Mary Oliver was posted to Britain as Canadian liaison officer to the Government Communications Headquarters.

46 See above note 33.

47 Memorandum on the mission to Canada by Father Kotowski, 14 May 1943, AMAE, Guerre 1939-45, 1246. This was apparently sent to Algiers by diplomatic bag or safe hand. Mackenzie King had concluded two years earlier that the papal delegate to Canada was fascist-leaning and an admirer of Franco. WLMK diary, 15 May 1941.

48 See entire file and especially Stone to Wrong, 4 May 1944, NAC, RG25, 2168, 53-MS-40C.

49 Bonneau to Diplofrance, 13 Aug. 1944, AMAE, Guerre 1939-45, 1246. As this is on a telegraph form, it was sent by cable or wireless and therefore certainly intercepted in its encoded form.

50 Bonneau to Diplofrance, 9 Sept. 1944, ibid.

51 Bonneau to Diplofrance reporting conversation with Robertson, 22 Sept. 1944, ibid. See the Canadian view of this matter in NAC, RG25, Acc1989-90/029, 48, 160s.

CHAPTER TEN

1 WLMK diary, 29 Oct., 31 Oct. 1943.

2 Y Committee minutes, 10 Dec. 1943, NAC, RG24, 8125, NSS-1282-85(2). Most of what follows is from subsequent meetings of the committee.

3 Kendrick, "Report on Discussions Held in Washington March 1944," CSE doc. 1760. The other CSE documents dealing with the Met Unit are too numerous to list.

4 VMI, William Friedman papers, photo 058.

5 The decisions of the conference are listed in Y Committee minutes, 31 March 1944, NAC, RG24, 8125, NSS-1282-85(2). It was styled the "2nd J.A.C. Conference."

6 "Examination Unit history," pp. 73-74.

7 Y Committee minutes, 31 March 1943, NAC, 8125, NSS-1282-85(2).

8 "Visit of OIC to Washington," 12 June 1944 and "Visit of OIC-4 to Admiralty," 31 May 1944, NAC, RG24, 8057, NSS-1225-100/81(1-2). The context in which "BRUSA" is mentioned suggests that the "BRUSA agreement," so often cited by other authors, only applied during wartime to wireless intelligence sharing between the U.S. Navy/Op-20-G and the Admiralty/Government Code & Cipher School (Bletchley).

9 The U.S. Navy was supplying a daily signal of "results derived from cryptanalysis and traffic analysis...." Y Committee minutes, 21 April, 5 May, 1944, NAC, RG24, 8125, NSS-1282-85(2). See also de Marbois to ACNS, 29 March 1945, ibid.

10 Stone, "Memorandum on Most Secret Intelligence," 4 March 1944, CSE doc. 1744. The deleted portions of this document are quoted in Stone to Murray, 6 May 1944, NAC, RG24, 8125, NSS-1282-85(2). Robertson sent the memo to Mackenzie King the same day that he received it. CSE doc. 1743.

11 "... recommendation made to you and which you approved that a higher direction should be given to our general participation in the field of cryptography and very secret intelligence...." Robertson to Prime Minister, 28 March 1944, CSE doc. 1763. The deletions are *in Washington* and *the United States Navy*. This memo is also initialled as "Read - K" by Mackenzie King. On May 5 Stone told the Y Committee that the Prime Minister had approved the proposal.

12 "Memo on organization of secret intelligence in Canada," 1 May 1944; Y Committee minutes, 5 May 1944, NAC, RG24, 8125, NSS-1282-85(2). Stone to deputy minister DND, 29 April 1944, CSE doc. 1785.

13 Stone to "Bill," 3 May 1944, CSE doc. 1804. Keenleyside to Wrong, 27 July 1944, NAC, RG25, 90-91/008, 178, 50065-40(1). The reports themselves from Oct. 22, 1942 to July 16, 1944 are in NAC, RG25, 3212-13, 5357-A-40. This collection is still

closed but the coincidence of the final date cited in the finding aid suggests that External Affairs stopped receiving them after Keenleyside's negative report. Hinsley, *British Intelligence* vol. 2, p. 55 also says that BSC was winding down its "collecting intelligence" function at this time. It would appear that the British were not much interested in the BSC's efforts either.

14 See various "American secret sources" reports from 25 Dec. 1944 to 17 May 1945 in NAC, RG25, Acc89-90/029, 3, 2-T(s); NAC RG25, Acc90-91/008, 169, 50055-40. These are either addressed to Norman or bear his initials. The OSS apparently had adopted the ABC-0123 evaluation system of the British described by Ewen Montagu, *Beyond Top Secret U* (London: Peter Davies, 1979) p. 25. For the Russian attaché and reports out of China specifically obtained by espionage see Keenleyside to Odlum, 2 Aug. 1944, NAC, MG30, E300, R33. For an OSS spy in the Vatican see NAC, RG25, Acc89-90/029, 32, 45-B(s). For Norman's announcement of the deal with the OSS see Examination Unit committee minutes, 11 Nov. 1942, CSE doc. 000391-92.

15 Gagnon (assistant Postal Censor) to Stone, February-March, 1943, NAC, RG25, G1, 1930, 724-AT-39. The subsequent description of the problems involving the Peruvian Consul is all from correspondence in this file.

16 WLMK diary, 12 May 1944. This passage is omitted from *The Mackenzie King Record* with the editor's incredible comment, p. 683, that the Prime Minister's notes of the conversations that day "are, in fact, not very interesting."

17 WLMK diary, 15 August 1943. Omitted from *The Mackenzie King Record.*

18 Churchill to COS, 6 July 1944, PRO, PREM3/89.

19 Bryden, *Deadly Allies*, pp. 195-96, from documents in NAC and NARA.

20 The foregoing is more fully described in Bryden, *Deadly Allies*, pp. 123-27, 193-95, and is entirely derived from documents in archives in Ottawa and Washington.

21 F. W. Winterbotham, *The Ultra Secret* (London: Harper & Row, 1974), pp. 123-24.

22 Michael A. Smith to John Bryden, 17 Dec. 1991, National Security Agency file J9415-90.

23 Message to Canadian Minister, Washington, 21 April 1944: "Gilbert Robinson of the Examination Unit is leaving [*blank*-14] on Saturday and will report to you sometime on Monday. He is going [*blank*-4] to talk to some of his opposite numbers in [*blank*-17]." CSE doc. 1792. The first deletion is obviously *for Washington* since that is where the message was sent. Now compare this to an earlier document which reads: "The Chairman agreed to a proposal made by the Unit that we seek closer cooperation [*blank*-17] in our [*blank*-6] work. This had been suggested by them and would be considered in more detail by the Secretary [Robinson] on a forthcoming visit [*blank*-13]." The second deletion is obviously *French* (plus two spaces) because the Examination Unit was only working on Japanese and French messages. The third deletion is obviously *to Washington*. Examination Unit Committee minutes, 28 March 1944, CSE doc. 252.

24 "History of MIS," circa autumn, 1944, NARA, RG457, SRH-041. B-Section of Special Branch dealt with Japanese military intercepts and C-Section with British-supplied German ENIGMA decrypts. See reference to "diplomatic texts" from

Britain in VMI, William Friedman papers, 110, SRH-132.

25 Examination Unit committee minutes, 23 May 1944, CSE doc. 234. "We are now sending [*SSA*] decodes of all [*French*] messages in low grade diplomatic codes which are received here. In return they send us translations of Vichy messages of similar grade. This arrangement avoids duplication of work on material which [*Arlington*] wishes to leave unread...." Kendrick to Glazebrook, 20 June 1944, CSE docs. 1947-53. The italicized words were deleted from this document. See also, Robinson to Glazebrook, 16 June 1944, CSE doc. 1924-26. The deletions are *French traffic, with Washington*, and so on.

26 Examination Unit committee minutes, 28 June 1944, CSE doc. 230. "Report of Operation of Exchange Agreement," 25 July 1944, CSE doc. 1940. Examination Unit Committee minutes, 9 August 1944, CSE doc. 228. "Examination Unit history," p. 78. Glazebrook to Robertson, 8 September 1944, CSE doc. 1052-53. The second, third, fouth and fifth deletions are *diplomatic, diplomatic, France* and *French*.

27 VMI, William Friedman papers, 110, SRH-153.

28 Caffery arrived in Paris Oct. 18, 1944. PRO, FO371/41959.

29 Article on Glazebrook, *Windsor Star*, 3 April 1946.

30 Wrong to Robertson, 9 June 1944, CSE doc. 1064.

31 Kendrick to Glazebrook, 20 June 1944, CSE doc. 1947-53. The Examination Unit now was larger than the pre-war Government Code and Cipher School.

32 Glazebrook to Robertson, 25 August 1944, CSE doc. 1056-7. The italicized words were deleted from the document. Letter-count and the fact that the Examination Unit then only had Japanese and French sections makes it certain that the deletions are the word *French*.

33 Glazebrook to Robertson, 8 Sept. 1944, CSE doc. 1052-3.

34 Examination Unit committee minutes, 20 Sept. 1944, CSE doc. 224-27.

35 Glazebrook to Robertson, 20 Sept. and 5 Oct. 1944, CSE docs. 1049-51. Memorandum to (blank), 6 Oct. 1944, CSE doc. 1047-48. Memorandum to Robertson, 1 Nov. 1944, CSE doc. 1039-40. The identity of [*blank*] as U.K. DMI is derived from the Y Committee minutes, 15 and 21 Sept. 1944. The identity of the DMI is derived in turn from Commander Little, who remembered meeting him in Britain at a meeting of the U.K. Joint Intelligence Committee in 1943 and from Philby, *My Silent War*, p. 84. Sinclair later became head of MI6 which presumably accounts for why he is never actually named in Hinsley, *British Intelligence*, vols. 1-4.

36 Robinson to Robertson, 2 Nov. 1944, CSE doc. 1906-08. (Punctuation corrected).

37 Stone to Glazebrook, 27 Nov. 1944, CSE doc. 1031-32. It is hard to see how Menzies could make these promises, since the sharing of postwar diplomatic decrypts would have required the agreement of the Foreign Office and, undoubtedly, the Prime Minister. There are many deletions in this document, but Menzies can be identified because the person Stone talked to is referred to by a single blanked-out letter. Menzies was the only person involved in British special intelligence whose commonly used code-name consisted of only one letter—"*C*".

38 "Plans for the Future of the Examination Unit," 8 Dec. 1944, CSE doc. 1027-29. The italicized words were deletions and are derived by letter count and the context of other documents.

39 Examination Unit committee minutes, 14 December 1944, CSE doc. 212-14. The italicized words are deletions.

CHAPTER ELEVEN

1 Solly Zuckerman, *From Apes to Warlords* (London: Hamish Hamilton, 1978), p. 103.

2 NRCA, transcript of C. J. Mackenzie taped interview, undated.

3 Churchill to Cadogan, 13 April 1944, *The Second World War: Closing the Ring*, vol. 5, p. 705.

4 Wright, *Spycatcher*, p. 186.

5 Andrew Boyle, *The Fourth Man* (New York: Dial Press, 1979), p. 215.

6 Jolliffe to Rivett-Carnac, 8 November 1944, NAC, RG2(14), 5749, 110. Rivett-Carnac to Joint Intelligence Committee (JIC), 11 Jan. 1945, NAC, RG24, 2469, S715-10-16-1-3(4). O. W. Wren, "Report on Visit to OpNav," 3 November 1944, RG24, 8057, NSC-1225-100/81(2).

7 Minute 750, "Wireless Intelligence," as enclosure Mjr. Sirluck to Col. Murray, 23 Aug. 1945, NAC, RG24, 2469, S715-10-16-1-3(4). The Joint Intelligence Centre for the Pacific War drew on the resources of Arlington, the Government Code and Cipher School, the Discrimination Unit in Canada, Central Bureau in Australia, the Wireless Experimental Centre in India (New Delhi), and Southeast Asia Command. Ibid. It appears to have been formed at Arlington in mid-1944, probably as a result of the Allied conference on Japanese communications described in Chapter 10.

8 "Final processing of material is carried out in the Joint Intelligence Center, and out of the common pool the General Staffs and Diplomatic Branches of each participating country draw processed intelligence," Minute 750. Ibid.

9 Robertson to Pearson, 12-13 Oct. 1944, CSE docs. 1912-13, 1877. (For the identification of Sinclair in these documents see above, Chapter 10, n35). Glazebrook to Robertson, 19 Oct. 1944, CSE doc. 1875. Norman to [*blank*], 27 Nov. 1944, CSE doc. 1853.

10 Norman continued to receive OSS reports as late as May 17, 1945. See American Secret Sources, "Russo-Japanese relations," 17 May 1945, initialled by Norman, NAC, RG25, Acc89-90/029, 3, 2-T(s). The valuations in this document run as low as C-4, indicating that some of the information is hardly to be believed. Also see OSS reports on Manchuria, 1943-45, NAC, RG25, Acc77-78/87, 6, MI103-106.

11 O. W. Wren, "Report on Visit to OpNav," 3 Nov. 1944, NAC, RG24, 8057, NSC-1225-100/81(2). "Addresses and signatures" were sought because they were especially useful for cryptanalysis.

12 "... diplomatic or commercial messages which bore on the situation in France and

the Low Countries." VMI, William Friedman papers, 110, SRH-153. Note regarding Denniston scribbled on file folder, early 1945, PRO, FO371/50209. This file was otherwise gutted of its contents. See also NSA 1993 release of 1945 Diplomatic Summaries at NARA. This collection shows that by the end of the war the United States was reading the diplomatic traffic of the major neutral countries in Europe and the Middle East.

13 Y Committee minutes, 8 Sept. 1944, NAC, RG24, 8125, NSS-1282-85(2).

14 Y Committee minutes, 5 Jan. 1945, NAC, RG24, 8125, NSS-1282-85(1).

15 Glazebrook to Robertson, 19 Jan. 1945, CSE doc. 1024-5. Note to file by Robinson, 3 Feb. 1945, CSE doc. 1023.

16 De Marbois to ACNS, 29 March 1945, NAC, RG24, 8125, NSS-1282-85(1).

17 Glazebrook (for Robertson) to Pearson, 19 March 1945, CSE doc. 990-91.

18 "Each telegram received by the French section....is registered on its arrival.... Separate series have special pages (i.e. messages going from Paris to Washington are on a different page from those going from Washington to Paris, and also from those going from Paris to any other post)." "Examination Unit history," p. 84. This part of the history was completed for May 25, 1945, long after Vichy had ceased to exist. Fifteen per cent of the Joint Machine Unit's time was then being spent on French traffic. JMU time distribution report, 9 April 1945, NAC, RG24, 8125, NSS-1282-85(1).

19 Robinson to [*blank*] at Arlington, 9 May 1945, CSE doc. 967-68.

20 Examination Unit decrypts J-4780, J-4790, J-4784, CSE.

21 JIC minutes, 30 May 1945, NAC, RG24, 2469, S715-10-16-1-3(4).

22 Glazebrook to Stone, 14 June 1945, CSE doc. 0950.

23 JIC minutes 25 June 1945, NAC, RG24, 2469, S715-10-16-1-3(4). Glazebrook memorandum, 7 July 1945, CSE doc. 0944-45. Glazebrook to Stone, 9 July 1945, CSE doc. 0941-43.

24 Robertson to Secretary of COS, 13 July, 15 August 1945, CSE docs. 0934-35.

25 For Pope's involvement see Glazebrook to Robertson, 28 Feb. 1945, CSE doc. 1004-05. Glazebrook to Pope, 9 March 1945, CSE doc. 996-7. Glazebrook to Pope re. attached memo to CGS about the closing of the Examination Unit, 7 April 1945, CSE doc. 986-88.

26 Pope diary, 2 May 1945, NAC, MG27(III), 4, 2.

27 The Examination Unit was intercepting and decrypting the exchanges between Tokyo and the Japanese embassy in Moscow at this time. See reference to JNO and RTZ in NAC, RG24, NSS-1282-85-1 and decrypts from Sato, the Japanese ambassador to Russia. As to a possible reason why Hope burst into tears, see below.

28 David McCullough, *Truman* (New York: Simon & Schuster, 1992), pp. 437-39.

29 Sato to Tokyo quoted in Diplomatic Summary, 22 July 1945, VMI, William Friedman papers, 110, SRH-040. The plan to destroy Japan's rice crop is in Baron Bernstein, "The Birth of the U.S. Biological Warfare Program," *Scientific American*, June 1987, p. 120.

30 Stimson's actions and the subsequent events at Potsdam described below are mainly

taken from the excellently documented account in Richard Hewlett and Oscar Anderson, *The History of the United States Atomic Energy Commission: The New World, 1939/1946* (University Park: Pennsylvania State University Press, 1962), pp. 361-407. External Affairs learned from "American Secret Sources" on May 17, 1945, of the Emperor's intention to send a peace mission to Moscow. Herbert Norman note to file, NAC, RG25, Acc89-90/029, 3, 2-T(s).

31 Unless otherwise indicated, the intercepted messages cited below are from the Magic/Diplomatic Summaries in NARA, RG457, SRS-1740-plus. The parallel collection of Diplomatic Summaries in NARA, RG457, SRH-040 is not to be trusted, having apparently been subjected to creative editing.

32 Field Marshall Viscount Alanbrooke (COS) diary, 23 July 1945, quoted in Arthur Bryant, *Triumph in the West* (London: Collins, 1959), p. 477.

33 Lengthy report from Allen Dulles, OSS chief in Switzerland, sent by Charles Cheston, OSS deputy director, to Miss Rose Conway for forwarding to the President, copies to the Chiefs of Staff and the Secretary of State, 2 Aug. 1945, NARA, RG226, 180, A3304, reel 36. This document notes that all such reports were going directly to the President.

34 Victor Graham, taped interview, 1990. The Germans were certainly aware the Americans were working on the bomb. See the request to a spy for details on heavy water, cyclotrons and "atom splitting and isotope separation" in Cologne to South America, 2 Nov. 1943, NARA, RG457, SRIC-2577. They could have disclosed their knowledge to the Japanese representatives in Berlin. By the time of Potsdam, however, the Japanese did not know an atomic bomb was actually ready for use. Morawetz to Glazebrook, 18 Oct. 1945, CSE doc 352.

35 See "J" series of decrypts ending with J-4911, CSE. The Diplomatic Summary for July 29, 1945, is in NARA, RG457, SRS-174-plus. There is no way of knowing whether this file contains all the summaries that were issued up to this date.

36 WLMK diary, 10 Sept. 1945. Omitted from *The Mackenzie King Record*, vol. 3 (1970). Failing to include this passage in the published version of the diaries is surely either a monumental error in judgment, or deliberate.

37 Moran, *Churchill*, pp. 301-02. Lord Moran was "deeply shocked by this ruthless decision" adding, "I once slept in a house where there had been a murder. I felt like that here."

CHAPTER TWELVE

1 Correspondence Aug.-Sept. 1945, NAC, RG2(14), 5760. There are thousands of excerpted letters, with names and addresses, in Defence and External Affairs files at the National Archives. These records will be just as valuable to future generations of Canadians as the nineteenth-century immigrant passenger lists are today. It is fortunate the Director of Censorship did not get his way.

2 Minute 750, 23 Aug. 1945, NAC, RG24, 2469, S715-10-16-1-3(4). The G-2 memoran-

dum of 11 Aug. 1945 is cited in James Bamfield, *The Puzzle Palace* (Boston: Houghton Mifflin, 1982), p. 44.

3   This last sentence is an assumption but surely a safe one. Japanese postwar diplomatic decrypts would have been sent to MacArthur's Counter-intelligence Corps and Norman was the appropriate specialist to receive them. Norman's assessments were greatly valued by MacArthur.

4   Minute 750, 23 Aug. 1945, NAC, RG24, 2469, S715-10-16-1-3(4).

5   JIC minutes, 27 Aug. 1945, ibid.

6   References to ULTRA in Canadian documents indicate that it was derived from one of at least two security gradings that existed above TOP SECRET. By 1944 it came to be applied to all wireless intelligence obtained from high-grade codes and ciphers, regardless of type or country of origin.

7   Nine-page (foolscap) Top Secret memorandum prepared by Col. Murray, 27 Aug. 1945, DHist, 193.009(D48). Security was tightened at DND's Directorate of History after I saw this document in 1990 for it was no longer present when I called the file in 1993. Fortunately, I had photocopied it.

8   WLMK diary, 6 Sept. 1945.

9   WLMK special diary, 6 Sept. 1945. Omitted from *The Mackenzie King Record,* vol. 3 (1970). As the special diary is collected with the main diary it is convenient to cite from each as though they are a single narrative.

10   *The Mackenzie King Record,* vol. 3, p. 10. There is absolutely no documentary evidence to support the insertion of Stephenson's name here, and much that contradicts it within a few pages of this quotation in the original diary. Nevertheless, this erroneous assertion that the "head of the Secret Service" was Stephenson continued to be accepted as fact as late as 1990. See J. L. Granatstein and David Stafford, *Spy Wars: Espionage and Canada from Gouzenko to Glasnost* (Toronto: Key Porter, 1990), p. 56.

11   WLMK diary, 7 Sept. 1945. Only the first portion of this quotation is in *The Mackenzie King Record,* vol. 3, p. 11. The editors of this volume also took it upon themselves to correct the original diary's consistent misspelling of Stephenson as Stevenson. This, and similar textual changes or spelling corrections—Seigniory instead of Seignory, for example, or Robertson instead of R.—often appear in quoted passages in books on the Gouzenko affair, even though the writers only cite them by date in their notes, thus giving readers the impression that the original diary has been used rather than *The Mackenzie King Record.*

12   H. Montgomery Hyde, *The Quiet Canadian: The Secret Service Story of Sir William Stephenson* (London: Hamish Hamilton, 1962), pp. 229, 232.

13   Wright, *Spycatcher,* p. 282. All this suggests that Stephenson was unavailable when Robertson tried to reach him. He appears to have arrived on the scene several days later and then only to provide Dwyer with a telekrypton machine for secure communications with New York for onward transmission by BSC cable to London.

14   Interview with George Glazebrook and elaborated on by Don Page, External Affairs historian, quoted in John Sawatsky, *Gouzenko: The Untold Story* (Toronto: Macmillan, 1984), pp. 46-47. This version of events has Stephenson and Robertson meeting

the night of Sept. 6 at the Royal Ottawa Golf and Country Club. It does not fit with the details given by Hyde/Stephenson.

15 Stafford, *Camp X*, pp. 250-257. This author interviewed some of the people who wrote the history at Stephenson's direction.

16 The errors derived from the "BSC History," in William Stevenson, *A Man Called Intrepid* (1976) are legion and have been noted by other authors many times. Earlier chapters of this book illustrate even more of them.

17 Seigniory Club membership list and members' card file, the Seigniory Club, Hotel Montebello, Montebello, Quebec. The green ink on the documents resisted photocopying, suggesting that the chiefs of MI6 traditionally used the colour because it could not be photographed. Pens with similar inks invisible to black and white film are still used today in photo-typesetting. The train route from Ottawa to the United States passed through Montebello and Montreal, so there was ample opportunity for a stopover in the latter city. The hotel register for the Ritz-Carlton during the war could not be located.

18 Stone to Glazebrook, 3 Sept. 1945, CSE doc. 0924. The italicized words are deletions letter-counted and filled in by the context. The word "Oshawa" is scribbled in the margin next to the *HYDRA* line. Menzies apparently included the United States in this visit to North America for FBI agent Robert Lamphere mentions having being introduced to him prior to 1949 in Robert Lamphere, The FBI-KGB War, (1986) p. 130.

19 "... and two telekrypton lines from Ottawa to New York, and Ottawa to Washington. (All have since been abandoned)." Aide-memoire for CGS from Col. Murray, 23 Oct. 1945, DHist, 193.009(D48). This document also has disappeared from this file since I viewed and photocopied it in 1990. See above note 7. Gouzenko arrived at Camp X in mid-October and remained there until February, according to interviews with his RCMP guards in Sawatsky, *Gouzenko*, pp. 58-67.

20 This description of the Soviet code-cipher system is taken from Lamphere, *The FBI-KGB War*, pp. 79-84. Lamphere was an FBI agent and was directly involved in work on these codes in 1945 with Martin Gardner at Arlington. He cautions on p. 79 that the National Security Agency asked him to withhold certain details of this incident.

21 The handicaps of one-time pad ciphers are well known, but for a contemporary description of their limitations as they affected the War Office W cipher and Canada's M cipher, see Instructions re. (Cipher) Office Routines and Procedures at Canada House by Maj. J. P. Page, 24 May 1941, NAC, RG24, 12,324, 4/ciphers/3.

22 "... and the telegrams he brought with him when he defected would have been a great help to Western decrypters." Interview with Kim Philby in Phillip Knightley, *Philby: The Life and Views of the K.G.B. Masterspy* (London: Andre Deutsch, 1988), p. 133.

23 For a fuller explanation of VENONA see Lamphere, *FBI-KGB War*, passim. Wright, *Spycatcher*, pp. 222-27.

24 Even if he had not taken a code book, Gouzenko had been a cipher clerk since 1941, so he would have known the numbers and meanings of a broad range of code words,

including many of those in the book obtained from the Finns. The Soviets changed their codes in May, 1945, and here again Gouzenko must have been helpful.

25 Robinson, "Blueprint for a permanent DU," 18 Sept. 1945, CSE doc. 0920-23.

26 "... a Joint Co-ordination Bureau which would digest and co-ordinate all military intelligence, including that derived from ULTRA." JIC meeting, 20 Sept. 1945, NAC, RG24, 2469, S715-10-16-1-3(5). For the proposal itself, see CJIC to CSC, 26 Sept. 1945, NAC, RG24, 6178, HQ22-1-43.

27 JIC meeting 12 Oct. 1945, NAC, RG24, 2469, S715-10-16-1-3(5).

28 Bamford, *Puzzle Palace*, p. 313 reports that the Government Code and Cipher School changed its name to Government Communications Headquarters (GCHQ) as part of a reorganization in 1943. However, Canadian documents indicate that while the British Y Committee was reorganized as the Signals Intelligence Board in November 1943, the Government Code and Cipher School continued to be referred as such until the postwar reorganization mentioned below. See Y Committee minutes, 19 Nov. 1943 and 1 May 1944, NAC, RG24, 8125, NSS-1282-85(2) and passim, NAC, RG24, 2469, S715-10-16-1-3(4-5).

29 Most of the foregoing on the visit by Travis is from the JIC meeting, 22 Oct. 1945, NAC, RG24, 2469, S715-10-16-1-3(5). But see also Glazebrook to Admiral G. C. Jones, 26 Oct. 1945, CSE doc. 0902. The deleted words in this document are: *Sir Edward Travis, Travis, United Kingdom* and *United States*.

30 Hinsley, *British Intelligence*, vol. 1, pp. 295-96. Churchill's persistent interference is well documented in various sources.

31 Hinsley, *British Intelligence*, vol. 1, p. 273; ibid, vol. 2, p. 21. Philby, *My Silent War*, p. 82.

32 R. V. Jones, *Reflections on Intelligence* (London: Mandarin Paperbacks, 1990), p. 15. William Friedman to Elizabeth, 19 August 1945, VMI, Elizabeth Friedman papers (unsorted).

33 Paraphrased from "Charter of U.K. JIC," 2 April 1948, NAC, RG2, 81, I-40. This essentially combined the roles of Britain's wartime Joint Intelligence Committee and the Security Executive, with the added responsibility of selecting wireless intercept targets. See also the reference to the British JIC in Wright, *Spycatcher*, p. 82.

34 Philby, *My Silent War*, pp. 70, 84-86. The "Jones" Philby mentions presumably is Captain Eric Jones, identified by William Friedman on the back of a photograph as "later ... director of GCHQ Britain." VMI, William Friedman papers, photo 525. Hastings as Denniston's successor is mentioned in an unsigned 17 July 1945 note on the file folder, PRO, FO371/W8744.

35 Aide-memoire for CGS from Col. Murray, Oct. 23, 1945; DHist, 193.009(D48).

36 Bryden, *Deadly Allies*, passim.

37 NRCA, C. J. Mackenzie taped interview, undated.

38 James Gibson, the External Affairs officer who worked for nine years in Laurier House and knew all of the Prime Minister's routines, stated flatly that the missing binder must have been deliberately taken after Mackenzie King's death. James Gib-

son, taped interview, 1991. The chances are strong that it was acquired by Defence Liaison Two and still exists either in External Affairs or the Privy Council Office.

39 Glazebrook, "Memorandum on postwar plans for intelligence and counter-intelligence," 3 Nov. 1945, CSE doc. 0898-0901. The first four deletions in this document are: *United Kingdom and the United States, Foreign Office, State Department* and *United Kingdom and the United States.* Under item one the references are to *ULTRA* intelligence. The reference to where the February meeting was to be held is also deleted but see references to Drake attending a Commonwealth communications conference in the U.K. in JIC minutes, 2 Feb. and 3 May 1946, NAC, RG24, 2469, S715-10-16-1-3(5).

40 "Proposal for the establishment of a National Intelligence Organization," Foulkes to Robertson, 22 Dec. 1945, NAC, RG24, 6178, HQ22-1-43.

CHAPTER THIRTEEN

1 Pearson to Mackenzie, 18 Feb. 1947, NAC, RG2, 83, I-50-5.

2 JIC minutes, 26 Jan, and 2 Feb. 1946, NAC, RG24, 2469, S715-10-16-1-3(5).

3 Ibid. By "position" they meant an actual receiver, a high-speed recorder and 4-5 operators per receiver on a 24-hour basis. They proposed the service responsibility for the 100 positions be shared on a 40-45-15 basis, navy-army-air force. JIC meeting (extraordinary), 6 Feb. 1946, ibid. The proposal went up to the Chiefs of Staff on Feb. 18.

4 For an External Affairs summary of world reaction see NAC, RG2, 54, I-40-3.

5 JIC minutes, 1 March 1946, NAC, RG24, 2469, S715-10-16-1-3(5). The definition of a "D notice" is from the British documents tabled at this meeting.

6 COS to Robertson and Heeney, 30 March 1946, NAC, RG2(18), C-30; Gill to JIC, 1 April 1946, NAC, RG24, 2469, S715-10-16-1-3(5); "Sigint History," CSE docs. 1178-79, 1220, 1183. As the senior civil servant in the Privy Council Office, Arnold Heeney represented the Prime Minister in discussions on intelligence.

7 Reference to Drake's report on the "Commonwealth Communication Conference" in JIC minutes, 3 May 1946, NAC, RG24, 2469, S715-10-16-1-3(5).

8 "Sigint History," CSE doc. 001228.

9 Memo (Top Secret) to Defence Committee of Cabinet, 8 Nov. 1946, NAC, RG2, 83, I-50-5.

10 Pearson to Mackenzie (Top Secret), 18 Feb. 1947; Mackenzie to Pearson, 26 Feb. 1947; Pearson to Heeney, undated; Heeney to Pearson, 19 March 1947. All in NAC, RG2, 83, I-50-5. Approval to hide the cost in the DRB was obtained from three ministers: St. Laurent (External Affairs), Claxton (Defence) and Abbott (Finance). There is no indication that the Prime Minister was consulted. The Director of the Defence Research Board was never told of the arrangement. O. M. Solandt, taped interview, 1991.

11   This is a surmise based on problems involving the U.S. Navy and the National Security Agency separately sending intelligence data to Britain circa 1953. NAC, RG24, 18,962, S1272-584/0. For the decisions of the London conference see memo to Defence Committee of Cabinet, 8 Nov. 1946 and subsequent correspondence from Pearson, NAC, RG2, 83, I-50-5.

12   For External Affairs setting targets and priorities for postwar Y, see "History and Activities of Operational Intelligence Centre," DHist.

13   For "CANUSA" and "BRUSA" see Hilborn, taped interview, 1991; Jones to Friedman, 13 March 1952, VMI, Elizabeth Friedman papers. I did not find any references in documents to what other writers refer to as the "UKUSA" agreement, leading me to suspect that this is an error in nomenclature arising from not knowing that there were two separate wartime Anglo-American agreements—one involving the U.S. Navy and one the U.S. Army. There was a further "telecommications conference" in the United States in 1947 but the only file I found on it does not mention signals intelligence. See NAC, RG2(18), 62, C-35-2.

14   Pearson to Travis, 19 Nov. 1946, NAC, RG2, 83, I-50-5. It was actually a British idea suggested at the October communications conference in London. It may be that France had taken back its transatlantic cable and, since commercial cables would have been too expensive for the volume of traffic involved, HYDRA was an economically attractive solution.

15   Pearson to Mackenzie, 18 Feb. 1947, NAC, RG2, 83, I-50-5. In order to do this, HYDRA was connected by private cable directly with Ottawa and Washington.

16   Bamford, *Puzzle Palace*, pp. 236-46, 331.

17   Correspondence regarding Cabinet Defence Committee, 19 Feb. and 5 March, 1946; Gill to COS, 25 Feb. 1946; Chiefs of Staff Committee extract 6 April 1946, NAC, RG24, 6178, HQ-22-1-43.

18   "Origin and function of the Joint Intelligence Bureau" prepared by A-2 of USAFE, 9 Oct. 1946, NAC, RG24, 6178, HQ22-1-43(1).

19   JIC (London) to JIC (Ottawa), 15 Nov. 1945, NAC, RG24, 2469, S715-10-16-1-3(5). Canmilitary to CSC (Ottawa), 23 March 1946; "History of Joint Intelligence Bureau," 6 April 1946. NAC, RG24, 6178, HQ22-1-43(1).

20   The Canadian JIB would "collect, collate and study overt intelligence and compare it with secret sources," Robertson to CSC, 2 May 1946; extract from CSC meeting, 7 Jan. 1947; CSC to Cabinet Defence Committee, 30 Jan. 30, 1947. All in NAC, RG24, 6178, HQ22-1-43. Ironically, the new head of the British Joint Intelligence Bureau, Major-General Kenneth Strong, felt the creation of a JIB to be a progressive, but still inadequate "first step toward the integration of Intelligence" in Britain. He much preferred the American decision to centralize intelligence in the CIA. Sir Kenneth Strong, *Intelligence at the Top: The Recollections of an Intelligence Officer* (London: Cassell, 1968) pp. 223-27. Strong describes the JIB concept in vague terms only.

21   Glazebrook to Crean, 1 Aug. 1946, NAC, RG25, 2116, AR418/2. JIC to CSC reporting on comment from External Affairs, 6 Aug. 1946, NAC, RG24, 6178, HQ22-1-43(1). Glazebrook was back at his teaching position at University of Toronto at this

time, but he continued to freelance for External Affairs on intelligence matters.

22 Passim, NAC, RG24, 6178, HQ22-1-43(3).

23 For the description of contact registers see "Visit of DNI to U.K. JIC," autumn 1943, and JIC minutes, 10 Oct., 18 Oct. 1944, NAC, RG24, 2469, S715-10-16-1-3(3-4).

24 The notorious Communist scientist Desmond Bernal would certainly have known about the contact registers. His job with Combined Operations involved the use of aerial photographs and he managed to visit Medmenham. Jones, *Reflections on Intelligence*, p. 60.

25 JIC "Service Intelligence," 17 Feb. 1947, NAC, RG24, 6178, TS22-1-44. The listing is taken verbatim from the document. "TS" on this file means Top Secret.

26 R. V. Jones, *Most Secret War* (London: Hamish Hamilton, 1978), pp. 493-97. DRB annual report, 20 Sept. 1951, NAC, RG24(F), 2425.

27 DSI(CIA) requests, Feb.-March 1950, NAC(F), 4117, 2-1-172-10. DSI(DRB) correspondence, 1953-54, ibid, 4133, 7-0-240.

28 "Information on Soviet Forces in East Germany" prepared by JIS for JIC and COS, 21 Jan. 1948, NAC, RG24, 2470, HQS-715-10-16-1-14.

29 For an account of some of the activities of the RCMP's Security Service during the 1950s, including the attempted bugging of the Soviet embassy, see Wright, *Spycatcher*, passim.

30 Crean to Hillenkoetter, 9 March 1949, NAC, RG24, 6178, TS-22-1-43(3).

31 Glazebrook to JIC, 24 Feb. 1949, ibid.

32 According to the finding aid, the file on DL2—still closed under the Access to Information Act—begins 14 Dec. 1948; NAC, RG25, Acc86-87/159, 9, 1086-L-1-40. The description of DL2 comes from G. W. Hilborn, taped interview, 1991.

33 Relations between DL2 and MI6 were cordial. One of Hilborn's duties during the 1950s was to compose Christmas greetings to "C".

34 Philby, *My Silent War*, pp. 112-13.

35 Dwyer moved to the Canada Council in 1957.

36 "Foreign Intelligence in Peacetime," Appendix E, 26 Sept. 1945, NAC, RG24, 6178, HQ-22-1-43(1).

37 Proposed by JIC on 22 Feb. 1946. "History of JIB," 6 April 1946, RG24, 6178, HQ-22-1-43. Glazebrook to Stone, 16 May 1946, NAC, RG25, Acc89-90/029, 69, 300-B(s).

38 Hillenkoetter to Crean regarding Angleton and Col. R. A. Schow, 23 May 1949; extract from JIC meeting, 13 Sept. 1949. Both in NAC, RG24, 6178, S-24-14-5. The Security Panel later became involved in working with the Communications Branch on the security of all forms of electronic communications, a very large field which is still a major interest of the Communications Security Establishment.

39 Correspondence beginning with Edwin Herbert to Charpentier, 13 Oct. 1945, NAC, RG25, 2686, 11229/40. Also empty file folders labelled "Censorship 1944-1949, 1941-1948," in NAC, RG2(14), 5761. The relevant files in Britain are closed but their titles disclose that cooperation extended into the 1950s. PRO, DEFE1/347, DEFE1/356-58.

40 Nicholson to DSI regarding letter from A. A. McLeod to Nigel Morgan, 5 May 1950, NAC, RG24(F), 4161, 201-159-301. For wartime security censorship see NAC, RG2(14), 5753, 206. See also undated note regarding files transferred from Censorship to External Affairs which mentions 57/1—"postwar use of subversive watch lists." NAC, RG2(14), 5761.

41 St. Laurent was regarded as so inexperienced that his public speeches were secretly vetted to prevent accidental "leakage." Heeney to Pickergill; Heeney to Claxton, 1 Nov. 1948, NAC, RG2(18), 81, I-40. There were no fears about Pearson.

42 Extract from CSC, 21 Jan. 1947, NAC, RG24, 6178, HQ-22-1-43. "Sigint History," CSE docs. 001185, 001230. See last paragraph of Pearson to C. J. Mackenzie, 18 Feb. 1947, NAC, RG2, 83, I-50-5 for the composition of the committee.

43 "Sigint History," CSE docs. 001185, 001211 and 001217. In 1972 the Joint Intelligence Committee became the Intelligence Advisory Committee, while also taking over the function of Communications Research Committee.

44 The Oerlikon information was Top Secret and derived either from espionage or, more likely, from intercepted communications. NAC, RG2, 81, I-40. For the other examples of secret intelligence, see NAC, RG24, 6178, TS-22-1-44.

CHAPTER FOURTEEN

1 Bamford, *Puzzle Palace*, pp. 133-45.

2 This is a safe assertion. As Cowgill's deputy in Section V of MI6 the British traitor Kim Philby regularly handled Abwehr decrypts, including those enciphered by the Abwehr's ENIGMA machine. Japanese decrypts pertaining to espionage also would have come to Section V.

3 I have not been able to find any authoritative reference to the breaking of any Communist postwar high-grade ciphers in any of the various intelligence histories consulted for this book. Wright in *Spycatcher*, p. 86, notes that in 1950s the ciphers of the Soviet embassy were "unbreakable."

4 Wright, *Spycatcher*, pp. 81-82.

5 This comment was made in the context of intercepting diplomatic traffic for the benefit of the President and State Department. Col. Alfred McCormack to Col. Carter Clarke, 15 April 1943, NARA, RG457, SRH-116.

6 "... we are now going through the labour pains of unification," Travis to Friedman, 7 December 1949, VMI, William Friedman papers, B-4/F-39.

7 Wright, *Spycatcher*, pp. 84-85, 110-11.

8 Wright, *Spycatcher*, p. 111.

9 G. W. Hilborn, taped interview, 1991. Hilborn did not remember handling Egyptian decrypts, but the interchanges of the other Arab states would certainly have given External Affairs a good idea of Nasser's attitudes and tactics.

10 Jones to Friedman, 2 Nov. 1956, VMI, William Friedman papers, B-4/F-39. Wright, *Spycatcher*, pp. 82-85.

11 Canadian JIC to British JIC, 1 Nov. 1945, NAC, RG24, 2469, S715-10-16-1-13(5)

12 Text of speech given by Solandt, 16 April 1947, NAC, RG24(F), 2425. This was a secret address to an unknown Ottawa audience which appears to have been accidentally included in a file of his public speeches. Solandt began his remarks by pledging his listeners to absolute secrecy.

13 U.S. Strategic Guidance memo EC 190/4, 13 Dec. 1949, NAC, RG24, 4117, 2-1-172-10. For the "threat to Malaya" see NAC, RG24, 6178, TS-22-1-44.

14 Mackenzie King called these "arrangements for peacetime security purposes ... in connection with exercises and tests of material of common interest" and that "no treaty, executive agreement or contractual obligation has been entered into." 10 Feb. 1947, NAC, RG25, 2153, unnumbered file. For CBW cooperation see NAC, RG24(F), 4133, passim.

15 External Affairs official statement, 9 Aug. 1951, NAC, MG26/N1, 10.

16 Interview with CIA officer Tom Braden quoted in John Ranelagh, *The Agency: The Rise and Decline of the CIA* (New York: Simon & Schuster, 1986), p. 157. It is probably no coincidence that Dwyer left his intelligence post with the Privy Council Office at this time (1957).

17 Most of the foregoing is derived by comparing "Sigint History" CSE docs. 001185, 001211, 001217, 001218, 001226, 001230, with the 1993 Government of Canada Telephone Directory.

18 Interview with former Defence Minister, Jean-Jacques Blais, *The Globe and Mail*, 3 June 1991.

19 Bill Robinson, "The Rise and Fall of Cryptanalysis in Canada," *Cryptologia*, vol. 16, 1, Jan. 1992, pp. 23-38. This is an excellent account of recent developments at CSE obtained from public documents. Interestingly, the CSE now employs about the same number of people as Britain's Government Communications Headquarters in 1945.

20 "Minutes of Proceedings and Evidence of the Special Committee on the Review of the CSIS Act and Security Offences Act," House of Commons, No. 27, 24 April 1990, pp. 5-6. Cited in ibid.

INDEX